Revealing the Christian Age is not just another commentary on Revelation, but is, as the subtitle clarifies, *"a Synthesis of the Prophets and Revelation."* By interweaving the messages of Daniel, Ezekiel and Isaiah, and to a lesser extent Jeremiah, with the message of Revelation, Fain demonstrates that the message of the prophets and Revelation is the story of the sovereign God working out his plan and purposes in human history, a history that culminates in the age of Christ the King. Fain also demonstrates a depth of knowledge of ancient history and employs it well to illuminate the biblical text. Fain's approach is panoramic, coherent, instructive. There is no consensus on Revelation, but one truth emerges from his study on which all should be able to agree: we are still living in the biblical story and we need to pay attention to the God who is the author of that story!

Dennis Connor, Raleigh, North Carolina

Neal Fain's *Revealing the Christian Age* holds exceedingly faithful to its subtitle, *A Synthesis of the Prophets and Revelation*. Page after page cites connections between Old Testament prophesies and the text of Revelation. Fain makes the case for a systemic, integrated reading of Scripture, for hearing God's singular voice from cover to cover. His respect for Scripture is both laudable and encouraging. *Revealing the Christian Age* will make you think and challenge you to read the text again. Are we hearing God accurately? Are we recognizing the allusions? Are we reading holistically? Are we letting the whole of Scripture aid our understanding? Fain has written a book well worth reading and discussing with fellow believers.

Dr. Bill Bagents, Heritage Christian University

Neal Fain has written a study of the Revelation and the Prophets entitled *Revealing the Christian Age*. The 348 page book is a substantial and enlightening contribution to the study of the Apocalypse. Using the full scope of the prophetic literature, brother Fain explores the first century meaning and modern-day significance of the book of Revelation.

Neal's previous study of *Prophecy Principles* equipped him to approach the events and symbols of the great Apocalypse. Neal uses apocalyptic images from all over the Bible to help him interpret what is read in Revelation. His technique makes sense and is highly effective. This approach reveals Neal's wide grasp of the prophetic literature of the Bible.

He views Revelation as predictive of events that will be fulfilled in the Christian age climaxed by the return of Christ.

Larry Murdock, Lawrenceburg, Tennessee

The sum of Your word is truth,
And every one of Your righteous
ordinances is everlasting.
Psa 119:160 NASB

Ask, and it shall be given you;
seek, and ye shall find;
knock, and it shall be
opened unto you:
Mtt 7:7 KJV

Also by this author:

*Prophecy Principles, The Background We Need
for Bible Prophecy and How It Works.*

*Jewish Chronicles, How the Jewish Nation Will
Turn in Faith to Rabbi Jesus of Nazareth,
Well Before the Second Coming!*

.

Revealing the Christian Age

A Synthesis of the Prophets and Revelation

A Much Abused Simple Story

A Bible Story ... in History

Neal Fain

AngleofEntry .com

Learning for the Journey

Cover Design by Neal Fain

ISBN 978-0-9786866-4-2

AngleofEntry.com
P. O. Box 384, Lawrenceburg, TN 38464

© 2018, by Neal Fain

Library of Congress Control Number 2018908311

Preface

This book is a sorting out of the foundational issues of studying the book of Revelation. This is a synthesis and overview of the prophets and the book of Revelation for understanding the Christian Age. This is *only* an overview. I thought of making the subtitle, "Strategic Issues from Scripture ..." This brief study hopes to outline the key parameters by which we should approach and study the book of Revelation, and view our present age. It is my intention to leave what is unknowable at this time as, well ... unknown ... and to tell you the outlines of what can be seen.

This not a "cover it all" book. It is impossible in a work of this nature to cover every true point or every sidetrack which has been proposed for the book of Revelation. Many good points have been made in many lessons and books on Revelation, and many tares also have been sown here, even from the very first. I will try to cover the main sidetracks, and deal with the principles of sound interpretation, with emphasis on what we may have missed.

The world of theological scholarship has a lot of its terms backward. When it is talking about "Biblical" theology, it is talking about how a book stands on its own, and what it means on its own, not assuming that is inspired, or related to any other books or the "Bible." If you are taking two or more books of the Bible together, assuming that they are coherent, and trying to determine what they are saying together, that is "systematic theology" in their nomenclature.

Accordingly this book is really not "Biblical Theology" in this backward sort of nomenclature, rather this book is part of systematic theology. This book assumes that the book of Revelation is part of the whole Bible, and that its message is not independent of the whole Bible.

The book of Revelation is not a stand-alone book. It is not whole without the Gospels or Genesis or Isaiah or the Psalms or Thessalonians, or really any of it. It is definitely not complete without the books of Ezekiel, Daniel, Zechariah, and the Psalms. To give an example, the study of New Testament prophecy is not without the book of Deuteronomy. For an overview of the Christian Age, the book of Daniel is especially necessary to put together a coherent "overview" of the Revelation and of our age.

However, this perspective is not justified here.

There are, or should be, prerequisites

to studying the book of Revelation. It would be helpful if you understood the general concepts about how prophecy works, and the subject matter it addresses before you begin reading this. However that is not an absolute require before reading this, for many of the basic concepts are reviewed all through this volume. My previous volume, *Prophecy Principles*, is a review of the basic concepts in Bible prophecy and the background with which we should be familiar. No, that does not mean that you are required to read that first. However if the reader is interested in reviewing some of the relevant background, it might be used as a reference, or a study guide, to review in greater detail say, the role of angels in prophecy, or the place of civil government, or the ancient mystery religions, or the importance of our own patience and perseverance, etc.

Regrettably, many both inside and outside of Christianity tend to take the Book of Revelation as a stand alone book, and do not start with an overall look at Scripture and how prophecy works, but instead approach the Book of Revelation as if it is unique, a stand-alone volume of God's Word that has nothing to do with anything which has gone on before. Many do this of all theological stripes. Starting this way, they begin with confusion over language and symbolism which they have not considered as having anything to do with anything else.

Also unfortunately with the book of Revelation, it is common for interpretation to supersede the text. Thus, what someone thinks it means, tends to supersede the text itself. Commentaries often starts with a thesis, and drive merrily in that direction, ignoring the text when it does not seem to fit. I hope to not do that. At times I will emphasize what the text does NOT say! It is my hope to so declare to you what the text says, that if some of my personal interpretations are wrong, this book will still be useful for studying what the text does say!

And What Is My Perspective?

Whether a person sees what they need to see, depends to a great extent on how they approach a subject. What you might call their "angle of entry."

It almost should be in this introductory material, but is in fact discussed on pages 14 and 15 of the text, under the heading, "So How Shall One Approach Revelation?" That is, as clearly as I can put it, the preconceptions which I bring to this task.

I believe that Jesus is the Christ and that He is presently reigning, even in this present period of amnesty. I have accordingly used the abbreviations BC and AD for Before Christ and for Anno Domini, the year of our Lord.

I have tried to realistically examine the evidence from a true Biblical perspective, taking note of what it actually tells, and accepting it when parts are not as clear as one might desire. Some things must be stated as mere possibilities, but not as anything to be dogmatically stated. At times the best we can do is to clearly outline the ambiguities with which we are presented, and assume that they are there for a reason, and to not try to artificially resolve them. I have tried to not be dogmatic where Scripture is not clear. The reader will be the judge of how successful I have been.

If I do my job as I hope to, this will treat Revelation as great living literature, *with a view to resetting the discussion on the book of Revelation.* I think Revelation is meant to enlighten and to be mulled over again and again in terms of our situations in history prior to the Second Coming. Should this end the study of this book? By no means. It is this author's hope, that by the end of this book, you will have the tools and the overview to begin the serious study of Revelation and the prophets of old.

The Table of Contents is an accurate guide to the lines of evidence which are pursued in this book.

About Quotations

It is of course a Liberal article of faith that the Bible documents are not genuine. This is never really proved, always asserted as a mandatory belief, even if the "proofs" are shot down. It is a well kept secret by our Establishment scholars, but the Bible documents actually stack up very well historically, as well or better than the Liberal icons of materialistic idolatry. Over and over, the quibbles about Bible books disappear into the dustbin of history. There are many good scholarly defenses of these books, and I clearly accept these books as authentic.

The "King James Version" KJV, is the default translation used in this volume. When the KJV is ambiguous, or even downright bewildering to the modern reader, then I have first used the New King James Version NKJV, then the NASB, and lastly other translations. Second place was given to the NKJV because it is probably the closest to the KJV of the modern translations. In truth both the NKJV and the NASB closely follow the KJV.

Truly, the issues discussed in this book are translation independent.

I have tried as best as possible to handle the citations for quotes within the text, while still trying to preserve readability (although a couple of true footnotes occur in the text). Bible books are cited in full, as for instance the book of "Genesis." Precise quotes are abbreviated, as for instance "Gen 1:31". Citations of other translations include The New International Version, 1984 (NIV), and the English Standard Version 2001 (ESV). The KJV, NKJV, NASB and the ESV use italics to identify words in the translation which do not occur in the original Hebrew or Greek, but which are needed for a good English sense. I have tried to preserve these italics in the text. *The NET Bible®*, has also been cited on occasion, as NET. *The World English Bible* (WEB), February, 2017 (a public domain, no copyright translation) has been used for quotes from the books of 1 and 2 Maccabees.

Where I have wanted to emphasize part of the text of a quote, a bold font has generally used, and such has generally been so noted after each citation. For clarity with *secular quotes* and my non-standard citation method, I have used quote marks even when indented.

Other Works: Ancient Jewish historian Flavius Josephus' *Antiquities of the Jews*, is quoted as *Antiquities*, and his *Wars of the Jews*, is quoted as *Wars*, with the standard Book and chapter and section numbers. I have used William Whiston's old translation as the most available, but there are good newer ones.

The Index

The book of Revelation sits at the intersection of many ideas. The index, *while far from perfect*, has been especially composed with a view to tracing the development of many of the concepts associated with this study, and it is hoped that it will be useful to the reader for thinking through the ideas that are involved.

And From You The Reader?

I ask a measure of your indulgence and patient reading. I readily admit that I will probably relay things that you might not like, or might not want to believe. In fact, the Bible *often* does that. Please remember that, "I am not sure I like that," or "I am not sure I believe that," is not really evidence, but may indeed sidetrack us from the straightforward message of the prophets. In my defense I will say that I have tried to make sure that my personal "thinks," and "perhaps," and "maybes," are clear, as mere possibilities to consider, but not as any "thus saith the Lord." And what have I told you? In the main I have merely told you *what* to look for, and not the "who," the criteria, but not the identification. To be forewarned is to be forearmed against the many seductive sidetracks of the Christian age, and the astounding nature of many things that are going on, and will yet happen.

And one more thing: Nothing here is new, either from Scripture or from history. These are merely things which are not generally realized.

Lastly let me say, the writing of this book has greatly increased my own faith, and my resolve to live for Christ, and do what is right in these troubling last days. May this writing also so bless you the reader!

And My Special Thanks

I owe special thanks to my very patient proof readers, especially to my daughter Alicia Hickman, and my dear friend from my Alaska days, Allen Houtz. Both are very sharp eyed, and made many excellent suggestions for improvement. If something still seems ragged or out of place, it is probably because I resisted their excellent counsel. Anything that is mistaken is clearly my own fault.

Others also made good suggestions, more than I should try to name, but one special one should be noted: my wife Cecilia, who has had to put up with my being almost totally absorbed with research and writing chores for a period of years. My thanks for her patience and support.

Bible Abbreviations

1Chron	1 Chronicles	Judg	Judges
1Cor	1 Corinthians	KJV	King James Version, 1611
1Jn	1 John		
1Kgs	1 Kings	Lam	Lamentations
1Pe	1 Peter	Lev	Leviticus
1Sam	1 Samuel	Lk	Luke
1Thes	1 Thessalonians	LXX	The "Septuagint," Ancient Jewish translation of the Hebrew Old Testament into Greek. Used by the early church for many centuries.
1Tim	1 Timothy		
2Chron	2 Chronicles		
2Cor	2 Corinthians		
2Jn	2 John		
2Kgs	2 Kings		
2Pe	2 Peter	Mal	Malachi
2Sam	2 Samuel	Mic	Micah
2Tim	2 Timothy	Mk	Mark
2Thes	2 Thessalonians	Mtt	Matthew
3Jn	3 John	Nah	Nahum
Acts	Acts	Neh	Nehemiah
Amos	Amos	NASB	New American Standard, 1995 ed.
Col	Colossians		
Dan	Daniel	NET	New English Translation, 2005
Deut	Deuteronomy		
ESV	English Standard Version 2001	NIV	New International Version, 1984
Eccl	Ecclesiastes		
Eph	Ephesians	NKJV	New King James Version, 1982
Esth	Esther		
Ex	Exodus	Num	Numbers
Ezek	Ezekiel	Obad	Obadiah
Ezra	Ezra	Phil	Philippians
Gal	Galatians	Philem	Philemon
Gen	Genesis	Prov	Proverbs
Hab	Habakkuk	Psa	Psalms
Hag	Haggai	Rev	Revelation
Heb	Hebrews	Rom	Romans
Hos	Hosea	Ruth	Ruth
Isa	Isaiah	Song Sol	Song of Solomon
Jas	James	Titus	Titus
Jer	Jeremiah	Zech	Zechariah
Jn	John	Zep	Zephaniah
Job	Job	WEB	World English Bible, February, 2017
Joel	Joel		
Jonah	Jonah		
Jos	Joshua		
Jude	Jude		

Table of Contents

I. How Revelation Came to be Distorted

"A light to bring revelation to the Gentiles,
And the glory of Your people Israel."
Lk 2:32 NKJV

That is what Jesus is. This verse in Luke 2 is part of a prophecy by the "just and devout," Simeon. And yes, that word "revelation" here is the same one used of the Revelation of Jesus Christ in Rev 1:1. The light of Jesus Christ will "reveal" the truth. But a great deal of disinformation has been sown here. Often you and I have absorbed it, and often propagated it.

It seems to be dogma, both inside and outside of the church, that this book *cannot* be understood, and you *should not* and *cannot* have any understanding of the end of our age! Many have been saying this even from the first! This is weird and confusing and what should be made of something so bizarre? You surely do not believe this? So what can anyone think of all of this?

"Apocalypticism"? Some seem to say, "I just do not believe something as bad as this could happen." Such is the language that is so often encountered when people talk about the book of Revelation. In this light, what should one think of the common approaches to the book of Revelation? Some of the confusion has its roots in old fashioned unbelief. For instance in ...

Refusing to Recognize God's Foresight and Wisdom.

Much of the guilt here must be laid at the footsteps of classical Liberalism. In the words of the Encyclopedia Britannica © 1994-2001, Liberalism "is closely linked with the idea of liberty or ... freeing ... the human spirit ..." and of the "maximizing of the individual's freedom to think, to believe, to express ..." not being limited by what others may think, or "God" may or might have thought. "The enemy was custom, tradition, institutions, social habit. They always sought to lift men from what Thomas Jefferson called 'the dead hand of the past.'" Many sought a separation from Christianity and all that it represented. Thus some who viewed themselves as very "scholarly" decided *a priori* to rule out God. They were often willing to believe there was no real "God," but most would not be dogmatic on that. However, even if "God" existed, many decided God was just "nature's God, and religion was universalized into a deism." The New Oxford American Dictionary calls deism,

> "belief in the existence of a supreme being, specifically of a creator who does **not** intervene in the universe. The term is used chiefly of an intellectual movement of the 17th and 18th centuries that accepted the existence of a creator on the basis of reason **but rejected belief in a supernatural deity who interacts with humankind.**" *(emphasis added)*

This is of course a very specific theological view, and also, since it is a negative (there is no "God" who interacts with mankind) it is *not* something which can be proved. You would have to be able to search the entire universe, looking for a "God," and then verify that He would *never* interact with us. Which "they" just cannot do. So here is counter-intuitive "scholarly" dogmatism, which they can never prove, and they want us to blindly accept.

So how do they deal with considerable evidence to the contrary? "They" just **refuse** *to believe* the evidence, no matter how good the evidence may be. Now that is real, open minded, scholarship!

After that, if you accept their *unprovable* **theology**, then they want you to believe *a priori*, that *if* there is a "God," since He is only our Creator, He obviously would not give a hoot about us, His creation, and would never communicate with us. Once again this is *unprovable* **theology**, again from "open-minded," "scholarly," Liberals. This is clearly assuming *a lot* about a Creator of whom they profess to know *nothing*. So there are already piling up quite a list of **theological** unprovables, before one gets very far.

Then if you come upon literature which professes to come from "God," and it tells us something about the future, and *it actually happened*—What must be assumed? *A priori* it must be assumed that the document **must be** false. No "God" would **ever** care about us (they tell us by implication), and if a document clearly forecast future events, then it must have been written *after* the fact. So they *assume* from the first. Then they try to prove (or sometimes just assume) a date for writing the prophecy which is later than the events that were successfully forecast. Here they have a problem with Scripture. Even if they posit a late date for certain Bible writings, they are almost invariably still unable to rule out all true prophecy. There are always little bits and pieces which they wish to ignore, but which they cannot deny, and are *not* excluded by their "theories." That is particularly true of some of Bible literature, including the books of Daniel and Revelation. They are quite willing to believe that *men* (like themselves, I might add) might use great forethought or foresight or skill, but are unwilling to believe that God could or would do so.

The common thought processes used when a Liberal approaches the book of Revelation is to assume what we might call "a late date" (a date which they think rules out true prophecy). Later, if the evidence does not quite fit their mold, often they force it to fit, and just ignore evidence that it does not fit their theories. Those of many theological stripes do that sometimes with Scripture, and to particular passages for which they have no explanation, although Revelation seems "favored" with such treatments. At times people do incredible mental gymnastics. Sometimes men will pick just one questionable idea about God and what He would or would not do, or one obscure verse of Scripture (take your pick), and develop a theory of what it means. Then they try to make the entire Word of God dance to the tune *they concocted* on a single, perhaps not very clear, verse. ***Beware of "one verse" theologies!***

At the last, what do you do if it positively does *not* fit? Well for the Liberals anyway, that often only shows how stupid the author of that Bible book really was. That evidence is just ignored, not worth dealing with. Such is common treatment, even from so-called "scholarly" sources.

None of this is really scholarly, accolades not withstanding. It is with such ignorance that Revelation is often approached. Of course such thinking can really give us a head start on confusion, and it generally does. Sometimes men, quite unnecessarily, shrink from the forms used in Bible prophecy.

Balking at the Symbolism

Most of the symbolism even in Daniel and Revelation is no different from the normal ranges of symbolism in Western literature, and that my friend is a very wide range. Just for a moment consider the mainly unexplained symbolism in Lewis Carroll's *Alice in Wonderland* (compare the original drawing to the right), or in much modern poetry! In comparison, Scripture gives us many leads in deciding how to treat its symbolism. To give an example, let us look at an important prophecy in a book we often do no consider a prophetic: the book of Psalms. Look at Psalm 22, a psalm of David. This psalm was considered from the view point of how prophecy works in my previous volume *Prophecy Principles*. Now let us look at it from a completely different point of view, to see how symbolic language works and whether or not we should be spooked by "symbolic" language. David starts off by saying,

> My God, My God, why have You forsaken Me?
>> Why are You so far from helping Me,
>>> And from the words of My groaning? Psa 22:1 NKJV

Perhaps we should note that David wrote many songs about his trials and

struggles, songs in which he is asking the Lord his God to deliver him. Most of these songs he wrote in the first person, just as he does this one. In this particular song he seems to feel completely overwhelmed, as if God had actually forsaken him, and he was pleading with God to take action and help him. So far, Psalm 22 is just like so many other psalms of David which we have. Some of these psalms even have historical prefaces before the start of the psalm, relating a psalm to this event or that in David's life. For instance look at the preface to Psalm 18, or Psalm 34.

You might say though, there is a strange thing about Psalm 22, a thing which did fit David's life at the point at when it was written, and which did *not* fit his life all the way to the end. David died in bed, an old man and full of years, as the story is told in 1 Kings 2. You see Psalm 22 pictures the author as dying a violent death at the hands of strangers. This is the One who says in the first person, "My God, my God, why have you forsaken **me**?" But of course, David did not die a violent death in the manner described in this psalm. In fact, he did not die at the hands of strangers at all. As was pointed out in *Prophecy Principles*, the things "which do not fit," are often the indicators that the text we have is speaking of someone else, and not the immediate subject of the psalm (compare Acts 8:34). To put it another way, the immediate subject (David in this case) is a type or symbol for someone else. In Psalm 22, these are the indicators that this psalm is not talking about David at all, rather it is of a second David who would die by crucifixion at the hands of his enemies, about a thousand years later, just as described.

Look at some of the symbolism. "I *am* a worm and no man," he says in Psa 22:6 KJV. Does he mean that he is not really writing this about a physical man ("not a man" literally), but about a species of worm, perhaps a *Phyla Annelida* (a segmented worm), or a *Nematoda* (a roundworm), or a *Platyhelminthes* (a flatworm), and not about *Homo sapiens* at all? Of course not. The very next line says he is, "a reproach of men and despised of the people." He means of course that he is being *treated* as if he were a worm to be destroyed. In fact such symbolic usage is even in the *Oxford New American Dictionary*. It speaks of a worm as "2 informal a weak or despicable person (used as a general term of contempt)." And that exactly fits our context. The author then says,

> Many bulls have compassed me: strong *bulls* of Bashan have beset me round. Psa 22:12 KJV

Is David out in the cow pasture? Are some mean male bovine creatures about to smash this "worm" out in the cow lot? It is known that David fought the lion and the bear (1 Samuel 17). Did he perhaps also fight a mean bull at some time? Who would take this so literally? Then David cannot make up his mind as to whether they are cows or lions, for he next says,

> They open wide their mouth at me,

As a ravening and a roaring lion. NASB

I have never seen a bull do that, intimidating though they can be. Okay David, which are they? Bulls or lions? Must we have a scholarly debate about this? Obviously not. Then in verse 15 the subject of the psalm dies.

> My strength is dried up like a potsherd,
> And My tongue clings to My jaws;
> You have brought Me to the dust of death. NKJV

Then David goes weird on us in the very next verse.

> For dogs have surrounded Me;
> The congregation of the wicked has enclosed Me;
> They pierced my hands and my feet. Psa 22:16 NKJV

So David says it is not bulls, and not lions, it is dogs! Should we debate this? He sticks with dogs again in verse 20, *but then says a sword kills him!*

> Deliver Me from the sword,
> My precious *life* from the power of the dog. NKJV

But how could a dog use a sword? Then he goes back to cows *and* lions in verse 21.

> Save Me from the lion's mouth
> And from the horns of the wild oxen!
> You have answered Me. NKJV

If you want to be a super literalist you can pick this apart, and express fright and revulsion at such bizarre language, all for nothing. Some express fright at the "dragon" imagery in the book of Revelation, yet our dictionary lists a dragon also as "derogatory a fierce and intimidating person." Or we might say a fierce and intimidating evil spirit? Might we not?

Besides a sort of paranoia at symbolic language, there exists another problem. Some act as if acknowledging that a passage has symbolic language, implies it is thus "meaningless." "Oh that is just symbolic," they say, as if to say, "Well, that does not really count!" Nothing could be further from the truth. To say that he is "a worm and not a man," is symbolic, but it is not meaningless. To say that the Pharisees and the kings who crucified Jesus were "dogs" or "a roaring lion," may be symbolic, but it is not meaningless. To say that a young man going out for an evening on the town is "a real wolf" is symbolic (despite using the word "real"), but it is not meaningless; and we quickly catch the meaning. Or for someone to say you are a "pig" or a "jackass" is once again symbolic, but it is not meaningless. Instead you ask, given the situation, what would this symbolism tell us about the subject.

Also, right beside highly symbolic language in Psalm 22, we have some very plain language describing the crucifixion of our Lord Jesus the Christ.

[15] My strength is dried up like a potsherd; and my tongue cleaveth to my jaws; and thou hast brought me into the dust of death. [16] For dogs have compassed me: the assembly of the wicked have inclosed me: they pierced my hands and my feet. [17] I may tell all my bones: they look *and* stare upon me. [18] They part my garments among them, and cast lots upon my vesture. [19] But be not thou far from me, O LORD: O my strength, haste thee to help me. [20] Deliver my soul from the sword; my darling from the power of the dog. Psa 22:15-20 KJV

In all, an awesome and poetic description of the crucifixion of Jesus a thousand years into the future from David; an instance of prophetic foresight which can hardly be denied, and which would be almost impossible for a man to arrange at the hands of his enemies. This is a description which includes both some very straight forward language and also some highly symbolic language, all together, right side by side, all very understandable, *unless you are* **determined** *to not understand.*

Or take Jesus language in Matthew 5

[13] "You are the salt of the earth; but if the salt loses its flavor, how shall it be seasoned? It is then good for nothing but to be thrown out and trampled underfoot by men.
[14] "You are the light of the world. A city that is set on a hill cannot be hidden. [15] Nor do they light a lamp and put it under a basket, but on a lampstand, and it gives light to all *who are* in the house. NKJV

Alright, "Time!" "Time Out!" Clear contradiction. Which are we? Are we salt, or are we light, or are we really men? This would clearly be a foolish conversation on Matthew 5. So is much of the fear and awe of the symbolism in prophecies, including the books of Daniel and Revelation.

There is no more reason to fear or cringe before the symbolism in Daniel or Revelation, than in the book of Psalms or the Sermon on the Mount. But you say, Oh, No! We might misunderstand something. Granted. Something like a "worm," maybe, you mean? Naturally, we can misunderstand symbolism, just as we can and often do. Just as when the boss gave us some instructions, and we took him too literally, and he said to us, "Oh, no! You did it just like I told you to do it!" So the "problems" with language, are just like the normal problems with language in everyday life, and not any more to be feared. Also there is ...

A Tendency to Assume Nothing is Original
in God's Word.

This is often an implicit assumption, not an explicit one. It should be re-membered that the human writers of Scripture often quote sources outside the Bible, in both the Old Testament and the New Testament. Paul is an example in Acts 17:28. Also we might quote Scripture when it says, "there is nothing new under the sun," Ecc 1:9.

God though is from beyond the sun. If you are testing something to see if its claims to be the Word of God are valid, this very weak assumption, is not a good place to start. Such assumptions might, and often do, make people "see things" which are not really there.

This assumption is generally followed by a tendency, if something is stated by a prophet of God, and also in, say, Hammurabi, then to automatically *assume* that the prophet copied Hammurabi, not the other way! The point seems to be that God was not the One who really said this or that. These presumptions neg-atively affects the interpretation of almost all of Scripture.

Confusing Revelation With False Prophecies:
"Apocalypticism"?

Scripture has continually been accompanied by false imitations, trying to pass them off as the Word of God, and so arranged to bring money or power or prestige or influence to whoever it is intended to help. Most of the forgeries are crude, and almost laughable, but such are often used to cause confusion about the Word of God. It is often as if one said, "Why many people have claimed to be prophets."

Occult forgeries, and occult fantasies are an everyday thing in life and have been for many thousands of years, and were even in Bible times.

Some clearly do not want us to *really* understand prophecy. They have other plans and these would conflict with descriptions outlined in Scripture. Jesus as Lord? Well maybe *they* want to be Lord. If they can twist the Scriptures so that you obey *them* rather than God, then they will be happy. So they "twist" away. God complained of such men through the mouth of Jeremiah.

> [25] I have heard what the prophets said, that prophesy lies in my name, saying, I have dreamed, I have dreamed. [26] How long shall *this* be in the heart of the prophets that prophesy lies? yea, *they are* prophets of the deceit of their own heart; [27] Which think to cause my people to forget my name by their dreams which they tell every man to his

neighbour, as their fathers have forgotten my name for Baal.
Jer 23:25-27 KJV

Not everyone who may disagree with you or me may be a con-artist trying to lead us astray, but there are plenty of con-artists around, and some of them may be at a carnival, and some on television, and some in offices or pulpits.

Even so, if someone wanted to deflect any natural inclination to actually *believe* what God has said in prophecy, an easy strategy would be to gather all of the so-called prophecy, both real and false, include the wacko on local television last week, and the Jewish screwballs and out-and-out phonies whom Jeremiah and Ezekiel and the other prophets had to face, and put them all in one big pot, *and treat them as if they were all of the same sort!*

This is actually part of the strategy which is implicitly used *against* believing the books of Revelation and Daniel even by a lot of the scholarly world. "Well, they all claim to be prophets don't they?" They all claim to foretell the future don't they? We will study them all in comparison. But of course, to put the Word of God in the same class with some swindler, whether low-class or high-class, whether ancient or modern, is not a reasonable comparison, though it is common. It is easy to *seem* to discredit the prophets of God if you put them in the same boat with phonies and reprobates. This sort of prejudicial strategy is often used both in "scholarly" literature and popular literature which seeks to discredit the book of Revelation.

These are not valid comparisons. What does the temple of God and the temple of idols have to do with each other, 2Cor 6:16. The prophets of God have nothing to do with these men. The Lord comments on the false prophets of Jeremiah's day, and it would apply to their legions down through history.

> [30] Therefore behold, **I *am* against the prophets**," saith the LORD, **"that steal <u>my</u> words <u>everyone from his neighbour</u>**. [31] Behold, I *am* against the prophets, saith the LORD, that use their tongues, and say, He saith. [32] "Behold, I *am* against those who have prophesied false dreams," saith the LORD, and do tell them, and cause my people to err by their lies, and by their lightness; yet I sent them not, nor commanded them: therefore they shall not profit this people at all, saith the LORD. Jer 23:30-32 KJV (*bold and underline emphasis added*)

Notice that the false prophets "steal my words," as also the scholars notice. It is a reality seen all through history. The phonies, just like real ministers of the Lord, just like the Devil in Matthew 4, quote actual prophecies of the Lord. Then comes the question of whether the supposed "Word of the LORD" really came from one of the false prophets or from the LORD?

So we are talking about a trail of questionable assumptions which often dog the study of prophecy. Assumptions which often seem to discredit the text before you ever get to analyzing its message. Then there is the ultimate side track.

Turning Heavenly Glory to an Earthly Glory

So we come to another huge source of distortion in prophecy. For many, who are fleshly minded, heaven is just not good enough. This is a built in dimension in Liberalism. Of Liberalism it has been written:

> "The axis of men's concerns shifted from the next world to this one, and from what had been laid down by tradition in the past to what men could achieve for themselves ...
>
> "The test of institutions became the question not of whether they were in the service of God but whether they ministered to the happiness of men." "Liberalism," *Encyclopedia Britannica,* © 1994-2001

The Occult very much intends to offer a New-World-Order here. It has been announced over and over, all the way from the *"Novus Ordo Seclorum"* and the *"Annuit Cæptis"* on the back of the United States one dollar bill (roughly speaking "The New Social Order" and "Our Enterprise is Successful), to by now thousands of would-be messiahs who have failed in the last two thousand years. This goes all the way from big failures like Frederick II of Sicily whom was discussed in detail in *Prophecy Principles*, to preachers and teachers and rabbis and politicians of whom most have never heard.

An Occult Messiah is clearly part of all of this. Some have debated back and forth about such things. Clearly not all of the debates have been public, but some of them have been.

Moses Hess (1812-1875) was an early proponent of socialism in Europe, and one of those who participated in the early debates as to how socialism/Communism should be developed. Many Germans have been noted as racists, and Hess also was a racist, but he was a Jewish racist. He was a friend and collaborator of Karl Marx and Frederick Engels, and he assumed that socialism would be a sort of precursor to the ultimate world-order, and he clearly believed the ultimate world-order would be Jewish. So how would the Messiah be chosen? Hess wrote,

> "Every Jew has within him the potentiality of a Messiah and every Jewess that of a Mater dolorosa." Moses Hess, translated by Meyer Waxman, *Rome and Jerusalem, A Study In Jewish Nationalism*, Bloch Publishing Co., NY, 1918, pg 45

The book was first published in 1862. It is mainly a cry for Jewish nationalism as the way to complete what he called "the goal of humanity, which the Jewish prophets termed the Messianic age," pg 75. Hess' book was mostly unnoticed in his time, but soon following his death became one of the fountainheads of Zionist thinking, leading to fully developed Zionism in the 20th century. Hess' view in essence was to first set up the kingdom of God, and whatever Jew was then put in charge ... Wh-a-a-a-Laah!, would become the messiah! In other words, being the king of the *messianic* kingdom would make you the *messiah*! So, per this view, it does not matter who is the messiah. Almost anyone will do (as long as he is a Jew in the view of Hess).

Many have also noticed the seemingly clear relationship between many of the popular leaders of premillennialism in America and of Zionist oriented groups trying to establish Hess' rule of the Jews over the earth.

A preoccupation with an earthly kingdom of glory in this world as some sort of heaven on earth has driven much of the discussion of the book of Revelation during the twentieth century. Much of this is **not** rooted in Scripture at all. Instead it is rooted in the Utopian ideals of Platonism and and Neoplatonism, as it traces down through Western history.

Premillennialism, the teaching that Jesus would personally return to earth to rule for a thousand years over a this-earth kingdom of the Jews, *prior to* the end of this world, rests on a very uneasy base in the New Testament. Some have actually claimed that God's plans for the world failed in the first century AD, and that Jesus will come again (before the Second Coming?) to sort of "try again." In fact, Jesus militantly rejected all attempts to make Him a king during his first coming.

> [14] Then those men, when they had seen the miracle that Jesus did, said, This is of a truth that prophet that should come into the world.
>
> [15] When Jesus therefore perceived that they would come and take him by force, to make him a king, he departed again into a mountain himself alone. Jn 6:14-15 KJV

Thus becoming a worldly ruler was very much a possibility in the first century AD, but was emphatically rejected. Jesus said plainly before Pilate

> Jesus answered, "My kingdom is not of this world: **if my kingdom were of <u>this</u> world, <u>then</u> would my servants fight, that I should not be delivered to the Jews**; but now is **my kingdom not from hence.**
> Jn 18:36 KJV (*bold and underline emphasis added*)

But many, both inside and outside of the church, emphatically want to make Jesus' kingdom one of this world, and want to tell us all of the details. It is true that when Jesus is delivering "the mysteries of the kingdom of heaven," in Mtt 13:11, that He tells us that "the field is the world," Mtt 13:38. However, later we are told of those who have been added to the church,

> [13] For He rescued us from the domain of darkness, and **transferred** us to the kingdom of His beloved Son, [14] in whom we have redemption, the forgiveness of sins. Col 1:13-14 (*emphasis added*) NASB

So then the kingdom is spiritual, not of this creation, literally not of this world. So what happened is what was intended.

> "But those things which God foretold by the mouth of all His prophets, that the Christ would suffer, He has thus fulfilled." Acts 3:18 NKJV

So the concept is one of a spiritual kingdom that is able to have the victory over all of the physical kingdoms.

> [20] And when he was demanded of the Pharisees, when the kingdom of God should come, he answered them and said, The kingdom of God cometh not with observation: [21] Neither shall they say, Lo here! or, lo there! for, behold, the kingdom of God is within you. Lk 17:20-21 KJV

It also must be admitted that there are yet some glorious times coming for Christianity during the Christian Age, when the Jews are converted to the worship of Jesus of Nazareth, as the Messiah He really is. Then it will come to pass,

> Now if their fall *is* riches for the world, and their failure riches for the Gentiles, how much more their fullness! Rom 11:12 NKJV

Indeed, glorious will be those results.

But a literal reign on this present earth of a thousand years? That idea rest precariously on six verses that do not even mention the "kingdom." Instead, the bulk of God's word rests on the understanding that Jesus is already ruling now, in the midst of his enemies, Psa 110:2; and He destroys rulers who displease Him *now*, Psa 2:10-12. And this reign must continue,

> [25] For he must reign, till he hath put all enemies under his feet. [26] The last enemy *that* shall be destroyed *is* death. 1Cor 15:25-26 KJV

The English phrase used here, "He must reign," is in the Greek "Present Active Infinitive." In other words, Jesus is already reigning, and *must* continue to reign until all enemies are put down. When Jesus arose from the dead, he said,

> "**All** authority has been given to Me **in heaven _and_ on earth.**" Mtt 28:18 (*emphasis added*) NKJV

How much authority? **All**! Would he need to come back to earth to exercise any more authority? Absolutely not! He can command ... or take out ... *anyone* He wishes, *even now*, **and often does!** This interval in between, what is it? It is time to repent and change. It is a period of amnesty.

> The Lord is not slack concerning his promise, as some men count slackness; but is longsuffering to us-ward, not willing that any should

perish, but that all should come to repentance. 2Pe 3:9 KJV

To worship just any Jew as the Messiah ... any Jew except Jesus of Nazareth, would be an abomination to any faithful Christian. Thus it is a built in dimension in Scripture to not focus on this world for answers, for it is ruined beyond redemption. But you and I can be redeemed if we are willing.

> Nevertheless we, according to his promise, look for new heavens and a new earth, wherein dwelleth righteousness. 2Pe 3:13 KJV

The end of this present universe will be in fire, and there is coming a new universe, a new heavens and a new earth, which is not dominated by sin and decay and death, what the physicists call entropy. It is there that the full reality of this kingdom will be seen. That is the promise of God to us. We are not looking at things which are seen. We are looking at the evidence that this really is the Word of the Lord, and having been convinced, trusting in its message.

> While we look not at the things which are seen, but at the things which are not seen: for the things which are seen *are* temporal; but the things which are not seen *are* eternal. 2Cor 4:18 KJV

No earthly kingdom, no earthly house or administration or refuge do we seek. We are looking for a permanent residence in another place, a much better place, a universe without entropy, a place which will never run down.

Those of you who are of the earth? Stand aside. We are not your competition. We desire no earthly kingdom. We only wish to save the few we can from the transient glory of a false kingdom of this world.

Trying to Make the Book of Revelation a Past Event

Many are concerned to neutralize the book Revelation, to make sure it is not considered as a book that is pertinent to anything that is going on now. This is often done for a variety of reasons. Some may do this for petty religious reasons. To many Revelation is just an inscrutable nuisance, of which they would like to dispose. Relegating it to the past is one way to do this.

The occult (hidden or semi-secret religion) naturally does not want the public or the church to be looking for their activity. It only makes their objectives more difficult.

One way to neutralize Revelation is to present all of its prophecies as having been already fulfilled in the past. Actually this is very difficult to do, since Revelation (and indeed, much of even the Old Testament prophets) is obviously recording what will lead up to the end of this universe. Unfortunately, most of these "past" "fulfillments" we are sold are grossly in violation of one part of the Scriptural qualifications or another, as shall be shown. Some of the best of them may qualify as additional "types" or symbols of the ultimate fulfillment. The caesars, the popes, Mohammed, Napoleon, or Hitler have often been favorites. Even if the sidetracks are alluring, and the audiences do not have enough understanding to crtique the ideas, there is always a certain uneasiness at what people sense as missing.

Treating Your Political Opponent as the "real" beast

Many major propaganda efforts have been made down through history, and even today, to make everyone believe that their political opponent, or adversary in war, is in fact the "real" beast of Revelation. This is often done to to give their side a certain amount of religious fervor.

Many of these are very believable orchestrations of available data. Why? Because many of these are indeed serious attempts by occult (hidden or semi-hidden) groups to install this little monster or that one, on the throne of the world. So quite often the proper links to the occult are all there, only ...

... only most of these attempts are like Bar Kokhba in the second century AD, or Shabbetai Zevi in the seventeenth century AD, or Adolph Hitler in the twentieth century. They often have made a good start, and then at some point their plans fizzled out, or they were overwhelmed.

There are many "antichrists" down through history, even down to including everyone who has denied Jesus is the Christ (1Jn 2:18, 22; 2Jn 7). (Perhaps including you and me at some point in our lives! Was Paul there at one time?) And there is also **"the antichrist of which you have heard that it is coming,"** 1Jn 4:3 NASB (and it is **"the"** in the Greek). The "man of lawlessness" in 2 Thessalonians 2, and "the beast" in Revelation are surely described as being the biggest antichrist who will ever appear. And these smaller monsters down through history? In truth none of them so far have been big enough, had wide enough success, to be the true "beast"/"man of lawlessness" of Scripture, as shall be shown.

So How Shall One Approach Revelation?

Many carefully conceal their presuppositions concerning this book. My presuppositions about the Book of Revelation are seven:

1. That it is inspired, and it is a foretelling of the Christian Age.

2. That it is in general understandable, but acknowledging that some details of the end of time may not be fully understood until near the end. *It is*

*an article of ̲f̲a̲i̲t̲h̲ **with some** that the book is not understandable and that any explanation must be rejected.* A big part of the problem is the astounding nature of the story that unfolds here. Perhaps it should be compared to something as simple as views on baptism. Poll a hundred people from a hundred different denominations and you may very well get a hundred different answers. It is not that the Scriptures on baptism are vague, or beyond understanding. *It is* that we often do not *like* the answers of Scripture because of our human theological or political views. So it is often with the book of Revelation.

3. That it should be interpreted in conjunction with, and in the light of, the rest of Scriptures. This is intended to be a true "use-the-full-Bible" approach to the interpretation of Revelation. I think this is the proper approach to use with every book of the Bible.

4. NOT classing the Book of Revelation as if it had any thing to do with the multitude of false prophecies and false prophets or their writings, either ancient or modern.

5. That the kingdom *was* (past tense) established in the first century, in accordance with Dan 2:44, Col 1:13, 1Cor 15:25-26, and many other passages. However, it should be acknowledged that we have not yet seen this kingdom in the fullness to which it will develop, 2Tim 4:18, 2Pe 3:13, etc.

6. That Jesus' kingdom is NOT of this present universe, Jn 18:36, etc., and NOT ̲a̲s̲s̲u̲m̲i̲n̲g̲ that any literal reign of Jesus here on earth, from an earthly throne, will ever occur. Even so, hopefully we are fully open to whatever the Lord our God will tell us. Many confuse prophecies of heaven, with prophecies of this present age.

7. That there will be a mass conversion of the Jewish nation to Jesus of Nazareth well before the Second Coming, and that it will bring astonishing benefits to the gospel and the world. The book of Romans and many Old Testament passages deal with this topic and the gospel of Luke also touches on it. This was briefly discussed in *Prophecy Principles.* This is not a topic of the book of Revelation itself, at least as far as I can see, but parts do touch on the subject. There is no stand alone book of the Bible, and Revelation is for sure not a stand-alone book.

Actually, most commentators on Revelation likewise have such a list of assumptions which some might seriously question. Many would not dare to layout their real presuppositions plainly, and hidden agendas abound, especially in the discussion of prophecy.

IF I have made a major mistake about the book of Revelation, it is probably right here, in one or more of the premises outlined above. However, there are some preludes and precursors we would do well to understand.

II. Prelude

> The unfolding of Your words gives light;
> It gives understanding to the simple.
> Psa 119:130 NASB

Driving Down the Road

Now suppose we are driving down the road. Sometimes it seems like this is "all of sudden," because we have forgotten how we got here, the route we took, even how or where we got the car or truck we are driving ... that has all faded into the background. We are thinking of the road we are dealing with, the traffic around us, behind us or before us. Sometimes it seems as if driving down the road at this particular moment *is* our life, and everything before or behind is of lesser consequence. We are just dealing ... you might say existentially ... with the road we are on.

Of course it makes sense to keep in mind the things we have been seeing on the road on this particular day. For example, the condition of the road on this particular day, and the car we saw a few miles back that slid off the road, the poor fellow. There seem to be extra police and troopers on this road today. What is my speed? Oh! You look down at the speedometer and are satisfied with your rate of speed. It always makes sense, wherever you are, to notice what is going on around you. The car in front, it looks like a little old lady ... she seems to be driving very timidly. You look up in the rear view mirror. That truck, you passed a few miles back, when he seemed to be in no hurry, and now he is on your bumper, acting as if he wants to push you a little faster down the road. There is no one on your right. A little foreign car is on your left. A teenager is driving. You cannot pull out into that lane, at least not right now. It pays to keep track of what is going on around you, when you are going down the road. If you are like me, you learned that in driving classes you took in high school. It always pays to be aware of your surroundings, both for driving safety and personal safety. Just look around. Be aware. Have a "heads up" attitude as they call it in basketball. If you are more systematic, then perhaps you have a routine. Look ahead, then behind, then to the right, then to the left.

A little history does not hurt. Knowing how the police have been enforcing the rules does not hurt. Joe was recalling the fine he got just going a little fast in a construction zone on Highway 70. It doesn't hurt to keep things like that in mind. A little current "history," paying attention to at least some of the rumors we hear, does not hurt.

Avoiding Wandering

Further it does not hurt to know the layout. A map. You may know from memory and experience all of the local layout where you live. If you are going somewhere new, a map, or a virtual map (like a GPS) is almost a necessity. At least it will *help you* to intelligently get where you want to go. It is definitely a great aid to avoid aimlessly wandering.

Avoiding Over-Control, Over-Steering

I remember some of the first lessons I learned was about steering. I was just a kid. I was trying really hard, and I was responding in a jerky sort of way to the road. What did they call it? Over-steering! Perhaps you remember doing the same yourself. Perhaps you were really concentrating on that little patch of pavement right in front of the car. It was pointed out to me that if I wanted to drive intelligently, I had to be looking way down the road, not at the pavement three feet in front of me. This meant that I was seeing what was going on with the traffic as much as a half a mile in front of me, and, at the same time, was taking in what was going on in between. This meant being well advised of a slow-down or a dangerous pot hole, long before I got to it.

Knowing how the police have been enforcing the rules does not hurt.

Over-control means a lot of useless wear and tear on your nerves, all for a poor way to drive down the road. The way to avoid over-steering was to be ever looking *way on down the road*, far before you get to those places yourself.

These are merely routines in doing a good job of driving down the road.

Life is Such a Journey

Sometimes we are only dimly aware of how what we see around us started. Even so, it makes sense to be aware of what is going on around us, and what has been going on in the recent past, and the rules and how they have been and are being enforced. It makes sense to be aware of what is happening in our immediate vicinity. Jesus said it very succinctly.

And what I say unto you I say unto all, Watch. Mk 13:37 KJV

Jesus even tells us of some particulars to beware of, and warns of the limitations of our own field of view. We will not know the day or the hour of Christ's coming. Beware of practicing our righteousness to be seen of men. Beware of false prophets. Even, "beware of men!" Mtt 10:17 (which is a long way from Liberalism's trusting in ourselves or in our fellow man). Do not be asleep at the wheel.

Therefore let us not sleep, as *do* others; but let us watch and be sober. 1Thes 5:6 KJV

However, that does not mean acting with fear and dread.

Watch ye, stand fast in the faith, quit you like men, be strong. 1Cor 16:13 KJV

We should talk to the Lord about things that bother us, realizing the Lord cares for His own, and that He is in control, and things cannot happen which are beyond His control.

Continue earnestly in prayer, being vigilant in it with thanksgiving; Col 4:2 NKJV

All of this is comforting, and well worth knowing. Still, it would be good to have an overview of our journey, a perspective which shows where we are, and where all of this is leading. Perhaps then we could avoid over-control, over-steering. We have that of course in prophecy, and especially for our age in the book of Revelation. We should not let ourselves be bamboozled into neglecting such perspective.

Naturally it makes sense to realize how we got where we are, and those things which have already been outlined. Then we would be better prepared to look ahead, on down the road. Scripture gives us this information.

A Fall and a Seed War

One of the first things we should understand in Scripture is that we are not in a normal situation. A disaster has happened of cosmic proportions. This disaster started with a revolt in the spiritual sphere of creation, seemingly even before man was created, but our information is sketchy here. However we are able to see some very important points in how things have developed.

We see first that man was made as a special part of creation. There were separate acts of creation. On the third day God created vegetation. On the fourth day great lights were lit to give light upon the earth. There were two great lights, one to rule the day and the other to rule the night, and stars were also made.

Then sea creatures were made on the fifth day. Then on the sixth day all sorts of land creatures and birds and insects and reptiles were made. Then came the crown of this physical world: man. Mankind was *made* to dominate God's creation.

> And God said, Let us make man in our image, after our likeness: and let them have dominion over the fish of the sea, and over the fowl of the air, and over the cattle, and over all the earth, and over every creeping thing that creepeth upon the earth. Gen 1:26 KJV

The commands of God to man are very specific.

> ... Be fruitful, and multiply, and replenish the earth, and subdue it: and have dominion over the fish of the sea, and over the fowl of the air, and over every living thing that moveth upon the earth. Gen 1:28 KJV

Is man lower than the angelic powers? Yes, for a while it is implied.

> Yet You have made him a little lower than God,
> And You crown him with glory and majesty! Psa 8:5 NASB

The word "God" in Psa 8:5 is literal. It is *elohim* אֱלֹהִים, although the KJV translates it as "angels." The direct inference is that man is intended to be just below God Himself. This is captured in the Jewish translation of the Old Testament into Greek, called Septuagint, in another way, and is so quoted in Heb 2:7.

> "YOU HAVE MADE HIM **FOR A LITTLE WHILE** LOWER THAN THE ANGELS;
> YOU HAVE CROWNED HIM WITH GLORY AND HONOR,
> NASB (*bold and underline emphasis added*)

The Jewish translators of the Greek Septuagint (which is often abbreviated as LXX) interpreted *elohim* in Psa 8:5 as making a reference to angels, and that is the way they translated it, and that is the way the author of Hebrews quotes it. So man was made to be "a little lower than God," and is **"for a little while** lower than the angels." It is obviously speaking of a dignity which man has not yet achieved, and one which Hebrews 2 indicates man will only achieve through Jesus Christ.

It would appear that this grant of power and authority to man was an offense to many of the majestic and powerful spiritual beings in the universe, those we call angels. It seems it was especially offensive to some of the most powerful beings in the universe, some of the hoovering, "covering angels" around the throne of God Himself. One of them decided to try to avenge himself on this upstart creature called "man."

So when Satan first appears in man's story, he is already opposed to God's plans: plans for man to rule, plans for man to rise from his temporary lowly station to a higher station. Satan first appeared as a reptile, a serpent, and "was more cunning than any beast of the field," NKJV. The serpent focused on the one he figured would be the most easily swayed, the one he thought would be most easily deceived. Paul tells us by inspiration that Adam was not deceived.

> And Adam was **not deceived**, but the **woman** being **deceived** was in the transgression. 1 Tim 2:14 KJV (*bold emphasis added*)

Adam then allowed himself to be led into sin by the woman with horrific results. The serpent was also cursed for its part in these things.

> And the LORD God said unto the serpent, Because thou hast done this, thou *art* cursed above all cattle, and above every beast of the field; upon thy belly shalt thou go, and dust shalt thou eat all the days of thy life: Gen 3:14 KJV

The woman was deceived, did wrong, and was cursed for her part.

> Unto the woman he said, I will greatly multiply thy sorrow and thy conception; in sorrow thou shalt bring forth children; and thy desire *shall be* to thy husband, and he shall rule over thee. Gen 3:16 KJV

The man was not deceived, but listened to his wife when he knew better, and likewise was cursed.

> [17] And unto Adam he said, Because thou hast hearkened unto the voice of thy wife, and hast eaten of the tree, of which I commanded thee, saying, Thou shalt not eat of it: cursed *is* the ground for thy sake; in sorrow shalt thou eat *of* it all the days of thy life; [18] Thorns also and thistles shall it bring forth to thee; and thou shalt eat the herb of the field; [19] In the sweat of thy face shalt thou eat bread, till thou return unto the ground; for out of it wast thou taken: for dust thou *art*, and unto dust shalt thou return. Gen 3:17-19 KJV

Man's little paradise was ruined, quite literally. The word "paradise" incidentally comes from the Greek word for a garden or a park, *paradeisos* παράδεισος. We first see it in the Greek translation of the Old Testament in Gen 2:15. And a creation long enmity began between the seed (descendant, masculine, singular, *zera* זֶרַע) of the serpent, and the seed (descendant, masculine, singular, *zera* זֶרַע) of the woman.

> And I will put enmity between thee and the woman, and between thy seed and her seed; Gen 3:15a KJV

Taken literally, there is a single male descendant of the serpent, and a single male descendant of the woman, who will be opposed to each other. The seed of the woman seems to be pointing to Jesus of Nazareth. Jesus was literally the seed of woman, not of man.

> And in the sixth month the angel Gabriel was sent from God unto a city of Galilee, named Nazareth, [27] To a virgin espoused to a man

> whose name was Joseph, of the house of David; and the virgin's name was Mary. ... [31] And, behold, thou shalt conceive in thy womb, and bring forth a son, and shalt call his name JESUS. [32] He shall be great, and shall be called the Son of the Highest: and the Lord God shall give unto him the throne of his father David:; [33] And he shall reign over the house of Jacob for ever; and of his kingdom there shall be no end. [34] Then said Mary unto the angel, How shall this be, seeing I know not a man? [35] And the angel answered and said unto her, The Holy Ghost shall come upon thee, and the power of the Highest shall overshadow thee: therefore also that holy thing which shall be born of thee shall be called the Son of God. Lk 1:26-27, 31-35 KJV

So Jesus was conceived by the Spirit of God coming upon Mary. He had no human father. Later when Mary's fiancé learned that she was pregnant, he made up his mind to quietly divorce her.

> [20] But while he thought on these things, behold, the angel of the Lord appeared unto him in a dream, saying, Joseph, thou son of David, fear not to take unto thee Mary thy wife: for that which is conceived in her is of the Holy Ghost. [21] And she shall bring forth a son, and thou shalt call his name JESUS: for he shall save his people from their sins. [22] Now all this was done, that it might be fulfilled which was spoken of the Lord by the prophet, saying, [23] Behold, a virgin shall be with child, and shall bring forth a son, and they shall call his name Emmanuel, which being interpreted is, God with us. [24] Then Joseph being raised from sleep did as the angel of the Lord had bidden him, and took unto him his wife: [25] And knew her not till she had brought forth her firstborn son: and he called his name JESUS. Mtt 1:20-25 KJV

In addition there is a seed of Satan, masculine singular, Gen 3:15. That is part of this story, both in our subject, the book of Revelation, and also in many other Scriptures.

> it shall bruise thy head, and thou shalt bruise his heel.
> Gen 3:15b KJV

There is more to the story, but this is the real beginning of the story of the book Revelation, and of our trip down the road of life. A story of two descendants, two seeds, of very different natures.

A God-Man From Above Our World

It is clear from Scripture that a special man is going to come to this earth: a God-man. So it will be that He will be called Immanuel, which means "God is with us," Isa 7:14. This is described in many ways and in many places in the Old Testament, but perhaps never so dramatically as in Isaiah chapter 40.

Do not worry, comfort My people. Jerusalem should not worry, because this will bring an end to her warfare, God says in Isa 40:1. A couple of reasons are outlined here. First her sin has been taken away. God's people have received some punishment, in fact "double for all her sins," God says in Isa 40:1. So when the final comfort comes there has been some punishment for the sins of God's people.

There is though another reason for God's people to rejoice. You see, God Himself was going to come to His people. Isaiah says there will be an announcement of God's arrival in the desert, Isa 40:3. Everything will have to be prepared for God's arrival, and then "the glory of the LORD shall be revealed," and "all flesh will see *it* together," Isa 40:5 KJV.

Before we go very far in this passage we quickly come to understand that some of this is speaking of the very end of time: "that her warfare has ended," and that "**all flesh** will see it together." All warfare being ended and literally all flesh seeing God together is something which will only be at the end of time when all nations are gathered before the Lord, Matthew 25, and Isaiah 24. So at least some of this passage seems to point to the very end of this universe, in the period of the grand release from all unrighteousness. That also is the normal pattern in much of prophecy. Prophecy will show the end of things, which is the goal of the immediate things which are being predicted. Also, however, there are earthly things in this passage which precede the eternal things.

Isaiah 40 is announcing literally "God" coming, and it talks about preparing for that, and it says to announce all of this from high mountains. So who is this "God" for whom the preparations will be made? Is this some lesser deity, some lower "god"? Absolutely not! This is the same "God,"

> Who has measured the waters in the hollow of His hand,
>> Measured heaven with a span
>> And calculated the dust of the earth in a measure?
>> Weighed the mountains in scales
>> And the hills in a balance? Isa 40:12 NKJV

What is the entire world compared to this God who will come?

> [15] Behold, the nations *are* as a drop of a bucket, and are counted as the small dust of the balance: behold, he taketh up the isles as a very little thing. [16] And Lebanon is not sufficient to burn, nor the beasts thereof sufficient for a burnt offering. [17] All nations before him are as nothing;

and they are counted to him less than nothing, and vanity.
Isa 40:15-17 KJV

Now God Himself cannot be seen by human eyes and have the beholder live. The apostle John says,

No man hath seen God at any time. If we love one another, God dwelleth in us, and his love is perfected in us. 1Jn 4:12 KJV

God said it Himself in Ex 33:20.

But He said, "You cannot see My face; for no man shall see Me, and live." NKJV

Moses even reminded Israel that they had seen no form at Mount Sinai.

"Take careful heed to yourselves, for you saw no form when the LORD spoke to you at Horeb out of the midst of the fire," Deut 4:15 NKJV

When Paul describes the presence of the Living God, he says,

who alone has immortality, dwelling in unapproachable light, whom no man has seen or can, to whom be honor and everlasting power. Amen. 1Tim 6:16 NKJV

Job even said that if God came by him, he would not be able to detect it.

"Were He to pass by me, I would not see Him;
Were He to move past me, I would not perceive Him."
Job 9:11 NASB

But Isaiah also says of this "God" who will come, and for whom all of these preparations are made,

... O Jerusalem, bearer of good news;
Lift it up, do not fear.
Say to the cities of Judah,
"Here is your God!" Isa 40:9 NASB

Astoundingly it is describing God coming, not just from heaven, but to *Judah!* It goes on to say that God is going to come with might, and will bring the re-payments for both good and evil. Again, this points ultimately to the end, but also it points to the cities of Judah saying, "Here is your God," clearly indicating a presence which is to be seen. It clearly says that God will tend to His flock and will "gently lead those that are with young." Isa 40:12 KJV. So there is God, the real God, the all powerful creator God, who will be seen here on earth. And He is to be seen by many in Judah.

This is not the only passage in the Old Testament which points to God com-ing to earth and being seen here on earth, and some "messenger" preparing the way for God to come. In fact, one of the passages could arguably refer to two messengers. Look at Malachi 3:1.

> "Behold, I send My messenger,
>> And he will prepare the way before Me.
>> And the Lord, whom you seek,
>> Will suddenly come to His temple,
>> Even the Messenger of the covenant,
>> In whom you delight.
>> Behold, He is coming,"
> Says the LORD of hosts. NKJV

If we look closely at this passage, we see first of all that it is God Himself who is speaking, and He is going to send "My messenger," and "My messenger" will clear the way for "the Lord" to come to "His temple." *So truly "God" is going to appear in Judah,* and while it seems to imply in Isaiah 40 that He will appear in the wilderness, here it clearly states that indeed He "will suddenly come to His temple"!

At best it seems like convoluted language. God refers to Himself coming, and then He describes coming to "His temple," as if "He" were a third person! This third person then seems to be "the messenger of the covenant," almost as if it was speaking of a new covenant. Then God goes on to speak of this third person as if He is God Himself, and His anger is so great that none can resist Him, and says He will purify "the sons of Levi."

> 2 "But who can endure the day of His coming?
>> And who can stand when He appears?
>> For He is like a refiner's fire
>> And like launderers' soap.
> 3 He will sit as a refiner and a purifier of silver;
>> He will purify the sons of Levi,
>> And purge them as gold and silver,
>> That they may offer to the LORD
>> An offering in righteousness." Mal 3:2-3 NKJV

So "God" Himself coming to Judah is not an isolated topic in Scripture.

Several centuries after this, a wild man called John the Baptist came preaching in the wilderness areas of Judah.

> 4 Now John himself was clothed in camel's hair, with a leather belt around his waist; and his food was locusts and wild honey. 5 Then Jerusalem, all Judea, and all the region around the Jordan went out to him 6 and were baptized by him in the Jordan, confessing their sins. Mtt 3:4-6 NKJV

The historian Luke tells us that this was in the fifteenth year of Tiberius Caesar, Lk 3:1. Now John the Baptist was a cousin of Jesus of Nazareth, and was born a few months before Jesus was born, Luke 1. Their mothers knew each other. When the boy John was born, his father had prophesied by the Holy

Spirit that his son was to prepare the way for the LORD God.

> And thou, child, shalt be called the prophet of the Highest: for thou shalt go before the face of the Lord to prepare his ways; LK 1:76 KJV

The chief priests and scribes sent men to John the Baptist to determine who he was claiming to be. John immediately said that he was not the Christ. They asked if he were Elijah, and he said he was not Elijah. They asked if he were the great prophet of Deuteronomy 18, and he said "No." Who are you then? And John answered,

> ... "I *am*
>> "*The voice of one crying in the wilderness:*
>> '*Make straight the way of the LORD,*" ' as the prophet Isaiah said."
> Jn 1:23 NKJV

So John's answer was *that he was the voice crying out to prepare the way for God to come* (from Isa 40:3), so that men could see the LORD in Judah. Then the very next day John saw Jesus coming to him, and John said Look at the Lamb of God who takes away the sins of the world! Rabbi Jesus of Nazareth is that One for whom John the Baptist was sent to prepare the way. Jesus of Nazareth is that "LORD," that Yahweh, who is coming according to Isa 40:3, 5, 7, and 10. An extraordinary man, this One, Jesus of Nazareth, must be. So John the Baptist says,

> This is he of whom I said, After me cometh a man which is preferred before me: for he was before me. Jn 1:30 KJV

Jesus did start His ministry *after* John did, but then John strangely says that "He existed before me," NASB when in fact John was born first! Unless ... is John speaking of Jesus as some sort of pre-existing "God"? Could He mean such a thing? Something else John said was likewise strange. John was born first, and they were relatives, but John says that he did not recognize Jesus! As Jesus? Or did he not recognize Jesus as *the* "God" who would come? However John does say that he was told to baptize men to prepare the way for Him. He also was told that whoever he sees the Holy Spirit descending upon and remaining ... this is the One who would baptize in the Holy Spirit. So John was testifying that Jesus was "the Son of God," Jn 1:30-34.

It is strange indeed that a God-man was to come. God in the flesh! Born of the seed of woman!

And a Demonic Man From Satan

Ezekiel chapters 27 and 28 are concerned with a merchant empire, a city state, that of the city of Tyre, on the Mediterranean coast of Palestine, north of Galilee. These chapters are a lament over Tyre and over her king. Tyre was a very powerful merchant empire, living by conducting trade all over the Mediterranean world. Chapter 27 mentions Tyre trading with Tarshish (Spain), Aram (Syria), Persia (Iran), Egypt, and on and on. Tyre was fabulously wealthy, but our subject is specifically the king of Tyre, in Ezekiel chapter 28.

It is only in Ezek 28:12 that the ruler of Tyre specifically called a king. In Ezek 28:1 he is called a leader, or some translations say a prince. Obviously he has the authority of a head of state, but also this is one very arrogant little king. He thinks he is a god.

> ... 'Thus saith the Lord GOD, Because thine heart is lifted up **and thou hast said, I *am* a God**, I sit *in* the seat of God, in the midst of the seas; yet thou *art* a man, and not God, though thou set thine heart as the heart of God: Ezek 28:2 (*bold emphasis added*)

We will come back to this in a little bit, but first it should be noticed that although he says he is "a god," *he is really just a man!* That is a very important point in light of what we will see later in this same passage.

Also this leader of Tyre is a very smart man. It seems that no secret is a match for him, verse 3. By wisdom he has gathered great riches, verses 4 to 6. However God says He will bring foreigners upon him, the most ruthless of men, and this "god" will die, go down to the pit of death, Ezek 28:7-8. God taunts this little nobody.

> [9] Wilt thou yet say before him that slayeth thee, I *am* God? but thou *shalt be* a man, and no God, in the hand of him that slayeth thee. [10] Thou shalt die the deaths of the uncircumcised by the hand of strangers: for I have spoken *it*, saith the Lord GOD!
> Ezek 28:9-10 KJV

Where then did this "man" get his start, this "man" who is about to be killed by foreign enemies? At this point God really astounds us. God speaking through the mouth of Ezekiel says that this "man" got his start in Garden of Eden! *Literally that is what He says!* In the beginning he was full of wisdom and said "I *am* of perfect beauty." He was decorated with all sort of precious stones, because,

> Thou hast been in Eden the garden of God; every precious stone was ... prepared in thee in the day that thou wast created.
> Ezek 28:13 KJV

So this "man" was a "created" being, not a "god," and there was a day on which he was created, and he was in the Garden of Eden, which had passed

The Ruins of Ancient Tyre, former center of a merchant empire.

away some thousands of years before. Who exactly *was* in the Garden of Eden? Then God astonishes us again, and tells us that this "man" was also an angel in heaven.

> Thou *art* the anointed cherub that covereth; and I have set thee *so*: thou wast upon the holy mountain of God; thou hast walked up and down in the midst of the stones of fire. Ezek 28:14 KJV

A cherub is an especially powerful type of angel. It seems like a deliberate contradiction. Wait a minute! Was he *really* a man or *really* an angel? This passage seems to indicates the king of Tyre was one of the four powerful angelic creatures who covered the throne of God, as pictured for instance in Ezekiel chapter one, and Revelation chapter four. That is to say that he was one of the most powerful *creatures* **ever** **made**. He was blameless at first.

> Thou wast perfect in thy ways from the day that thou wast created, till iniquity was found in thee. Ezek 28:15 KJV

It was through the abundance of his trade that he sinned, so God says He threw him out of heaven and down to the "ground," the earth, the land, Ezek 28:17. Then it goes on and talks about this king of Tyre having fire come out from within him and destroying him, Ezek 28:16-19.

This also seems a contradiction. In Ezek 28:7 it says this king of Tyre was killed by the swords of strangers/foreigners. Then Ezek 28:18-19 says this cherub is destroyed by fire coming up from within him!

These are some of the footprints of a "type" or symbol in Scripture, that is to say, when some things do not seem to fit. Such things are often the clue that the main subject (the king of Tyre) is symbolic of someone else.

So *if* the king of Tyre is a type, to whom does this type or symbol point?

It seems to point to some "man," who is also an angel, a "cherub," Satan who was in the Garden of Eden. **He is a man, and he is Satan.**

We will come back to Tyre as a type later on in our studies, but this points to **a descendant of Satan, a seed of the serpent, Gen 3:15.** If you miss this theme in Scripture, then you will not be prepared for what the book of Revelation tells us.

III. Precursor and

Continuing Conflicts?

We have already seen that there is an age-long enmity between man, and the seed of Satan, and these conflicts have significance for our daily lives even to the end of the age. Are there other continuing themes which have a bearing on the text of our subject, the book of Revelation? Indeed there are. In fact there are many, but our focus in this section will be on one particular set of texts: some of the visions in the book of Daniel.

Mighty Empires Announced: A Series of Visions

We have already noticed, the weaknesses of the flesh have often caused man to turn aside. God had wanted man to live for Him. He had wanted man to,

> ... Be fruitful, and multiply, and replenish the earth, and subdue it: and have dominion over ... every living thing that moveth ... Gen 1:28 KJV

Purpose? Serve the Lord, spread out and fill up the earth, subdue it, and make it serve the gracious purposes of God. But even after surviving the flood Noah's descendants, our ancestors, purposefully tried to turn aside. Even at that time, men were still all of one "tribe" of men

> [1] And the whole earth was of one language, and of one speech. [2] And it came to pass, as they journeyed from the east, that they found a plain in the land of Shinar; and they dwelt there. [3] And they said one to another, Go to, let us make brick, and burn them throughly. ... [4] And they said, Go to, let us build us a city and a tower, whose top may reach unto heaven; and let us make us a name, lest we be scattered abroad upon the face of the whole earth. Gen 11:1-4 KJV

There are some good points in being unified of course. But if men are inclined toward evil purposes? It is clearly not good to be unified in a drift toward evil purposes. There was already institutionalized some punishment for sin, in the commands to Noah and his descendants. God gave a command to all of Noah's descendants that,

> [6] Whoso sheddeth man's blood, by man shall his blood be shed: for in the image of God made he man. [7] And you, be ye fruitful, and multiply; bring forth abundantly in the earth, and multiply therein. Gen 9:6-7 KJV

Thus God's commission to man was repeated, with the addition of a duty to punish the evil doer. This is comparatively recent history. All of this happened in the third millennium BC, and we, all men, are from these roots. This occurred on what was then the fertile plains of "Shinar," the area that was later known as Babylon, and what is today southern Iraq. The Lord then considered what was happening.

> [5] And the LORD came down to see the city and the tower which the children of men builded. [6] And the LORD said, Behold, the people *is* one, and they have all one language; and this they begin to do: and now nothing will be restrained from them, which they have imagined to do. Gen 11:5-6 KJV

So yes, God agrees that in being unified, "now nothing which they purpose to do will be impossible for them," NASB. Only being unified against the purposes of God is NOT a good thing. So the Lord acted, with age-lasting effects.

> [7] Go to, let us go down, and there confound their language, that they may not understand one another's speech. [8] So the LORD scattered them abroad from thence upon the face of all the earth: and they left off to build the city. [9] Therefore is the name of it called Babel; because the LORD did there confound the language of all the earth: and from thence did the LORD scattered them abroad upon the face of all the earth. Gen 11:7-9 KJV

In this way "Babel" and Babylon, and mankind organizing to work at cross-purposes to God, became an age-long theme, symbolically surfacing again in the western empires of the first millennium BC, which we consider next.

So to do justice to the book of Revelation we need to start with the book of Daniel. One of the most ridiculous things we could do is start with the book of Revelation as some sort of stand-alone book. Where should we really start? Actually in the book of Genesis as we have shown. After that one of the most immediate jumping off points would be in the book of Daniel, although indeed, the book of Revelation is not really independent of any of the rest of Scripture. Remember:

> The **sum** of Your word is truth,
> And every one of Your righteous rules endures forever.
> Psa 119:160 ESV (*bold emphasis added*)

Trying to be Sensitive to What the Text Actually Says

Unfortunately, the book of Daniel is in many ways like the book of Revelation in many of its human interpretations. Men tend to take a position, then interpret the book according to their view, *and if by any chance, parts of the book contradict their view,* **then they tend to ignore those parts as either wrong, or as without meaning.** Then they often try to force their interpretation on an unwilling text. Likewise, we must sadly add, *many* tend to do this, both believers and unbelievers, Liberals and Conservatives, both scholars and the unlearned.

There is a good reason *not* to do this. This was discussed in detail in *Prophecy Principles*, laying out the principles which Scripture tells us we should use in interpreting prophecy. The little things which "do not fit," or do not seem to fit, or which seem "exaggerated," are often the signal that the immediate subject is symbolic (a Bible "type," *tupos* τύπος, or a pattern or a shadow) of some other subject, which corresponds to it. (Which in Greek is often the "anti-type," *anti-tupos* ἀντίτυπος, which is translated this way in 1Pe 3:21 NKJV, and as "copies" in Heb 9:24 in the NKJV, and as "figures of the true," in the KJV.

In my earlier work I used 2 Samuel 7 and the prophecies of a son of David who will build the temple of the Lord, as an illustration of these things. I showed that the text itself gave hints that this prophecy was not just about Solomon. Other texts can also be used to illustrate these things, and I used Psalm 22 about David and about Christ, in the first section of this book to illustrate these principles.

So having seen there is something more than David, then we patiently wait and watch. Watching! That is an important part of God's plan, that we should be watching, and that is the very thing which God's enemies want to prevent us from doing: watching. *They do not wish to be seen!*

Lord help us all, both writer and reader, both believer and unbelievers, to learn these lessons, and use discernment in reading, and wait patiently for whatever You have to say. Amen.

This section is an overview of parts of the book of Daniel to see how it works and relates to the book of Revelation.

Nebuchadnezzar's Dream

In the book of Daniel, Daniel has been sent as a captive from Judah to Babylon. He was in one of the first shipments of captives to Babylon. The Babylonians, though often cruel masters, were intent on creating a lasting world empire, and wanted to merge their holdings into a stable, integrated, whole. So Daniel and some of his friends from the Judean aristocracy, were taken as young men to be trained "for serving in the king's court," Dan 1:4. Their trainers and tutors in Babylon seem from this story to have been intelligent and open-minded men, anxious to help their charges. Daniel especially progressed rapidly. In Daniel chapter two a crisis occurs in the court, and Daniel is called upon to interpret a dream of Nebuchadnezzar, king of Babylon. Daniel modestly claims no ability of his own in this matter.

> But there is a God in heaven that revealeth secrets, and maketh known to the king Nebuchadnezzar what shall be in the latter days. ...
> Dan 2:28 KJV

In his dream Nebuchadnezzar had seen a large and splendid statue of a man, a statue made mainly of various metals. The head was made of gold, the breast and arms were made of silver, its belly and thighs were made of bronze, its legs were made of iron, and its feet were made partly of iron, and partly of clay. Then while Nebuchadnezzar was watching in the dream, a stone was cut out of a mountain without hands, and it struck the statue on its feet and crushed it. The statute fell and the iron and the silver and the bronze and the gold were all crushed to pieces, ground to powder by the stone cut without hands, and completely blown away. Then the stone became a great mountain and filled the entire earth, Dan 2:31-35.

At this point Daniel started giving the interpretation, and he described the statue as picturing four major world empires for the entire area of the ancient Mediterranean and western Asian world. Again, I am but summarizing. The head of gold represented the kingdom of Babylon, with Nebuchadnezzar as the "king of kings" for the ancient world of that time, Dan 2:37.

After Babylon will come another kingdom, inferior to Babylon, but still very rich, characterized by silver. That would be the Medo-Persian empire, which conquered the Babylonians in the 6th century BC, with the two arms of silver representing the Medes and the Persians.

After the Medes and Persians would come a kingdom of bronze, stronger but not as rich. That would be the Greeks with their bronze weapons and armor. The Greeks under Alexander the Great conquered the Medo-Persian empire in the 4th century BC.

After the Greeks "the fourth kingdom shall be strong as iron: forasmuch as iron breaketh in pieces and subdueth all things:" Dan 2:40 KJV. That would be the Roman empire, which conquered the Greeks in the second century BC. All the same, the foundations of this fourth kingdom are weak. Its foundations, its feet, are described as being made of a mixture of iron and clay, and of course, iron and clay do not mix. So the feet of this image are weak.

No dates are given in this farseeing prophecy. This dream and its interpretation occurred in the 6th century BC. (Nebuchadnezzar died in 562 BC). Unbelievers try to post date this prophecy to the 2nd century BC, but that still does not rule out true predictions here. (The Liberals like to try to post-date many prophecies, to rule out any real predictions.)

Consider for instance the two legs of the fourth kingdom. The Roman Emperor Diocletian (who ruled from 284–305AD), did not formally divide the Roman Empire until 286 AD; centuries after this prophecy was given (and five centuries after the fictitious post dating of the prophecy)! And was the fourth kingdom, the Romans, stronger than the third kingdom, the Greeks? Gibbon in his *Decline and Fall of the Roman Empire*, traces the fall of the Roman Empire to the 1400's AD. In opposition, even the ancient historian Livy noted that the Greek rule had lasted for a mere 150 years, from beginning to end, *The History of Rome*, Book XLV. 9.

Nor does such post dating account for the last part of the prophecy. In the days of the fourth kingdom, the Roman Empire, the strongest of the four as outlined in this prophecy, it says,

> And in the days of these kings shall the God of heaven set up a kingdom, which shall never be destroyed: and the kingdom shall not be left to other people, *but* it shall break in pieces and consume all these kingdoms, and it shall stand for ever. Dan 2:44

This fifth kingdom was "a stone ... cut out without hands." That is to say, it is not of human origin or working. It will be a kingdom "the God of heaven set up." This kingdom crushes all of these previous structures, and makes them disappear, but will itself last forever.

Now this fifth kingdom does not correspond to any secular successor kingdom to the Roman Empire. Historian Edward Gibbon, who was militantly anti-Christian, treats Christianity as one of the causes of the *Decline and Fall of the Roman Empire* in his six volume work (published 1776-1788). To accurately forecast such a thing in even the second century BC, much less in the sixth century BC, would indeed be an incredible thing in human terms.

It appears that the "kingdom" which would crush all of these ancient empires was Christianity. A spiritual kingdom was thus to come in the days of the Roman Empire, and bring these phases of ancient empires to a close, and even crush them, which it did. This prophecy anyway, does *not specifically* tell *when* all these things will happen, only that it will happen in the days of the Roman Empire. Prophecy *generally* does not tell us specific times, but only assures us that this or that will *certainly* happen, and **plainly God intends for us to watch for these things**. In our present case, there is some greater definition given. In the last part of Daniel chapter 9 there is a prophecy of "Seventy Sevens" of years. The prophecy is open to some variations of interpretation, but in general terms it points to this spiritual kingdom as coming between the first century BC and the first century AD. This prophecy is discussed in detail in my earlier volume *Prophecy Principles* in the chapter on "Daniel's Visions."

Lastly let us note that this prophecy in Daniel 2 says that this spiritual kingdom which will arise in the days of the Roman Empire, will fill the entire earth, Dan 2:35. But it has not *yet* **filled** the *entire* earth. **So even now, this prophecy is still in the process of being *completely* fulfilled.** And it will be ... completely. Scripture cannot be broken, Jn 10:35.

Lets now look at some of Daniel's other visions, in our case taking them in ascending order of general complexity.

A Ram and a Goat

If we do not take a look at a comparatively simple prophecy such as Daniel chapter 8, then we will never be ready for what we see in the book of Revelation. We are apt to be stunned by the imagery we will see, and clueless for how to approach it. Indeed, that is how many people are when they come to the book of Revelation, because so many, both believers and unbelievers, tend to treat Revelation as a stand-alone book. Daniel chapter 8 though, tells us how to treat some of these things. We can go even further, Daniel 8 is ideal for this purpose.

Daniel chapter 8 is dated as "In the third year of the reign of king Belshazzar," and would by our calendar be about 551 BC. Daniel saw a vision of a powerful ram with two horns. The two horns were long but one was longer than the other, and the longest horn came up last. This ram went around butting down all other creatures to the north and the south and the west. None could stand before him. He did whatever he wanted to do, and he "magnified himself," Dan 8:3-4.

In this vision Daniel saw a male goat coming from the west, and this male goat had a prominent horn between his eyes. This goat came up to the ram, and charged him, and shattered his two horns so that the ram was not able to resist him. This male goat greatly exalted himself, but as soon as he was successful, the large prominent horn was broken off, and in its place four notable horns came up toward the four winds of heaven.

At this point we should look ahead toward the end of the chapter and see some of the clues for interpretation. It is an angel who gives Daniel the keys to the interpretation, and thus gives us some of the keys for understanding the book of Revelation. First the angel says something strange to which we will have to return later.

> He said, "Behold, I am going to let you know what will occur at the final period of the indignation, for it pertains **to the appointed time of the end.**" Dan 8:19 NASB (*bold emphasis added*)

We are not there yet, but at least from our point of view, this story *does **not*** "pertain to the appointed time of the end." Are we then dealing with a Biblical "type"? Perhaps. We will come back to that later. But let us look further.

> [20] "The ram which you saw, having the two horns—*they are* the kings of Media and Persia. [21] And the male goat *is* the kingdom of Greece. The large horn that is between its eyes is the first king. [22] As for the broken *horn* and the four that stood up in its place, four kingdoms shall arise out of that nation, but not with its power." Dan 8:20-22 NKJV

So before we go further, let us apply these keys to what we have read in Daniel 8 so far. Notice that the prophecy is talking about kingdoms, and it discusses them under the imagery of animals, or in Dan 8:4 it calls them "beasts." In this way we see that **a beast can represent an empire or kingdom.** And that **horns can represent kings or lines of kings.** The horns of the ram represent the kings of the Medes and the Persians. The Medes were dominant in this empire at first, but they were later replaced by the Persians. The Persians were more powerful rulers, and lasted all the way to the end. Thus, "the two horns *were* long, but one *was* longer than the other, with the longer one coming up last," Dan 8:3.

The prominent horn on the goat represents the first king of this great empire, Alexander the Great (and in fact Alexander was sometimes represented in ancient times as a man having horns like a goat). Thus a **"horn,"** representing power**, can also symbolize an *individual* king, in this case Alexander the Great.** Of course Alexander died right at the height of his successes ("the great horn was broken," Dan 8:8), and his empire was divided up among his leading generals, into four kingdoms, all of whom are well known in history. They are:

1. Antipater and Cassander, joint rulers Greece
2. Lysimachus, who took control of what we call Asia Minor.
3. Seleucus I Nictor (literally, the "Victor," who is the first "king of the North") who took over greater Syria
4. Ptolemy I Lagi Soter (literally the "Great Savior," the first "king of the South") who took over Egypt

The Ptolemies of Egypt lasted the longest of these dynasties. The last Ptolemy ruler of Egypt was the famous Cleopatra who allied herself with the Roman general Mark Anthony. She committed suicide when they lost the battle of Actium to the man later known as Caesar Augustus. Those things were in the first century BC, but that is another story.

The story in Daniel 8 now concentrates on one particular king of the Seleucid line of kings of Syria. The Seleucids in fact ended up ruling Asia Minor and almost all of what we would call the Middle-East *except* the prosperous Ptolemies in Egypt. Daniel 8 describes a special horn.

Alexander the Great represented on an ancient coin as having the horns of goat.

> **And out of one of them** came a little horn which grew exceedingly great toward the south, toward the east, and toward the Glorious *Land.* Dan 8:9 NKJV (*bold emphasis added*)

Daniel 8, anyway, does not specifically tell us which of the four "horns" produced this "little horn." However, if we take Daniel 8 literally, this "little horn," implying a ruler who is not especially significant, will even cause some of the angels in heaven to fall. The phrase "the Glorious *Land*" seems to refer to Israel. And of this little horn it says,

> And it grew up to the host of heaven; and it cast down some of the host and some of the stars to the ground, and trampled them.

Dan 8:10 NKJV

The "hosts of heaven" indicates the armies of heaven. In many Old Testament passages "hosts," *tsava*, צָבָא, indicates armies, as in for instance Gen 21:32 where the NASB translates it as "army" and the KJV translates it as "host." So incredibly, it seems to be talking about an *unimportant* ruler of Syria making some angels in heaven fall, and be trampled down! Far be it from me to question the Word of God, but this seems at the very least to be exaggerated language to apply to some minor Seleucid king of the second century BC! Of course, exaggerated language is one of the indicators of something being a Bible "type," being symbolic of someone or something, else. It goes on to speak of this little horn.

> Yea, he magnified *himself* even to the prince of the host, and by him the daily *sacrifice* was taken away, and the place of his sanctuary was cast down. Dan 8:11 KJV

It describes this king as making himself "equal with the Commander of the host" NASB and it is talking about the "hosts of heaven," so it is talking about this king making himself equal to God! Then it says,

> And an host was given *him* against the daily *sacrifice* by reason of transgression, and it cast down the truth to the ground; and it practised, and prospered. Dan 8:12 KJV

Casting "truth to the ground"? This is powerful language being used here. It seems to be talking about a particular king of one of these four lines of rulers of the Greek empires as taking away the daily sacrifices to the Lord, at some particular future time. If so, this could only refer to one man, Antiochus IV Epiphanes, who only ruled from 175 to 164 BC. Is that a match here?

We will come back to Daniel 8 and discuss these culture wars shortly, and they are very significant for the book of Revelation. First though, lets look at another vision of the future in the book of Daniel.

Four Great Beasts, Daniel 7

We are trying to get perspective on how language is used in literature like the book of Daniel. We have used Daniel 8 as a springboard to see how God wishes us to understand such language. Perhaps now we prepared to look at the vision in Daniel chapter 7. This is in the first year of Belshazzar king of Babylon, Dan 7:1. That would be, say, about 553 BC. Daniel saw in his vision the four winds of heaven stirring up the sea, and four "beasts" coming up out of the sea. *"Beasts" as we have noted can indicate nations or kingdoms in Scripture.*

The first beast was like a lion and had the wings of an eagle, but then its wings were clipped and it was lifted up on its hind feet like a man, and given the mind of a man.

The second beast was like a hungry bear, raised up on one side, and eating three ribs, Dan 7:5.

Then a third beast was like a leopard, which had four wings on its back, and it had four heads (a very strange leopard, right?). Already, when we look ahead to chapter 8 we see what seems to be parallels to the description of the kingdoms given there. Before we read any further we are apt to think that the leopard represents the kingdom of Greece which was to come as described in Daniel 8, and was to be divided four ways.

Then we come to the fourth beast.

Figures of winged lions were common in the ancient East. This image is from Nineveh.

> ... dreadful and terrible, and strong exceedingly; and it had great iron teeth: **it devoured and brake in pieces, and stamped the residue with the feet of it**: and it was diverse from all the beasts that were before it; and it had ten horns. Dan 7:7 KJV (*bold emphasis added*)

Now we are seeing Daniel 7 as a parallel to both Daniel 8 and Daniel 2. In Daniel 2 the fourth kingdom which would come was characterized by iron legs and feet made of iron mixed with clay. It would seem that the fourth beast in Daniel 7 is also the Roman Empire. Then there is also a strange passage in Daniel 7 about what is presumably the Roman Empire.

> I considered the horns, and, behold, there came up among them another little horn, before whom there were three of the first horns plucked up by the roots: and, behold, in this horn were eyes like the eyes of man, and a mouth speaking great things. Dan 7:8 KJV

Dan 7:19 says this beast has "claws of bronze" NASB. Does this indicate some overlap between the third and the fourth world empires? The ten horns of Dan 7:7, 20, would seem to overlap with the (ten?) toes of Dan 2:41-42. Let me say frankly that I do not know of anything *specifically* that Dan 7:8 refers to in the Roman Empire. Perhaps that is just my ignorance. Does it not refer to Rome, and is it then "typical"/a "type," a symbol, of something else which would happen later? Perhaps we should come back to this verse later. This is clearly a mystery, at least to most of us. Still it does seem that it is speaking of some particular "little" "horn" who is bragging about himself, who pulls up three other "horns" by their roots. That is to say, the entire dynasties upon which these "horns" are based, are completely destroyed. It still seems to be speaking of the days of the dreadful beast with iron teeth: the Roman Empire, but it also has similarities to the small horn in Daniel 8.

Then a grand court scene opens up in heaven

> 9 I beheld till the thrones were cast down, and the Ancient of days did sit, whose garment *was* white as snow, and the hair of his head like the pure wool: his throne *was like* the fiery flame, *and* his wheels as burning fire. 10 A fiery stream issued and came forth from before him: thousand thousands ministered unto him, and ten thousand times ten thousand stood before him: the judgment was set, and the books were opened. Dan 7:9-10 KJV

It *appears* that this is a court in session *in heaven* occurring *during* history! Then this beast is judged, and sentenced to death by this heavenly court—*within history!*

> 11 I beheld then because of the voice of the great words which the horn spake: I beheld even till the beast was slain, and his body destroyed, and **given to the burning flame**. 12 As concerning the rest of the beasts, they had their dominion taken away: yet their lives were prolonged for a season and time. Dan 7:11-12 KJV (*bold emphasis added*)

Then it speaks of other things happening before this heavenly court. Someone like a "Son of man" appears before the Lord, "the Ancient of Days." He is given a kingdom which includes the nations of the world, and his kingdom is one which will never pass away, Dan 7:13-14. Clearly this must be speaking of the kingdom which is supposed to come in the days of the Roman Empire, which we saw in Daniel chapter two. If you will remember, a spiritual kingdom it seemed to be, which would "stand for ever," Dan 2:44. And the *"one* like the Son of Man" in Daniel 7:13? He must be the ruler of this eternal kingdom. Indeed, Jesus often referred to himself as a "son of man" in passages like Mtt 9:6. Daniel then summarizes what this passage teaches.

> 17 These great beasts, which are four, *are* four kings, *which* shall arise out of the earth. 18 But the saints of the most High shall take the kingdom, and possess the kingdom for ever, even for ever and ever. Dan 7:17-18 KJV

Hm-m-m-m! The "great beasts ... are four kings." Then Daniel asked for more specific information about that terrible fourth beast.

> 20 And of the ten horns that *were* in his head, and *of* the other which came up, and before whom three fell; even *of* that horn that had eyes, and a mouth that spake very great things, whose look *was* more stout than his fellows. 21 I beheld, and the same horn made war with the saints, and prevailed against them; 22 Until the Ancient of days came, and judgment was given to the saints of the most High; and

the time came that the saints possessed the kingdom.

Dan 7:20-22 KJV (*bold emphasis added*)

The saints "receive" the kingdom in Dan 7:18, and take "possession" of the kingdom in Dan 7:22. Two different events? Jesus said the kingdom was at hand in Mtt 3:2. Does Dan 7:18-22 span the entire Christian age? Compare Col 1:13 with 2Tim 4:18.

Once again the subject is the "other" horn who deals with a certain ten horns, and who cuts off three horns, and makes war on the saints. The saints are the holy ones, those who are made holy by the blood of the sacrifice, those who are truly believers in the Lord their God. The Hebrew word is *qaddish* קַדִּישׁ, and the Greek word for saint is *hagios* ἅγιος, as in 1 Cor 1:2 where Paul says he is writing,

> Unto the church of God which is at Corinth, to them that are sanctified in Christ Jesus, **called *to be* saints**, with all that in every place call upon the name of Jesus Christ our Lord, both theirs and ours:
> KJV (*bold emphasis added*)

This little horn, with ten other horns, are making war on the saints "and prevailed against them;" Dan 7:21. It says this is from the ten horns of the fourth beast, but it is very like the little horn of Daniel 8. Notice that this little horn does not seem to be making war on a nation-state as such, but rather on the saints! Notice that this horn is winning this war against the saints, until God intervenes, "and the time came that the saints possessed the kingdom."

Thus we have at least two discussions in the book of Daniel about powerful rulers who oppose the people of God and who seem to win against them, and one description seems to be associated with the Greeks and one seems to be associated with the Romans. Are these separate persecutions which are being pictured? Or are these overlapping descriptions, overlapping symbolic pictures? Such is not unknown in prophecy. *Or is it both ways?* That is to say perhaps these are separate persecutions which are being described, *and* they are **both** symbolic of some greater persecution which will happen, or in Bible terms, they are "types," or "shadows," or "patterns," or pehaps even prototypes!

If you have already read ahead to the book of Revelation, written in the first century AD, during the days of the Roman Empire, it is easy to see the relevance of these prophecies of a little ruler who bands together with ten other rulers to make war on the saints. **To pretend that these prophecies somehow have nothing to do with the book of Revelation is ludicrous.**

But before that perhaps we need to backup and look at the grand scheme of the book of Daniel.

Synoptic Descriptions:

Clearly these visions in the book of Daniel are overlapping, synoptic visions. It is very plain that Babylon is pictured in the vision in Daniel chapter 2 and also in Daniel chapter 7. It is plain that the Medo-Persian Empire is pictured in Daniel chapter 2, and in chapter 7 and chapter 8. It is plain that the Greek Empire started by Alexander the Great is pictured in Daniel chapter 2, and chapter 7, and chapter 8. The four sections into which the Greek Empire was divided is pictured in both chapters 7 and 8. Lastly the Roman Empire is pictured in chapters 2, and 7. These are not the only places these kingdoms appear in the book of Daniel, but that is what we have seen in our examinations so far.

Each vision is different in nature. In Daniel 2 it is the image of a statue, with different kingdoms being represented by different parts of the statue. In Daniel 7 it is various beasts, with the fourth beast being unnamed, but it is described as great and terrible and very different from the others. In Daniel 8 the image is of a goat and a ram, and it is here that we receive specific clues as to interpretation, and are even given the names of two of the succeeding kingdoms, Medo-Persian and Greece. Because of this we are able with more confidence to know the interpretations of Daniel 2 and Daniel 7. It is also here in Daniel 8 that we are specifically told that horns often represent specific lines of rulers.

Other little clues also help us to see that the visions are overlapping. In both Daniel 7 and Daniel 8, the second kingdom of the Greeks is pictured as splitting into four parts. In Daniel 8 it is pictured as four horns coming up, to replace the single horn which has been broken off. In Daniel 7 the third animal, a leopard, has both four wings and four heads. I think most of us instinctively assume that they are just different representations of the same thing. Also the irons legs and feet of the fourth kingdom which "crushes and shatters all things" in Daniel 2, and the "large iron teeth" of the fourth beast in Daniel 7, instantly cause us to assume that these visions are parallel and overlapping. Similarities of association cause us to see these relationships, almost unconsciously.

One of the Biggest Mistakes We Make!

Let me be emphatic on this point. It would be foolishness to stack these visions end to end, and assume for instance, the vision in chapter 7 *follows* the vision in chapter 2 as a continuation of the story. And that the vision in chapter 8 tells us of things which will follow the events described Daniel chapter 7, and so on until the end of the book. That would be a foolish way to handle these texts.

It should be pointed out that parallel accounts is a common way that we are instructed through the prophets, by parallel, overlapping, stories. God commonly gives us more than one way to get a particular point. Sometimes one prophecy will tell us things that another one does not, but their accounts supplement each other so that we may more easily get the full picture. That is the way the New Testament is written also. Jesus' parables of the kingdom of heaven are intended to help us view what the kingdom of heaven will be like from more than one point of view, and were never intended to be stacked end-to-end.

However, sometimes people approach the book of Revelation as if we should put the visions end-to-end. Naturally, this is a disaster for understanding the texts of these "revelations."

Parallel-Overlapping-Progressive-Cumulative Descriptions

These visions complement each other. The vision for instance in Daniel 2 tells us some things about the fourth kingdom that we are not told in the other visions. The feet of the image are made of a mixture and iron and clay. So while the feet have considerable strength in them, there is also considerable weakness there also: the clay. The fourth kingdom is incredibly strong but its foundations, its feet, are also weak. That is something we are not told in the other visions.

The visions in chapters 7 and 8 tell us that the third kingdom of the Greeks will start out unified, but will end up being broken into four centers of power and authority. That is something we are not clearly told in Daniel chapter 2. And so on.

If we soon forget these obvious lessons, we will immediately get into trouble in the book of Revelation.

Destructive Culture Wars:
Antiochus IV and the Maccabees

This is just a synopsis of the life of Antiochus IV Epiphanes. There is much more to tell than can be included here, and the story is very much to the credit of the Jews who resisted their oppressions. It is a complicated piece of history, and Scripture and the historical records which we have do not always talk in the same terms. This is recorded in some detail in the books of 1 Maccabees and 2 Maccabees, with 1 Maccabees being generally credited as being a trustworthy history, and 2 Maccabees less so. These books, though not claiming to be Scripture, are well worth reading to understand this phase of Jewish history. Also much of this history is covered by historians such as Livy, Polybius, and Josephus.

Antiochus IV was the son of Antiochus the Great, ruler of the large kingdom of Syria, part of the Selucid dynasty, and one of what Daniel 11 calls "the kings of the North."

Antiochus the Great won the land of Palestine at the battle of Paneas (198 BC) from the Ptolemies, the rulers of Egypt (called "the kings of the South" in Daniel 11 because Egypt was south of Palestine). The Jews overall got along well with the rulers of both the North and the South, until the time of Antiochus IV. The father, Antiochus the Great, was an ambitious and capable ruler, who overextended himself, and brought great misery on both himself and his kingdom. Though he greatly outnumbered his enemies, he was defeated by the Romans at the battle of Magnesia in Asia Minor in the year 190 BC. As a result, Antiochus and all of Syria were burdened with heavy tribute to Rome (we would call them "reparation payments"). Additionally, he had to send some hostages to Rome, including his young adult son Antiochus IV.

Antiochus IV, as a young man, was a little on the wild side, and at times even erratic. Often he would escape his restraints, and though a prince, he would talk and eat and party with common people. He was very generous and liberal with gifts, but inconsistent, and often would give common people extravagant gifts, and important people simple gifts. He

Antiochus IV Epiphanes, a picture from an ancient coin.

sometimes even took baths in the public baths with common folks. He petitioned for election to a position as a Roman aedile or tribune, dressed up in a Roman toga, shook hands, hugged some people, and begged for their votes. Once elected he was very conscientious in judging from a Roman style ivory chair. Some thought that he was a little out of his head, Livy, *The History of Rome*, Book XLI. 20-22. No one knew how to take him, and many thought that he really did not know how to take himself.

His surname, "Epiphanes," according to the classical Greek-English Lexicon by Liddell and Scott (Seventh Edition, Harper and Brothers, NY, 1883) conveys the idea of one who is conspicuous and famous, and distinguished by great deeds. It was evidently a name given to Antiochus IV before he became king. Contrary to what some scholars have said, it does not by itself indicate divinity. Many have tried to picture Antiochus IV as thinking uniquely of himself as a "god," but these pictures are often overdrawn. Two centuries before Antiochus IV, the first of the Ptolemies named himself "Ptolemy I, Lagi Soter," or "Great Savior." Antiochus the Great's great-grandfather was named "Antiochus II Theos," or literally "Antiochus II God"! (He reigned from 261-246 BC, and is mentioned in Dan 11:6.) To say that one is distinguished or illustrious is mild by comparison!

In fact, Antiochus IV was very zealous in supporting the temples to various "gods." Livy notes that he started a temple to Jupiter Olympus at Athens, which was well conceived and magnificent, and another to Jupiter Capitolinus in Antioch, but neither were finished because of his short reign. Livy, Book XLI. 20. The ruins of one of these temples still remains.

He introduced gladiatorial games to Antioch, which some found offensive at first, but gradually accepted and liked, and he gave many young men a degree of eagerness to fight.

His older brother was king first, but he connived to overthrow him. A man by the name of Helidorius was instrumental in overthrowing the older brother, Seleucus IV Philopater, Dan 11:20. The Roman historian Livy, in his *The History of Rome*, pictures Antiochus IV as paying tribute (late), through emissaries to Rome, giving his apologies for it being late, and adding other offerings with the tribute. He expressed that he remembered the kindness which the Senate had shown him when as a young man he was a hostage in Rome for his father Antiochus the Great (AD 189 and following), and had lived as royalty and not as a prisoner, Livy, Book XLII. 6. Clearly, Antiochus IV was never able to merely do as he pleased

The Greek historian Polybius in his *Histories*, describes Antiochus IV as "energetic and daring in design, and worthy of the royal dignity, except as regards his management of the campaign near Pelusium," in his war with Ptolemy Philometer (Polybius, *The Histories*, Vol VI, translated by W. R. Paton, Harvard University Press, Cambridge, Mass, 1927, Book XXVIII, 18.1).

Then Antiochus IV decided to try to expand his territory and his income by conquering Egypt. He won a naval battle at Pelusium, crossed the Nile on a hastily built bridge, and was threatening Alexandria, Livy, *The History of Rome*, Book XLIV, 11.

The Ptolemies knew they were near defeat. They sent dirty and scraggly emissaries to Rome as from a defeat. They suggested that the Romans merely send diplomats to Antiochus in the desert outside of Alexandria, Egypt, and threaten war if Antiochus did not withdraw. They calculated that the mere thought of war with Rome would cause him to withdraw, such was the respect he had gained for the Romans during his time as a hostage there.

At first the Romans held back (they had plenty of commitments at the time), but finally sent Popilius Laenas with a small delegation. Antiochus was dictating terms of defeat to the Ptolemies (Livy, Book XLV. 11-12) when Popilius arrived at his camp in the desert outside Alexandria, Egypt.

When they met, Popilius Laenas refused to take the hand of Antiochus, and handed him a copy of the Roman Senate's counsel and said for him to read it first. The king read it, and said he would consult with his advisors on the matter. At this point Popilius drew a circle around Antiochus in the sand, and said he must answer before he left the circle or he would be at war with Rome. Antiochus was astonished by this bravado, and after some hesitation agreed. Then the Romans warmly extended their hand to him. Arrangements and times for withdrawal were agreed upon and the Romans stayed until that happened. Then the Romans went to see that the victorious Syrians evacuated Cyprus, where they had been successful in defeating the forces of the Egyptians. (This story is recorded in Livy's *The History of Rome*, Book XLV. 11-12, and also in Polybius' *The Histories*, Book XXIX. 27.1-13). Undoubtably Antiochus IV was very angry, but felt that he was helpless to oppose the Romans.

Then, having all of the expenses of a major war, but none of the loot to pay for it, Epiphanes decided to rob the temple at Jerusalem on his second return journey to Syria.

> [20] And Antiochus, after he had struck Egypt, returned in the hundred and forty and third year, and went up against Israel and Jerusalem with a great multitude, [21] and entered presumptuously into the sanctuary, and took the golden altar, and the candlestick of the light, and all that pertained thereto, [22] and the table of the show bread, and the cups to pour withal, and the bowls, and the golden censers, and the veil, and the crowns, and the adorning of gold which was on the face of the temple, and he peeled it all off. [23] And he took the silver and the gold and the precious vessels; and he took the hidden treasures which he found. [24] And when he had taken all, he went away into his own land, and he made a great slaughter, and spoke very presumptuously.
> 1 Maccabees 1:20-24 WEB

According to 2 Maccabees 5:21 he stole 1800 talents of gold and silver. Josephus says,

> So he left the temple bare, and took away the golden candlesticks, and the golden altar [of incense], and table [of shewbread], and the altar [of burnt offering]; and did not abstain from even the veils, which were made of fine linen and scarlet. He also emptied it of its secret treasures, and left nothing at all remaining; and by this means cast the Jews into great lamentation,
> Josephus, *Antiquities*, Book 12. 5. 4.250

Now in the Middle-East of Antiochus' time, Greek culture was winning the day, but it was a gradual win. In Judah many were turning away from Judaism to Greek culture. Antiochus was appointing the high priests in Jerusalem. The priests were bidding for the job, and one made a very high bid and in addition was offering to build a gymnasium where the men could exercise naked according to the Greek style. Many inroads were being made into Jewish culture. Josephus tells part of the story this way:

237 About this time, upon the death of Onias the high priest, they gave the high priesthood to Jesus his brother; for that son which Onias left [or Onias 4] was yet but an infant; and, in its proper place, we will inform the reader of all the circumstances that befell this child. 238 But this Jesus, who was the brother of Onias, was deprived of the high priesthood by the king, who was angry with him and gave it to his younger brother, whose name also was Onias; for Simon had these three sons, each of whom the priesthood came, as we have already informed the reader. 239 This Jesus changed his name to Jason; but Onias was called Menelaus. Now as the former high priest, Jesus, raised a sedition against Menelaus, who was ordained after him, the multitude were divided between them both. And the sons of Tobias took the part of Menelaus, 240 but the greater part of the people assisted Jason; and by that means Menelaus and the sons of Tobias were distressed, and retired to Antiochus and informed him, that they were desirous to leave the laws of their country, and the Jewish way of living according to them, and to follow the king's laws, and the Grecian way of living: 241 wherefore they desired his permission to build them a Gymnasium at Jerusalem. And when he had given them leave they also hid the circumcision of their genitals, that even when they were naked they might appear to be Greeks. Accordingly, they left off all the customs that belonged to their own country, and imitated the practices of the other nations. *Antiquities of the Jews*, Book 12. 5. 1. 237-241

Even so, evidently it was going too slowly for Antiochus. No doubt he realized that one of the weaknesses of his kingdom was the cultural divides between different subject populations, and nowhere were they greater than between Jews and gentiles. Antiochus decided to end this cultural divide between the Greeks and the Jews. So the culture war started.

41 And king Antiochus wrote to his whole kingdom, that all should be one people, 42 and that each should forsake his own laws. And all the nations agreed according to the word of the king; 43 and many of Israel consented to his worship, and sacrificed to the idols, and profaned the Sabbath. 44 And the king sent letters by the hand of messengers to Jerusalem and the cities of Judah, that they should follow laws strange to the land, 45 and should forbid whole burnt offerings and sacrifice and drink offerings in the sanctuary; and should profane the Sabbaths and feasts, 46 and pollute the sanctuary and those who were holy 47 that they should build altars, and temples, and shrines for idols, and should sacrifice swine's flesh and unclean beasts: 48 and that they should leave their sons uncircumcised, that they should make their souls abominable with all manner of uncleanness and profanation:
1 Maccabees 1:41-48 WEB

Then the desolating sacrilege was set up on the Jewish lunar month of Chislev 15, 168 BC, which overlaps our months of November and December.

> [54] Now on fifteenth day of Chislev, in the hundred forty and fifth year, they built an abomination of desolation upon the altar, and in the cities of Judah on every side they built *idol* altars. [55] And at the doors of the houses and in the streets they burned incense. [56] And they tore in pieces the books of the law which they found, and set them on fire [57] And wherever was found with any a book of the covenant, and if any consented to the law, the king's sentence delivered him to death.
>
> 1 Maccabees 1:54-57 WEB

According to Josephus they offered a pig on the altar, *Antiquities*, Book 12. 5. 4. 253. Even women and children were put to death for minor infractions of these rules. However "many in Israel were fully resolved and confirmed in themselves not to eat unclean things." 1 Maccabees 1:62.

This was the beginning of a long and bitter cultural war in Judea and Galilee. Gradually the Jews gained strength, and obtained additional arms from the enemy by guerrilla warfare. Finally, although greatly outnumbered, the Jews were able to win some major battles against the Syrians. Finally they were able to recapture Jerusalem, cleanse the temple, and reestablish the daily sacrifices.

> [47] And they took whole stones according to the law, and built a new altar after the fashion of the former; [48] and they built the holy place, and the inner parts of the house; and they hallowed the courts. [49] And they made the holy vessels new, and they brought the candlestick, and the altar of burnt offerings and of incense, and the table, into the temple. [50] And they burned incense upon the altar, and they lighted the lamps that were upon the candlestick, and they gave light in the temple. [51] And they set loaves upon the table, and spread out the veils, and finished all the works which they made.
>
> [52] And they rose up early in the morning, on the five and twentieth day of the ninth month, which is the month Chislev, in the hundred and forty and eighth year [53] And offered sacrifice according to the law upon the new altar of burnt offerings, which they had made.
>
> 1 Maccabees 4:47-53 WEB

1 Maccabees goes on to say that the Jews decided to celebrate this cleansing and reestablishment of worship at the same time every year. So came about what in the New Testament is called the "Feast of Dedication" (Jn 10:22), and which modern Jews called Hanukkah. Like Easter, Hanukkah is also calculated by a lunar calendar, not our regular solar calendar, and this is why these feasts fall on different days every year.

Finally, the Jews began winning victory after victory against the Syrians. Antiochus was driven to desperation.

[27] But when king Antiochus heard these things, he was full of indignation: and he sent and gathered together all the forces of his realm, an exceedingly strong army [28] And he opened his treasury, and gave his forces pay for a year, and commanded them to be ready for every need. [29] And he saw that the money failed from his treasures, and that the tributes of the country were small, because of the dissension and plague which he had brought upon the land, to the end that he might take away the laws which had been from the first days; [30] and he feared that he should not have enough as at other times for the charges and the gifts which he gave aforetime with a liberal hand, and he abounded above the kings that were before him. [31] And he was exceedingly perplexed in his mind, and he determined to go into Persia, and to take the tributes of the countries, and to gather much money. 1 Maccabees 3:27-31 WEB

Antiochus left a man by the name of Lysias in charge while he was gone, but he lost even more battles to the Jews under their leader Judas Maccabeus ("Judas the Hammer"). Later Antiochus wished to rob the sanctuary of Artemis in Elymais, but was prevented by local "barbarian tribes," and died at Tabae in Persia, very shaken, just a little on the crazy side, Polybius, Book XXXI. 9.1-4.

The war between Syria and the Jews continued, with the Jews gradually winning, and the Maccabees establishing the Hasmonean dynasty. This dynasty ruled Judah until the Roman general Pompey took Jerusalem in 63 BC. Herod the Great in the first century BC married a beautiful lady named Mariamne of the Hasmonean dynasty, but later had her and the last of the Hasmoneans murdered.

This concludes a very brief overview of the life of Antiochus IV Epiphanes, for the purpose of now comparing his life to the prophecies of Scripture, and in looking for either fulfillments or "types." **Now we consider whether Antiochus IV Epiphanes fits Daniels prophecies.**

Unfinished Business

Daniel 8 and Antiochus Epiphanes

First let us look again at the last half of Daniel 8, then go to Daniel 11.
We have seen how in Daniel 8 it speaks of a "little horn" who,

It even magnified *itself* to be equal with the Commander of the host; and it removed the regular sacrifice from Him, and the place of His sanctuary was thrown down. Dan 8:11 NASB

Then if we look at the history of Antiochus IV, he *did* remove the sacrifice from before the Lord in Jerusalem, and he did dismantle the sanctuary to the

Lord in Jerusalem, and *perhaps* made himself equal to the Commander of the host of heaven. Dan 8:11 could be construed as true of Antiochus, or could be regarded as a little exaggerated. It also said of this little horn,

> And an host was given *him* against the daily *sacrifice* by reason of transgression, and it cast down the truth to the ground; and it practised, and prospered. Dan 8:12 KJV

The worship of Jews was given over to oppressors, because of "transgression" among God's people it says in Dan 8:12. Perhaps to wake them up. Clearly the last prophet of the Old Testament, the prophet Malachi, testified to the unfaithfulness of Israel, later in the 400's BC. Also we know from the New Testament prophets, including Jesus Himself, that the situation had not gotten better by the first century AD. *So being given over to Antiochus because of transgression is very believable.*

> And it grew up to the host of heaven; and it cast down *some* of the host and *some* of the stars to the ground, and trampled them. Dan 8:10 NKJV

But the host of heaven, the armies of heaven, being handed over to Antiochus "on account of transgression"? It could be true, but it sounds like exaggerated language. Then the last part of Dan 8:12, "and it practised, and prospered," is definitely **not** true of Antiochus. His reign was only a short ten or eleven years. Antiochus' major schemes in Egypt, Palestine, and in trying to rob a temple in Persia, did NOT work, and instead of leading him to prosper, it led to his undoing.

Consider at this point what Scripture says about how long the period of time for these events was to be.

> [13] Then I heard a holy one speaking, and another holy one said to that particular one who was speaking, "How long will the vision *about* the regular sacrifice apply, while the transgression causes horror, so as to allow both the holy place and the host to be trampled?" [14] He said to me, "For 2,300 evenings *and* mornings; then the holy place will be properly restored." Dan 8:13-14 [1] NASB

[1] In Dan 8:14 the text of the NASB, ESV, NET, NIV, etc., are clearly more accurate to the Hebrew than the KJV and the NKJV. The Hebrew is quite literally *ad* (until) **erev** (evening) **boquer** (moring) עַד עֶרֶב בֹּקֶר, There are no articles here in the Hebrew text, and no "and" is there, and the word "day" or "days" is **not** there. So it is literally "until evening morning 2,300." The KJV and the NKJV takes the phrase to mean 2,300 "days", and **paraphrase** the text **instead of translating it**. So the Hebrew phrase **could be** taken as 2,300 days (as in the KJV), **or it could be** taken to mean 1,150 evenings plus 1,150 mornings, for a total of 2,300. These would be radically different interpretations. It would be useless for your author to try to be dogmatic here. I leave it to the reader to think it out and try to determine which period of time fits where. Lastly, I might ask, in light of the seemingly intended ambiguity, is perhaps a double meaning involved here?

It is clearly talking about the daily sacrifices to the Lord, as described in Ex 29:38-42, and there was both a morning and an evening sacrifice. So if the daily sacrifices are to be stopped for "2,300 evenings and mornings," then it *could be* taken as 1,150 days. The following addresses how 1,150 days might apply in the days of Antiochus Epiphanes.

As we pointed out earlier, Epiphanes started building the altar to Zeus on the lunar month of Chislev 15, 168 BC, 1 Maccabees 1:54. Antiochus had a pig sacrificed on the altar to Zeus on the lunar month of Chislev 25, 168 BC, 1 Maccabees 1:59. Judas Maccabeus then reestablished the sacrifices to the Lord on Chislev 25, 165 BC, 1 Maccabees 4:52-53. As Josephus observes,

> [320] Now it so fell out, that these things were done on the very same day on which their divine worship had fallen off, and was reduced to a profane and common use, **after three years' time**; for so it was, that the temple was made desolate by Antiochus, **and so continued for three years**. ...
>
> [322] And this desolation came to pass according to the prophecy of Daniel, **which was given four hundred and eight years before**; for he declared that the Macedonians would dissolve that worship [for some time]. *Antiquities.* 12. 7. 6. 320, 322 (*bold emphasis added*)

Chislev 25, 168 to Chislev 25th, 165 would be exactly three lunar years.

But the prophecy is not given in years but is in essence given in days, 1,115 days. A common solar year, for the commonly used calendars of the times of which we speak, would 365 days (or 12 months of 30 days each, plus 5 days). Thus three years by a solar calendar would be 3 x 365 = 1,095 days. That is close to 1,115 days of Daniel. Add then the 10 days between the stopping of sacrifices on the old altar of the Lord in the temple on Chislev the 15th (1 Maccabees 1:54), and then you have 1,105 days, which is very close to the 1,115 days of Dan 8:14.

However, the records in 1 Maccabees, 2 Maccabees, and Josephus, are in *lunar years!* A lunar month in our own times is approximately 29 and 1/2 days. A lunar year of 12 months then would be approximately 354 days, with an extra month being thrown in every three years or so, to keep the lunar calendar in synchronization with the solar seasons of the year. So every three years or so they would have a lunar year of about 383 and 1/2 days.

*The bottom line is that we **may** not have enough information to exactly figure out all of this.* Additionally, when we get this close in figuring things, questioning Scripture aside, we should remember that one or more of our historical records may be in error, *our* calculations of the calendars may be in error, or we may have picked some false assumption in any one of these areas, without being aware of where and how it happened. At times, a big dose of humility is the best cure for getting carried away with how much we supposedly know.

However, the figures in Dan 8:14 and the figures we can readily get from history are very close. In fact so close that a casual reader might readily agree that this passage is talking about the events which occurred around Antiochus Epiphanes. When you have a Biblical type at work, for instance in 2Sam 7:12-16 where Solomon is symbolic of Jesus the Christ, most would readily agree that the passage applied to Solomon, as indeed Solomon was claiming in both 1 Kings and 2 Chronicles, but it would have seemed that perhaps some exaggerated language was involved. Only as time progressed would the missing parts of the prophecy tend to stand out more.

Also there are other factors to notice in Daniel 8. An angel is told to explain this vision to Daniel (Dan 8:16), and the angel Gabriel tells Daniel that this vision is about **"the time of the end,"** Dan 8:17. This also is perplexing, because Antiochus Epiphanes is not about the end of *anything!* This Greek king was not about the end of time, or the end of the Mosaic covenant, nor the end of gentile overlordship of Palestine (although there was some reprieve from the gentiles under the Maccabees). So what is this about? Also it does not sound like something a forger would invent of the times of Antiochus Epiphanes, *after the fact!* The angel then makes all of this even more emphatic by saying,

> He said, "Behold, I am going to let you know what will occur **at the final period of the indignation,** for *it* pertains to the appointed time of the end. Dan 8:19 NASB (*bold emphasis added*)

An early second century BC deceiver, accurately knowing what had happened to Antiochus Epiphanes (and the prophecies in Daniel 8 do reflect knowledge of what was to happen), would also know that none of these things were "the time of the end" of anything, and would not write such nonsense as a forgery. Only if these texts were already in place from the time of Daniel, and were following the Biblical pattern of types, and Antiochus Epiphanes was symbolic of someone who would come at the "time of the end," would this make any sense.

How does the angel at this point explain this "little horn"?

> [23] And in the latter time of their kingdom, **when the transgressors are come to the full,** a king of fierce countenance, and understanding dark sentences, shall stand up. [24] And his power shall be mighty, **but not by his own power**: and he shall destroy wonderfully, **and shall prosper, and practise, and shall destroy the mighty and the holy people.** [25] And through his policy also he shall cause craft to prosper in his hand; and he shall magnify *himself* in his heart, and by peace shall destroy many: he shall also stand up against the Prince of princes; but he shall be broken without hand. Dan 8:23-25 KJV (*bold emphasis added*)

"Without hand" KJV, thus "without human agency," NASB. Let us consider this part of the description in the light of our information about Antiochus Epiphanes. In general terms we might say this fits him. It says this will occur, "When transgressors are come to the full," and as we have seen that *could* very well apply to Antiochus. He did "destroy many while *they are* at ease." You might say he caused "deceit to proper," at least for a while. In a way it does seem he died of natural causes, so you might say that he was "broken without human agency." ***On the other hand,*** it might be argued that it was the opposition of human beings which *caused him* to "be broken." In other words, there was some human agency.

Despite that, there are fine points even here we might question. Once again it says that he will "prosper and perform *his will*" Dan 8:24 NASB, which as we have seen *does **not** apply* to Antiochus Epiphanes short reign of ten or so years. In that line you could argue that he never actually destroyed "the mighty and the holy people." ***So parts seem to fit Epiphanes, and other parts do not seem to!***

Then we come to the superficially parallel account at the end of Daniel chapter 7.

Daniel 7 and the Ten Horns and Another Horn

We have already seen that our best clues to the intention of Daniel's visions was in Daniel chapter 8 where it clearly identifies the second and third kingdoms following Babylon as the Medo-Persian Empire, and the Greek Empire. It is well to point out that not only history, but also Daniel treats the Medo-Persian Empire as one entity (the two horns of the ram, as we have pointed out). The Medes and the Persians were *not* two separate empires as the Liberals try to pretend in their commentaries on the book of Daniel. That of course means that the fourth kingdom, which Daniel asks about in Dan 7:15-16, is emphatically the Roman empire, NOT the Greeks who were clearly pictured as the leopard with four wings and four heads in Dan 7:6, of whom Antiochus Epiphanes was a little king in one of those four branches of the Greek Empire.

So we come to the last part of Daniel 7.

> [19] Then I would know the truth of the fourth beast, which was diverse from all the others, exceeding dreadful, whose teeth *were of* iron, and his nails *of* brass; *which* devoured, brake in pieces, and stamped the residue with his feet; [20] And of the ten horns that *were* in his head, and *of* the other which came up, and before whom three fell; even *of* that horn that had eyes, and a mouth that spake very great things, whose look *was* more stout than his fellows.
> Dan 7:19-20 KJV (*bold emphasis added*)

Remember that the little horn of Daniel 8 has to do with the *third kingdom* of the Greeks, and that the ten horns and "the horn which had eyes and a mouth uttering great *boasts*" is clearly of the *fourth kingdom*, the Romans. It does not here really call this special horn a "little horn." We saw earlier that a horn can be either a kingdom, or a dynasty, or an individual king (as Alexander the Great is the "conspicuous horn between the eyes" of the goat in Daniel 8:5, which is later broken off, Dan 8:8). So it seems this "horn which had eyes and a mouth uttering great *boasts*," seemingly indicates an individual king.

This particular individual horn then has some relationship with ten particular horns/kings or dynasties. This horn with eyes and mouth then causes three of these horns to fall, Dan 7:20.

The explanation given by the angel is that the special bragging horn and the ten horns are emphatically of the fourth kingdom of iron, Dan 7:23-24. The ten horns are ten kings, and that special horn will come to power after they come to power. The special horn will be different, and will "subdue three kings."

Subduing Three Kings/Shepherds, Zechariah 11

At this point, talking about the special horn subduing three kings in Dan 7:8, 20, 24, I am led to think of the prophet Zechariah's discussion of the worthless shepherd. Kings in Scripture are sometimes referred to as horns in prophecy (as has been shown), but are also commonly spoken of as shepherds of the people they rule over. For instance, in 2Sam 5:2 it speaks of God choosing King David to shepherd Israel, and there are many other examples.

Zechariah has a running commentary over several chapters in his book of prophecy, about both the good shepherd (Jesus the Christ), and also about an unnamed "worthless shepherd." In Zech 11:4 Zechariah is commanded to take up the implements of a worthless shepherd, to pasture "the flock *doomed* to slaughter," Zech 11:4. So Zechariah did what he was told.

> [7] So I pastured the flock *doomed* to slaughter, hence the afflicted of the flock. And I took for myself two staffs: the one I called Favor and the other I called Union; so I pastured the flock. [8] **Then I annihilated the three shepherds in one month**, for my soul was impatient with them, and their soul also was weary of me.
> Zech 11:7-8 NASB (*bold emphasis added*)

All we can say at this time is, Wow! So here is one particular worthless shepherd/king, who gets tired of three other shepherd/kings, and kills them, so it seems to imply. It gives us other details also. These three shepherds are all destroyed in one month.

We have to ask: Could this be the three ribs in the mouth of the bear in Dan 7:5, speaking of the Medo-Persian Empire? Zechariah was prophesying in the days of the Medo-Persian kings. *Or* could this be the same three kings/ horns who are uprooted/fall/subdued in Dan 7:8, 20, 24, pictured as being in the days of the Roman Empire? Zechariah does not tell us when this will happen, but more details are given about this worthless shepherd. No one has come up with a convincing case for someone who fulfills either the text at the end of the vision in Daniel 7, or the prophecy of Zechariah.

At this point in our discussion we will have to leave this as merely a question, but we will come back to the Worthless Shepherd of Zechariah in our study of the book of Revelation.

Wearing Out the Saints, for Three-and-a-Half Years

Then we are told again that this special horn will speak out against God, "the Most High," and will "wear out the saints," and will intend to change the law and the times, Dan 7:25. And the law, and the times, *and the saints*, it says will be given into this special horn's "hand For a time and times and half a time," Dan 7:25 NKJV.

It is talking about how long this special horn will be successful in his operations, and how long the persecution of the saints will last. Various arguments have been given as to how to interpret this "time, times, and half a time." To make this discussion shorter, let it be conceded that most people think this term "a time" refers to a year. "Times" then would refer to two years (in Semitic languages the plural is often used to refer to a pair), and a half a time would refer to half a year. Thus "time, times, and half a time," would mean three and one-half years. The Jews tend to take the phrase this way, and even the Liberals do. Thus the very liberal, *The New Oxford Annotated Bible*, Oxford University Press, Oxford, New York, 1973-1991, which is sort of a touchstone for the Liberal seminary crowd, automatically thinks this refers to Antiochus Epiphanes, and says in the note to Dan 7:25, "*A time, times, and half a time* indicates three and a half years (see 4:36), approximately the time of Antiochus persecution," pg 1269.

It is a logical way to interpret this phrase, and it makes sense in context. Most of the efforts to prove this interpretation *from the Old Testament* are inconclusive, even though the interpretation itself seems very sensible. For the Christian though, the clincher is that this same phrase time, times, and half a time is used in Rev 12:14. That phrase is then explained as "forty-two months" (three and a half years) in Rev 11:2, and Rev 13:5, and in the immediate context it is explained as "one thousand two hundred and sixty days" in both Rev 12:6, and also in Rev 11:3 NKJV (that is to say, forty-two months of thirty days each, 42 X 30 = 1260). Each month having thirty days was the custom in those days. 42 months times 30 days each equals 1,260 days, or 3-1/2 years. Also James says that the period of drought in Elijah's time was "three years and six months," Jas 5:17.

The similarities are too much to be coincidental. This special horn rules / ruins for three and half years. Just the fact of using the exact same period of time of 3-1/2 years in both Daniel and Revelation, with both speaking of coming of a "beast" from the Roman Empire, would seem to indicate either 1.) both are speaking of the same events in the days of the Roman Empire, or 2.) either one or the other, or both, are speaking of *rulers who will arise in the days of Roman Empire* who are *symbolic* of some final horn who is to be one who "[21] ... made war with the saints, and prevailed against them; [22] Until the Ancient of days came, and judgment was given to the saints ..." Dan 7:21-22 KJV.

Always remember: when there is a *symbol*, a "type," in prophecy and also *an ultimate fulfillment*, **both** are spoken of as fulfilling the prophecy. So if Antiochus is intended to be symbolic of someone who will come later, then parts of the prophecy will only fit Antiochus, and parts will only fit the person-place-or-thing symbolized, and parts will fit both the symbol and the thing symbolized, but perhaps in different ways. Finally, **both** *would be spoken of as fulfillments!* For instance Solomon and Jesus, 2Sam 7:12-16, 1Kgs 8:19-20, Heb 1:5.

Jumping ahead in our analysis, let me say that there have been many attempts to identify the ten kings, either in Antiochus IV Epiphanes times, or in Roman times, or modern times, but all of these attempts have so far been speculative and inconclusive. If a true symbol is involved, then this factor of ten kings will become plainer as other factors in the symbols become apparent.

But the court of heaven will sit in judgment and this special horn will be "destroyed forever," Dan 7:26 NASB, but the kingdom of the saints will be an everlasting kingdom, Dan 7:27.

Yes, **there are many similarities** to the story of Antiochus Epiphanes. **Also there are differences,** and the period of time involved is *similar*, but **not exactly the same,** in Daniel 7 and Daniel 8, and in ancient history.

The Kings of Daniel 11

There is much more to talk about in the book of Daniel than I can cover in this book. I am concentrating on those parts of Daniel which may have special relevance to New Testament prophecies, especially the book of Revelation. Now let us take a short look at Daniel chapter 11. Daniel 11 is a continuation of a vision which starts in Daniel 10. That chapter is dated as "In the third year of Cyrus king of Persia," Dan 10:1. Thus we see that this was written after the Medes and the Persians took Babylon (see Dan 5:30). That would be the year 536 BC or there about. We are concentrating on only part of the text, as it might apply to our studies.

The angel gives a brief summary of the remaining years of the Medo-Persian Empire, leaving out some of the less important rulers. Then the angel discusses the coming of Alexander the Great and how his kingdom will be divided "toward the four points of the compass," but not to his own descendants, Dan 11:4.

Then the angel turns to a discussion of two of those lines of kings which succeeded Alexander the Great. Those lines would be the descendants of the first "king of the North," Seleucus I Nictor, who ruled Syria, which was "North" of Israel; and the first "king of the South," Ptolemy I Lagi Soter, who ruled Egypt, which was "South" of Israel.

The text of Daniel 11 then forecasts the back and forth of the kings of the North and the kings of the South, from 323 BC to 175 BC, a period of about 150 years, in Dan 11:5-20. This is such a convoluted story that no one could have guessed this sequence of events. For an overview we have included here a

Kings of the North
(North of Palestine: Syria Asia Minor)
The Seleucids
Dan 11:5 Seleucus I Nictor 311-280 BC
(At first a commander of Ptolemy I)
Antiochus I Soter 280-261 BC

Kings of the South
(South of Palestine: Egypt)
The Ptolemies
Ptolemy I Lagi Soter
323-285 BC
Ptolemy II Philadelphus
285-246 BC. Commissioned a Greek translation of the Old Testament, the same translation used by the early church

Dan 11:6 Antiochus II Theos 261-246 BC
----marries----------------------------
(after divorcing Laodice)
Dan 11:7 Seleucius II Callinicus
(246-226 BC)

Bernice, daughter of Ptolemy II
Dan 11:7 Ptolemy III
Eugeretes I 246-221 BC

Dan 11:10 Seleucus III Ceraunus 226-223 BC

Dan 11:11 Ptolemy IV
Philopator
221-203 BC

Dan 11:10,11,16-18 Antiochus III (The Great) 223-187 BC, takes Palestine away from the Ptolemies, 198 BC

Dan 11:17, His daughter, Cleopatra *marries ------->*
Dan 11:20 his son **Seleucus IV Philopater** 187-175 rules

Dan 11:14 Ptolemy V
Epiphanes 203-181 BC

Dan 11:21,27,28-35 Antiochus IV Epiphanes, 175-164 BC
replaces his brother, invades Egypt, & is turned back by Rome, he

Dan 11:25,27
Ptolemy VI Philometer
181-146 BC

1. Takes away the daily sacrifice, Dan 8:9-13
2. Is a stern faced, master of intrigue, destroys the holy people, Dan 8:23-26
3. Dan 11:31 Sets up an abomination that causes desolation

But 4. Dan 11:36-45 ???? This part doesn't fit what we know about Antiochus Epiphanes, or any ancient ruler.

chart from *Prophecy Principles* about the kings of the North and the kings of the South, and their reigns and relationships. That chart is a good summary in order to get an overview of Daniel 11. For details of this period of time, there are many good commentaries, and also many good histories from ancient times, including Polybius, and Livy, and as far as these events touch the Jews, also Josephus. That is not a complete list, but it is a good place to start. *These things did not happen in the dark, or in a corner, so there is a lot of information about this period of history.* As a matter of fact, most events in this period of time we can date to within a year (hence some of the variations you will see from various sources for dates), and some of these events we can date to the very day when the events happened, because of ancient astronomical observations. Most of the details here are aside from the purpose of this study.

Then starting in Dan 11:21 the prophet seems to discuss that notorious king of the North, Antiochus IV Epiphanes. He was following Seleucus IV Philopater, Dan 11:20,

> "And in his place shall arise a vile person, to whom they will not give the honor of royalty; but he shall come in peaceably, and seize the kingdom by intrigue." Dan 11:21 NKJV

In other words, he was not really supposed to be king, but he was able to seize the throne. Then we read more details about Epiphanes.

> "He shall enter peaceably, even into the richest places of the province; and he shall do *what* his fathers have not done, nor his forefathers: he shall disperse among them the plunder, spoil, and riches; and he shall devise his plans against the strongholds, but *only* for a time."
> Dan 11:24 NKJV

Next is described the beginnings of Epiphanes' expeditions against Egypt.

> "He shall stir up his power and his courage against the king of the South with a great army. And the king of the South shall be stirred up to battle with a very great and mighty army; but he shall not stand, for they shall devise plans against him." Dan 11:25 NKJV

Then it describes his final expedition against Egypt.

> [29] "At the appointed time he shall return and go toward the south; but it shall not be like the former or the latter. [30] For ships from Cyprus shall come against him; therefore he shall be grieved, and return in rage against the holy covenant, and do *damage*.
> "So he shall return and show regard for those who forsake the holy covenant." Dan 11:29-30 NKJV

Kittim (NASB, etc.) is a term, originally referring only to Cyprus, but which came to be used in Hebrew for any foreigners coming in ships. You can consult various Hebrew Lexicons on the subject. Here it seems to refer to the Romans, and the face-off in the Egyptian desert between Antiochus IV and the Roman emissary, Popilius Laenas, which we described earlier, a well known event from ancient history. Then it points out that when he returned from Egypt he became angry at the Jews who insisted on holding to the Mosaic covenant. Next the prophecy describes his destruction of the worship of the LORD God, and the setting up of an altar, and evidently also an image, of the Greek "god" Zeus.

> "And forces shall be mustered by him, and they shall defile the sanctuary fortress; then they shall take away the daily *sacrifices*, and place *there* the abomination of desolation." Dan 11:31 NKJV

This is the original text of the widely discussed "abomination of desolation," and it seems first to refer to setting up a pagan idol in the temple of the LORD Himself, a detestable act which is said to make everything desolate. (And yes, it is singular in Hebrew, "**the** abomination.") In context with Antiochus IV it would refer to the war which these actions started, which indeed ruined many people's lives for many years. This all *seems* to speak of Antiochus.

> [33] "And those of the people who understand shall instruct many; yet *for many* days they shall fall by sword and flame, by captivity and plundering. [34] Now when they fall, they shall be aided with a little help; but many shall join with them by intrigue. [35] And *some* of those of understanding shall fall, to refine *them*, purify *them*, and make *them* white, **until the time of the end**; because *it is* still for the appointed time." Dan 11:33-35 NKJV (*bold emphasis added*)

In a way this could be construed to describe what happened at first with the institution of the worship of Zeus. It does seem to speak as though a Jew would need some insight to know that these things were wrong. Really? Would not *any* Jew know that these things were contrary to the Mosaic Covenant? Then it gives a reason why some fall with no one to help them. It says these things happened to them "to refine *them*, purify *them*, and make *them* white *until the end time*"!

Although we might question a point here or there up to this place in Daniel 11, with verse 36 the account clearly goes beyond anything history talks about. Now look closely at what Daniel tells us will happen.

Dan 11:36 once again tells us that this king will do as he pleases, and will say outrageous things against the Lord God. This prosperity will continue until it seems, that [God's] (implied) indignation is completed. Who is the indignation against? It seems it is against God's people, and so their enemies in the form of this king are able to afflict them. And it has already been discussed how Antiochus IV was *not* able to do whatever he wanted.

Next it says that he will have no regard for the god of his fathers, or regard any other god, Dan 11:37. We have likewise shown that this also does not fit Antiochus. He was involved in the construction of more than one temple to pagan "gods." This verse says of other "gods," that "he will magnify himself above them all." There is no doubt Antiochus was an arrogant man, as in fact many kings and presidents and dictators have been. But to say of Epiphanes that "he will magnify himself above all"? At the very least this seems to be exaggerated language. Then it does mention a "god" he honors.

> [38] "But in their place he shall honor a god of fortresses; and a god which his fathers did not know he shall honor with gold and silver, with precious stones and pleasant things. [39] Thus he shall act against the strongest fortresses with a foreign god, which he shall acknowledge, *and* advance *its* glory; and he shall cause them to rule over many, and divide the land for gain." Dan 11:38 NKJV

This is a plainly puzzling passage, and does not appear to fit anything we know about those times.

Then it speaks of this king of the North having a war against the king of the South.

> "At the time of the end the king of the South shall attack him; and the king of the North shall come against him like a whirlwind, with chariots, horsemen, and with many ships; and he shall enter the countries, overwhelm *them*, and pass through." Dan 11:40 NKJV

If speaking of Antiochus IV, this would be speaking of now a third invasion of Egypt, after the second one in which he was stopped by the Romans in Dan 11:29-30. Clearly, no such invasion happened. Then it goes on to say he will enter the glorious land, and many countries will fall, Dan 11:41. However, as we have seen, Antiochus *already had* the "Glorious land" of Israel. Then it goes on to describe his success against Egypt.

> [42] "He shall stretch out his hand against the countries, and the land of Egypt shall not escape. [43] He shall have power over the treasures of gold and silver, and over all the precious things of Egypt; also the Libyans and Ethiopians *shall follow* at his heels." Dan 11:42-43 NKJV

He did have initial success in his first and second invasions of Egypt, as we have shown, but the Romans finally told him to go back home or he would be at war with Rome, and he did go back, and these following events never happened to Antiochus. Then it describes him being stopped.

> "But news from the east and the north shall trouble him; therefore he shall go out with great fury to destroy and annihilate many."
> Dan 11:44 NKJV

Only it was not news from the East or North which disturbed Antiochus. Rather it was from the West, from Rome. Then it describes him coming to his end.

"He will pitch the tents of his royal pavilion between the seas and the beautiful Holy Mountain; yet he will come to his end, and no one will help him." Dan 11:45 NASB

So this passage says that his camp will be set between Mount Zion in Jerusalem and the Mediterranean, and he will die there with no one to help him. This plainly does not describe Antiochus IV Epiphanes, in either gentile histories or Jewish histories. Both the Greek historian Polybius, and the Roman historian Livy say he died in Tabae in Persia, as we previously discussed. The Jewish historian of the book of 2 Maccabees goes further and give many details of his death, and even pictures him as coming to repentance for many of the wrongs he had committed, 2 Maccabees 9:4-28. Quite a difference! This passage in Daniel 11 may bear some relationship to that passage "... But he will be broken without human agency." Dan 8:25 NASB, which likewise we noted *perhaps* does not really describe the ruin of Antiochus IV.

To summarize: Dan 11:36-45 does not match Antiochus Epiphanes or *any* ancient ruler whom we know.

These are some pretty stark contrasts. On one hand we might just decide that this is a false prophecy and dispense with it as best we can, as the Liberals do. On the other hand, *these seem to be very **deliberate variations** from those things which happened in ancient times.* So deliberate in fact as to cause one to wonder about whom they are speaking. Remember, Daniel does **not** *specifically* mention Antiochus Epiphanes, although he fits much of these prophecies, as has been shown. As we have pointed out repeatedly, these are often the signs that one person, place, or event is being used as symbolic of another person, place or event. We should also point out that Josephus, writing toward the end of the first century AD, wrote of Antiochus stopping the worship of the Lord our God in Jerusalem,

> And this desolation came to pass according to the prophecy of Daniel, which was given four hundred and eight years before; for he declared that the Macedonians would dissolve that worship [for some time].
> *Antiquities.* 12. 7. 6. 322

The Jewish historian Josephus, writing in the first century AD, plainly views the book of Daniel as authentic, as being from the sixth century BC, and as accurately describing Antiochus IV's destruction in the second century BC, which was recent in historical terms.

We should remember that the history given in Dan 11:1-35, though not anything a natural person would guess ahead of time, was well known history in the Mediterranean world, and that many records of these things survive to our own day. These were turbulent times internationally. The things as described in Dan 11:1-35 would have been near impossible to foresee, and then would have been more clear as they were beginning to unfold. If Daniel 11 was written around 536 BC, and many of the things concerning Antiochus IV were being fulfilled in the second century BC, yet some of the things in the end of chapter 11 were lacking, there would still be enough authenticity in the passage for it to survive as part of Scripture, and people would then continue to look for those things which were lacking. On the other hand, if Daniel 11 was written in the second century BC, just before Antiochus died, and the rest proved to be a fraud ... it would have been thrown away immediately, rejected as clearly a fraud, as much current prophecy literature ends up, and never would have survived as being part of Scripture.

Still there is a need to take one more look at the book of Daniel.

The Time of the End, Daniel 12

It is easy to forget, looking at the English chapter divisions, that Daniel chapters 10 through 12 are all part of a single vision. Therefore Daniel 12 is merely a continuation of the vision in Daniel 11. So look at what the angel tells Daniel in chapter 12.

> "At that time Michael shall stand up,
> The great prince who stands *watch* over the sons of your people;
> And there shall be a time of trouble,
> Such as never was since there was a nation,
> *Even* to that time.
> And at that time your people shall be delivered,
> Every one who is found written in the book." Dan 12:1 NKJV

So what is the time when Michael the archangel will stand up for God's people? It seems to be at the time when the special king in Dan 11:45 "shall come to his end" between Jerusalem and the Mediterranean. It is a time of great stress, but more than that, it is the time when "**Every one** who is found written in the book," "**shall be delivered**"! Written in the book? What book? It seems to be speaking of a book in which God writes the names of all who are His, all who are saved. Moses spoke of this book of the Lord, and asked that he be taken out of this book rather than Israel in his day.

> [32] Yet now, if thou wilt forgive their sin–; and if not, blot me, I pray thee, out of thy book which thou hast written. [33] And the LORD said unto Moses, Whosoever hath sinned against me, him will I blot out of my book. Ex 32:32-33 KJV

Other prophets also spoke of this book, such as David, where he called it the book of life.

> Let them be blotted out of the book of the living, and not be written with the righteous. Psa 69:28 KJV

Astoundingly, the angel says that "**every one**" in this book will be rescued **at this time**. So this has to be talking about literally the end of time, right after this special king comes to his end. And so the angel continues to speak of these times.

> [2] And many of them that sleep in the dust of the earth shall awake, some to everlasting life, and some to shame *and* everlasting contempt. [3] And they that be wise shall shine as the brightness of the firmament; and they that turn many to righteousness as the stars for ever and ever. Dan 12:2-3 KJV

It is clearly speaking here of the resurrection of the dead at the end of time, and some at that time will shine like the sun, and some will rise to everlasting shame and contempt.

But not all of the book of Daniel was *intended* to be understood *before* "the time of the end."

> But thou, O Daniel, shut up the words, and seal the book, *even* **to the time of the end**: many shall run to and fro, and knowledge shall be increased. Dan 12:4 KJV (*bold emphasis added*)

So if there are some mysteries here, and there are, then many of them are not *intended* to be cleared up until *just before the end of time!* So Daniel is told to "shut up the words and seal the book." It was not **all** *intended* to be understood either in Daniels day, nor in our day (unless we are right at the end of time!).

Daniel and others wanted to know when all of these things would be over. "How long *will it be* until the end of *these* wonders?" Dan 12:6.

> Then I heard the man clothed in linen, who was above the waters of the river, when he held up his right hand and his left hand to heaven, and swore by Him who lives forever, that *it **shall be*** for a time, times, and half *a time*; and when the power of the holy people has been completely shattered, all these *things* shall be finished. Dan 12:7 NKJV (*bold emphasis added*)

That my friends is a lot to say, and all in a single verse. How long will it be until all of these things are over? The angel says it will be 3-1/2 years, "time, times, and half *a time*," just as in Daniel 7. As has been pointed out, the period of Antiochus' persecution of God's people was pretty close to *only* three years!

What then is the sign that the 3-1/2 years are over? " ... when the power of the holy people has been completely shattered, all these *things* shall be finished." That is to say, when the people of God are completely shattered/destroyed, then this period of 3-1/2 years will come to an end. Again let us point out that the people of God were not shattered at the end of Antiochus' devastations. Instead, it was Antiochus who was shattered. **So either this is a false prophecy,** very crudely written after the fact, **or Antiochus was intended from the first to be symbolic.** Symbolic of one who will come near "the time of the end," who will actually shatter "the power of the holy people."

> And I heard, but I understood not: then said I, O my Lord, what *shall be* the end of these *things*? Dan 12:8 KJV

Do not imagine you are alone in thinking that some of this is hard to absorb. Daniel himself had trouble absorbing all of this, so why should you and I feel bad? Then again, what will be the outcome of all of this?

> And he said, "Go thy way, Daniel, for **the words** *are* **closed up and sealed till the time of the end.** Dan 12:9 KJV (*bold emphasis added*)

In other words, **not all of this is *supposed* to be understood until the end the age!** These words are *deliberately* concealed from us, sealed *until* the end of the age, and intended to be understood then.

So you ask, Why study all of this now? Why not just wait until "the time of the end," and then we will study these things when they can be understood? Alright. When will that be, my friend? We are commanded to be watching for these things now, so we would know where to study at that time. In any other condition, we will be blind-sided by these things when they come. Right? I think that is true.

Then looking at the way these things are presented to us, what would we make of the intentions of the author, the Lord our God? It appears the Lord wishes us to be alert, and looking for the indications of "the time of the end," so we would be prepared, and clothed with our Lord. If we did that, then we would be,

> Not forsaking the assembling of ourselves together, as the manner of some is; but exhorting one another: and so much the more, **as ye see the day approaching.** Heb 10.25 KJV (*bold emphasis added*)

There are things to see and understand as we come close to the time of end, as we glean information from both Daniel and many other prophecies of both the Old and the New Testaments. The angel then tells Daniel,

> Many shall be purified, and made white, and tried; but the wicked shall do wickedly: and none of the wicked shall understand; but the wise shall understand. Dan 12:10 KJV

In other words, a lot of things have to happen first, and many people will come to the Lord. However, when the end of this universe comes, if we are walking in darkness, if we are acting wickedly, we never understand these things even when it is most needful. Then comes one more set of days of time.

> And from the time that the daily sacrifice shall be taken away, and the abomination that maketh desolate set up, *there shall be* a thousand two hundred and ninety days. Dan 12:11 KJV

1,290 days from the time that the regular sacrifice is stopped and the "abomination of desolation" is set up? That emphatically does NOT fit the story of Antiochus IV.

To review this history, as best as your author can see it:

• Antiochus began to rule in 175 BC, as agreed by most historians (**the 137th year of the Greeks**, acording to 1 Maccabees 1:10).

• Antiochus was rebuffed by the Romans in Egypt. Angry, on the way back from Egypt, he entered and plundered the temple, 1 Maccabees 1:20-24, 2 Maccabees 5:21. This was **143rd year according to 1 Maccabees** 1:20, and **Josephus** *Antiquities*, Book 12. 5.3.246.

• "And after two years fully expired" 1 Maccabees 1:29, and Josephus *Antiquities*, Book 12. 5. 4.248 says it was the **145th year of the Greek kings**. Antiochus returned to Jerusalem and plundered the city, and set up a fortress near the temple in Jerusalem.

• The sacrifices to the Lord were stopped, and the "abomination of desolation," the statue of Zeus, was set up by Chislev the 15th, the 145th year, 1 Maccabees 1:54.

• On Chislev 25th of this very same year, a mere ten days later, a pig was sacrificed to an idol of Zeus on the altar in the temple at Jerusalem, 1 Maccabees 1:59.

• Then three years later Judas Maccabeus cleansed the temple in Jerusalem and reestablished the sacrifices to the Lord, on Chislev the 25th of **the 148th year** of the Greeks, 1 Maccabees 4:52.

There may be some problems here, however this chronology seems reasonable, and is in any event sufficient for this study. The real issue is that none of this is close to the 1,290 days (43 months of 30 days each) of Dan 12:11!

There is another point to make here. Suppose a forger was writing up the history of Antiochus Epiphanes in the early second century BC. Suppose he knew all the history of Antiochus which we know, except he did not know how or when he died. He would never write something so at variance to events as this. This 1,290 days would not fit anywhere in the second century BC!

However, it does say there will be 1,290 days between stopping the sacrifices and the setting up of the "abomination of desolation," and the end? It seems to imply that. Then two more things are said.

> "Blessed is he who waits, and comes to the one thousand three hundred and thirty-five days. " Dan 12:12 NKJV

Now we have 1,335 days. That would be about 44-1/2 months. When does this period of time start, or the 3-1/2 years for that matter? Where does that fit in? Not in the second century BC. As a close though, Daniel is assured that this does not apply to his own time.

> "But you, go your way till the end; for you shall rest, and will arise to your inheritance at the end of the days." Dan 12:13 NKJV

So ends our special purpose look at some the prophecies of Daniel, all for the purpose of showing how parts of Daniel, and indeed other passages in the Old Testament, relate to the book of Revelation.

And Oh Yes! The Abomination of Desolation

First we should notice that it clearly *seems* that this is speaking of the placing of a pagan idol in the very temple of God, and of this being such a heinous crime (an abomination, something detestable) that it ruins everything (it brings desolation and ruin on everyone). Thus the object reference in Dan 11:31 seems to be to Antiochus IV.

> "And forces shall be mustered by him, and they shall defile the sanctuary fortress; then they shall take away the daily *sacrifices*, and place *there* the abomination of desolation." NKJV

The reference to Antiochus IV seems clear, and it seems to be tellings us of what was later recorded in the histories of Josephus, 1 Maccabees and 2 Maccabees, and other histories.

This would then relate this verse to those things we read about the "little horn" in Daniel 8. That also is plain enough. In contrast to this, there seems to be at least a verbal relationship to the very last verse of Daniel 9.

> And he shall confirm the covenant with many for one week: and in the midst of the week he shall cause the sacrifice and the oblation to cease, and for the overspreading of abominations he shall make *it* desolate, even until the consummation, and that determined shall be poured upon the desolate. Dan 9:27 KJV

We have not discussed the prophecy at the end of Daniel 9, although it is discussed in *Prophecy Principles*. The word "abomination" is the same in Dan 11:31, Dan 12:11, *and in* Daniel 9:31. It is the Hebrew word *shiqqutz* שִׁקּוּץ. And the word desolate is also the same in all of these verses. The Hebrew for "desolate" which is used in these passages is the word *shamem* שָׁמֵם.

Daniel 9 is primarily concerned with when the Christ would come, but as you can see, the end of the prophecy seems to overlap our present subject. The problem is that the prophecy in Daniel 9 *does NOT concern the Greeks, but the Romans!* So we are back to the same overlap which seemed to be implied in Daniel 7, where also there, part of the prophecy reminded us of the little horn of the Greeks in Daniel 8, *but was speaking of Roman times!* One might assume that these were contradictory indications, but we are not assuming that. We are assuming instead that Scripture is trying to tell us something, and that Antiochus IV is symbolic of someone worse, who will come in, shall we say, "Roman times." Also we must remark, in an extended sense, we are in "Roman times." Our law in the Western world, and our government, and to some degree, much of our culture, are in truth Roman in character.

Now Jesus in Matthew 24 was speaking of three subjects: 1.) When will the first century AD temple be destroyed? 2.) What are the signs of Jesus' coming again, and 3.) What will be the signs of the end of the age? Mtt 24:1-3. In typical prophecy fashion, Jesus in Matthew 24, went back and forth talking about all three of these issues, not in any strict order.

Then we see that Jesus speaks in the first century AD, about the abomination of desolation as something *which has NOT happened yet!* (In other words, Antiochus IV *IS* symbolic of someone who will come later in history!) Further, Jesus speaks of the appearing of the abomination of desolation as something which all believers will recognize, and that will be the time to RUN FOR ALL YOU ARE WORTH, NOT LOOKING BACK, NOT GOING BACK INTO THE HOUSE FOR **ANYTHING**, but to just run and hide as best you can.

Roman Standard Bearers

> [15] When ye therefore shall see the abomination of desolation, spoken of by Daniel the prophet, stand in the holy place, (whoso readeth, let him understand:) [16] Then let them which be in Judaea flee into the mountains: [17] Let him which is on the housetop not come down to take any thing out of his house: [18] Neither let him which is in the field return back to take his clothes. Mtt 24:15-18 KJV

Actually Jesus says even more than this about these terrible times, and it goes on for several verses.

Obviously, the destruction of the temple in Jerusalem of which Jesus spoke in 30 AD, occurred in the Jewish revolt against the Romans which occurred from AD 66 to 70. These are well recorded events in history. At the end of the siege of Jerusalem, after the temple was destroyed by fire, the Roman general Titus and some of his troops, met in the temple compound (but **not** in the Holy of Holies), in a sort of private ceremony, carrying with them their standards (their "flags" so to speak), which had on them idolatrous images, including of Jupiter/Zeus. They then burned incense to their "gods," and offered a pig as a sacrifice of praise to their "gods" for giving them the victory. This is very similar to the picture which we have of the Roman Emperor Trajan a few years later on page 69, about to sacrifice a pig, in thanks for victory. Surely these idolatrous images of these pagans *were* an abomination to the True and Living God !

Scripture does not say so, but some people say that *the sacrifice in the temple area*, in Roman times, *was the "abomination of desolation"* of which both Daniel and Jesus spoke. There is just one problem with this idea. The sacrifices in the temple area in the first century by Titus and his troops, **were too late for people to run from *anything*.** The city and the temple had already been destroyed and most of the Jews in Jerusalem were *already* dead. This occurred too late to be a sign of a time to run for your life!

So we come to a crisis:

1. Perhaps this is just a false prophecy, and this false prophecy has failed. That is what many unbelievers and Liberals think.

2. Perhaps Jesus is speaking of another greater abomination which will occur later in history, *which **will be** a sign to run,* a little before Jesus' Second Coming. This idea does **NOT** require you to be a premillennialist. It does *not* require you to believe that Jesus will rule a literal kingdom here on earth *before* the end of time. It does require you to believe that Jesus *will* come again! It does require you to believe God's prophetic Word.

3. If the events of Titus and his soldiers do not fulfill the abomination of desolation, **perhaps they _also_ are merely *another* "type"/"shadow"/"pattern" of the end events**. Another symbol, another type, of that which is yet to come. Similarly there were multiple symbols of Jesus before He came. He was to be like Moses, and like Solomon, and like a sacrificial lamb! And He was to be a mighty warrior like David!

So perhaps, just perhaps, the *real* abomination of desolation is yet to come. Perhaps we will run into him under different symbolism in the book of Revelation. Perhaps. If so, we should also run into trails of evidence leading us to reexamine some of the passages we have already studied.

The Emperor Trajan and his soldiers offering incense and about to sacrifice a pig, as a an offering of thanks to their gods for a victory. This image is taken from Trajan's Column in Rome, depicting events which occurred around the end of the first century AD.

So Again, Why is This Pertinent to the Book of Revelation?

We should remember that the entire context of Scripture should be kept in mind when interpreting any Scripture, especially the book of Revelation.

Besides, the book of Daniel and the book of Revelation plainly overlap in some of their subject matter. For instance, they specifically overlap in speaking of the Roman Empire. The book of Revelation was written of things which "would soon come to pass" Rev 1:1, and it was written *during the times of the Roman* Empire, which was also written about in the book of Daniel. Also because Daniel seems to have unfulfilled symbols ("types") in its stories. Lastly they overlap because *both books* in some detail *speak of the time of the end.*

For us to attempt to leave out the prophesies of especially Daniel or Zechariah in

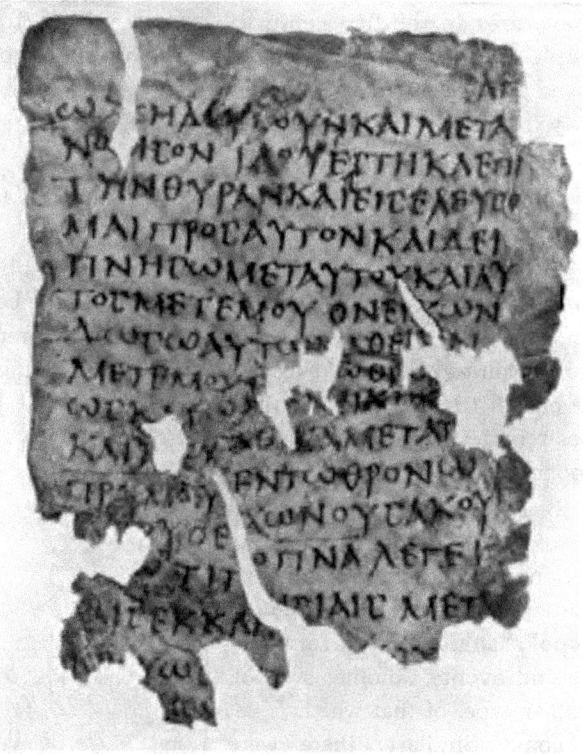

Shown actual size, the pages are 2-7/8 by 3-3/4 inches, from a pocket copy of Revelation found in Egypt, dated in the 300's AD. Shown is page 33, Rev 3:19 to 4:1. It is numbered 0169, and it is located in Princeton, NJ.

any discussion of the book of Revelation and the end of the universe, is just foolishness that we never should have considered in the first place.

Remember these studies as we approach the book of Revelation.

IV. Letters to God's Churches

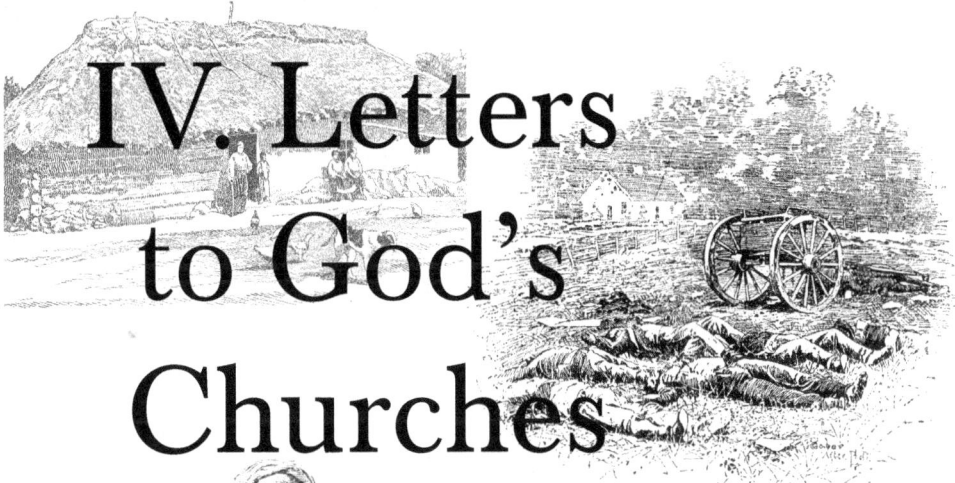

Revealing What Must Soon Take Place, Rev 1:1-3

The announcement of the purpose of the book of Revelation is at the beginning of the prophecy.

> The Revelation of Jesus Christ, which God gave Him to show to His bond-servants, the things which must soon take place; and He sent and communicated it by His angel to His bond-servant John,
> Rev 1:1 NASB

This book is revealing things. That is what the foreword says. This book is often called the Apocalypse, and that comes from the word "Revelation" or *apokalupsis,* ʼαποκάλυψις. Many people only associate the book of Revelation with a very negative view of history that is leading to destruction. A while back I heard a popular talk-show host talking about the subject, and this host said he did "not believe in "apocalyptic" anything." He plainly did not know what apocalypse meant, and associated it with a very negative view of history, in which he did not believe.

It is true that the book of Revelation describes terrible times which will come upon the earth. It implicitly treats these things, not as things which *had* to happen, but rather, because of men's hardness of heart, and refusal to repent, as things which *will* happen. I must ask: if men pursue destructive courses of action, and if these actions do indeed lead to the destruction of man, is that God's fault? Should God sugar-coat the pill for us? *Should God tell that everything will be alright even if we refuse to do what is right?* Should God tell us that nothing will go wrong, when things often do go wrong? Should God tell us that nothing bad will happen to the righteous, when in fact, if we cling to righteousness, we will suffer persecution from those refusing to do what is right? Scripture obviously tells us the truth about these matters.

> Yes, and all who desire to live godly in Christ Jesus will suffer persecution. 2Tim 3:12 NKJV

So ALL who even just "desire" to live godly will be persecuted.

Judgment *does* come on both men and nations, all through history, as clearly told in both the Old and the New Testaments, and as is indeed sensed by many people down through history. Sin carries with it its own punishment, and also there will be a final judgment. For every idle word we will give an account.

> For we must all appear before the judgment seat of Christ; that every one may receive the things *done* in *his* body, according to that he hath done, whether *it be* good or bad. 2Cor 5:10 KJV

Again, Paul tells Christians that they should be,

> in no way alarmed by *your* opponents — which is a sign of destruction for

them, but of salvation for you, and that *too,* from God. Phil 1:28 NASB

In other words, the very fact of our standing fast, and not being scared by wicked men, will be a sign to them of their destruction. There will be good things which will come upon the righteous, and evil things which will fall on those who refuse to repent, and *before* the end of time, men will go through many severe trials, which are outlined in Scripture, which reveals what will happen.

Is this really a twisted view of history ... *or is this just a sober overview of what will happen in the Christian age?* What would be a sober view of the Christian age? I cannot help but think of the Roman historian Tacitus' introduction to *The History,* one section of his history of the Roman Empire. Here is the way he tells us about his subject.

> "I am entering on the history of a period rich in disasters, frightful in its wars, torn by civil strife, and even in peace full of horror."
> *The Complete Works of Tacitus,* translated by Church and Brodribb, The Modern Library, NY, 1942, pg 420.

That phrase could easily have been written of many periods of the multi-century fall of the Roman Empire, and also of much of the Middle Ages, as most would acknowledge. Also it could have been written of the 20th century AD, and its two World Wars, and Holocausts! In fact, much worse things have been written of the 20th century and its disasters and wars and famines. The reader can easily find quotations by current historians of modern history which are much like this. Has God misled us? **Is everything really alright? Or are we a disaster in the making,** which God will deliver us from if we will submit to His One and Only Son, Jesus of Nazareth? I think God is giving us a solemn and thoughtful overview of the Christian Age, so that we will be under no delusions, and so that we will be ready for those things which we will not be able to change.

The first verse of Revelation says that Jesus Christ is doing the revealing. He is revealing this message "to His bond servants" NASB, that is to say, to His slaves! The Greek word is *doulos* δοῦλος, the regular word for slave. Almost all the translators, from King James' times forward, have shunned a clear translation of the word "slave." It was an offense to them. But there it is. The great men of God all the way down through history have been called 'slaves' of God. Sometimes that is translated 'servant' in our Bibles, but the original word is 'slave'. The Apostle John is a slave to Jesus Christ, Rev 1:1. Paul the Apostle is a slave of God, Titus 1:1. The Apostle James is a slave of God, Jas 1:1. Moses is called a slave of God, 2Kgs 18:12. The great men of God all through history have been slaves of God, *unashamedly* bound to serve and obey Him, and not the least bit embarrassed of being slaves to what is right and good and just and merciful and all powerful.

More than that, it says that He is revealing "what must soon take place" NASB. What does that mean, "soon take place"? Obviously it means that these are things which will begin soon in human terms. Soon at least in the sense of beginning in a few years, if not a few months. Not far off in human terms. Perhaps it also means "soon" in divine terms. We might compare it with the "perish quickly" of Joshua in Jos 23:16. Although there were many periods of punishment in between, it was nearly eight hundred years later when they finally went into captivity.

> For a thousand years in thy sight *are but* as yesterday when it is past, and *as* a watch in the night. Psa 90:4 KJV

In this book we are studying events which end with the end of time, the end of this present universe, and the beginning of a new universe in which sin and death are not operating principles. In the long stretch, even the end of the world will not be far off. We die, we sleep some days in the grave, then one day comes a trumpet call which will quite literally wake the dead ... at the end it will seem as nothing, as just a few days. So quite possibly this also speaks of "soon" as the end of all things in this present universe, which is swiftly coming upon us all.

Also these are things are "communicated," "signified," to God's slave, John the Apostle. The Greek word is *sāmainō* σημαίνω, from the Greek word for a sign. It has the idea of communicating by signs or symbolism, of indicating by visual representations what will be coming down the road. It is a fitting representation of what we will see in the book of Revelation. This visual representation then was communicated by Jesus' angel to this slave John,

> who bore witness to the word of God, and to the testimony of Jesus Christ, to **all** things that he **saw**. Rev 1:2 NKJV (*bold emphasis added*)

Clearly it is saying that John the son of Zebedee told us "all" that he saw. Then it gives us a blessing. Blessed is the one who reads and hears this prophecy and who "heeds" it, Rev 1:3. The Greek word is *tāreō* τηρέω, which literally means to keep something, to watch over it, even to guard it. In context it obviously means blessed is the one who obeys these words. So we see this is a book to obey! "The end of all things is at hand," 1Pe 4:7 KJV.

To understand, to grow, or to be first, we must first be a slave to what is right, Mtt 10:24-25. We need to circumcise our hearts, Rom 2:29; so that we can see and feel and know how to walk rightly.

On the other hand, many will be seeing and hearing ... but never understanding, Mtt 13:14-15. They will never understand according to Daniel 12:10. Sin blinds, darkness blinds, John 12:35-36a. Refusing to hear ... well that obviously blinds, and keeps you from hearing the words that will deliver your life from death, and your soul from pain, and your body from the traps that men set.

What if you do not understand what this book is about, what then?

Well two distinct possibilities are that either 1. You are not using your light to open the book ... or 2. You are not understanding because you are not walking in the light, 1Jn 1:6-7. We need the light to see. It is said again at the end of this book. God sent his angel to show his servants, once again, "the things which must shortly be done," Rev 22:6 KJV. Then Jesus at the very end of the book, after telling us in multiple ways what the end of this present universe will be like, tells us,

> Behold, I come quickly: blessed is he that keepeth the sayings of the prophecy of this book. Rev 22:7 KJV

It is a prophecy. A prophecy to heed, to obey.

To The Seven Churches, Rev 1:4-8

John is writing the record of this revelation, this revealing, to the seven churches that are in Asia:

> ... Grace be unto you, and peace, from him which is, and which was, and which is to come; ... Rev 1:4b KJV

This is in one way a letter. A letter written at a particular time, to some particular places in what is now part of Asia Minor, actually the large southwestern quarter of what is today western Turkey. This letter is from John the Apostle. The date is probably around 95 AD, but that is just an educated guess. And this letter is from God, "and from the seven Spirits which are before his throne;" Rev 1:4c. This is the One "which is, and which was, and which is to come" God is described in Ex 3:14 as "I AM THAT I AM," KJV. He is God Almighty; Gen 17:1. Before the mountains were born He was "God," Psa 90:2. They will perish, but You remain; Psa 102:25-27.

> ... I, the LORD, the first, and with the last; I *am* he. Isa 41:4 KJV

> ... before me there was no God formed, neither shall there be after me. Isa 43:10 KJV

This letter is from God Himself, and this letter is from Jesus, Rev 1:5. He is *the* faithful witness.

> "Most assuredly, I say to you, We speak what We know and testify what We have seen, and you do not receive Our witness." Jn 3:11 NKJV

He has been in heaven. He has literally seen it all, without reservation, and told men the important facts of life.

> "For I have not spoken on My own *authority*; but the Father who sent

Me gave Me a command, what I should say and what I should speak."
Jn 12:49 NKJV

"What He has seen and heard, of that He testifies; and no one receives
His testimony." Jn 3:32 NASB

I have many things to say and to judge of you: but he that sent me is
true; and I speak to the world those things which I have heard of him.
Jn 8:26 KJV

He is also firstborn from the dead, Rev 1:5. The first born is an appointed position. The position of heir, the position of preeminence. Esau was born first,
but the *position* was *given* to Jacob. The Lord says of the Christ,

Also I will **make him** my firstborn, higher than the kings of the earth.
Psa 89:27 (*bold emphasis added*)

Reuben, for instance, the physical firstborn of Jacob, lost his inheritance because of a sin against his father.

Now the sons of Reuben the firstborn of Israel, (for he *was* the
firstborn; but, forasmuch as he defiled his father's bed, his birthright
was given unto the sons of Joseph the son of Israel: and the genealogy
is not to be reckoned after the birthright.) 1Chron 5:1 KJV

So it was that Jesus was chosen for preeminence. He is the ruler of the
kings of the earth, Rev 1:5. He is *now*. Let all kings bow down before him, and
all nations serve Him, Psa 72:11. All things were placed under his feet.

[20] ... when he raised him from the dead, **and set** *him* **at his own right
hand** in the heavenly places, [21] **Far above all principality, and
power, and might, and dominion**, and every name that is named, not
only in this world, but also in that which is to come: [22] **And hath put
all *things* under his feet**, and gave him to be the head over all things ...
Eph 1:20-22 KJV (*bold emphasis added*)

Then you are a king? Pilate said to Him in Jn 18:37. Yes, He is king,

For unto us a child is born, unto us a son is given: and the government
shall be upon his shoulder: and his name shall be called Wonderful,
Counsellor, The mighty God, The everlasting Father, The Prince of
Peace. Isa 9:6 KJV

In Daniel's visions we saw Him as one like a son of man, approaching the
Father to receive an eternal kingdom, Dan 7:13-14. That is Jesus the Christ. The
kings of the earth will conspire against this Supreme Ruler, take counsel against
Him, Psa 2:1-2. But He will smash them like a clay pot, Psalm 2:9. The judges
and rulers on the earth would do well to tremble before Him, Psa 2:10-11. His
anger against them is often swiftly kindled, Psa 2:12. He alone is King of Kings,
and Lord of Lords.

He has both loved us and released us from the power of our sins, by His very own blood, Rev 1:5. He has made Christians to be followers of His, both Jews and gentiles.

> Peter said to Him, "You shall never wash my feet!" Jesus answered him, "If I do not wash you, you have no part with Me." Jn 13:8 NKJV

But of us it is said,

> .. But you were washed, but you were sanctified, but you were justified in the name of the Lord Jesus and by the Spirit of our God.
> 1Cor 6:11 NKJV

It was promised a long time ago that God would make His people into a kingdom of priests, and a holy nation.

> And ye shall be unto me a kingdom of priests, and an holy nation. These are the words which thou shalt speak unto the children of Israel.
> Ex 19:6 KJV

Isaiah said that God's people would be called priests of the LORD, Isa 61:6. However, holiness is something that Israel studiously avoided, and a nation of priests ... ? One would have to do away with Moses Law to ever have that. Many swore Moses Law could never pass away, even though it would have to in order to fulfill Ex 19:6, and for the great prophet to tell us new laws which we must do, Deut 18:15-19. But one day that Great Prophet did take the Law of Moses away, nailing it to a cross, Col 2:14. Then that Great Prophet took those of Israel who would listen, along with those of the nations who would listen, and made them,

> [9] ... a chosen generation, a royal priesthood, an holy nation, a peculiar people; that ye should shew forth the praises of him who hath called you out of darkness into his marvellous light: [10] Which in time past *were* not a people, but *are* now the people of God: which had not obtained mercy, but now have obtained mercy. 1Pe 2:9-10 KJV

Thus He has "made us unto our God kings and priests:" Rev 5:10, as was originally promised. He ordained such power for them in this kingdom as can be scarcely imagined. It is a kingdom which is not of this *kosmos*/world, not of this universe, Jn 18:36; but rather it relates to a perfect universe which is yet to come, where sin and death and entropy are not operating principles. But it is a universe for which we now prepare, while He prepares to roll-up and put away the present order which has been ruined, Heb 1:10-12.

He has *all* authority, Mtt 28:18. There is none missing. He does not need more authority to do what He must do. He can and will straighten out this mess. He does rule *now* in the midst of His enemies, Psa 110:2. To Him be the glory and power, and both the right to and the reality of eternal rule, literally, and figuratively.

Now of this LORD, clouds and thick darkness surround Him, Psa 97:2.

> He lays the beams of His upper chambers in the waters;
> He makes the clouds His chariot;
> He walks upon the wings of the wind; Psa 104:3 NASB

The LORD is riding His swift chariot. He is coming to the Egypt of this world, and the images themselves will tremble at His coming, Isa 19:1. He is coming on the clouds, Rev 1:7.

> And then shall appear the sign of the Son of man in heaven: and then shall all the tribes of the earth mourn, and they shall see the Son of man coming in the clouds of heaven with power and great glory.
> Mt 24:30 KJV

After worms have destroyed my skin, ... I will see God, Job said in Job 19:26-27. At His mockery of a trial, Jesus told the high priest who was examining Him that he would in the future see Jesus, standing at the very right hand of God, Mtt 26:64. You and I will also see Him! A detail of soldiers was formed: an execution squad. They stripped and mocked Him, and beat Him. Then they took Him to the place of execution, nailed Him up, and waited. Every eye will see Him, even those who executed Him.

On a hill far away, in the mountains of Heaven itself, a guidon, a standard, a flag, will be raised.

> **All inhabitants of the world** and dwellers on the earth:
> When he lifts up a banner on the mountains, you see it;
> And when he blows a trumpet, you hear *it*.
> Isa 18:3 (*bold emphasis added*)

Then when that signal is raised, and that trumpet is sounded, men will be in turmoil as never before, as the dead are raised, and the universe itself starts to pass away.

> [25] **And there shall be signs** in the sun, and in the moon, and in the stars; and upon the earth distress of nations, with perplexity; the sea and the waves roaring; [26] **Men's hearts failing them for fear**, and **for** looking after **those things which are coming on the earth**: for the powers of heaven shall be shaken. [27] And **then** shall they see the Son of man coming in a cloud with power and great glory.
> Lk 21:25-27 KJV (*bold emphasis added*)

All the tribes of the earth will be dreading the facing of the God whom they had ignored and despised. He is the "Alpha and Omega," the beginning and the end, Rev 1:8. He is everything. Literally everything. He was something before *anything* existed. He will fill the fullness of everything, even if you and I become nothing. Our only hope for something lasting is with Him.

In the beginning was the Word, and the Word was with God, and the

Word was God. Jn 1:1 KJV

Jesus Christ the same yesterday, and to day and forever. Heb 13:8 KJV

The secret of the LORD *is* with them that fear him; and he will shew them his covenant. Psa 25:14 KJV

If you are not afraid, you don't have good sense. The Lord is slow to anger and mighty in power, but He will by no means clear the guilty. If men will not turn, they will bear their own sins forever.

There is a fountain opened for men. A fountain that takes away the sins of men. That fountain is open for you and for me, that we might stand entire at the last, confident and washed of all pollution.

Jesus Appears, Rev 1:9-20

"I, John, who also am your brother," John writes in Revelation 1:9 KJV. He assumes you know who He is and what he is. He is the apostle Jesus loved. The one who stood by him at the cross. He stayed in Jerusalem for many years, and then according to most accounts, moved to the city of Ephesus in what is modern South-Western Turkey, in what many now call Asia Minor.

The emperor at this time was Titus Flavius Domitianus, known as Domitian, who was emperor from AD 81-96. Domitian was a son of Titus Flavius Vespasianus, who is known as Vespasian. His dad had first been a Roman general. It was his dad and his older brother who captured Jerusalem from the Jewish rebels in the revolt which began in 66-67 AD. It was during the siege of Jerusalem that Vespasian had left the field of battle to make an attempt to become Emperor of Rome, during the turmoil which followed the death of Nero. Vespasian's first son, Titus Flavius Vespasianus, known as Titus, had been left to complete the conquest of Jerusalem in 70 AD. Father and son, Vespasian and Titus, were sober, intelligent, level headed rulers. Vespasian restored order to the Roman Empire, and established the Flavian dynasty, and ruled to 79 AD. Titus also was credited with being a good Emperor, but only lived as Emperor until 81 AD. It was Titus who built the Colosseum in Rome, the ruins of which still stand today.

The second son, Domitian, was very power hungry and somewhat on the erratic side. Even his dad and his older brother commented on these things. He was a very harsh and demanding ruler, very particular that he be honored as he thought he should be, and was generally despised by the Roman aristocracy.

The worship of kings as some sort of "gods" had begun in Asia. The Greeks had become used to various kings of Egypt and Syria claiming they were gods. It seems to have been first in Asia that some of the provinces offered "worship" to the Emperors of Rome as a way to flatter their rulers. The first Roman Emperors, a little self-consciously, perhaps a little uneasily, accepted such "honors." We can see how such things sometimes start. Part of the story of Herod Agrippa I is told in Acts 12. He was a grandson of Herod the Great, the one who had tried to murder the infant Jesus in Matthew 1. Herod Agrippa I was king of Judea from 41 to 44 AD, and had already had some conflicts with Christianity and had put to death the original apostle James in Acts 12:1-2. The historian Luke tells us of this Herod,

> [20] And Herod was highly displeased with them of Tyre and Sidon: but they came with one accord to him, and, having made Blastus the king's chamberlain their friend, desired peace; because their country was nourished by the king's *country*. [21] And upon a set day Herod, arrayed in royal apparel, sat upon his throne, and made an oration unto them. [22] And the people gave a shout, *saying, It is* the voice of a god, and not of a man. Acts 12:20-22 KJV

They said it, the crowd did, that this was "the voice of a god and not of a man." Herod did not say it. And the crowd? There is a good chance they had been paid by local authorities. They were shills, meant to spark approval in the crowd, set to flatter the speaker and bring his approval of the city. Here we learn also the frequent significance of silence. It is true silence is sometimes golden. Sometimes though it is cowardly, and can of itself have great significance. We see this in some of the regulations concerning oaths in the Law of Moses.

> [3] If a woman also vow a vow unto the LORD, and bind herself by a bond, *being* in her father's house in her youth; [4] And her father hear her vow, and her bond wherewith she hath bound her soul, and her father shall hold his peace at her: then all her vows shall stand, and every bond wherewith she hath bound her soul shall stand. [5] But if her father disallow her in the day that he heareth; not any of her vows, or of her bonds wherewith she hath bound her soul, shall stand: and the LORD shall forgive her, because her father disallowed her. Num 30:3-5 KJV

So silence, in Scripture and in life, may mean nothing, or can have the significance of de facto approval. Sometimes, if something is greatly in error, we have the *obligation* to speak out, and to not do so is wrong. So it says of this incident,

> Then immediately an angel of the Lord struck him, because he did not give glory to God. And he was eaten by worms and died. Acts 12:23 NKJV

The Jewish historian Josephus also tells this story in his *Antiquities of the Jews,* Book 19, chapter 8. He tells us,

[344] On the second day of which shows he put on a garment made wholly of silver, and of a contexture truly wonderful, and came into the theatre early in the morning; at which time the silver of his garment being illuminated by the fresh reflection of the sun's rays upon it, shone out after a surprising manner, and was so resplendent as to spread a horror over those that looked intently upon him; [345] and presently his flatterers cried out, one from one place, and another from another (though not for his good), that he was a god; and they added, "Be thou merciful to us; for although we have hitherto reverenced thee only as a man, yet shall we henceforth own thee as superior to mortal nature." [346] Upon this the king did neither rebuke them, nor reject their impious flattery. But, as he presently afterwards looked up, he saw an owl sitting on a certain rope over his head, and immediately understood that this bird was the messenger of ill tidings, as it had once been the messenger of good tidings to him; and fell into the deepest sorrow. A severe pain also arose in his belly, and began in a most violent manner.

Josephus tells us he died some five days later.

Domitian had no uneasiness at being worshipped. He began to insist on being called "dominus et deus" ("master and god"), which was to the Roman aristocracy arrogant and false and stupid. These things showed up in both big and small things. The Roman historian Suetonius says that when Domitian decided to take back a wife he had divorced, he said it was a "recall to my divine bed." Some of his letters he began to start with the words, "Our Lord and God instructs you to do this!" *Suetonius, The Twelve Caesars*, translated by Robert Graves, Penguin Books, NY, 1989, pgs 308-309.

In the years 93 to 96 AD he became a literal terror to everyone he saw as opposing him, whether Roman or Christian or Jew. In 95 AD he had his Christian first cousin, Titus Flavius Clemens executed, and he had his sister, Domitilla Flavia, who was also a Christian, banished to the island of Pandateria. Perhaps it was at about this time that the old man, John the apostle, who was probably well into his nineties, was banished to the island of Patmos. Shortly after Domitian's death John was released, and spent his last years in Ephesus. Domitian was murdered September 18, 96 AD, and the Roman senate was glad to see him go.

But on this day, John is still in exile because of the gospel, on the island of Patmos, off of what is today the Mediterranean coast of Turkey. John says that he, like many others, had undergone the stress of persecution, and was, like many others, standing fast in the faith, Rev 1:9. God does test us, and we do need such things so that we can become what we should become.

And Moses said unto the people, Fear not: for God is come to prove you, and that his fear may be before your faces, that ye sin not.
Ex 20:20 KJV

For sure, everyone who even just *wants* to live godly in Jesus Christ *will be* persecuted, 2 Tim 3:12. The more ardently we hold to Him, and the more truly we understand and apply His Word to our speech and our lives, the more implacably will the world oppose us, and even at times seek to destroy us. In times of peace it often seems as if no one would bother us. Still, even in those times, there are men who stand firm in their faith, and are murdered for such, although most never recognize that it was because of their faith that they died. The world never wishes to call attention to such incidents. They treat the deaths as coming on them for foolish stubbornness when most submitted to the will of others. It is through many tribulations we enter the kingdom, Act 14:22. If you are trying to enter glorious life forever without any hardships, you are trying to do what cannot be done. Even the Son of God Himself learned obedience "by the things which he suffered," Heb 5:8 KJV. Even riches in this life involve some risk and some hardship, and much more does the life to come.

John was in the Spirit on what he calls "the Lord's day," Rev 1:10. The Sabbath is on the seventh day of the week. Our Lord arose on the first day of the week, Jn 20:1. That became the normal day for worship of all the churches of the Lord, Acts 20:7, the Lord's day. That also became the time to make donations to the Lord's work, 1Cor 16:2. As your author writes this passage, there is no longer a Lord's Day in America. Even in the church of our Lord in the 21st century, many at best have "the Lord's hour," perhaps. But the Lord's Day? No, most American's say that Sunday is "my day," and forget the Lord who is the source of this rest from labor.

But John was in the Spirit on the Lord's Day. "In the Spirit." What does that mean? We often think of mysterious influences of the Spirit of God, and of the Lord taking over someone's consciousness, or enabling a person to do "miraculous" things. "Miraculous"! There is an ambiguous term. The real Bible terms are "powers," "signs," and "wonders." The use of the Latin-English term "miracle" is an interpretation, and such was discussed in *Prophecy Principles*. The other side of this is seen in Ephesians 5.

> And be not drunk with wine, wherein is excess; but be filled with the Spirit; Eph 5:18 KJV

Notice that according to this verse you can *decide* to be filled with the Spirit! If you have the Spirit, you can decide to do this, and do it. A person can decide to not get drunk, and not get drunk, and can decide to be filled with the things of the Spirit, and then be filled with the Spirit. Of course this is logical if you understand that Christians have the Spirit of God living in them,

> Or do you not know that your body is the temple of the Holy Spirit who is in you, whom you have from God, and you are not your own? 1Cor 6:19 NKJV

So what would being "in the Spirit" mean from this point of view? It would mean setting your heart on the things of the Spirit, Rom 8:5-6. It would mean setting your heart on things above, Col 3:2-4. It would mean setting your eyes on Jesus, Heb 12:2. It would mean filling your mind with the things of God, and making up your mind, to do the things of God. Not to discount what the Holy Spirit can and often does cause to happen, being filled with the spirit is something you can do, and that we should do in order to live properly before the Lord, Eph 5:18. It is a presence we should nurture, not snuff out.

And John heard a loud voice behind him, like the voice of a trumpet, and telling him to write what you see to the seven churches, Rev 1:10. The churches are named: places of various renown in what is today South-Western Turkey.

Of course dreams have often been used by the Lord our God to communicate to men. Here however John is instructed to "write what you see"! These messages are being primarily transmitted to John through what he will "see," and he is to record for us what he will "see." This "Revelation" is called a "vision" in Rev 9:17. Perhaps we should take the "seeing" quite literally. In Luke chapter one an angel "appeared" to the priest Zacharias, all while he was very much awake, and he "saw" the angel, Lk 1:11-12. (It is the same way in the Greek.) Then when Zacharias came out and was unable to speak, the crowd that was waiting for him understood "he had seen a vision," Lk 1:22 KJV. All of which was very much happening in real time, while Zacharias was very much awake and conscious. We are not really told any more details of John's vision as it relates to current space and time off the coast of Asia Minor.

Many prophets have been told such things. "Write the vision" it says in, Hab 2:2 KJV. A revelation is something that can be written down and read and understood. The "voice" mentions churches that were in existence in the province of Asia in the first century.

Then he saw a symbolic vision of Jesus in Rev 1:12-16. This is no doubt what he really saw, but the elements seem to be intended to be symbolic, instead of literally what Jesus actually looks like in heaven. In truth, a spirit does not have a physical body like we have. When Jesus rose from the dead you have read what happened in Lk 24:37-39.

> [37] But they were terrified and affrighted, and supposed that they had seen a spirit. [38] And he said unto them, Why are ye troubled? and why do thoughts arise in your hearts? [39] Behold my hands and my feet, that it is I myself: handle me, and see; for a spirit hath not flesh and bones, as ye see me have. KJV

The seven lampstands of Rev 1:12, remind us of the temple lamps of the Old Testament, in for instance Ex 25:37. Many people picture this like a Jewish gold menorah. There were gold candlesticks in a vision (?) in a dream (?) in Zech 4:2.

Then John saw someone "like the Son of man," Rev 1:13. There is no "the" here in the Greek. It seems to indicate that the being he saw, at first glance looked like a man. The "son of man" is also a term for Jesus. We first see it in Ezekiel, when Ezekiel as a type of the Christ, is called by the Lord God "Son of man", in passages like Ezek 2:3. We might even say that is the normal way that God addresses Ezekiel in the book. Then we see it in the book of Daniel, "one like the son of man", approaching God in heaven to receive an eternal kingdom.

A Jewish Menorah Lamp

> I saw in the night visions, and, behold, *one* like the Son of man came with the clouds of heaven, and came to the Ancient of days, and they brought him near before him. Dan 7:13 KJV

A son of a man is of course a man. Jesus repeatedly calls Himself "the Son of man." And he was a true man. According to Phil 2:6 Jesus had the true inner nature or form of God, and He *also* had the true inner nature of a man, Phil 2:7. For the Son of Man did not have a physical home on earth, Mtt 8:20.

We see this "son of man" in Revelation 1 dressed somewhat like an exalted and wonderful high priest, beyond what may be in this life. The high priests of the Old Testament wore a chest piece called an ephod, Ex 28:6-8, and a great waist band, Ex 39:4-5. In this vision, we see His head and hair and mouth, Rev 1:14. His hair was white as snow, and His eyes were like fire, and His feet glowed like bronze in a furnace, and His voice was powerful beyond what is human on earth, Rev 1:15. God's voice was like that in a vision of Ezekiel in the Old Testament, Ezek 43:2. In His right hand are seven stars. A sword is coming out of His mouth, Rev 1:16. This is as clear an indication that this is a symbolic representation as we could possibly ask for. What is the implication of this. I think it is that the only weapon he needs is to speak to make something be so. Isaiah writes of the Christ with singular pronouns in Isaiah 49, not really speaking of himself.

> [2] And he hath made my mouth like a sharp sword; in the shadow of his hand hath he hid me, and made me a polished shaft; in his quiver hath he hid me; [3] And said unto me, Thou *art* my servant, O Israel, in whom I will be glorified. Isa 49:2-3 KJV

The sword of the spirit is the Word of God, and that is what we see symbolized.

> And take the helmet of salvation, and the sword of the Spirit, which is the word of God: Eph 6:17 KJV

"For the word of God *is* living and powerful," Heb 4:12 NKJV. The picture is of one who is great and astonishing beyond anything on this earth. He was shining as bright as the sun. John says he fell at His feet, Rev 1:17.

Do not be afraid, is what Isaiah was told in Isa 41:10. If you are His you need not be afraid. Be afraid only of not submitting to Him. Only the LORD is the first and the last.

> Thus saith the LORD the King of Israel, and his redeemer the LORD of hosts; I am the first, and I am the last; and beside me there is no God. Isa 44:6 KJV

Notice the turns of language in Isa 44:6. It is the LORD speaking, that is to say Yahweh, Yehovah. This Yahweh is also King of Israel *and* "his Redeemer"! Further this one, "his Redeemer," is "the LORD of hosts." There is not a God but Him (singular), and He is the beginning and the end of everything, and He has mastery over everything. He was dead but is alive. He has the keys of death and Hades.

Then our LORD repeats what He has said earlier. Write down the things which you see. They are about the things which will take place later, "hereafter." Then He explains the stars and lampstands, Rev 1:19-20.

The stars are the angels of the churches, Rev 1:20. The word for messenger and the word for angel is the same, in Hebrew. They are also the same in Greek. The word angel, which is the Greek word *angelos* ἄγγελος, just means messenger, in fact just any old messenger. It can be a regular human messenger, or it can mean a special spirit messenger made by God for His own purposes, and who is God's messenger to carry out God's will.

So which are these messengers in these early chapters of the book of Revelation? Some argue that these are just human messengers. Who then would be a human messenger to a church? It could be their preachers. The preacher brings God's message to the congregation, the assembly, the church.

On the other hand, the spiritual beings called angels are associated with 'stars' in Scripture. This is easily seen in Job 38 when it is talking about creation.

> When the morning stars sang together, and all the sons of God shouted for joy? Job 38:7 KJV

A High priest wearing an ephod.

We will likewise see such an association in our study of the book of Revelation.

We should not forget that angels exist to take care of Christians, as we see in Heb 1:14. Angels are appointed to take care of various groups and even nations. So in the book of Daniel there is an angel named Michael who stands guard over God's people, Dan 12:1. In Daniel 10 we see that there are angelic princes for the various nations. So there is an angelic prince for Greece and for Persia, and they sometimes even oppose each other, Dan 10:10-21.

So most of our translations say that these are "the angels of the churches." Angels sent from God to care for the churches, is entirely reasonable from a spiritual point of view.

The other side is that maybe these letters are addressed to "messengers" of the churches, and the letters are supposed to be delivered to these churches! In truth, this may not be an "either" "or" situation, and we may not need to seek a dogmatic solution.

And the seven lampstands are the seven churches. The fact that the churches are lights in this world, is something most understand. You are the light of the world, Jesus said, and then compares us ... well, to lampstands.

> [14] Ye are the light of the world. A city that is set on an hill cannot be hid. [15] Neither do men light a candle, and put it under a bushel, but on a candlestick; and it giveth light unto all that are in the house. [16] Let your light so shine before men, that they may see your good works, and glorify your Father which is in heaven. Mtt 5:14-16 KJV

The church's mission is to deliver this message of light and salvation to the entire world.

> [19] Go ye therefore, and teach all nations, baptizing them in the name of the Father, and of the Son, and of the Holy Ghost: [20] Teaching them to observe all things whatsoever I have commanded you: and, lo, I am with you alway, *even* unto the end of the world. Amen.
> Mtt 28:19-20 KJV

It is here that we come to one last element of how we should treat these letters to the seven churches. Many, especially of the "scholarly" sort, object to the many symbolic elements, or allegorical elements, in Scripture. They argue that these were never intended by the original authors, and were foisted on the text later, in an attempt to make it "work," when (they would say) it did not really work in the first place. These detractors often point to how many have in the past gotten carried away with allegorical interpretations, and turned a sober and plain text into a mishmash of nonsense. Your author of course agrees that many have indeed gotten carried away with improper symbolic interpretations.

On the other hand notice that Scripture *often* uses symbolism to teach us about future things, and that it cannot be avoided in the text. For instance, about

1400 BC Moses said,

> The LORD thy God will raise up unto thee a Prophet from the midst of thee, of thy brethren, like unto me; unto him ye shall hearken;
> Deut 18:15 KJV

Now you or I may or may not like this text, but it is clearly a text in which the great prophet Moses says that many centuries later God is going to send a great prophet, indeed the Messiah, who will be *like* Moses. Moses is intended to be symbolic of this greater prophet to come, *and there are many such passages.*

There are also many passages where exaggerated language is used to prophesy about some comparatively near event, as we have shown. So exaggerated in fact, as to be really false if only talking about the near events. *So false as to be immediately discredited, unless there is sufficient ambiguity to make us question the first application as **ever** really sufficient to be the object of the text.* But Scripture cannot be broken, Jn 10:35. If we are determined to rule out symbolism, then we are often forced to treat the original author as some sort of imbecile, not sophisticated enough to talk about the time of day, and clearly not intelligent enough to write something like Scripture which has had so much influence for generations. So for instance, David wrote many psalms which we can identify with his life and the ups and downs of a very gifted ruler. Also David wrote Psalm 22, again in the first person, describing a first person-death, and, yes, even a veiled reference it seems to a resurrection, which *never* happened to David himself. So how should we take the Psalm? It does not seem to be the product of insanity or hallucination. It is breath-taking and awe inspiring in its beauty, and its passion. It is stunning in its message about, apparently, someone else. Even the unbelieving Jews acknowledged that this Psalm was of the Christ, and the chief priests and scribes and elders even mockingly quoted Psa 22:8 to Jesus on the cross in Mtt 27:43, as if to say, You fool! You think *you* are this beloved One who trusts in God! You cannot get away from the symbolic implications, and it is those things which, strangely and seemingly deliberately, do not fit David, that are the tipoff of a greater symbolism, and another, greater, prophet.

Or again, look at some of the "parables" in Matthew 13, and Jesus' explanation of the story of the "tares of the field" as an allegory of the end of this present universe.

> [37] ... He that soweth the good seed is the Son of man; [38] The field is the world; the good seed are the children of the kingdom; but the tares are the children of the wicked *one*; [39] The enemy that sowed them is the devil; the harvest is the end of the world; and the reapers are the angels. [40] As therefore the tares are gathered and burned in the fire; so shall it be in the end of this world. [41] The Son of man shall send forth his angels, and they shall gather out of his kingdom all things that offend, and them which do iniquity; [42] And shall cast them into a

furnace of fire: there shall be wailing and gnashing of teeth. [43] Then shall the righteous shine forth as the sun in the kingdom of their Father. Who hath ears to hear, let him hear. Mtt 13:37-43 KJV

It is easy to see that in fact Scripture continually talks about the future, in a confident fashion, using symbolism both implicitly and explicitly. That seems to be the norm. Often the more unusual the events or places to be described, the more unusual is also the symbolism. Might we be able to abuse this symbolism? Yes. Should we be able to profitably use this symbolism, to see the author's intent. Yes, again, we should be able to.

Here then is the curious thing. Almost all commentators reading these first three chapters all but automatically read them as if these churches are symbolic of churches throughout the Christian age. They might not say as much, but that is how they instinctively treat these passages. Any intelligent reader and researcher almost immediately recognizes that these locations are of actual places in history, about which we can know and understand something. And the churches? Soon we realize that we know something of these churches from the book of Acts and Paul's letters. Still almost everyone realizes that the messages have a wider application than just these seven church ... so they by nature treat these churches as types, symbolic, of churches throughout the Christian age. Even if they do not mention the concept of "type" and "anti-type" or of allegory, preachers and commentators on these early chapters of Revelation almost instinctively tend to treat these churches in this way.

ST. PAUL'S TRAVELS

English Miles

— · — · — 1st Journey   ┄┄┄┄┄┄ 3rd Journey
              2nd Journey   ············ 4th Journey

Also notice that each "letter" really covers the entire Christian age. Each letter starts off with where that church is now, about 95 AD, and ends with where this leads to eternally. There is some unusual symbolism, in part because in moving from this present universe to a new one without entropy or sin or death, we are dealing with an entity we can scarcely comprehend, having lived our entire lives in a universe dominated by sin and death and things running down.

Again, Jesus alone has the keys of death and Hades, Rev 1:18. He alone is the key to escape from death.

> ²² And the key of the house of David will I lay upon his shoulder; so he shall open, and none shall shut; and he shall shut, and none shall open. ²³ And I will fasten him *as* a nail in a sure place; and he shall be for a glorious throne to his father's house. Isa 22:22-23 KJV

There is no way out of the mess we are in, other than through Jesus. The other solutions presented to us, are, in the final analysis, unfruitful dead ends.

Jesus' Letter to Ephesus, Rev 2:1-7

Unto the angel of the church of Ephesus ... Rev 2:1 KJV

And what again does "angel " mean?

In the New Testament the Greek word *angelos* ἄγγελος, means either an ordinary messenger, or an angel. In the NASB it is translated angel (86 times), angel's (2 times), angelic (1 time), angels (80 times), messenger (4 times), and messengers (3 times). So the Greek word is used mainly in the New Testament as referring to angelic creatures. However *angelos* is also used of Rahab the harlot receiving messengers, in Jas 2:25. It is used of human messengers, of those sent by John the Baptist in Lk 7:24. Also Jesus sends his disciples as messengers, Lk 9:52, and there can be messengers of Satan, 2Cor 12:7.

In addition let us note that in the Old Testament, the Hebrew word is *malak* מַלְאָךְ, and is used for both angels and men as messengers. In the NASB it is translated: ambassadors (2 times), angel (101 times), angels (9 times), envoys (1 time), messenger (24 times), and messengers (76 times). It is used when Moses sent messengers to the King of Edom in Num 20:14, and when Joshua sent messengers to look in Aachan's tent in Jos 7:22, and when Abner sent messengers to David, 2 Sam 3:12. Priests are represented as messengers of God in Mal 2:7. Also messengers are ambassadors in the NASB in Isa 30:4, and Isa 33:7. Jesus is seen as a messenger of the covenant in Isa 42:19. There are many other such references which you can find for yourself, and you do not need to know Hebrew or Greek. Needed is a good concordance or Bible program with links to the Greek and Hebrew words in English.

Jesus holds absolute power over the churches. He holds absolute power over the churches and over the stars. He holds them in His hand, in His right hand, Rev 2:1. He *walks* among the lampstands, the churches, Rev 1:20. The churches, the lampstands, are meant to provide light, light to this world, Mtt 5:14-16. Light is what this world needs, but if you have a lamp that will not function as a light, you throw it away. You remove it. You take it to the dump. So it is with the churches.

Ephesus was a rich and powerful port city in what was the Roman province of Asia, that is to say, almost the entire South-Western section of what is today Turkey. It was a center of both government and commerce with a harbor which reached out to the Mediterranean Sea, to the entrance itself at Melitus, where Paul met the elders of the church of Ephesus in Acts 20:17. This harbor, over the centuries, silted up, and now Ephesus is many miles inland, and is no longer significant as a port, or a city. Ephesus had a famous temple to Artemis/Diana (*Artemis* ῎Αρτεμις is what the Greek in Acts 19:24 says) which was of tremendous size and wealth, and was rated as one of the seven wonders of the world. The theater in Ephesus, which is still standing, was one of the largest in the ancient world, and capable of holding over 25,000 people, and it figured prominently in the riot which is detailed in Acts 19. The population of the city in the first century may have been well over 300,000.

When Paul first passed through the region he had been forbidden by the Holy Spirit to preach there (Acts 16:6-8), and he passed on to Macedonia and Greece. He later returned and preached for two years, and the whole province of Asia heard the Word from there. (Acts 19:10)

Magic At Ephesus

Ephesus had a large population of Jews and also had been tremendously influenced by occult religion, witchcraft, and magic. The gospel had a powerful impact on these things.

> [18] And many who had believed came confessing and telling their deeds. [19] Also, many of those who had practiced magic brought their books together and burned *them* in the sight of all. And they counted up the value of them, and *it* totaled fifty thousand *pieces* of silver. [20] So the word of the Lord grew mightily and prevailed. Acts 19:18-20 NKJV

There are good things about the church at Ephesus. Jesus knows about the church in Ephesus, Rev 2:2-3. He knows their deeds, and their hard labor (and that's what the Greek words emphasize: labor that produces sweat and agony). The NIV says "hard work."

The Ephesians cannot stand evil men, and have tested those who claim to be apostles but are not. Paul speaks of such false men in passages like 2Cor 11:13-15. Incredibly, this is an on going process. Paul became an apostle in about the year 35 AD, approximately 5 years after the others became apostles, and he said that becoming an apostle at that time was like being a child being born out of due time, 1Cor 15:7-8. Yet we have even now people who are trying

The magnificent temple to Artemis/Diana at Ephesus was
one of the seven wonders of the ancient world.

to claim that they are legitimate apostles. We need to be like the church at Ephesus. We need to find them false. We need to test the spirits, 1Jn 4:1.

> If anyone comes to you and does not bring this teaching, do not receive him into your house, and do not give him a greeting; 2Jn 10 NASB

More than good works, and more than spiritual discernment, the Ephesians have patiently worked on, and withstood their opposition, and carried on the labor which they had to do.

The Importance of Love

But Jesus has something against them: "that you have left your first love," NKJV. As human beings we understand these things in life and marriage situations. We may respect and honor someone, dutifully toil for them, carefully fulfill our daily routines ... but may have lost that passion and commitment which we had at first ... for a husband or wife, a friend, or a political figure.

Love, as we know, is the most important thing, 1Cor 13:1-3. What then is labor and patience, and many other good works, if we do not love the Lord? Many things in society may affect our relationship with God, and may sap its impact.

> "And because lawlessness will abound, the love of many will grow cold.." Mtt 24:12 NKJV

Jesus said it as a prophecy. It is true. Even just the moral chaos around us may subtly undermine true allegiance and faithful commitment. Maybe that was happening to the Ephesians as it often happens to us. Jeremiah speaks of when God's people had fallen from the love that they once had.

> ² "Go and cry in the hearing of Jerusalem, saying, "Thus says the
> LORD:
>> 'I remember you,
>> The kindness of your youth,
>> The love of your betrothal,
>> When you went after Me in the wilderness,
>> In a land not sown.
> ³ "Israel *was* holy to the LORD,
>> The firstfruits of His increase. ... Jer 2:2-3a NKJV

But what love is it speaking of in Rev 2:4? Is it speaking of their love for Christ ... or their love for their fellow men? We are not actually told in our text, but it implies the issue is their love for Christ. The key, the glue that holds things together is our love for Christ. Their "first love."

So Jesus tells them to remember the spiritual heights from which they had fallen and to repent! Rev 2:5 Remember! Remember where you were. Remember the love and commitment you had. Even if you have many works and labor, it will never be the same as that motivated by pure love and devotion.

Moreover, if the Ephesian do not return to their first love and do the deeds which they did at first? God will remove them as a church, remove them as a light to the world. Such things happen all along in history. It appears that often a new planting of the Word must occur for the love and devotion to the pure message to once again thrive.

Hating Works of Lawlessness

But the Ephesians have this in their favor. They hate the Nicolaitans, whom Jesus also hates, Rev 2:6. We will talk about the Nicolaitans later, but they basically are of the immoral parts of the occult working in the church. A part teaching anarchy and immorality and wild living as acceptable in the Lord. It is to the Ephesians credit that they cannot endure these people. There is no tolerance of evil in Ephesus. Listen to David who said,

> ²¹ Do I not hate them, O LORD, who hate You?
>> And do I not loathe those who rise up against You?
> ²²   I hate them with perfect hatred;
>> I count them my enemies. Psa 139:21-22 NKJV

There are two sides of the coin to remember here. One that it is often easier to hate what is evil than to love what is good. The other is that it is indeed good to hate what is evil.

Regaining Access to the Tree of Life

If you have any ears, you need to hear what the Spirit of God says to the churches. Here the letter hastens to the end of time.

> He that hath an ear, let him hear what the Spirit saith unto the churches; To him that overcometh will I give to eat of the tree of life, which is in the midst of the paradise of God. Rev 2:7 KJV

It is Jesus speaking from Rev 1:17, and it is also the Spirit of God speaking. This is the One True God speaking. Man originally had access to the tree of life, Gen 2:9, and lost it. What leads to life? It is wisdom.

> She is a tree of life to them that lay hold upon her: and happy *is every one* that retaineth her. Prov 3:18 KJV

It is righteousness.

> The fruit of the righteous is a tree of life,
> And he who wins souls is wise. Prov 11:30 NKJV

It is hoping and trusting in the Lord.

> Hope deferred makes the heart sick,
> But desire fulfilled is a tree of life. Prov 13:12 NASB

It is controlling your tongue.

> A wholesome tongue *is* a tree of life,
> But perverseness in it breaks the spirit. Prov 15:4 NKJV

Man can once more gain access to the tree of life, and once again live in the Paradise of God, Rev 22:1-2. We need to do what is right and be patient.

> 7 Rest in the LORD, and wait patiently for Him;
> Do not fret because of him who prospers in his way,
> Because of the man who brings wicked schemes to pass.
> 8 Cease from anger, and forsake wrath;
> Do not fret—*it* only *causes* harm.
> 9 For evildoers shall be cut off;
> But those who wait on the LORD,
> They shall inherit the earth. Psa 37:7-9 NKJV

Revelation is not some sort of secret plan for Christians to wipe out the wicked. Some of the wicked assert this, and then wish you to hate this message as they do. Rather this is a message for Christians to do what is right, and patiently wait for the Lord to make all things right.

> But he that shall endure unto the end, the same shall be saved. Mtt 24:13 KJV

> Now unto him that is able to keep you from falling, and to present *you*

faultless before the presence of his glory with exceeding joy, Jude 24 KJV

For whatsoever is born of God overcometh the world: and this is the victory that overcometh the world, *even* our faith. 1Jn 5:4

Smyrna, the faithful church, Rev 2:8-11

To the angel of the church in Smyrna, Rev 2:8. It is "the first and the last," the One who was dead but who came to life, who is speaking.

Smyrna was a rich city, and one of the loveliest cities of ancient Asia. Smyrna had originally been established about 1000 years before Christ, but had been destroyed by the Lydians about the time of Isaiah. Then after the death of Alexander the Great, one of his generals, Lysimachus, one of the fours horns on the goat of Greece in Daniel 8, came to rule over this area, and he reestablished Smyrna as a beautiful well planned city. It lay on one of the key trade routes through the Roman province of Asia. Smyrna became an early ally of Rome, and was always faithful to Rome. She was a beautiful, wealthy, and prosperous city. It is now Izmir in western Turkey.

I know your works, your tribulation, Rev 2:9. He knows of the poverty of this church in midst of this wealthy city. The word for poverty which is used here is *ptocheia* πτωχεία, which means that you have absolutely nothing, you are destitute, completely impoverished. You are a beggar. You ain't got a thing! It it is the word used in 2Cor 8:9 when it says of Jesus, "for your sakes he became poor," KJV. The Christians in this rich city, seem to be an impoverished minority. Blessed are you who are poor Jesus says in Lk 6:20.

> ... **Hath not God choose the poor of this world** rich in faith and heirs of the kingdom which he hath promised to them that love Him?
> Jas 2:5 KJV (*bold emphasis added*)

However Jesus says this church is rich, but it is clearly not in gold and silver. In the midst of opulence and riches the Christians at Smyrna had been afflicted. This word is in other places in translated tribulation. It is a word that basically means to be under pressure, to be under stress.

The True Jew, and Jesus Christ

As an important trade center, Smyrna also had a large contingent of Jews. Jewish merchants were already becoming a force in the world, so that there was a large contingent of Jews in an important trade center was natural. As in other places, instead of receiving the Savior and King of all men, they rejected Jesus the Christ, the one promised to Abraham, Isaac and Jacob. Now a true Jew is one who is spiritual, a Jew of the heart, those who submit to the Holy Spirit of God. So the apostle Paul said,

> 28 For he is not a Jew, which is one outwardly; neither *is that* circumcision, which is outward in the flesh: 29 But he is a Jew, which is one inwardly; and circumcision *is that* of the heart, in the spirit, and not in the letter; whose praise is not of men, but of God. Rom 2:28-29 KJV

However, again and again, the Jews of the Roman world tried to prevent the spread of the gospel, beginning with the early church in Jerusalem, Act 5:27-28, 40-41. Also the Jews frequently tried to stir up governments against Christianity in places like Antioch in Act 13:50, and at Iconium in Act 14:2, 5, and they did it also at Lystra, Act 14:19, and at Thessalonica in Act 17:5. Paul says of the men of his own nation,

> 15 Who both killed the Lord Jesus, and their own prophets, and have persecuted us; and **they please not God, and are contrary to all men:** 16 **Forbidding us to speak to the Gentiles that they might be saved,** to fill up their sins alway: for the wrath is come upon them to the uttermost. 1 Thes 2:15-16 KJV *(emphasis added)*

I think it is in the light of these things that Jesus speaks of those who say they are Jews and are not in Rev 2:9. It is a falsehood that they call themselves Jews, because they really are not. To begin with, even nominally, they subscribe to a man

Smyrna

made religion from the Pharisees, an Old Testament denomination, not really a manifestation of the Law of Moses. As Jesus pointed out to them before His death,

> 45 "Do not think that I shall accuse you to the Father; there is *one* who accuses you—Moses, in whom you trust. 46 For if you believed Moses, you would believe Me; for he wrote about Me. 47 But if you do not believe his writings, how will you believe My words?" Jn 5:45-46 NKJV

Many Liberals of our own day think that you can believe the New Testament of Jesus Christ, yet reject the so-called "myths" of Moses' Law. Here Jesus says something different. He says that if you do not really believe, say those early chapters of Genesis, then how can you ever believe what Jesus has to say. And so it is to this day.

The Jews, Gnosticism and Satan

Beyond that, Jesus says they are really of the synagogue of Satan, Rev 2:9. Those who reject the true and beloved Messiah are not of God. There is a long confrontation in John 8 between Jesus and the scribes and the Pharisees in the temple. Jesus says He is speaking the things which He has seen with His Father, and they are doing the things they have heard from their father. Jesus knew they were plotting to kill Him. They answered that Abraham was their father. Jesus says that if Abraham was really their father (and Jesus means spiritually) then they should do the works that Abraham did, but instead, here they are trying to murder the Messiah whom God had sent. The Jews are also speaking spiritually, and answered,

> ... We be not born of fornication; we have one Father, even God.
> Jn 8:41 KJV

Now these Jews had heard His message of peace. They had seen the powerful works which He had done, works which they could not deny, even in their writings in the Talmud later. In despair they acknowledged the many signs He was performing, Jn 11:47. When the Jews recorded their opposition they did not deny His powerful works, rather they attributed them to evil magic. Many had believed, even among the ruling authorities, Jn 12:42. So it was to many a political struggle, a struggle to prevent any *personal* loss of power. They even discussed putting Lazarus to death because Jesus had raised him from the dead, Jn 12:10. Jesus said that if God were their Father they would love Him.

> [44] Ye are of your father the devil, and the lusts of *your* father ye will do. He was a murderer from the beginning, and abode not in the truth, because there is no truth in him. When he speaketh a lie, he speaketh of his own: for he is a liar, and the father of it. [45] And because I tell *you* the truth, ye believe me not.
> [46] Which of you convinceth me of sin? And if I say the truth, why do ye not believe me? [47] He that is of God heareth God's words: ye therefore hear *them* not, because ye are not of God
> Jn 8:44-47 KJV

This passionate and obstinate opposition to Jesus continued. It was not enough that they refused to believe. It was important *to them* that **no one believe**. So everywhere they tried to stir up governmental opposition to the faith, as for instance in Corinth in years 51-52 AD in Acts 18. Men who reject Jesus the Messiah are not true Jews. Whether they are Jews or gentiles, they are of Satan, Jn 8:42-44, Eph 2:1-2. That included all of us at one time.

There is also another side of this development among the Jews leading up to the first century. Many gloss over it, but it is a development in Judaism which truthfully cannot be ignored. That is the development of the occult among the Jews. Sir William Ramsay has this to say.

> "The Jews were too clever for their fellow-townsmen. They regarded with supreme contempt the gross obscene ritual and the vulgar super-stitions of their neighbors; but many of them were ready to turn those superstitions to their own profit; and **a species of magic and sooth-saying, a sort of syncretism of Hebrew and pagan religious ideas**, **afforded a popular and lucrative occupation** to the sons of Sceva in Ephesus and **to many another Jew** throughout the Asiatic Greek ci-ties." Ramsay, W. M., *The Letters to the Seven Churches of Asia, And Their Plan in the Apocalypse*, Hodder and Stoughton, 1904, London, pg 142-143 (*bold emphasis added*)

Actually the Jewish playing with the occult was much more than that, even from earlier Old Testament times. Isaiah writes of Jews who are,

> 3   A people who provoke Me to anger continually to My face;
> Who sacrifice in gardens,
> And burn incense on altars of brick;
> 4   Who sit among the graves,
> And spend the night in the tombs;
> Who eat swine's flesh,
> And the broth of abominable things is *in* their vessels;
> 5   Who say, "Keep to yourself,
> Do not come near me,
> For I am holier than you!'
> These *are* smoke in My nostrils,
> A fire that burns all the day. Isa 65:3-5 NKJV

In other places Isaiah speaks of Jews entering a covenant with death so that death and destruction would have no hold on them.

> Because you have said, "We have made a covenant with death,
> And with Sheol we are in agreement.
> When the overflowing scourge passes through,
> It will not come to us,
> For we have made lies our refuge,
> And under falsehood we have hidden ourselves."
> Isa 28:15 NKJV

So we are talking about serious *evil* occult activity among many of the pre-exilic Jews. But God says He will annul their covenant.

> "Your covenant with death will be annulled,
>> And your agreement with Sheol will not stand;
>> When the overflowing scourge passes through,
>> Then you will be trampled down by it." Isa 28:18 NKJV

This preoccupation continues after the exile. The Lord speaking through the prophet Malachi says,

> And I will come near to you to judgment; and I will be a swift witness against the sorcerers, ... Mal 3:5 KJV

Ramsay mentions the Jewish exorcists in Acts 19. We see the Jewish magician Bar-jesus in Acts 13, and there is much more to tell of the subject. The seeking of decidedly evil power is noted in Isa 28:15, and became a signature trait among many of the Jewish Gnostics. Modern Jewish historians of the Jewish occult, like Gershom Scholem, trace some Jewish worship of evil back to Jewish Gnosticism of the early centuries both before and after Christ. At times Scholem calls this "the left hand path." When speaking of the later development of the Jewish Kabbalah, Scholem says,

> "the central ideas, as well as many details, go back as far as the first and second centuries."
> Gershom Scholem, *Kabbalah*, New American Library, NY, 1974, pg 15

In fact, a few Jews believed that it was the evil "god" Satan who actually created the world. Jewish historian Heinrich Graetz comments,

> "Beneath this highest of all beings they set the Creator of the world (Demiurge), whom they also called Ruler. To him they assigned the work of creation; he directed the world, he had delivered the people of Israel, and given them the Law."
> Graetz, *History of the Jews*, Vol 2, pg 375

In this way the evil "god" was treated as the actual creator of the world. ("Samael" or "Simyael" are names used for Satan "the blind god," Scholem, *Kabbalah,* pg 385, 386). Under much so-called "Jewish" or "Christian" Gnosticism, the "god" of the Old Testament was Satan, and the God of the New Testament was the spiritual First Cause. There are shades of these ideas in much of so-called "Christian" or "Jewish" theology: the "God" of the Old Testament is viewed as being bad; the God of the New Testament is viewed as good.

This is too large a topic to cover in this overview of Revelation, but suffice it to say that some Gnostics, both of the Jews and of the nations, turned to a formal worship and service of Satan.

Using Judaism as a Facade

Is this in fact what Jesus is talking about when He speaks of "those who say they are Jews and are not, but are a synagogue of Satan"? This is a powerful strain throughout history, a "mystery of lawlessness" 2Thes 2:7, *which cannot be avoided* in the book of Revelation. This is another reason why the secret followers of these mysteries hate the book of Revelation and try to undermine its study.

Further, if that is what Jesus it talking about, what should we make of it? First of all remember that Jesus is NOT anti-Jewish. As Jesus remarked to the Samaritan woman,

> Ye worship ye know not what: we know what we worship: for salvation is of the Jews. Jn 4:22 KJV

While the rejection of their own Messiah by the Jews was clearly forecast in the Old Testament (as for instance in Isa 8:14-15, and many more passages), so also both the Old Testament and the New Testament forecast the eventual conversion of the Jews to Jesus of Nazareth (Deut 30:5-6, Lk 13:35, and many other passages). So, once again, if Jesus is literally speaking about some sort of "Jewish" "church" of Satan, what should we make of it? This is what we should make of it: **These are men who say they are Jews, but who are not *really* Jews!** This is not some sort of anti-Jewishness: *these men* **are not _really_ Jews.** This is something for both Jews and gentiles to recognize.

It is not out of order to point out that one of the greatest false messiah's of the Christian age came from Smyrna: a Jewish false-christ Shabbetai Zevi (or Sevi), 1626-1676 AD.

Finally it must be said, even if we find this line of evidence distasteful, it is still there, even without the book of Revelation. It is a very potent and important line of evidence in history. Also see that this evidence is not actually against the Jews, or even against Pharisaism, but against Satanism.

All of that line of evidence aside, the anti-Christian streak among the Jews very much continued. In the middle of the next century there was an outstanding martyr to Jesus Christ at Smyrna. We have some historical records of the persecution of the church in Smyrna in the 2nd century AD, and the death of an overseer of the church of Christ in Smyrna, a man by the name of Polycarp. He died on Saturday, February 23, 155 AD. Much opposition was stirred up against him, but he refused to offer incense in worship of Caesar. Then at last, when it came time to burn him alive, the Jews were eager in their assistance.

> "This, then, was carried into effect with greater speed than it was spoken, the multitudes immediately gathering together wood and fagots out of the shops and baths; the Jews especially, according to custom, eagerly assisting them in it."
> *The Martyrdom Of The Holy Polycarp*, Chapter 13

So it has been throughout the Christian age, that those who should have been the chosen sons and priests of the Most High God, became instead its most implacable opponents. Do not be afraid, Jesus tells the Christians at Smyrna, Rev 2:10a. Sometimes we forget,

> ... and that we must through much tribulation enter into the kingdom of God. Acts 14:22 KJV

Those who promise that if we will just accept Jesus, then all will go well for us on earth, preach a lie. The book of Revelation is a witness against that lie, and so is Acts 14:22, and many other passages. However, God does take care of His own. Do not be afraid of the troubles which are coming to you.

> [4] And I say unto you my friends, Be not afraid of them that kill the body, and after that have no more that they can do. [5] But I will forewarn you whom ye shall fear: Fear him, which after he hath killed hath power to cast into hell; yea, I say unto you, Fear him. [6] Are not five sparrows sold for two farthings, and not one of them is forgotten before God? [7] But even the very hairs of your head are all numbered. Fear not therefore: ye are of more value than many sparrows.
> Lk 12:4-7 KJV

> These things I have spoken unto you, that in me ye might have peace. In the world ye shall have tribulation: but be of good cheer; I have overcome the world. Jn 16:33 KJV

The devil will put some of you in prison Jesus says to this church in Asia. They will be tested and have much trouble for ten days, Rev 2:10.

The devil is always looking for someone to devour, 1Pe 5:8. Our struggle is not against flesh and blood, Eph 6:12. We are really fighting against Satan and the demonic powers surrounding him, to whom all of us at times have fallen prey. Their power over us was through the fear of death, but Jesus has removed their power to destroy us forever, Heb 2:14-15.

Be faithful even unto death, Rev 2:10. Even to the point of losing your job? Even to death? Even to the point of losing your house? We have to live don't we? Even to the point of death? We have to get along with these people a little. We have to compromise a little! Even to death! We have to eat! Paul says with food and raiment we should be content. But if necessary ... even unto death! They will lay hands on you and persecute you. Lk 21:12, 16-19 ... but by standing firm "you will gain your lives."

> He that loveth his life shall lose it; and he that hateth his life in this world shall keep it unto life eternal. Jn 12:25 KJV

> And they overcame him by the blood of the Lamb, and by the word of their testimony; **and they loved not their lives unto the death**.
> Rev 12:11 KJV

It is to he who overcomes. The overcoming is not by our own strength, it is not human will or human assistance. It is by faith, 1Jn 5:4-5.

Now everyone is going to die once. This body will fail. Something will malfunction, or it will be injured in an accident or calamity. But the second death is not for everyone. It is only for those whose names are not in the book of life, Rev 20:12-15. If you suffer the second death, you will be existing ... but not living. You will be feeling ... but not alive. You will have death and decay forever.

Hell is described in Isa 66:24.

> "And they shall go forth and look
> Upon the corpses of the men
> Who have transgressed against Me.
> For their worm does not die,
> And their fire is not quenched.
> They shall be an abhorrence to all flesh." NKJV

But for those alive in Christ Jesus, for those who overcome, the second death, of eternal rot and decay and burning in the fires of hell, will have no power.

You do not have to be well to do to have everlasting life and blessings. Our Lord had nothing bad to say about this impoverished band of saints in a very well to do city. And once again, this letter also ends with the end of the age.

> He that hath an ear, let him hear what the Spirit saith unto the churches; He that overcometh shall not be hurt of the second death. Rev 2:11 KJV

To the church at Pergamum, Rev 2:12-17

It was an ancient and famous city. The town still exists and is now called Bergama in Turkey. It is on the river Caicus, at the top of a high conical hill, about sixty miles north of Smyrna, and you could look way off and see the Mediterranean in the distance.

It had been a capital city for nearly 400 years in ancient times. This area had been switched back and forth between Lysimachus of Asia Minor and the Seleucus I of the kingdom of Syria. Both are mentioned in Scripture in the book of Daniel, as two of Alexander the Great's generals, two of the fours horns on the goat of Greece in Daniel 8. In 282 BC there had been a revolt and the Attalid kingdom had been formed with Pergamum as its capital. When King Attalus III died, he willed his kingdom to the Romans in the year 133 BC, as being the very best thing he could do for his people. It was one of the first places where a temple to the Caesars was later built.

Pergamum had one of the most famous libraries of ancient times. In fact our word 'parchment' comes from the name Pergamum. The son of Attalus I,

Pergamum from a distance.

the Greek king Eumenes, in the second century BC, was trying to build a more famous library than the one in Alexandria. He tried to hire away one of Egypt's top librarians, Aristophanes of Byzantium. Ptolemy of Egypt had Aristophanes put in prison to prevent this, and put an embargo on papyrus for making books. So king Eumenes had parchment invented (out of animal skins) to make books ... and this eventually won out ... and many of the oldest Bibles were made on parchment. They finally developed a library of some 200,000 volumes, which the Roman general Mark Anthony gave to the last Cleopatra.

God, and Zeus, and Satan

Also we should remember some of the foundations of history. The seed of woman was prophesied in Genesis. From the seed of woman, that is, the offspring of woman, will come the redemption of man, Gen 3:15. Of Abraham it was said, through your seed all the nations of the earth will be blessed, Gen 12:2-3, 7. So there was a seed. There was a line. There was a godly offspring through Isaac and Jacob and through them a king of David's line came. Finally there came the very son of God himself, born of a virgin, Mat 1:22-23. And it was 'seed' singular, not 'seeds' plural, Gal 3:16.

There has been persecution. There has been death. Many have been faithful even unto to death. A special statement is made here. Jesus says to this church, I know where you live, where Satan's throne is, Rev 2:13.

A huge altar of Zeus was in Pergamum. It was a magnificent structure, high on the hill, and was an altar, but from a distance was said to look like a throne. Many think this altar is the key to this passage. It is easy to document occult associations of Zeus with Satan. However, also Paul quotes a poem originally written of "Zeus" (Aratus *Phaenomena*, or Cleanthes *Hymn to Zeus*, both written in the third century BC) as referring to the real Lord God, Acts 17:28. Also the worship of Asclepius, known as 'the Pergamene god', was there. He was the god of healing, and the temples of Asclepius were as close to hospitals as anything in the pre-Christian world. It was a combination of faith healing and medicine. Further Asclepius was associated with the serpent. On the other hand there were also temples to other "gods" in Pergamum.

The serpent has always been associated with knowledge, and has often been associated with healing. In Gen 3:4, he says 'Ye shall not surely die'. He really promises a fuller life, and fuller knowledge. You will know more things. Even today, the serpent is involved in many of the the normal symbols for medicine. But these things alone don't seem to justify calling Pergamum the place where Satan has his throne.

And Where Did Satan Live in 95 AD?

So let us notice some things, based on this text. Satan does have a seat/throne, and it is at Pergamum in the first century! In Matthew 4 Satan offers his throne and power to Jesus. What a victory that would have been for Satan! Jesus, while not denying Satan's right to offer it, refuses the invitation.

Asclepius' rod (above), with a serpent, is seen in modern medical symbolism. The magical caduceus staff (top left), associated with the god Hermes, is also with serpents and is also associated with medicine (U. S. Army Medical Corps symbol, bottom left).

> [8] Again, the devil took Him up on an exceedingly high mountain, and showed Him all the kingdoms of the world and their glory. [9] And he said to Him, "All these things I will give You if You will fall down and worship me." [10] Then Jesus said to him, "Away with you, Satan! For it is written, *'You shall worship the LORD your God, and Him only you shall serve.'* "
> Mtt 4:8-10 NKJV

It is easy to see that Satan really *wishes* to be worshipped as if he were God. He is willing to offer great rewards to obtain that worship from men, and seemingly is allowed to do such things within certain limits. He is the God of this world, 2 Cor 4:4. He is "the prince of the power of the air" KJV, and we all followed him at one time, Eph 2:2-3. Further, the whole world is under his power,

1Jn 5:19; and he does have a seed, Mtt 13:38-39.

But who is this seed of serpent? Both the woman and the serpent have a singular "seed" in Gen 3:15.

Then let us notice that Scripture says that the one we call Satan was once the king of Tyre, or that king was symbolic of Satan. From Ezekiel 28.

> [11] Again the word of the LORD came to me saying, [12] "Son of man, take up a lamentation over the king of Tyre and say to him, 'Thus says the Lord GOD,
>
>> "You had the seal of perfection,
>> Full of wisdom and perfect in beauty.
>
> [13] "You were in Eden, the garden of God;
>
>> Every precious stone was your covering: ...
>> And the gold, the workmanship of your settings and sockets,
>> Was in you.
>> On the day that you were created
>> They were prepared.
>
> [14] "You were the anointed cherub who covers,
>
>> And I placed you *there*.
>> You were on the holy mountain of God;
>> You walked in the midst of the stones of fire.
>
> [15] "You were blameless in your ways
>
>> From the day you were created
>> Until unrighteousness was found in you.
>
> [16] "By the abundance of your trade
>
>> You were internally filled with violence,
>> And you sinned;
>> Therefore I have cast you as profane
>> From the mountain of God.
>> And I have destroyed you, O covering cherub,
>> From the midst of the stones of fire. Ezek 28:11-16 NASB

Is it literal? I don't *think* so. Do we really think that the ancient king of Tyre was literally in the garden of Eden? To that I would answer No! Then again, could this king of Tyre be the "was" of the special man of Satan in Rev 17:8, 11? Also notice that the terms in which the city of Tyre is described in Ezek 27:3b-7, and the following is very similar to the way Babylon is described in Revelation 18!

But all of that aside, here is a special statement about a king, an ancient king, a real king, and this king is identified with Satan, or at the very least, this ancient king is symbolic of, is a "type" of, Satan! Notice also that according to the book of Revelation Satan does give his throne to a man. Satan is identified with a "dragon" in Rev 12:9, where it identifies him as "the great dragon ... that old serpent called the Devil and Satan." And it says of this dragon,

[1] And the dragon stood on the sand of the seashore.
Then I saw a beast coming up out of the sea, ... [2] ... **And the dragon gave him his power and his throne and great authority**.
Rev 13:1-2 NASB (*bold emphasis added*)

There is much more to discuss, but most of the discussion will be left for later. However notice that this leads to the worship of Satan (the dragon), and worship of this "beast."

[3] ... And all the world marveled and followed the beast. [4] **So they worshiped the dragon** who gave authority to the beast; and they worshiped the beast, ... Rev 13:3-4 NKJV (*bold emphasis added*)

Also we should notice that Paul talks in 2 Thessalonians chapter 2 about some things which have to happen *before* Jesus comes again. These things are so big that Paul treats them as things which those who live on this earth could not possibly miss. Well what in the world is it Paul?

A man, *anthrōpos* ἄνθρωπος, will be "revealed" (it is the verb form of the word "revelation," *apocaluptō* ἀποκαλύπτω) 2Thes 2:3, and this man,

... opposeth and exalteth himself above all that is called God, or that is worshipped; so that he as God sitteth in the temple of God, shewing himself that he is God. 2Thes 2:4 KJV

Now those of Satan are very offended at the concept of Jesus of Nazareth being exclusively *the* God. But this "man" described in 2 Thessalonians 2 demands worship as *the* one and only God. Also this "man," who demands worship from the entire world, is,

Even him, whose coming is after the working of Satan with all power and signs and lying wonders, 2Thes 2:9 KJV

So here is a "man," described very similarly to the man in Revelation 13, who receives Satan's approval and support and is worshipped by "all the world," Rev 13:3-4. Wow! Coincidence? Hardly! No more so than the "Branch" in Isa 4:2, and the "man" called "The Branch" in Zech 6:12, and Branch of David in Jer 33:15, and the shoot or stem or tender plant of Jesse in Isa 11:1 and 53:2, are to be considered a "coincidence."

This "man" will be *personally* destroyed by Jesus' second coming.

... whom the Lord shall consume with the spirit of his mouth, and shall destroy with the brightness of his coming: 2Thes 2:8 KJV

So, whatever your theories are about "signs," the appearance of this "man" who is to be worshipped by *all* of the lost of this world (2Thes 2:9-11, Rev 13:8), **is a precondition to the second coming of Christ!** And that is the purpose for which Paul writes 2 Thessalonians chapter two.

[1] Now we request you, brethren, with regard to the coming of our Lord

Jesus Christ and our gathering together to Him, [2] that you not be
quickly shaken from your composure or be disturbed either by a spirit
or a message or a letter as if from us, to the effect that the day of the
Lord has come. [3] Let no one in any way deceive you, for *it will not come*
unless the apostasy comes first, and the man of lawlessness is revealed,
the son of destruction, 2Thes 2:1-3 NASB

Admittedly, you may or may not believe this passage, *but that **is** what it says.*
And these are not your author's words, "but ... as it is in truth, the word of
God," 1Thes 2:13. If you or I trivialize this into something that is of no signifi-
cance, then we have to ask, what then does 2Thes 2:1-3 really mean, and why did
Paul write 2 Thessalonians 2 *at all?*

Also this "man" in 2 Thessalonians 2 is supported by a mystery religion, a
special type of secret or semi-secret religion, which was already in existence in
the first century AD. "For the mystery of lawlessness is already at work;" 2Thes
2:7a NKJV. (The KJV here translates it as "iniquity." Of course lawlessness is sin,
1Jn 3:3, but the best reading here is "lawlessness.") There is an extended
discussion of mystery religions and their traits in *Prophecy Principles*, but the key
point is that there is a mystery religion which is in existence in the first century
AD, which will continue to exist until it produces this "man of lawlessness"
whom the entire world will have to worship.

Then there is the last point, and the key one for our text in Rev 2:13. Paul
speaks of this "man" as if he were ready to be revealed in the first century. He
is ready to be worshipped by the entire world, but something from God is holding
him back. Something which Paul had talked to the Thessalonians about, but of
which we know nothing.

And you know **what** restrains him **now**, so that in his time he **will be**
revealed. 2Thes 2:6 NASB (*bold emphasis added*)

Therefore this "man" is ready to be worshipped by the entire world **in the
first century**, but he is being held back by lack of the just-right conditions.
Still it is, "that he might be revealed in his time," KJV. Another "man"? A dynasty? A Satanic "seed"?

Surely these passages alone are compelling Scriptural evidence for the existence in even the first century AD of a certain awesome Satanic man. A "man
of lawlessness" who will "be revealed in his time." And Rev 2:13 says that the
church in Pergamum lives "where Satan's throne is." Does this relate to the magnificent temple of Zeus? I don't know, but I do not have a particular reason to
think so.

You may say, why bring up all of this concerning the book of Genesis, and
Jesus temptation, and the book of 2 Thessalonians? The answer is: did not these
things come before the book of Revelation? Are they not part of the background to be considered in understanding the book of Revelation?

A great deal of art and craft and bluster goes into "Establishment interpretation" to make sure that these verses are *not* even discussed, and for sure are *not* taken at face value, but they are still there.

There is a special seed of Satan, just as there is special seed of God.

Some have noticed the parallels between the Son of God and 'the man of lawlessness'. Two roughly parallel seeds, but they are really the antithesis of each other. One is about life and lawful behavior even to the point of suffering an unjust death. The other is about lawlessness and is destructive in his very character. We shall see more about this later.

It does say *that Satan lived at Pergamum*, "where Satan dwells" NKJV and that Satan's seat/throne is there, Rev 2:13. Once again, *you may not like what Jesus said*. Is it possible that this is merely symbolic language, without any real meaning? Yes, I suppose it is possible, but this is pretty dramatic language, and, as we have pointed out, Pergamum was *not* overall any more pagan than many other places in the ancient world, including in the Roman province of Asia. Additionally, as we have shown, there are lines of collateral evidence from Scripture and from history, that would support the idea of taking these statements literally. Part of the resistance to taking this literally would be a general rationalistic tendency in the modern world to not really believe Scripture, or to not take the idea of a literal Satan as true. However, the Bible is a book about the reality of both the physical and the spirit world, and it definitely states that Satan is a very real and powerful spiritual creation who has led a revolt against God Himself. Also the "seed" or descendant of the woman is a very literal thing. It is the man Jesus the Christ who was born of the Holy Spirit of God and of the woman Mary! It would be up to the detractor to **prove** that Jesus is speaking symbolically, and that the symbolism is meaningless. These are some very dramatic statements of what is going on, especially when we take these statements at face value.

Luring People to Sin

Additionally we can see that the church at Pergamum has gone through some difficult times, and they held the line even in the days when the faithful saint Antipas was killed, here at this place where Satan dwells, Rev 2:13. Nevertheless, Jesus has a few things against them.

Some there hold to the teachings of Balaam, who lured people to sin to bring a curse on them, Rev 2:14. A very Satanic sort of activity: Luring to sin! This luring to sin in the Old Testament was by placing stumbling blocks before God's people. Balaam in the Old Testament started off as a prophet of God who spoke regularly with God. He was a gentile, but he started off as a remarkable man of God. A king, Balak, hired Balaam to bring a curse on Israel for *a huge sum of silver and gold*. Balaam tried to bring a curse on Israel, but he could not, because there was no sin found in the camp of Israel at that time which might provide *the grounds* for a curse. In the case of the original Balaam, who still wanted to earn all of that silver and gold, he taught the Moabite women to lure the Israeli men to sin, in order to bring God's curse upon them, so that Balak would be able to defeat Israel in war. So this **error of Balaam *has***, from the first, ***governmental and political overtones***. The story is told in Numbers chapters 22 through 31. The key to the sin of Balaam is given in Num 31:16.

> Behold, these caused the children of Israel, through the counsel of Balaam, to commit trespass against the LORD in the matter of Peor, and there was a plague among the congregation of the LORD. KJV

When Peter summarizes the error of Balaam in his second letter, he says that the false teachers of his time (and indeed the entire gospel age),

> ... are gone astray, following the way of Balaam the son of Bosor, who loved the wages of unrighteousness; 2Pe 2:15 KJV

And Jesus in Revelation 2 says that some in Pergamum,

> ... hold the doctrine of Balaam, who taught Balac to cast a stumblingblock before the children of Israel, to eat things sacrificed unto idols, and to commit fornication. Rev 2:14 KJV

If you think it through, this is a dazzling picture of ***spiritual warfare*** in order to win ***physical wars***. Here are men of God of the highest character and spirituality, who are suborned/seduced into helping worldly rulers wage war against their enemies, so that the enemy will be defeated in battle! Shades of "Raiders of the Lost Ark"! In this case, *some* in the first century church in Pergamum were involved in these things! In this place where Satan dwells! Also some in the church at Pergamum hold to the occult doctrines of the Nicolaitans, Rev 2:15

The message to the church from Christ is to repent or else. Or else, Christ will come upon these errant brothers quickly,

> ... and I will make war against them with the sword of My mouth. Rev 2:16 NASB

How effective can that be? If you ask that, you obviously have no idea.

> By the word of the LORD the heavens were the heavens made; and all the host of them by the breath of his mouth. Psa 33:6 KJV

He can do absolutely *anything* by merely speaking it to be. Woe to the one who is at war with his Maker!

> He who has an ear to hear, let him hear ... Rev 2:17 NKJV

Then Jesus relates all of this to the end of time. To the one who overcomes, God will give him the bread of heaven to feed on, and a new name, which no one else knows, Rev 2:17. That last part seems to reference magical practices of using names, where they often needed the name of the victim in order to be able to place a curse on him. Those who are with Jesus will be above where a curse on them will be effective.

To Thyatira, Rev 2:18-29

To the angel of the church in Thyatira, from Him whose eyes are like fire, and whose feet are like polished bronze, Rev 2:18. Notice the description is similar to that of the angel described in Daniel 10.

> [5] I lifted my eyes and looked, and behold, a certain man clothed in linen, whose waist *was* girded with gold of Uphaz! [6] His body *was* like beryl, his face like the appearance of lightning, his eyes like torches of fire, his arms and feet like burnished bronze in color, and the sound of his words like the voice of a multitude. Dan 10:5-6 NKJV

The city of Thyatira was not anything special as a town. It was a trade center, in the middle of a valley, and it was very hard to defend. It was a garment, pottery, and brass working center. There was a lot of dyeing of cloth there. If you remember, Lydia, the seller of purple cloth, was from Thyatira, Act 16:14. Thyatira was on the road between Pergamum and Sardis. The road then travelled to Philadelphia and Laodicea. It was part of the kingdom of the Attalid kings which was willed to the Romans in 133 AD. It was the least important of the towns these letters were written to.

A Church That Held Firm

I know your deeds, your love and faith Rev 2:19, and good things were said about their work for the Lord. In fact their service to the Lord, their persistence and their good works were greater than they had been at their first conversion to the gospel. That is very good and dramatic. The tendency is great for men in a sinful world to drift away from what is right. We may know what is right, do it for a while, and then imperceptibly at first, slowly move away from doing what is right.

The church at Ephesus had been established somewhere around the years 53 to 55 AD. People from other towns seem to have spent some time there first, but in essence we can consider the church there as really established by the Apostle Paul during his two years in Ephesus, Acts 19:10, for it says "that all they which dwelt in Asia heard the word of the Lord Jesus, both Jews and Greeks," KJV. Imagine being part of a church established by the Apostle Paul himself. But a mere forty years later Ephesus had good deeds but did not still have the love for Jesus she once possessed. Thyatira in contrast still had her love for Christ, and had actually increased her works and her service.

Thyatira

The Problem of Tolerating Wickedness

No persecution is mentioned against the church at Thyatira. We can infer that the women of the congregation are very active. Jesus says He has something against them ... toleration!

You tolerate the woman, who is called Jezebel, Rev 2:20. The name Jezebel is obviously symbolic. The original Jezebel died in 2 Kings 9, and she is indeed symbolic of militant pagan wickedness and warped religion. She was the daughter of Ethbaal king of the Sidonians, and she led Ahab and all of Israel into sin, 1Kgs 16:31. She freely murdered anyone she wished, and promoted the evil religion of Baal. Baal worship involved religious prostitution and the sacrifice of infants. In the Old Testament Jezebel is presented as seductive evil personified and in the end, her conduct invited punishment from God in *this world*.

Our text about Thyatira has overtones of what was later called Gnosticism. Among the Jewish Gnostics there was a tendency to act as if there were two "gods," two grounds of being, two "deities." One was the all good, all spirit "God," who was very remote and inaccessible. The other was the "creator" "god" who was evil enough to create our present world out of flawed and evil matter. So in their twisted thinking, the "creator" "god" of the Old Testament was actually Satan, as we have previously pointed out. These things are easy to document from history, and even from some New Testament commentaries. The rest of the story is that the heroes of the Gnostics were often those men who opposed the "god" of the Old Testament (their words not mine). So Jewish historian Heinrich Graetz, in his *History of the Jews*, describes some of these things this way.

"One sect called themselves Cainites, for no other reason than that its disciples, in defiance of the Biblical narrative, regarded the fratricide Cain as superior to Abel. The Cainites also honored the depraved Sodomites, Esau, in spite of his savagery, and the ambitious Korah. The Ophites and Naasites were filled with similar love of opposition to the Biblical accounts, but they assigned to it a better motive than that of the Cainites. **They took their name from the Greek word Ophis and the Hebrew Nahash (Naas) serpent**, and honored this animal very highly, **because in the Bible the serpent is considered as the origin of evil**, and, according to the ideas of those times, was looked upon as the symbol of evil, and **as the form taken by Satan**. The Ophites gave thanks to the serpent, by whose means the first human pair were led into disobedience against God, and thus to the recognition of good and evil and of consciousness in general."

History of the Jews, Philadelphia, Jewish Publication Society of America, 1891-1898,Vol 2, pgs 374-375 (*bold emphasis added*)

So there was a strain in Jewish-Gnosticism of a very militant worship of evil, and rejection of all that is good! The overtones of such sects have already been seen in this discussion of religion in Asia.

So here is a woman "who calls herself a prophetess" NKJV, and who leads some to commit fornication and to eat in worship things sacrificed to idols. Jezebel leads Jesus' "slaves" aside (that is the word in Rev 2:20, *doulos* δοῦλος, which is translated as "servants" in the KJV, and as "bond-servants" in the NASB). The text calls her Jezebel. This would fit right in with these Satanic Gnostic cults who idolized the wicked men and women of the Old Testament. Her doctrine was the "so-called deep secrets" of Satan, Rev 2:24 NIV. It would seem that this woman has become a Christian, and claims prophetic gifts. Possibly she was Jewish. That would fit these times.

Toleration can be a problem. Of God it says, the wrong doers cannot stand before Him. He cannot stand them we might say.

> The foolish shall not stand in thy sight: thou hatest all workers of iniquity. Psa 5:5 KJV

I cannot stand your worship services, God says of some in Amos' time.

> [21] I hate, I despise your feast days, and I will not smell in your solemn assemblies. [22] Though ye offer me burnt offerings and your meat offerings, I will not accept *them*: neither will I regard the peace offerings of your fat beasts. [23] Take thou away from me the noise of thy songs; for I will not hear the melody of thy viols. [24] But let judgment run down as waters, and righteousness as a mighty stream.
> Amos 5:21-24 KJV

Some things God will not tolerate, and there are things we should not tolerate.

Tolerating a child who misbehaves can be a problem.

> Discipline your son while there is hope,
> > And do not desire his death. Prov 19:18 NASB

A king who tolerates wickedness can be a problem.

> Take away the wicked *from* before the king, and his throne shall be established in righteousness. Prov 25:5 KJV

> A wise king sifts out the wicked,
> > And brings the threshing wheel over them. Prov 20:26 NKJV

Tolerating sin can be a problem.

> Righteousness exalteth a nation: but sin is a reproach to any people. Prov 14:34 KJV

As a nation we are not to tolerate evil, rather we are to punish it so that the nation as a whole will not come under condemnation.

> [19] "... Thus you shall purge the evil from among you. [20] The rest will hear and be afraid, and will never again do such an evil thing among you." Deut 19:19-20 NASB

We are being taught a lot of mandatory toleration of *everything* in the early 21st century. Even so, everyone agrees that some things should not be tolerated. Even the liberals agree that Nazism should not be tolerated. What we should or should not tolerate must be determined by the truth of God. Unfortunately, we are increasingly in a society that can tolerate *anything* but righteousness, anything but truth. Toleration can be good, or it can be deadly.

The Ephesians were highly praised because they could not tolerate evil men, Rev 2:2. And the church in Thyatira is condemned because they tolerate evil, and unfaithfulness to God in fornication,

> For, lo, they that are far from thee shall perish: thou hast destroyed all them that go a whoring from thee, Psa 73:27 KJV

Jesus described the Jews of His generation as an evil and adulterous generation, Mtt 13:39. That could be interpreted both literally and spiritually.

Then we come to the problem of eating meat offered to idols. Plainly we are not to prostitute ourselves to other gods. As Moses commanded,

> [15] Lest thou make a covenant with the inhabitants of the land, and they go a whoring after their gods, and do sacrifice unto their gods, and *one* call thee, and thou eat of his sacrifice; [16] And thou take of their daughters unto thy sons, and their daughters go a whoring after their gods, and make thy sons go a whoring after their gods. Ex 34:15-16 KJV

And although the worship of God through images is wrong, an image, of any "divinity" or so-called "god" is in reality nothing. It is merely metal or stone or plastic or perhaps even flesh.

> [4] As concerning therefore the eating of those things that are offered in sacrifice unto idols, we know that an idol *is* nothing in the world, and that *there is* none other God but one. [5] For though there be that are called gods, whether in heaven or in earth, (as there be gods many, and lords many,) [6] But to us *there is but* one God, the Father, of whom *are* all things, and we in him; and one Lord Jesus Christ, by whom *are* all things, and we by him. 1Cor 8:4-6 KJV

Among both pagans and Jews of the first century, sacrifices in temples were part of the support of priests. If, for instance, a young bull was offered, part would be burned on the altar, part would be eaten by the worshipper at a sacrificial meal in the temple, and the rest might go to the family of the priest, or might be sold for money to support the priest at a meat market (called a "shambles," in the KJV 1Cor 10:25). Indeed, almost all of the meat available for sale in most pagan cities had first been offered to some so called "god."

> [10] For if anyone sees you who have knowledge eating in an idol's temple, will not the conscience of him who is weak be emboldened to eat those things offered to idols? [11] And because of your knowledge shall the weak brother perish, for whom Christ died?
> 1Cor 8:10-11 NKJV

There is also the reality that the sacrifices of pagans are offered to demons. The full context of 1 Corinthians 10 is perhaps appropriate. First is that we should not participate in worship to images.

> [20] Rather, that the things which the Gentiles sacrifice they sacrifice to demons and not to God, and I do not want you to have fellowship with demons. [21] You cannot drink the cup of the Lord and the cup of demons; you cannot partake of the Lord's table and of the table of demons. [22] Or do we provoke the Lord to jealousy? Are we stronger than He? 1Cor 10:20-22 NKJV

The second is that although the meat is just meat, we should not behave in a way that will be a snare to others. We should not behave in a way that will cause others to think that worshipping images is of no concern.

> [23] All things are lawful for me, but not all things are helpful; all things are lawful for me, but not all things edify. [24] Let no one seek his own, but each one the other's *well-being*.

> [25] Eat whatever is sold in the meat market, asking no questions for conscience' sake; [26] for *"the earth is the LORD'S, and all its fullness."*
> 1Cor 10:23-26 NKJV

So how should we handle this, if a pagan invites us to a meal?

[27] If any of those who do not believe invites you *to dinner*, and you desire to go, eat whatever is set before you, asking no question for conscience' sake. [28] But if anyone says to you, "This was offered to idols," do not eat it for the sake of the one who told you, and for conscience' sake; for *"the earth is the LORD'S, and all its fullness."* [29] "Conscience," I say, not your own, but that of the other. For why is my liberty judged by another *man's* conscience? [30] But if I partake with thanks, why am I evil spoken of for *the food* over which I give thanks? 1Cor 10:27-30 NKJV

It seems this Jezebel is both leading Christians to commit fornication ("immorality" in some translations), and also to treat the worship of other "gods" as not really being evil. All of these are of course explosive issues in a society which is actually worshipping demons, and in which almost all of the meat God has given men to eat, has at some point been in a pagan temple ritual.

God has given this Jezebel time to repent, but she does not seem to want to repent. God gives men, even very wicked men, time to repent, Rev 2:21; and so should we. Next we see that often God sends suffering in our age to cause people to repent. God is going to send sickness on this Jezebel and those who commit adultery with her, *unless* they repent, Rev 2:22.

Discipline. We need to count all hardship as discipline from God according to Heb 12:7. God also sends death in our age to cause people to repent.

"I will kill her children with death, and all the churches shall know that I am He who searches the minds and hearts. And I will give to each one of you according to your works." Rev 2:23 KJV

So people will know that the Lord is God. Our God *still* acts in history.

But to the rest of those at Thyatira, who do not hold the deep secrets of Satan, God is not going to place any other load on them, Rev 2:24. The "so-called deep secrets" of Satan NIV! That is what the Satanic occult is all about, and it is quite often not limited to worshipping demons and fornication. It is a very real, but subterranean, power in our world. Most of the church at this place has had the good sense to stand aside from this nonsense, but they never should have tolerated it in the church. Now they just need to hold on to what they have in Jesus Christ, Rev 2:25.

Lastly, once again Jesus relates all of this to the end things of this universe. Hold on he says, and Jesus will give Christians authority over the nations, Rev 2:26-27. This seems to be a reference to Psalm 2:8-9.

[8] 'Ask of Me, and I will give You
     The nations for Your inheritance,
     And the ends of the earth for Your possession.
[9]   You shall break them with a rod of iron;
     You shall dash them to pieces like a potter's vessel.'" NKJV

The writer of the book of Hebrews applies Psalm 2 to Jesus (Heb 1:5b), and surely it does apply to Him. However there is something else. Christians become part of Christ. They become His body.

> ²² And hath put all *things* under his feet, and gave him *to be* the head over all *things* to the church, ²³ Which is his body, the fulness of him that filleth all in all. Eph 1:22-23 KJV

This is in fact the basis of our salvation.

> I am crucified with Christ: nevertheless I live; yet not I, but Christ liveth in me: and the life which I now live in the flesh I live by the faith of the Son of God, who loved me, and gave himself for me.
> Gal 2:20 KJV

So in Revelation 2 Jesus applies Psalm 2 to Christians, and this of course is something spoken by the prophets,

> But the saints of the most High shall take the kingdom, and possess the kingdom for ever, even for ever and ever. Dan 7:18 KJV

Judgment will begin at the house of God. This is part of what Jesus told us in the gospels.

> ²⁸ And Jesus said unto them, Verily I say unto you, That ye which have followed me, in the regeneration when the Son of man shall sit in the throne of his glory, ye also shall sit upon twelve thrones, judging the twelve tribes of Israel. ²⁹ And every one that hath forsaken houses, or brethren, or sisters, or father, or mother, or wife, or children, or lands, for my name's sake, shall receive an hundredfold, and shall inherit everlasting life. ³⁰ But many *that are* first shall be last; and the last *shall be* first. Mtt 19:28-30 KJV

Then,

> ² Do ye not know that the saints shall judge the world? and if the world shall be judged by you, are ye unworthy to judge the smallest matters? ³ Know ye not that we shall judge angels? how much more things that pertain to this life? 1Cor 6:2-3 KJV

Of the wicked the psalmist writes,

> As sheep they are appointed for Sheol;
> Death shall be their shepherd;
> And the upright shall rule over them in the morning,
> And their form shall be for Sheol to consume
> So that they have no habitation. Psa 49:14 NASB

To achieve rich and permanent rewards we must serve the Lord with patience and perseverance. We must live for the Lord and not for ourselves.

Jesus has received all authority, Mtt 19:18. At the right time He will commission us, He will give us the morning star! Rev 2:28. He who has an ear, let him hear what the Spirit says to the churches, Rev 2:29. God says He takes no pleasure in the death of the wicked, Ezek 33:11

To the church at Sardis, Rev 3:1-6

From Him who has the seven Spirits of God, Rev 3:1a.

The Danger of Complacency

Sardis was a city that had been great. It had been in the past a powerful city, a city that could withstand almost any attack. It was built on a high plateau, with very steep sides that were 1500 feet high. It was almost impossible to assault and capture. It was also a very rich city. The most famous of the kings of Sardis was Croesus. He was so rich that the old saying "Rich as Croesus," came from him. The great Greek lawgiver Solon visited him, and saw all the wealth, and dazzling magnificence of the place but also saw the false self-confidence and the moral weakness of both the king and the people. King Croesus had it all and needed no more, and so it was here that Solon said, "Call no man happy until he is dead." (William Barclay, *The Revelation of John, Vol 1*, Westminster Press, 1960, p143).

Thus twice in the next few hundred years, in a totally unexpected occurrence during a war, Sardis was captured and plundered by an enemy. On both occasions a handful of enemy soldiers secretly climbed the mountain and walls at night, and found the walls completely unmanned, so confident were they in their position and security. Pride and excessive self-confidence kills. Sardis was no longer a leading city.

Jesus says to the church in this city, a church in which many had probably heard the preaching of the apostles within the previous 40 years, and many of whom had probably also heard the Apostle John at Ephesus,

> 'I know your works, that you have a name that you are alive, but you are dead.' Rev 3:1b NKJV

Sometimes people go to sleep spiritually. There are people who have been alive spiritually, but who later drift away. Some people are like King Solomon, who in his old age had the pleasures and luxuries of life get to him, 1Kgs 11:4-6. We see this lapse into luxury again in 1 Kgs 15:3 of King Abijam of Judah. Or like Amaziah of Judah.

> He did right in the eyes of the LORD, yet not with a whole heart.
> 2Chron 25:2 NASB

It can happen when you do not think it is possible. Samson didn't realize that the Lord had left him, when they sheared his head in Judg 16:20. Gray hairs can appear spiritually.

> 8 "Ephraim has mixed himself among the peoples;
>   Ephraim is a cake unturned.
> 9   Aliens have devoured his strength,
>   But he does not know *it*;
>   Yes, gray hairs are here and there on him,
>   Yet he does not know *it*.
> 10   And the pride of Israel testifies to his face,
>   But they do not return to the LORD their God,
>   Nor seek Him for all this. Hosea 7:8-10 NKJV

For just as the body without the spirit is dead, so also faith without works is dead, Jas 2:26. Indeed, all of us were dead at one time, in our trespasses and sins, Eph 2:1. Then in times of stress we can again fall into sin and die a death which can last forever. Women, for instance, generally have more self-control in sexual matters. Even so, it is very easy after the loss of a husband, for a widow to desire the pleasures of fornication.

> 5 Now she who is a widow indeed and who has been left alone, has fixed her hope on God and continues in entreaties and prayers night and day. 6 But she who gives herself to wanton pleasure is dead even while she lives. 1 Tim 5:5-6 NASB

This is not picking on widows. The same is true of any of us who fall into fornication, 1Cor 6:9-10. Again, at Sardis is a church within arms reach of the apostles which has drifted away from the faith, *all while maintaining the outward appearances of fidelity.* Evidently most in Asia still think of this church as faithful to the Lord our God. It is not that it requires some sort of super-human fidelity. It is that it requires attention to what we are doing or not doing, and it requires keeping our focus on the Word of God. I think sometimes of the requirements to survive extreme cold. They say that freezing to death is an "easy" way to die. You just go to sleep and never again wake up in this world. What then is the solution for spiritual sleep? Sometimes you have to struggle against just drifting away to sleep ... and to eternal death.

Coming Like a Thief

> Be watchful, and strengthen the things which remain, that are ready to die: for I have not found thy works perfect before God. Rev 3:2 KJV

So those at Sardis need to wake up before they are beyond recovery. They need to remember what was preached to them, and they need to obey those things and repent. We need to avoid waiting until punishment comes to begin repenting. We need to not wait until the message comes to us in a drunken party, as it did to King Belshazzar.

> "'TEKEL' — you have been weighed on the scales and found deficient. Dan 5:27 NASB

Do not wait for punishment to come, before you think about turning.

> But the end of all things is at hand: be ye therefore sober, and watch unto prayer. 1 Pe 4:7 KJV

That is not something which is impossible, but it does require focus. Satan is trying to destroy you. Repent! Change your mind about following your old ways. That is what repentance really is, changing your mind about how you will live. Finally, as John the Baptist says, "Therefore bear fruits worthy of repentance," Mtt 3:8 NKJV.

If you do not keep watch?

> [42] "Watch therefore, for you do not know what hour your Lord is coming. ...
> [48] "But if that evil servant says in his heart, "My master is delaying his coming,' [49] and begins to beat *his* fellow servants, and to eat and drink with the drunkards, [50] the master of that servant will come on a day when he is not looking for *him* and at an hour that he is not aware of, [51] and will cut him in two and appoint *him* his portion with the hypocrites. There shall be weeping and gnashing of teeth."
> Mtt 24:42, 48-51 NKJV

Here then is a key principle: our Lord Jesus will come unexpectedly, either in history, or at the end of history, *for those in sin*. Sin blinds us. Makes us unable to see and to judge and to understand what may be swiftly coming upon us. Nor should we assume that all judgment starts at the end of time. There is also judgment in time. So Jesus says to the assembly at Sardis,

> ... Therefore **if** you do not wake up, I will come like a thief, and you will not know at what hour I will come **to you**. Rev 3:3 NASB

IF you do not wake up. It is the same throughout Scripture. If we are spiritually awake, we will see what is coming. Noah knew and saw what was coming. Lot and his daughters knew what was coming. We may not know the exact day or hour the Master will arrive, but if we are awake, we will know what is coming. Thus Paul says in 1 Thessalonians 5.

> [1] But concerning the times and the seasons, brethren, you have no need that I should write to you. [2] For you yourselves know perfectly that the day of the Lord so comes as a thief in the night. [3] For when they say, "Peace and safety!" then sudden destruction comes upon them, as labor pains upon a pregnant woman. And they shall not escape. [4] **But**

you, brethren, are not in darkness, so that this Day should overtake you as a thief; 1Thes 5:1-4 NKJV (*bold emphasis added*)

This is why, among other things, the book of Revelation was written. So we will know what is coming down the highway. Did you not believe it? For that you will have great sorrow later. Regret for not being awake and alert. Still there are always some who pay attention. Isaiah said it well.

> Except the LORD of hosts had left unto us a very small remnant, we should have been as Sodom, and we should have been like unto Gomorrah. Isa 1:9 KJV

In the midst of a drifting church, there are some who are right with the Lord.

> 'But you have a few people in Sardis who have not soiled their garments; and they will walk with Me in white, for they are worthy.'
> Rev 3:4 NASB

It is like having the sense to keep your clothes clean when you are about to meet the president or the King of Glory. Even in the midst of sin and great unfaithfulness, God does reserve some people for Himself, Rom 11:4-6. They have not gotten dirty.

> [17] And they shall be mine, saith the LORD of hosts, in that day when I make up my jewels; and I will spare them, as a man spareth his own son that serveth him. [18] Then shall ye return, and discern between the righteous and the wicked, between him that serveth God and him that serveth him not. Mal 3:17-18 KJV

Sardis is the church that has fallen asleep, that has confidence in what they had done in the past. Sardis is the "has been" church.

Again Jesus comes to things of the end. If we stay awake, if we pay attention to our business, Jesus will *never* blot us out of the book of life. There is a book of life. The Lord said of ancient Israel when they rebelled against Him, that He was ready to destroy them. Moses then pled in their behalf, and offered himself in their place for punishment.

> [32] Yet now, if thou wilt forgive their sin—; and if not, blot me, I pray thee, out of thy book which thou hast written [33] And the LORD said unto Moses, Whosoever hath sinned against me, him will I blot out of my book. Ex 32:32-33 KJV

Of those who betray the Christ it says in Psalm 69.

> [27] Add iniquity unto their iniquity: and let them not come into thy righteousness. [28] Let them be blotted out of the book of the living, and not be written with the righteous. Psa 69:27-28 KJV

Everything is recorded in the Lord's books.

[15] My frame was not hidden from You,
>When I was made in secret,
>*And* skillfully wrought in the lowest parts of the earth.
[16] Your eyes saw my substance, being yet unformed.
>And in Your book they all were written,
>The days fashioned for me,
>When *as yet there were* none of them. Psa 139:15-16 NKJV

Even our tears are recorded there, Psa 56:8. This is clearly describing "mega-data" which will even put our giant international cartels and intelligence agencies to shame. There were some people at Philippi who were in the book of life, Phil 4:3.

>And whosoever was not found written in the book of life was cast into the lake of fire. Rev 20:15 KJV

If we are faithful, He will confess our name before His angels in heaven. Imagine Jesus pointing you out, and saying, This one is My faithful servant! If we have any ears we should listen to what the Lord says. God is seeking you and me, but we have to listen. He will give you white clothes to wear. What do we need **to coverup** the sinful selves we have been? Jesus is the answer.

>[26] For ye are all the children of God by faith in Christ Jesus. [27] For as many of you as have been baptized into Christ **have put on Christ**.
>Gal 3:26-27 (*bold emphasis added*) KJV

Do we have any ears? We should listen to what our Lord is saying to the churches.

To the church at Philadelphia, Rev 3:7-13

To the angel of the church in Philadelphia write, Rev 3:7. Philadelphia was the youngest of the seven cities of Asia to which Jesus was writing.

It is to the east and inland of Sardis and Smyrna. It was situated on an important trade route, and an important Roman post-road passed through there. This city pushed Greek culture and arts, and was successful enough that even before New Testament times the Lydian language was no longer spoken there. Its name meant: the city of brotherly love, and it was named by a King Attalus, who really loved his brother Eumenes. These Pergamen kings were always loyal to Rome. They supported Rome in the battle of Magnesia against Antiochus III and in the Roman struggle to dominate Asia Minor.

As it is with parts of western Turkey today, the area had been subject to regular and sometimes strong earthquakes, and several times it received funds from Rome for rebuilding. It had many temples and religious festivals. Later becoming a fully Christian city, it was still important, although trade routes in the area changed from being directed to Rome, to being directed to Constantinople. It was one of the last Christian cities to fall to the Turks, in the late 1300's. It is now called the town of Alasehir in western Turkey.

This is of course a very special message to Philadelphia, from Jesus, the One who is holy and holds the keys of the house of David, Rev 3:7. There was to be one from the house of David who was to rule *everything*. He was to come as a child, and there was to be "Of the increase of *his* government and peace *there shall be* no end, upon the throne of David, ..." Isa 9:7 KJV. He was to be given the very ends of the earth as His possession, Psa 2:8. All of the kings of the earth are advised to worship this Son of God (Psa 2:7) with fear and trembling, lest they be destroyed in a moment of anger, Psa 2:11-12. It also speaks of these things in Isaiah 22. He is the One who will control David's "house," his dynasty, his endless possessions.

> [22] And the key of the house of David will I lay upon his shoulder; so he shall open, and none shall shut; and he shall shut, and none shall open. [23] And I will fasten him *as* a nail in a sure place; and he shall be for a glorious throne to his father's house. Isa 22:22-23 KJV

Jesus was the One to have this throne of his father David, Lk 1:32. These are the keys to heaven and to eternal power itself. He can set you free and no one can bind you, or He can shut the door in your face, and there is no hope outside of His house. Jesus is *the* important One.

> Neither is there salvation in any other: for there is none other name under heaven given among men, whereby we must be saved.
> Acts 4:12 KJV

Jesus is the one who can help you and no one can negate it.

> [38] For I am persuaded, that neither death, nor life, nor angels, nor principalities, nor powers, nor things present, nor things to come, [39] Nor height, nor depth, nor any other creature, shall be able to separate us from the love of God, which is in Christ Jesus our Lord.
> Rom 8:38-39 KJV

There have been times and places where the gospel could be and was influential near the bastions of power. As Isaiah prophesied, one day there would be kings and queens who would serve the Lord with a full heart. Near Nero, there were those of Caesars household who were Christians (Phil 4:22). They had at least the prospect of influencing those in power. But the assembly in Philadelphia? It really had no influence, and very little power. They were, in worldly terms, totally insignificant. The media of their day would disdain to even mention them, but they kept Jesus' word, and never denied His name.

A Poor but Faithful Church

It was not a worldly strong church or a worldly strong people who were at Philadelphia. Strength, worldly strength, manly strength ... was not the key here, but God could supply whatever they needed. Our Lord talked to Paul along these lines.

> [9] And He has said to me, "My grace is sufficient for you, for power is perfected in weakness." Most gladly, therefore, I will rather boast about my weaknesses, so that the power of Christ may dwell in me. [10] Therefore I am well content with weaknesses, with insults, with distresses, with persecutions, with difficulties, for Christ's sake; for when I am weak, then I am strong. 2Cor 12:9-10 NASB

That does not mean we should not be faithful or strong in our beliefs.

> Be on the alert, stand firm in the faith, act like men, be strong.
> 1Cor 16:13 NASB

However, human power is really not the key. It is not our "will power" which will save us. Sometimes men are frustrated because God has not given *men*, good men, even at times righteous men, the victory. In fact, at times it seems to be that God will *not* give "the right side" the victory, when it might seem that their victory is "necessary" to justice and righteousness ruling. God does not depend on us, nor does He "need" us. **"Nor is He served by human hands, as though He needed anything,"** Act 17:25 NASB. **We** think **we** *have to* win, but God wants to make it clear that it is not by our power when we win.

> Then he answered and spake unto me, saying, This *is* the word of the LORD unto Zerubbabel, saying, **Not by might, nor by power, but by my spirit,** saith the LORD of hosts. Zech 4:6 KJV (*bold emphasis added*)

Not having worldly power is not a liability to this insignificant church. The key is holding on to Jesus regardless of our power. Do not be afraid, "thou worm Jacob," God said to the church in Isaiah's day.

> [14] fear not, thou worm Jacob, *and* ye men of Israel; I will help thee, saith the LORD, and thy redeemer, the Holy One of Israel. [15] Behold, I will make thee a new sharp threshing instrument having teeth: thou shalt thresh the mountains, and beat *them* small, and shalt make the hills as chaff. ... [20] That they may see, and know, and consider, and understand together, that the hand of the LORD hath done this, and the Holy One of Israel hath created it. Isa 41:14-15, 20 KJV

Fake Jews of the Synagogue of Satan

There are also fake Jews of the synagogue of Satan at Philadelphia, Rev 3:9. But what is a 'synagogue'? It is like the word 'church' and could even be used as a synonym. It means an assembly, a group coming together for a meeting. Church means to be 'called out' for a meeting. Synagogue means to 'lead together' for a meeting. They are very similar words. Here again it is a synagogue of Satan. There are two possibilities here:

1. That Judaism itself is of Satan. But how would we react to such possibility? We cannot call the Law of Moses evil or of Satan, as some would. The law is of itself good.

> Wherefore the law *is* holy, and the commandment holy, and just, and good. Rom 7:12 KJV

It gives us the knowledge of when we have done wrong, Rom 7:7. The alternative of course is to not know when we are hurting ourselves, to not understand when we are burning ourselves, to not recognize when we have mutilated our image and disfigured our appearance. That would be a curse. It would be like a person without feeling in their hands to know when they are being hurt. In a way Jews and gentiles who reject the messiah Jesus Christ are of Satan. That was discussed in the section about the church in Smyrna, and the section about the confrontation between Jesus and the leaders of the Pharisees in Jn 8:42-44. So, in one sense *all of us* once were of Satan.

> [1] And you *He made alive*, who were dead in trespasses and sins, [2] in which you once walked according to the course of this world, according to the prince of the power of the air, the spirit who now works in the sons of disobedience, Eph 2:1-2 NKJV

Ah, that spirit which is now working among all men who are disobedient. **All of us were once there!** But if we are talking about the true religion of Moses' Law, it is a law of the acceptance of the great prophet of Deuteronomy 18.

2. A second possibility of the text is that there is *an* assembly (a part and not the whole) of what men call "Jews," that is of Satan, that worships and serves the evil one. I leave it to you to judge. Still, however you take it, this synagogue is described in the most severe terms, and says that they claim to be Jews but are not, and are of the synagogue of Satan. Also the continued existence of a cult of Satan is a historical fact. Lastly, it is clear from the book of Revelation that during the Christian age there will come a time when *all* men will worship the dragon, the Devil or Satan, directly, Rev 13:3-4, etc. **Again, I think the Lord is speaking of some who use Judaism as a facade, but who really worship Satan!**

The Victory of the Faithful

At this point then look at what our text says. The LORD God will also make those of synagogue of Satan to come and bow at their feet, and will make them know that God has loved them, Rev 3:9. I will make them fall at your feet, He says. That is the same thing said in many prophecies. Jesus was from the first to rule in the middle of His enemies

> [1] The LORD said unto my Lord, Sit thou at my right hand, until I make thine enemies thy footstool. [2] The LORD shall send the rod of thy strength out of Zion: rule thou in the midst of thine enemies. Psa110:1-2 KJV

You remember of course,

> For the time *is come* that judgment must begin at the house of God: and *if* it first *begin* at us, what shall the end *be* of them that obey not the gospel of God? 1Pe 4:17 KJV

It has already been discussed, Christians will at the last judge both angels and men under Jesus Christ, 1Cor 6:2-3. The people of the Egypt of this world will bow before God's children as they did before Moses, Ex 11:8.

> [7] Thus says the LORD, the Redeemer of Israel *and* its Holy One,
>> To the despised One,
>> To the One abhorred by the nation,
>> To the Servant of rulers,
>> "Kings will see and arise,
>> Princes will also bow down,
>> Because of the LORD who is faithful, the Holy One of Israel
>> who has chosen You." ...
>
> [23] "Kings will be your guardians,
>> And their princesses your nurses.
>> They will bow down to you with their faces to the earth
>> And lick the dust of your feet;
>> And *you* will know that I am the LORD;
>> Those who hopefully wait for Me will not be put to shame."
> Isa 49:7, 23 NASB

All who despise you will come bowing to you.

> [14] The sons also of them that afflicted thee shall come bending unto thee; and all they that despised thee shall bow themselves down at the soles of thy feet; and they shall call thee, The city of the LORD, The Zion of the Holy One of Israel.
> [15] Whereas thou hast been forsaken and hated, so that no man went through *thee*, I will make thee an eternal excellency, a joy of many generations. [16] Thou shalt also suck the milk of the Gentiles, and shalt suck the breast of kings: and thou shalt know that I the LORD *am* thy

Saviour and thy Redeemer, the mighty One of Jacob. Isa 60:14-16 KJV

How much more then these vile Satanists!

These passages of course bridge from the gospel age to the age to come in heaven. Those who are faithful will be spared from the great test!

> Because thou hast kept the word of my patience, I also will keep thee from the hour of temptation, which shall come upon all the world, to try them that dwell upon the earth. Rev 3:10 KJV

There are a couple of principles here. The first is that we all must be tested.

> 4   The LORD *is* in His holy temple,
> The LORD'S throne *is* in heaven;
> His eyes behold,
> His eyelids test the sons of men.
> 5   The LORD tests the righteous,
> But the wicked and the one who loves violence His soul hates.

Psa 11:4-5 NKJV

Or again,

> The refining pot is for silver and the furnace for gold,
> But the LORD tests hearts. Prov 17:3 NASB

The second principle here is that we *can* avoid many tests. Josiah was spared from a great test. The Lord said to him,

> 19 "because your heart was tender, and you humbled yourself before the LORD when you heard what I spoke against this place and against its inhabitants, that they would become a desolation and a curse, and you tore your clothes and wept before Me, I also have heard *you*," says the LORD. 20 Surely, therefore, I will gather you to your fathers, and you shall be gathered to your grave in peace; and your eyes shall not see all the calamity which I will bring on this place." ' " So they brought back word to the king. 2Kgs 22:19-20 NKJV

Wow! Here humility and a repentant attitude is the key. Jesus instructs us to pray to be spared.

> Watch ye therefore, and pray always, that ye **may be accounted worthy to escape all these things** that shall come to pass, and to stand before the Son of man. Lk 21:36 KJV (*bold emphasis added*)

It is something to be prayed about. Sometimes, if you are worthy, you can be spared from a great test. However, goodness alone does not mean that you will be spared. Job was very good, but was not spared from testing. Jesus was perfect but was not spared from testing, Mk 1:12. Even so, if you are really faithful, if you patiently endure despite being small in strength, you can be spared a lot of big testing. Much further testing *may not* be necessary! You will already have proven to be true. You will be ready to be received by the Lord. So it is good to pray, "And do not lead us into temptation, but deliver us from evil" Mtt 6:13. In Revelation 3 Jesus pointedly says that there is a special testing which is about to come on the entire world, to test everyone, but the church at Philadelphia, because of their faithfulness, will be spared. Stunning! Is Jesus talking about a world-wide mandate for emperor worship? That would seem to me to fit. Also He says I am coming soon. Hold on to what you have, Jesus says in Rev 3:11, so that no one steals your crown.

"Quickly." "The time is at hand," Rev 1:3. These are clearly relative statements. Thus, as we have already pointed out, on one hand, Revelation seems to speak of these things starting to happen "soon" in human terms. Additionally these things go on even to the end of time, as Revelation clearly points out. Then at the end, even in our human terms, it will have seemed to all have happened "soon." However there are multiple indications of some period of time before these things are over.

> "But while the bridegroom was **delayed**, they all slumbered and slept." Mtt 25:5 NKJV (*bold emphasis added*)

> "But if that evil slave says in his heart, 'My master is **not coming for a long time**,'" Mtt 24:48 NASB (*bold emphasis added*)

Seemingly speaking of a distant "last days," Peter speaks of some mocking the fact that Jesus *seems* to be delayed.

> [3] Know this first of all, that in the last days mockers will come with *their* mocking, following after their own lusts, [4] and saying, "Where is the promise of His coming? For *ever* since the fathers fell asleep, all continues just as it was from the beginning of creation."
> 2Pe 3:3-4 NASB

Peter goes on to call attention to fact that time is not the same with transient men and an Eternal Father.

> But, beloved, be not ignorant of this one thing, that one day is with the Lord as a thousand years, and a thousand years as one day. 2Pe 3:8 KJV

This would seem to be a reference to Psa 90:4. Then Peter goes on to say that God is not slow as some count slowness, but He is just being patient with us, and giving us time to repent, 2Pe 3:9. Also there are indications of nearness, at least in some sense, and these are predominant.

> Do not complain, brethren, against one another, so that you yourselves may not be judged; behold, **the Judge is standing right at the door**. Jas 5:9 NASB (*bold emphasis added*)

> Let your gentle *spirit* be evident to all men. **The Lord is near**. Phil 4:5 NASB (*bold emphasis added*)

We can win, we can overcome with help from the Lord.

No temptation has overtaken you except such as is common to man; but God *is* faithful, who will not allow you to be tempted beyond what you are able, but with the temptation will also make the way of escape, that you may be able to bear *it*. 1Cor 10:13 NKJV

Watch and pray, that ye enter not into temptation: the spirit indeed is willing, but the flesh is weak. Mtt 26:41 KJV

If we overcome, God will make us a pillar of His temple made without hands, a temple made of living stones, a temple made up of men.

[4] To whom coming, *as unto* a living stone, disallowed indeed of men, but chosen of God, *and* precious, [5] Ye also, as lively stones, are built up a spiritual house, an holy priesthood, to offer up spiritual sacrifices, acceptable to God by Jesus Christ. 1Pe 2:4-5 KJV

Then, once again, Jesus comes to end things. He says He will write His name on you, and you will never be separated from His presence, Rev 3:12. You will be in the paradise of God forever. You will be in the presence of good and awesome power forever, and it will all be on your side! You will live in the perfect place, the heavenly, the "new Jerusalem," forever.

The church in Philadelphia is one of only two churches in rich and prosperous first century Asia Minor whom the Lord did not in any way rebuke! It can be done, but often we focus on transient things which will soon pass away.

If you have ears listen to what the Spirit says to the churches. It is Jesus who is speaking in this letter, and it is the Spirit who is speaking to the churches. Are you listening? Rev 3:13.

To the church at Laodicea, Rev 3:14-22

To the angel of the church in Laodicea write, Rev 3:14. And who is writing this? It is the ultimate "Amen, the faithful and true Witness, the Beginning of the creation of God."

A Prosperous, Confident, and Unfaithful Church

Laodicea was an important city of what was called Phrygia. It was founded by Antiochus II. It was on the great Roman road from Ephesus to the far east. It was located in the Lycrus river valley, about 12 miles North-West of the small town of Colossae, and far more important as a city center than Colossae. Sir William Ramsay in *The Letters to the Seven Churches of Asia, and Their Place in the Plan of the Apocalype*, 1904, remarks that "to the Greeks "Phrygian" often stood in place of "Laodicean.""

Paul mentioned Laodicea when he wrote to the Colossians in Col 4:16. The Laodiceans probably received the gospel at the same time as the other cities of Asia, at approximately the same time as the Colossians, as depicted following Paul's preaching in the synagogue in Ephesus in Act 19:8-10.

Laodicea was a great road hub and a great financial and commercial center. It was very very rich and prosperous. It was also a clothing center, and a medical center. It was famous for its rich and luxurious woolen garments, especially of black. Also Laodicea's medical schools were famous for their eye salve, and it medicinal wines and baths. Laodicea had a very mixed population and a large segment of Jews. At one point the Roman governors of this area were alarmed at the amount of money that was going from this area to pay the temple tax in Jerusalem, so they actually instituted currency controls to keep from losing so much money to Jerusalem.

If we want to understand what a lot of the Greek speaking world was like at this time, we might compare it to what can be seen in Antioch of Syria, as it was in the fourth century AD. There is a time difference here from the first century, but not as many cultural differences. It was in many ways much like America today. The city of Antioch had good schools and several outstanding churches. The greatest of them was begun by the Emperor Constantine and finished by Constantius. The famous Greek preacher Chrysostom preached there. The people of Antioch were Syrians, Greeks, Jews, and Romans, but the Asiatic element prevailed, including a large population of Jews. In the late 300's AD, the whole population amounted, as Chrysostom states, to about 200,000 of whom one half were nominally Christians. The people of Antioch were into luxury, greed, pleasure, the circus and the theater. What they called the circus, we would call chariot races and gladiatorial combat.

Chrysostom said, "So great is the depravity of the times, that if a stranger were to compare the precepts of the gospel with the actual practice of society, he would infer that men were not the disciples, but the enemies of Christ."

Gibbon describes the morals of what we would call "Christian" Antioch:

> "The warmth of the climate disposed the natives to the most intemperate enjoyment of tranquility and opulence, and the lively licentiousness of the Greeks was blended with the hereditary softness of the Syrians. Fashion was the only law, pleasure the only pursuit, and the splendor of dress and furniture was the only distinction of the citizens of Antioch. The arts of luxury were honored, the serious and manly virtues were the subject of ridicule, and the contempt for female modesty and reverent age announced the universal corruption of the capital of the East. The love of spectacles was the taste, or rather passion of the Syrians; the most skillful artists were procured from the adjacent cities. A considerable share of the revenue was devoted to the public

amusements, and the magnificence of the games of the theater and circus was considered as the happiness and as the glory of Antioch."
Decline and Fall of the Roman Empire, Vol 2, Chapter 24, Part 1

We might also add that homosexuality was rampant, and there was a lot of male effeminacy, which was perhaps implied in Gibbon's quote.

In this sort of situation, what was church like? The church of Antioch was strained by church fights for 85 years (330-415), in which there were three main parties in the disputes.

In fact Laodicea's attitude toward religion is typical of many who are well to do. Like many Americans. I know your deeds, Jesus says, Rev 3:15. The Laodiceans are not cold toward religion. They are just not so hot! They do not want to reject the true and living God. They do not want to formally neglect the work of the Lord. They just have bigger fish to fry. More important things to tend to ... than just the Lord God. Don't worry, we haven't forgotten the Lord. But I have a meeting tonight. I have a ball game. You wouldn't believe what my job takes out of me.

Neither Hot Nor Cold

You are neither cold or hot! Rev 3:15a. Some people drink iced coffee, and many people drink hot coffee. But have you ever had a cup you had put cream and sugar in ... and you forgot it ... and went to take big sip and found it lukewarm? Or a soft drink that is now warm and flat?

I wish you were either cold or hot! Rev 3:15b. I wish you would either get in or get out. I wish you would really be dedicated, or get completely out of my sight.

So this is what I will do! Jesus says in Rev 3:16, I will spit you out. Whew! Glad to get rid of that! And so God does to many of us. Spits us out!

The Laodiceans say, "I am rich .." Rev 3:17a. I have become wealthy and I don't really need a thing. I have a job. I work hard. I have a house and a car. I've got groceries on the table. I'm not really in need. But you are not realizing, Rev 3:17b. You don't realize that you are wretched. The Greek word is *talaipōros* ταλαίπωρος, and it means to be miserable, distressed. It means to be in a horrible, pathetic situation. To be sad and weak and in want. And the Laodiceans are not only wretched, but they are also miserable. The Greek word is *eleeinos* ἐλεεινός, and it means someone who really deserves to be pitied, and who really needs someone to have mercy on them, *not* someone who is independent and self-sufficient and needs no one. Additionally these Laodiceans are poor—and the Greek word for poor here, *ptoōhos* πτωχός, does not just mean someone who doesn't have much money. It meant a beggar. Someone crouching and bowing before others in order to get a handout. And the Laodiceans are also blind—a beggar who cannot even see, that doesn't even know what is happening. Lastly they are naked. They have nothing to properly protect and cover their needs.

Sometimes we don't realize we are naked, rumpled, unbuttoned, unzipped, our slip is showing. Our ancestors Adam and Eve didn't know!

> [7] And the eyes of them both were opened, and they knew that they *were* naked; and they sewed fig leaves together, and made themselves aprons. ... [9] And the LORD God called unto Adam, and said unto him, Where *art* thou? [10] And he said, I heard thy voice in the garden, and I was afraid, because I *was* naked; and I hid myself. [11]   And he said, Who told thee that thou *wast* naked? Hast thou eaten of the tree, whereof I commanded thee that thou shouldest not eat?
>
> Gen 3:7, 9-11 KJV

Do you know when you are vulnerable? Already the Corinthians thought they were rich and prosperous. And they were—compared to the poor apostles, 1Cor 4:8-10. Do you really know where you are! Do you really know what your situation is? Jesus says woe to you who are comfortable.

> [24] "But woe to you who are rich, for you are receiving your comfort in full. [25] Woe to you who are well-fed now, for you shall be hungry. Woe *to you* who laugh now, for you shall mourn and weep. [26] Woe *to you* when all men speak well of you, for their fathers used to treat the false prophets in the same way." Lk 6:24-26 NASB

Get yourself some gold from the Lord, so that you can really be rich, and some clean clothes to cover up your nakedness, and eye salve from me, and use it on your eyes, Jesus says, Rev 3:18. The real source of wealth is Jesus, and He is the only true source of any riches either here or in the beyond. He came to help the spiritually sick and needy.

> There is one who pretends to be rich, but has nothing;
> > *Another* pretends to be poor, but has great wealth.
>
> Prov 13:7 NASB

Those I love I rebuke and discipline, Jesus says in Rev 3:19. We do need discipline.

> It is for discipline that you endure; God deals with you as with sons; for what son is there whom *his* father does not discipline?
>
> Heb 12:7 NASB

And if we do not have discipline from the Lord? The KJV is the translation to really get a feel for this passage.

> But if ye be without chastisement, whereof all are partakers, **then are ye bastards,** and not sons. Heb 12:8 KJV (*bold emphasis added*)

We are being disciplined for a reason!

Laodicea

But when we are judged, we are chastened of the Lord, that we should not be condemned with the world. 1Cor 11:32 KJV

In contrast to Philadelphia and Smyrna, about whom Jesus has nothing *bad* to say, here is a first century church about whom Jesus does not have anything *good* to say. Here I am, our Lord says in Rev 3:20. I'm knocking and trying to get you to open. Are you hearing? Are you listening? If you will open up I will come in and I will eat with you, and you will eat with Me.

Again Jesus speaks of last things. To him that overcomes, he will sit down with Jesus on His throne of all creation, just as Jesus overcame and sat down with His Father on His throne, Rev 3:21-22. We have to overcome. We cannot just give in to inaction and sin. To Cain there was fitting counsel.

> 6 So the LORD said to Cain, "Why are you angry? And why has your countenance fallen? 7 If you do well, will you not be accepted? And if you do not do well, sin lies at the door. And its desire *is* for you, but you should rule over it." Gen 4:6-7 NKJV

You cannot just lay down. You cannot just give up. You cannot just show up every once in a while, or on the other hand just depend on merely showing up.

You will sit on a throne as a ruler one day. You will rule with the saints one day, 1Cor 6:2-3. Beside Jesus we will rule.

> 1 Ho, every one that thirsteth, come ye to the waters, and he that hath

no money; come ye, buy, and eat; yea, come, buy wine and milk without money and without price. [2] Wherefore do ye spend money for *that which is* not bread? and your labour for *that which* satisfieth not? hearken diligently unto me, and eat ye *that which is* good, and let your soul delight itself in fatness. [3] Incline your ear, and come unto me: hear, and your soul shall live; and I will make an everlasting covenant with you, *even* the sure mercies of David Isa 55:1-3 KJV

We need to repent and change and follow. We need to be clothed with Jesus, 'put on' Jesus in baptism, Gal 3:27; and then be zealous, be hot, for His service.

If so be that being clothed we shall not be found naked. 2Cor 5:3 KJV

V. Visions of
of
Heaven,
Revelation
4-7

A Throne in Heaven, Revelation 4

Jesus has sent His messages to the churches. John is seeing a vision, a vision of heaven itself. John is being called up there to see some things. John saw a door which was open in heaven. He also heard a voice like the one he had heard at first. A voice that was like a trumpet, a voice like many waters, so it seems. Also the voice was telling him to come up to heaven, and this one will show him, reveal to him, what was to take place later, Rev 4:1-2. It is a continuation of the promises in Rev 1:1.

John is going to where God dwells. He is going to the special place God, so to speak, "lives," even though He is present in every place. David said it well.

> [7] Whither shall I go from thy spirit? or whither shall I flee from thy presence? [8] If I ascend up into heaven, thou *art* there: if I make my bed in hell, behold, thou *art there.* [9] *If* I take the wings of the morning, *and* dwell in the uttermost parts of the sea; [10] Even there shall thy hand lead me, and thy right hand shall hold me. [11] If I say, Surely the darkness shall cover me; even the night shall be light about me. [12] Yea, the darkness hideth not from thee; but the night shineth as the day: the darkness and the light *are* both alike *to thee.* Psa 139:7-12 KJV

Similarly, when Paul is speaking of God at the Areopagus in Athens, he says about God's presence.

> For in him we live, and move, and have our being; as certain also of your own poets have said, For we are also his offspring. Acts 17:28 KJV

In context Paul does **not** say that God **is** *everything* as in pantheism and popular occult literature. Rather God *made* everything.

> [24] God that made the world and all things therein, seeing that he is Lord of heaven and earth, dwelleth not in temples made with hands; [25] Neither is worshipped with men's hands, as though he needed any thing, seeing **he giveth to all life, and breath, and all things**;
> Acts 17:24-25 KJV (*bold emphasis added*)

Yes, He is *not* everything, but He *made* everything and He is omnipresent, He is *in* everything. But His temple in heaven is where He lives.

> And the temple of God was opened in heaven, and there was seen in his temple the ark of his testament: and there were lightnings, and voices, and thunderings, and an earthquake, and great hail.
> Rev 11:19 KJV

There is a throne there. It is in heaven, Rev 4:2-3. John says he was immediately there and saw "One" who sat on the throne, brilliant and beautiful in appearance, and the throne was surrounded by a rainbow like an emerald. Jasper is a red, opaque crystal. Sardius, a ruby or carnelian, is likewise red. The

Lord is in His Holy Temple; the Lord is on His heavenly throne, Psa 11:4. The Lord is often pictured as looking down from heaven to see what is going on.

> [2] The LORD looked down from heaven upon the children of men, to see if there were any that did understand, *and* seek God. [3] They are all gone aside, they are all together become filthy: *there is* none that doeth good, no, not one. Psa 14:2-3 KJV

Isaiah saw the LORD on His heavenly throne in Isa 6:1-3. Angels, specifically seraphim, stood above Him, each one having six wings, and crying out "Holy, Holy, Holy is the LORD of hosts." Isaiah likewise heard a voice and the casing of the door of the temple trembled at the sound of the voice.

In Revelation 4 the elders of God's people worship Him there, Rev 4:4; and they surround the throne with their twenty-four thrones, and are wearing white clothing and gold crowns. They are pictured here as being humans. Man is a chief part of God's creation. It is man who has been given to rule over all of God creation in the world to come, Heb 2:5-6. Man has been made for a little while, a little lower than the angels, but he has been given a special position of honor, and *everything* has been put under man's control, Heb 2:7. As God said at first,

> And God said, Let us make man in our image, after our likeness: and let them have dominion over the fish of the sea, and over the fowl of the air, and over the cattle, and over all the earth, and over every creeping thing that creepeth upon the earth. Gen 1:26 KJV

Heb 2:8b makes the point that there is nothing in God's creation that was left out from being under man's control. There are several facts to make note of here. The first is that God intended for man to control *everything*, and second that God commissioned him to seek that sort of control.

> And God blessed them, and God said unto them, Be fruitful, and multiply, and replenish the earth, and subdue it: and have dominion over the fish of the sea, and over the fowl of the air, and over every living thing that moveth upon the earth. Gen 1:28 KJV

Next is that men instinctively seek control over all of their environment, yes even including such elusive things as all of the insects of the world, and the fish of the sea, and the weather, and even outer space and the universe as a whole, which man dreams of coming to control. Then there is the last thing to notice

> ... But now we do not yet see all things subjected to him. Heb 2:8 NASB

Ah! What an understatement. Man works. He tries, but still finds more things than he would like to be outside his control, in fact very resistant to his control. Man began with tilling and keeping that perfect garden which was set somewhere in what is today northern Iraq or south-eastern Turkey. Man then ruined much of his situation in refusing the outlines of God's grant of power and control, and the struggle continues today with our jobs of working to master our environment, and our fighting bugs in the kitchen, and our struggles to dominate this or that aspect of our environment, either on an individual scale, or on a national or world-wide scale. So, no, we do not see man as having achieved that power yet. But what do we see?

However we see Jesus coming that man may attain what God has desired man to achieve, Heb 2:9. It is through Jesus the Christ that man realizes his ordained destiny in righteousness and truth. So Jesus likewise was made for a little while, a little lower than the angels, that he might taste death for each of us, and bring us to our rightful place in a world to come that will not be subject to sin and death and decay. Yes, man, for whatever are God's reasons, is at the very core of God's plans for the universe.

This throne of God in Revelation 4 is the very center of power.

> And out of the throne proceeded lightnings and thunderings and voices: and *there were* seven lamps of fire burning before the throne, which are the seven Spirits of God. Rev 4:5 KJV

Around the Lord our God was a sea of glass, and the throne is surrounded by powerful creatures that were full of eyes all around them. Similarly, in all of the visions of God's throne He is surrounded by awesome creatures, and the similarities in these creatures are easily seen. In Revelation 4 the first creature is like a lion, the second like a calf, the third had a face like a man, and the fourth was like an eagle, and they all had six wings each, and were full of eyes. We have already noted that in Isaiah 6 the seraphim each had six wings. In Ezekiel 1 in the "visions of God" which Ezekiel saw, there were "four living beings" which looked like men. These man-like creatures each had four wings and four faces. They had the face of a man in front, the face of a lion on the right, and the face of a bull on the left, and the face of an eagle behind. Additionally there was awesome evidence of great power.

> [13] As for the likeness of the living creatures, their appearance *was* like burning coals of fire, *and* like the appearance of lamps: it went up and down among the living creatures; and the fire was bright, and out of the fire went forth lightning. [14] And the living creatures ran and returned as the appearance of a flash of lightning. Ezek 1:13-14 KJV

In Isaiah 6 the awesome creatures are called "seraphim" and in Ezekiel 10 they are called "cherubim," evidently two different orders of angels. Are the prophets indicating some of both of these types of creatures are near the throne? We also know that angelic creatures can take on more than one form. When the evil angel Satan first appears in the Paradise of God here on earth, it is in the form of a snake, Genesis 3. When the Lord appears to Abraham with two angels in Genesis 3 it says "he lift up his eyes and looked, and, lo, three **men** stood by him," Gen 18:2 KJV. Then Abraham prepares his guests a meal, and they ate of it! There is more to tell in all of these accounts, and both the diffe-rences and the similarities are striking. The question I think naturally comes up: how should we take these "visions" of God and the creatures surrounding God? The first thing is that these are obviously symbolic visions, and it is easily seen that some of the traits seen are overlapping. God is not a material being that is some part of our creation.

> God *is* a Spirit: and they that worship *him* must worship him in spirit and in truth. Jn 4:24 KJV

However, when Jesus rose from the dead, He made a point of His fleshly resurrection.

> Behold my hands and my feet, that it is I myself: handle me, and see; for a spirit hath not flesh and bones, as ye see me have. Lk 24.39 KJV

But in Revelation 4, and Isaiah 1, and Ezekiel 1, and Ezekiel 10, the Lord is portraying to the men of this world, other-worldly beings and settings. With what words or images should the Lord our God and His court be portrayed? They are called creatures. The Greek word literally means "living things," *zōon* ζῶον. They are not called beasts, *thārion* θηρίον, as the man in Revelation 13 is called. These are not wild brute beasts. The KJV is misleading here. They are what are called angels. They are powerful angels, awesome creatures of incre-dible strength and ability. Symbolically they have the intelligence of men, the strength of an ox, the ferociousness of a lion, and the audacity and speed of an eagle. Everyone in heaven is honoring God, and, like the creatures surrounding the throne Isaiah saw, are continually proclaiming the holiness and majesty of God, Rev 4:8-9.

> Who *is* like unto thee, O LORD, among the gods? who *is* like thee, glorious in holiness, fearful *in* praises, doing wonders? Ex 15:11 KJV

> [6] or who in the heaven can be compared unto the LORD? *who* among the sons of the mighty can be likened unto the LORD? [7] God is greatly to be feared in the assembly of the saints, and to be had in reverence of all *them that are* about him. [8] O LORD God of hosts, who *is* a strong LORD like unto thee? or to thy faithfulness round about thee?
> Psa 89:6-8 KJV

God is overwhelming, astounding. Just read about when He appeared on Mount Sinai. There was thunder and lightning.

> [16] And it came to pass on the third day in the morning, that there were thunders and lightnings, and a thick cloud upon the mount, and the voice of the trumpet exceeding loud; so that all the people that *was* in the camp trembled. ... [18] And mount Sinai was altogether on a smoke, because the LORD descended upon it in fire: and the smoke thereof ascended as the smoke of a furnace, and the whole mount quaked

greatly. Ex 19:16, 18 KJV

They trembled with fear, and stood at a distance, and asked Moses to represent them before the Lord, Ex 20:18. The elders saw a vision of God in Ex 24:9-11. This was not anything you and I have ever seen. God is perfect in all His ways

> *He is* the Rock, his work is perfect: for all his ways *are* judgment: a God of truth and without iniquity, just and right is he. Deut 32:4 KJV

And for us who have so many both visible and hidden blemishes, God is a terrifying prospect to meet. He made everything, and knows everything.

> For by him were all things created, that are in heaven, and that are in earth, visible and invisible, whether *they be* thrones, or dominions, or principalities, or powers: all things were created by him, and for him: Col 1:16 KJV

Those who will not honor God will not stay in the place John saw, where God dwells. The devil used to be there, as seen in Job 1:6-7, although he had already turned away from submitting to God. The devil or Satan was a lesser, but also an awesome creature as described in Ezekiel 28. But sin was found in him, Ezek 28:15, 17, and he lost his place among the righteous. As Jesus was going to Jerusalem and to His murder, He saw Satan falling from heaven, Lk 10:18.

Those who are in heaven worship and serve not themselves, rather they serve The Most High God! God *is* the greatest.

> [11] Thine, O LORD, *is* the greatness, and the power, and the glory, and the victory, and the majesty: for all *that is* in the heaven and in the earth *is thine*; thine *is* the kingdom, O LORD, and thou art exalted as head above all. [12] Both riches and honour *come* of thee, and thou reignest over all; and in thine hand *is* power and might; and in thine hand *it is* to make great, and to give strength unto all. [13] Now therefore, our God, we thank thee, and praise thy glorious name.
> 1Chron 29:11-13 KJV

If you do not love to worship and serve the Most High God, you will not want to be in heaven, Rev 4:9-11. You would not be happy there! He won't force you to go. But of course by your separation from Him you separate yourself from the One and Only Source of Life. The devil wasn't happy there. But many will be. It will be the most astonishing and mind blowing experience you have ever thought of. God will be marveled at among those who believe,

> When he shall come to be glorified in his saints, and to be admired in all them that believe (because our testimony among you was believed) in that day. 2Thes 1:10 KJV

Amazing! Just imagine! David said there was just one thing that he asked.

⁴ One thing have I desired of the LORD, that will I seek after; that I may dwell in the house of the LORD all the days of my life, to behold the beauty of the LORD, and to enquire in his temple. ⁵ For in the time of trouble he shall hide me in his pavilion: in the secret of his tabernacle shall he hide me; he shall set me up upon a rock. ⁶ And now shall mine head be lifted up above mine enemies round about me: therefore will I offer in his tabernacle sacrifices of joy; I will sing, yea, I will sing praises unto the LORD. Psa 27:4-6 KJV

I will be satisfied then, David says.

As for me, I will behold thy face in righteousness: I shall be satisfied, when I awake, with thy likeness. Psa 17:15 KJV

Job knows that he will see Him himself.

²⁵ For I know *that* my redeemer liveth, and *that* he shall stand at the latter *day* upon the earth: ²⁶ And *though* after my skin *worms* destroy this *body*, yet in my flesh shall I see God: ²⁷ Whom I shall see for myself, and mine eyes shall behold, and not another; *though* my reins be consumed within me. Job 19:25-27 KJV

Isaiah says we will see Him in "a far distant land" in the NASB in Isaiah 33:17. The NIV says in "a land that stretches afar." Both ideas are in line with what we know of these things. Isaiah goes on to say we will no longer have the terror of evil men hanging over us. But who can get there? Who can live with a consuming fire? Who but those who walk righteously, who speak with honesty and compassion, who adamantly will never take a bribe, who have not lived lives of bloodshed or loved wickedness, Isa 33:15.

He shall dwell on high: his place of defence *shall be* the munitions of rocks: bread shall be given him; his waters *shall be* sure. Isa 33:16 KJV

Thou art worthy, O Lord, to receive glory and honour and power: for thou hast created all things, and for thy pleasure they are and were created. Rev 4:11 KJV

So the start of seeing what *will be*, is seeing the Mighty God in heaven, and His Son, the Lamb. You start on that road by repenting, by believing in Jesus, and being baptized for the forgiveness of your sins.

Worthy is the Lamb, Revelation 5

John is seeing a vision of heaven. He has been called up to heaven to see what must take place after this, Rev 4:1. He has seen a throne scene in heaven, with mighty creatures surrounding the Most High God. Micaiah said he saw the Lord sitting on his throne in heaven, and all of the armies of heaven standing by Him on every side, 1Kgs 22:19. Also John the apostle saw Him.

Then John sees a scroll at the right hand of the throne, a scroll written on both sides, a scroll that is sealed, that no one can read, Rev 5:1. There is a similar thing in Isaiah 29. A scroll is given to one man, but he says he cannot read. The scroll is given to another man, and he says, "I cannot read it because it is all sealed up, Isa 29:11.

Many writings have been sealed in the past, and some of them have remained sealed, have remained unread, at least at this point. For instance in Dan 12:4, 8, Daniel is asking what will be the outcome of all of the visions he had seen, and he is told that the words are sealed, Dan 12:9-10. Sealed until the time of the end ... but the wicked will never understand. So some things are sealed, they are not intended to be understood until a certain time. And no one was able to read the scroll, Rev 5:2-4. No one above or below could read this. Not even the powerful creatures or angels. No one. Sometimes when things are hidden from us, we must be patient and wait a while, as in Isa 8:16-17. Isaiah speaks there of God hiding Himself from His people, even though Isaiah has given them signs in himself and the children he has borne. At times we must be patient, and not be arrogant in seeking discovery. We must carefully seek, much like the prophets of old.

> [10] Of which salvation the prophets have enquired and searched diligently, who prophesied of the grace *that should come* unto you: [11] Searching what, or what manner of time the Spirit of Christ which was in them did signify, when it testified beforehand the sufferings of Christ, and the glory that should follow. 1Pe 1:10-11 KJV

In the vision in Revelation 5 John starts to cry thinking of the things hidden there which he would like to see. There are some things that are still sealed. For instance, parts of the book of Daniel, and the voice of the seven thunders in Rev 10:4 are still sealed. **But the book of Revelation over all is *not* sealed, Rev 22:10**, because the lion of the tribe of Judah is about to open it. He has that ability and foresight.

The tribe of Judah has always been the select tribe. You are a lion's cub, O Judah, Jacob said in Gen 49:9-10.

> [9] Judah *is* a lion's whelp: from the prey, my son, thou art gone up: he stooped down, he couched as a lion, and as an old lion; who shall rouse him up? [10] The sceptre shall not depart from Judah, nor a lawgiver

A sealed scroll from ancient times.

from between his feet, until Shiloh come; and unto him *shall* the gathering of the people *be*. KJV

A shoot, a tender "rod" /Branch/stem, will come from the stump of Jesse.

> [1] And there shall come forth a rod out of the stem of Jesse, and a Branch shall grow out of his roots: [2] And the Spirit of the LORD And there shall come forth a rod out of the stem of Jesse, and a Branch shall grow out of his roots: LORD; Isa 11:1-2 KJV

So while the tree of David's house still stood, in the time of Isaiah, Isaiah says that tree will later be cut down, it will be laid waste, but later God will bring the tree back to life from David's roots. Jeremiah says God will raise up a righteous Branch of David. It called Him a shoot from the roots of Jesse in Isaiah 11 NASB. This One will be a good and just king. As in Isaiah He will be wise and insightful, and He will make Israel secure, Jer 23:5-6. Jesus of Nazareth is His name. He is King of Kings and Lord of Lords. This Jesus, this shoot from the root of David, was to be given everlasting authority.

> [14] And there was given him dominion, and glory, and a kingdom, that all people, nations, and languages, should serve him: his dominion *is* an everlasting dominion, which shall not pass away, and his kingdom *that* which shall not be destroyed. ...
>
> [18] But the saints of the most High shall take the kingdom, and possess the kingdom for ever, even for ever and ever. Dan 7:14, 18 KJV

Then when He came it was said,

> And hath raised up an horn of salvation for us in the house of his servant David; Lk 1:69 KJV

The elders in heaven said that He is able to open the scroll, this one, this Lion of the tribe of Judah, this root of David is able. What then does John see of this Lion? He saw a Lamb which looked as if it had been sacrificed. A lamb with seven horns and seven eyes which we are told are the seven Spirits of God. All of this is in the center of the throne, Rev 5:5-6. Seven is the perfect number symbolically. The lamb has the perfect number of horns and eyes. He is perfect in power and perfect in vision. Clearly a metaphorical picture of Jesus.

Do angels look after men? Yes they do, Mtt 18:10. It says the same in Heb 1:14. So what is the perfect number of angels to look after you? A children's lullaby says,

"When at night I go to sleep,
Fourteen angels watch do keep,
Two to whom is given
To guide my steps to heaven."

So the song says that twice the perfect number of angels are available. So it says symbolically God has abundantly provided for the protection of His little ones. Symbolic? Yes! But also true, as is this picture of Jesus in Revelation 5.

John the Baptist, when he saw Jesus coming, said look, the Lamb of God who takes away the sins of the world, Jn 1:29, 36. It was as a lamb in Isaiah 53 that Jesus was led to the slaughter. It pointed there to oppression and a court masquerading as justice, which is of course a clear picture of what happened to Jesus, Isa 53:7-8. Jesus is our sacrifice. He is our passover lamb, 1Cor 5:7. The lamb of God He is. So it was that God has exalted him to the highest place, that before Him *all* would bow, and *all* would confess Him as the absolute Master and Lord, Phil 2:9-11.

This lamb then took the scroll from the right hand of the One on the throne, Rev 5:7. Then all fell in worship before the Lamb, all of them having harps and golden bowls of incense which we are told are the prayers of the saints. And they glorify Him.

> Bless the LORD, ye his angels, that excel in strength, that do his commandments, hearkening unto the voice of his word Psa 103:20 KJV

He is worthy! He was sinless, Heb 4:15.

> [22] Who did no sin, neither was guile found in his mouth: [23] Who, when he was reviled, reviled not again; when he suffered, he threatened not; but committed *himself* to him that judgeth righteously: 1Pe 2:22-23 KJV

When He was cussed, He cussed not again. The elders and the living creatures sang a new song. Worthy is this lamb to open the seals, for He was slain, and has redeemed us to God by His blood, us of every tribe and nation and people and tongue. He has made us into kings and priests before the Lord, and we shall reign/rule over God's creation. He does wonderful things, Psa 98:1-2.

> [1] O sing to the LORD a new song!
> For He has done marvelous things;
> His right hand and His holy arm have gained Him the victory.
> [2] The LORD has made known His salvation;
> His righteousness He has revealed in the sight of the nations. NKJV

It was said from the first that God's people would be a kingdom of priests, Ex 19:6. That is you and me as you well know from 1Pe 2:9-10.

> [9] But ye *are* a chosen generation, a royal priesthood, an holy nation, a peculiar people; that ye should shew forth the praises of him who hath called you out of darkness into his marvellous light: [10] Which in time

past *were* not a people, but *are* now the people of God: which had not obtained mercy, but now have obtained mercy. KJV

And the angels too sing this song, and soon all of heaven is filled with joyful voices!

Saying with a loud voice, Worthy is the Lamb that was slain to receive power, and riches, and wisdom, and strength, and honour, and glory, and blessing. Rev 5:12 KJV

They are coming with Him at the last day, Jude 14. They will be sent out with a trumpet sound to collect his saints from one end of the heavens to the other, Mtt 24:31. Then it will come true that all of creation will honor Him, the lamb that was slain, Rev 13:8. So it pictures everyone honoring the Lamb, Rev 5:13-14.

The lamb is opening the scroll, He is opening the book of Revelation. He is not hiding it, He is not sealing it, He is *un-sealing* it. The book of Revelation is an unsealed book. It is a revelation, not a hiding! So the apostle John sees things coming out of the book, Rev 6:1. A seal is open. The contents are revealed. You and I can read the contents and know as opposed to not knowing.

He signified these things by His angel it says in the KJV in Rev 1:1. In the NASB it says he communicated it to his servant John. Like the parable of the sower, it is in symbolic form, but we know what the future will be.

⁹ Who shall be punished with everlasting destruction from the presence of the Lord, and from the glory of his power; ¹⁰ When he shall come to be glorified in his saints, and to be admired in all them that believe (because our testimony among you was believed) in that day.
2Thes 1:9-10 KJV

Now why would someone not like this Revelation, this revealing of the future? Unless ... unless somehow we do not *like* this message to God's saints. Many of those who object to the message of Revelation treat it as "intending" to "predict" some of the Roman emperors, and failing miserably. Even so, they bristle at the message as if it points to still existing entities which they think should be protected. Sometimes you can even detect a bit of indignation at the message. Perhaps sometimes we do not *like* a message which points to God's wrath falling on evil doers. It is difficult to tell, but we may not be comfortable with the idea of God who is active throughout the ages in dealing with His creation. We might want to pretend that we are sovereign and not the LORD our God, and that we can do as we please. Maybe we do not *like* its *pointing* to *certain* age-long forces working against Christians and indeed against all men. Possibly we do not *like* its pointing to a world-powerful pseudo-messiah to come. Perhaps!

The First Six Seals, Revelation 6

A fundamental question we face as we come to Revelation 6, is how should we deal with the seals of this next section of the book. What is it talking about, and how should we understand this section? First let us look at seals themselves as a subject.

Seals are used to close something so it cannot be tampered with. In this way the tomb of Jesus was sealed, probably with a quick-drying clay seal, to prevent tampering with the tomb, Mtt 27:66. Seals are also used as a mark of ownership. We shall also see that kind of usage in the very next chapter of Revelation. Further, it is also like our sealing of an envelope to keep others from reading or tampering with our mail.

Now to get our perspective, remember that the first section of Revelation was chapters 1-3, which pictured some churches of Asia as typical of churches and their struggles throughout the Christian age. Then we saw the next section of Revelation started in Revelation chapter 4. First of all it pictured all of heaven as worshipping and serving the Lord God of heaven and His Christ continually. Then we saw that there was a book, a scroll, written inside and out, but it was sealed with seven seals, so we might say the book was sealed with seven stickers of ownership of the book and its message, Rev 5:1. Now who is qualified to break the seal on our mail, to tear open the envelope enclosing our mail? Why, we are! But no one was worthy to break these seals, and tell us the message of the scroll, except Jesus Christ, the very lamb of God, Rev 5:5. And why was He worthy? He has bought and paid for us with His very own blood, Rev 5:9.

*You and I are **bought and paid for**, if* we belong to Christ, 1Cor 6:19-20. We as Christians do not belong to ourselves, if we have life in us. If we deny our Lord's *right* to control us, then we have cheated Jesus Himself, the LORD who both made, and bought us. What then is our Lord showing us? It seems He is showing us the dominant powers which are at work in our world. Jesus *owns* our age. The first seal is opened and John hears a noise like thunder, and the four living creatures *zōon* ζῶον (not "beasts" as in the KJV) say, Come and see what will be. The first power working in the Christian age is Jesus Himself. John saw one riding a white horse, and He has a crown on His head and bow in His hand. The first horse is not war and desolations. That is the second horse. The first horse, the primary power of world history, is Jesus going forth conquering and to conquer, Rev 6:1-2. The LORD is a man of war.

> "The LORD is a warrior;
> The LORD is His name." Ex 15:3 NASB

He has endured and does patiently endure the children of wrath who have rejected and opposed and slain Him. He has no fear. Nothing can overcome Him. It is a white horse which we see being ridden here. We have a very similar picture of Jesus in Rev 19:11-16. Jesus is pictured in Psalm 2 as ruling over the nations in the Christian age. God speaks of Jesus as born.

> I will declare the decree: the LORD hath said unto me, Thou *art* my Son; this day have I begotten thee. Psa 2:7 KJV

Then God speaks of giving this "Son" the very ends of the earth as His possession.

> Ask of me, and I shall give *thee* the heathen *for* thine inheritance, and the uttermost parts of the earth *for* thy possession.. Psa 2:8 KJV

Nevertheless, Jesus' has a rule *within* history. At the end of history, at Jesus second coming, Jesus will hand His rule *back* to the Father.

> [24] Then *cometh* the end, when he shall have delivered up the kingdom to God, even the Father; when he shall have put down all rule and all authority and power. [25] For he must reign, till he hath put all enemies under his feet. 1Cor 15:24-25 KJV

When Paul says that Jesus "must reign," in Greek that is the ***present active*** *infinitive*. It is continuous action *in the **present tense!*** (The Greek is *dei gar auton Basileuein* δεῖ γὰρ αὐτὸν βασιλεύειν. To paraphrase, it literally says "necessary for him to be reigning as a king.") I call Psalm 2 the New Testament psalm of Christ's rule, for that is what it is. Scripture picturing Jesus as ruling now as a king, and continuing to rule *until* He puts *all* of His enemies under His feet, as also does these first few verses in Revelation 6. So when it pictures Jesus in Psalm 2 as smashing His enemies, it is picturing what is going on in history *now!*

> Thou shalt break them with a rod of iron; thou shalt dash them in pieces like a potter's vessel. Psa 2:9 KJV

So rulers and judges are advised to submit to Him and please Him, if they want to stay alive and rule,

> Be wise now therefore, O ye kings: be instructed, ye judges of the earth. Psa 2:10 KJV

You thick-headed rulers, you had better pay attention. How blessed are all of those who worship and serve Him.

> Serve the LORD with fear, and rejoice with trembling. Psa 2:11 KJV

Treat Jesus with reverence and rejoice before Him with *trembling!*

> Kiss the Son, lest he be angry, and ye perish *from* the way, when his wrath is kindled but a little. Blessed *are* all they that put their trust in him. Psa 2:12 KJV

You rulers had better do homage to "the Son" NOW, before He gets angry with you and smashes you NOW! "In the way"! Jesus is sitting on His throne with His Father now.

To him that overcometh will I grant to sit with me in my throne, even **as I also overcame, and am set down with my Father in his throne**. Rev 3:21 KJV

"Overcame" and "sat," both referring to *past actions*. He rules over the kings of the earth now, Rev 1:5. He does not wait for some mythical future kingdom. He rules and smashes those displeasing to Him **now**! And He will continue to rule, until He puts down all obstacles and opposition, 1 Cor 15:25-26. So the first and primary power working in the Christian age is Jesus our Lord. We are looking at the primary powers of the Christian age. Jesus rules and conquers those who oppose Him.

The next seal is conflict between men. No peace.

> ³ When He opened the second seal, I heard the second living creature saying, "Come and see." ⁴ Another horse, fiery red, went out. And it was granted to the one who sat on it to take peace from the earth, and that *people* should kill one another; and there was given to him a great sword. Rev 6:3-4 NKJV

There is a second horse riding through the Christian age which we see here, a red horse of conflict, I suggest symbolizing anger and blood. This is conflict which even leads at times to death. It is the kind of conflict we may even see in our families. Jesus says He did not come for peace, but for conflict. We were united in sin before Jesus first coming, and He comes to break up that unity in doing what is evil.

> ³⁴ Think not that I am come to send peace on earth: I came not to send peace, but a sword. ³⁵ For I am come to set a man at variance against his father, and the daughter against her mother, and the daughter in law against her mother in law. ³⁶ And a man's foes *shall be* they of his own household. Mtt 10:34-36 KJV

Jesus comes to break up our bondage to Satan and to sin and death, and separate a people for Himself, for goodness and righteousness. This separation will involve some conflict with Satan and those who through bondage stand with him. Some of the conflict is because the gospel is dividing Satan's kingdom, is it not? Some of the conflict is also because of pleasures warring in our bodies.

> What is the source of quarrels and conflicts among you? Is not the source your pleasures that wage war in your members? Jas 4:1 NASB

So we graspingly desire and murder, Jas 4:2. I think we can include robbery and gang fights here, and also we can probably include the fighting between husband and wife as to who will get what pleasures, especially when the pleasures conflict with each other. Why then do we not have life? Life in this world is often driven by conflicts because of our sins, which includes the murders and wars and desolations on the evening news. When all the time we could have had it all, *if* we had stood with our Lord, and *asked*, Jas 4:3.

Next is the black horse of famine, Rev 6:5. On this black horse is a rider carrying a pair of scales. John then heard a voice coming from the center of the living creatures proclaiming a measure of wheat for a denarius, and three measures of barley for a denarius. Now a denarius was a silver coin about the size of an American dime, which was a day's wages for many centuries. Now wheat is better eating and better bread, and more nutritious, than say barley, which is not as tasty, nor as nutritious. Wheat has always been a preferred grain, both in ancient times and modern times.

Now if a quart of wheat costs a days wages, it is pretty hard to feed your family with that, Rev 6:6. On the other hand, if you can buy 3 quarts of barley with a day's wages, it might fill you up, but it wouldn't be as satisfying, or nutritious. Famine stalks many nations during the Christian age, as it says here. The form of punishment that falls on men who are unwilling to repent is not only conflict, as with the second horseman, the red horse of conflict, but it also the black horseman of short food supplies and famine. ***Unfulfilled needs are part of punishments*** **which fall on a sinful world, and is clearly pictured in this section.**

There is an episode that is told concerning the recovery of Japan after World War II. General Douglas MacArthur, one of the key architects of the conquest of Japan, was in essence arguing for the economic rehabilitation of Japan. He was arguing for allowing them to once again sell to the world market place, and he said the options were for America to allow that, or for America to endlessly support Japan, or ... starvation. One of the statements he made was that, "No weapon, not even the atomic bomb, is as deadly in its final effect as economic warfare. The atom bomb kills by the thousands, starvation by the millions." *Supreme Commander, MacArthur's Victory in Japan*, Harper Collins, NY, 2014, pgs 221-222. Often such economic warfare is very deliberate. Sometimes a tyrant uses it to subdue his own people, as for instance the Communists did with the rebellious Ukraine in the 1920's and 30's. They sealed off the Ukraine, and deliberately exported all the food from that productive country, leaving the population to starve, as several million did. It is another of the basic forces at work in the Christian age. Revelation is telling the truth.

Next is the horse of death and destruction, Rev 6:7-8. An "ashen horse" is the way it is described in the NASB, and as a "pale horse" as in the KJV and the NIV. And the result is death and destruction ruling over men, including sickness, plagues, famine, rats, mice, ants, locusts, and flies. When it speaks of God punishing men for their sins in the Old Testament, similar devices are mentioned as being used by the Lord. The Lord says,

> [12] When they fast, I will not hear their cry; and when they offer burnt offering and an oblation, I will not accept them: but I will consume

them by the sword, and by the famine, and by the pestilence. ...

¹⁶ And the people to whom they prophesy shall be cast out in the streets of Jerusalem because of the famine and the sword; and they shall have none to bury them, them, their wives, nor their sons, nor their daughters: for I will pour their wickedness upon them.
Jer 14:12, 16 KJV

The prophet Ezekiel speaks in general terms of such punishments as come on men in history, and the question of saving any righteous men among them?

¹³ Son of man, when the land sinneth against me by trespassing grievously, then will I stretch out mine hand upon it, and will break the staff of the bread thereof, and will send famine upon it, and will cut off man and beast from it: ¹⁴ **Though these three men**, Noah, Daniel, and Job, were in it, they should **deliver but their own souls by their righteousness**, saith the Lord GOD. Ezek 14:13-14 KJV (*emphasis added*)

So we are not looking at something new in history, or any new reaction against sin by the Lord our God. The Lord is the same yesterday, today and forever, Mal 3:6. When the whole world was into depravity in the days of Noah, the whole world perished with the exception of eight people. How are men killed? By violence (the sword), by famine, by disease, and by wild animals, Rev 6:8. Authority is given to death and hades *over a fourth of the earth*. Picture the famines you hear about in the evening news. Picture the wars and desolations you hear about. Picture the concentration camps of the Nazis which killed their millions, and of the Communists who at one time ruled one-third of our world and who in the 20th century killed well over a hundred-million people. These are not just ancient or medieval things of which it speaks. Actually these things are also very modern.

Above and beyond what men may do, Scripture clearly teaches that the Lord our God often uses natural disasters to discipline nations. You may even question whether God disciplines men within history, but that is a frequent topic of Scripture, and not just in the book of Revelation.

⁸ Understand, ye brutish among the people: and ye fools, when will ye be wise? 9 He that planted the ear, shall he not hear? he that formed the eye, shall he not see? ¹⁰ **He that chastieth the nations, shall He not correct?** he that teacheth man knowledge, *shall not he know?* ¹¹ The LORD knoweth the thoughts of man, that they are vanity.
¹² **Blessed is the man whom You chasten, O LORD, and teachest him out of thy law;** ¹³ That thou mayest give him rest from the days of adversity, until the pit be digged for the wicked.
Psa 94:8-13 KJV (*bold emphasis added*)

In Psalm 94 it is all in the context of turning nations from sin, so that they might live. Also it is sometimes specifically environmental disasters, as is seen in Psalm 107.

> [33] He turneth rivers into a wilderness, and the watersprings into dry ground; [34] A fruitful land into barrenness, **for the wickedness of them that dwell therein.** [35] He turneth the wilderness into a standing water, and dry ground into watersprings. [36] And there he maketh the hungry to dwell, that they may prepare a city for habitation; [37] And sow the fields, and plant vineyards, which may yield fruits of increase. [38] **He blesseth them also, so that they are multiplied greatly;** and suffereth not their cattle to decrease. [39] Again, they are minished and brought low through oppression, affliction, and sorrow. [40] **He poureth contempt upon princes, and causeth them to wander in the wilderness, _where there is no way_.** [41] Yet setteth he the poor on high from affliction, and maketh him families like a flock. [42] The righteous shall see it, and rejoice: and all iniquity shall stop her mouth. [43] Whoso is wise, and will observe these things, even they shall understand the lovingkindness of the LORD. Psa 107:33-43 KJV (_bold emphasis added_)

Here it is picturing God using tremendous environmental changes to both curse or bless a people as might be appropriate. **If we look carefully at Scripture we see that these themes in the book of Revelation are earth-age long profiles of how God deals with either the righteous or the wicked.** Thus we see in the book of Job that God uses the weather, both ways, both to judge or to bless.

> [26] "Behold, God is exalted, and we do not know _Him;_
>   The number of His years is unsearchable.
> [27] "For He draws up the drops of water,
>   They distill rain from the mist,
> [28] Which the clouds pour down,
>   They drip upon man abundantly.
> [29] "Can anyone understand the spreading of the clouds,
>   The thundering of His pavilion?
> [30] "Behold, He spreads His lightning about Him,
>   And He covers the depths of the sea.
> [31] **"For by these He judges peoples;**
>   **He gives food in abundance**.
> Job 36:26-31 NASB (_bold emphasis added_)

Once again, these are age long traits, from the garden of Eden to Noah and the flood, to the second temple ... to the end of the age. But there are other forces at work. Men are suffering for righteousness sake.

> And when he had opened the fifth seal, I saw under the altar the souls of them that were slain for the word of God, and for the testimony which they held: Rev 6:9 KJV

Jesus warned us that if we are faithful to Him, if we are like Him, men will persecute us like they did Him, Mtt 10:16-18. Of course *we already realize this*, and that is one reason sometimes we keep quiet about the truth when we should speak. We would rather watch TV than get beat up because we told someone the plain truth about the gospel. Jesus warns us about keeping quiet. It is by using our mouth for Jesus that we are saved

> [8] But what does it say? *"The word is near you, in your mouth and in your heart"* (that is, the word of faith which we preach): [9] that **if** you **confess with your mouth** the Lord Jesus and believe in your heart that God has raised Him from the dead, **you will be saved**. [10] For with the heart one believes unto righteousness, and **with the mouth confession is made unto salvation**. Rom 10:8-10 NKJV (*bold emphasis added*)

If you and I are like Christ, then the world will hate us just as it hated Christ, Jn 15:18-19. If we keep quiet, we are foolishly trading temporary trouble for eternal trouble. Those who have been murdered for Christ are asking, how long will it be Lord before you avenge us? Rev 6:10.

Again these are not new things in the book of Revelation, that men might be constantly suffering for doing what is right. The author of Hebrews, when speaking of the heroes of faith down through the ages, describes them in part this way.

> [37] They were stoned, they were sawn asunder, were tempted, were slain with the sword: they wandered about in sheepskins and goatskins; being destitute, afflicted, tormented; [38] (Of whom the world was not worthy:) they wandered in deserts, and *in* mountains, and *in* dens and caves of the earth. Heb 11:37-38 KJV

Once again we are not talking about something which is new to history. Rather it is a subject which will become more pointed as we move toward mankind's final spin out of control, in history. These suffering saints in Revelation 6 are given clean clothes and told to be patient for a little while before He avenges them, Rev 6:11.

Finally the Sixth Seal pictures the second coming of Christ and the end of our present universe. There are massive rumblings of the earth. The sun turns black and the moon turns to blood, and the heavens are tearing apart like figs shaken to the ground in a strong wind. The atmosphere is split in two, and *every* mountain and island is moved out of their place. It is not a wonder that men will be fainting at the overwhelming things they see overcoming our present universe, Lk 21:26.

Once again, these are not new "Apocalypse"/Revelations of things which are coming on our universe. Instead, this is a universal picture of the Second Coming in Scripture, such as for instance in Isaiah.

> [9] Behold, the day of the LORD is coming,

Cruel, with fury and burning anger,
To make the land a desolation;
And He will exterminate its sinners from it.
10 For the stars of heaven and their constellations
Will not flash forth their light;
The sun will be dark when it rises
And the moon will not shed its light.
11 Thus I will punish the world for its evil
And the wicked for their iniquity;
I will also put an end to the arrogance of the proud
And abase the haughtiness of the ruthless.
12 I will make mortal man scarcer than pure gold
And mankind than the gold of Ophir.
13 Therefore I will make the heavens tremble,
And the earth will be shaken from its place
At the fury of the LORD of hosts
In the day of His burning anger. Isa 13:9-13 NASB

Here it is clearly talking about the coming of the Lord God for the punishment of wickedness. It is not the same phraseology as in Revelation 6, but it is the same general concepts. Revelation 6 in this respect is once again not something new and strange to the Word of God. However, if we look closely at Isaiah 13 it clearly seems to point to some period of time being involved in the passing away of our present universe. Jesus does appear suddenly, as light flashes from one end of the sky to the other, Mtt 24:27. Every eye will see Him. Literally every eye which has ever existed, even the eyes of the those who crucified Him, Rev 1:5. Still there seems to be some time involved in all these things being rounded up. There is time in Isa 13:12 for men to become scarce, for not many to be yet left alive. There is time for men to fight each other in Isa 13:14-16. In Isaiah 24:17-18 it says that the one who runs away will fall into a pit, and the one who escapes the pit will be caught in a snare. Isaiah also says,

19 The earth is broken asunder,
The earth is split through,
The earth is shaken violently.
20 The earth reels to and fro like a drunkard
And it totters like a shack,
For its transgression is heavy upon it,
And it will fall, <u>never</u> to rise again.
21 So it will happen in that day,
That the LORD will punish the host of heaven on high,
And the kings of the earth on earth. Isa 24:19-21 NASB

So it seems a period of time is involved in this world passing away. Perhaps not years, but still some time is involved. Then all of sinful mankind will be gathered together and will be punished "after many days," Isa 24:22. Similarly, in Revelation 6 everyone has time to try to run and hide themselves from the Lord of Glory.

> [15] And the kings of the earth, and the great men, and the rich men, and the chief captains, and the mighty men, and every bondman, and every free man, hid themselves in the dens and in the rocks of the mountains; [16] And said to the mountains and rocks, Fall on us, and hide us from the face of him that sitteth on the throne, and from the wrath of the Lamb: Rev 6:15-16 KJV

Again, there will be time for those not immediately killed to *try* to run and hide, in the caves and rocks of the mountains, and they will be looking for almost anything to hide them from the Christ who is coming upon them with His mighty angels. This is a universal picture in Scripture of when the Lord comes to bring judgment on the earth, as in Isa 2:20-21.

> [20] In that day a man shall cast his idols of silver, and his idols of gold, which they made each one for himself to worship, to the moles and to the bats; [21] To go into the clefts of the rocks, and into the tops of the ragged rocks, for fear of the LORD, and for the glory of his majesty, when he ariseth to shake terribly the earth.   KJV

We are looking at the basic powers at work in the Christian age. Look around. Watch the evening news! Read history. This covers the entire Christian age! Everyone will realize who Jesus is when He comes, Rev 6:16-17. Everyone! Even the unbelieving! Are you ready for that day? Have you been redeemed, bought and paid for by Jesus? Are you living for yourself, *or* for Him? Are you a liar and a cheat, or a worker who belongs to the Lord?

God's Seal and Trouble, Revelation 7

We are continuing examining seals in this section. The discussion of seals began in Revelation 4 with a scene in heaven, and continued in Revelation 5 with a look at the book that had seven seals on it. It was asked who had the right to open those seals. If you remember, the answer was that Jesus had the right to open those seals, Rev 5:9.

We saw in Revelation 6 some of the powers which are working all through history, including Jesus Himself who is conquering all, as we saw in Rev 6:2. Then we saw a lot of different things working against sinful man in the Christian age. Instruments like conflict and quarreling and poverty and famine and war; and yes, even death and hades, Rev 6:8. Yes we even saw a picture of the second coming in Rev 6:15-17. But there are other things to be revealed from this book that was sealed. We have some of these other things revealed to us in chapter seven.

Four angels hold back the four winds.

> And after these things I saw four angels standing on the four corners of the earth, holding the four winds of the earth, that the wind should not blow on the earth, nor on the sea, nor on any tree. Rev 7:1 KJV

Why are they holding back these four winds, evidently damaging winds, about to strike the earth? It seems they do not *yet* want these winds of tragedy and harm to hurt the earth. You see, these winds, these angels, have the power to harm the earth and the sea, Rev 7:2. It would appear that the earth deserves to be harmed, deserves to be harmed by what it seems we would call the forces of "nature," and these powers are clearly under God's control.

God has brought tragedy on nature because of man's sin before. We see this first in Genesis 3. It is man who sinned, but the effect of this sin is to ruin the environment in which man lives.

> 17... Cursed is **the ground because of you**;
>   In toil you will eat of it
>   All the days of your life.
> 18 "Both thorns and thistles it shall grow for you;
>   And you will eat the plants of the field;
> Gen 3:17b-18 NASB (*bold emphasis added*)

Then we see it again, even becoming worse, when men's sins become worse.

> 5 Then the LORD saw that the wickedness of man *was* great in the earth, and *that* every intent of the thoughts of his heart *was* only evil continually. 6 And the LORD was sorry that He had made man on the earth, and He was grieved in His heart. 7 So the LORD said, "I will destroy man whom I have created from the face of the earth, both man and beast, creeping thing and birds of the air, for I am sorry that I have made them." 8 But Noah found grace in the eyes of the LORD. Gen 6:5-8 NKJV

It seems a principle in history that when mens's sins become bad, so does the environment in which they live, as we see in many passages like Isaiah 24.

> 4 The earth mourns *and* withers, the world fades *and* withers, the exalted of the people of the earth fade away. 5 The earth is also polluted by its inhabitants, for they transgressed laws, violated statutes, broke the everlasting covenant. 6 Therefore, a curse devours the earth, and those who live in it are held guilty. Therefore, the inhabitants of the earth are burned, and few men are left. Isa 24:4-6 NASB

But what of God's people? Are not they also on the earth? Though many are evil, are there not still some who are doing what is right? They surely should receive God's care. Let us seal the slaves of God with the seal of God! So wait a minute! Let's mark everyone who is a child of God. Let us give them the mark or the seal of God, before we unleash powers designed to bring punishment on sinful men.

> Saying, Hurt not the earth, neither the sea, nor the trees, till we have sealed the servants of our God in their foreheads. Rev 7:3 KJV

Now seals in this sense are marks of ownership. Like a stamp saying, this is the property of Joe Doaks, or this book belongs to George Smith or whoever. Or it would be like engraving your name on some valuable tool you have. You have seen the State seal on the bottom of State legal documents, and the king of Persia used his own seal to sign official decrees, as in Esth 8:8. Now the Lord our God has set His seal on Jesus Christ, Jn 6:27.

What is the Christian sealed with? He is sealed with the Holy Spirit of promise.

> [13] In Him you also *trusted*, after you heard the word of truth, the gospel of your salvation; in whom also, having believed, you were sealed with the Holy Spirit of promise, [14] who is the guarantee of our inheritance until the redemption of the purchased possession, to the praise of His glory. Eph 1:13-14 NKJV

The Lord gives us His Holy Spirit as a pledge, as a down payment on the eternal life which we have been promised.

> who also has sealed us and given us the Spirit in our hearts as a guarantee. 2Cor 1:22 NKJV

The word used for a "guarantee" or a "earnest" or a "pledge" in these verses is *arrabōn* ἀρραβών. It is a word used for a down payment or "earnest money" in buying something. God is giving us something to seal our deal. He is purchasing us out of sin and death, and purifying for Himself a people to do good works, and He is promising us eternal life. The pledge then, the seal of God's ownership of us, the guarantee of His promises to us, is the gift of God's Holy Spirit living in us. *Now we **have to have** the Holy Spirit of God to live forever.* It was the Holy Spirit in Jesus which raised Him from the dead, and it is this same Holy Spirit of God which will raise our corpses from the dead.

> But if the Spirit of Him who raised Jesus from the dead dwells in you, He who raised Christ from the dead will also give life to your mortal bodies through His Spirit who dwells in you. Rom 8:11 NKJV

If we have the Holy Spirit, the body may be dead because of sin, but our spirit is alive because of righteousness, Rom 8:10. How do you tell that you have the Holy Spirit? You will be able to tell by what you set your mind on.

> [5] For those who live according to the flesh set their minds on the things

of the flesh, but those *who live* according to the Spirit, the things of the Spirit. [6] For to be carnally minded *is* death, but to be spiritually minded *is* life and peace. Rom 8:5-6 NKJV

If we are being led by the Spirit of God, then we are sons of God, Rom 8:14. Many blessings follow from having this seal. We have not received a spirit of slavery, but a spirit of adoption by the Lord God our Father, and we call out to Him as Father, Rom 8:15-17. On the other hand, if we do not have the Spirit of God, if we do not have seal of God? Then we do not belong to Jesus, Rom 8:9. If we have the seal of God, we need to depart from all wickedness.

> Nevertheless the foundation of God standeth sure, having this seal, The Lord knoweth them that are his. And, Let every one that nameth the name of Christ depart from iniquity. 2Tim 2:19 KJV

So mark all of the slaves of God, says the angel in Rev 7:3. Once God's people have all been sealed, then it is alright to release these disasters upon the earth. God's people are identified and sealed, so that the Lord will know who is His, can care for and protect His own!

Then we see the symbolic number of those sealed: 144,000. It pictures 12,000 from each tribe of Israel, Rev 7:4. It seems to be picturing God's people as ancient Israel of twelve tribes, but of course the new Israel includes both Jews and gentiles. Paul says both Jews and gentiles have all been brought near in Jesus. Speaking of how the gentiles, those of the nations, used to be separated from salvation, Paul says,

> [12] *remember* that you were at that time separate from Christ, excluded from the commonwealth of Israel, and strangers to the covenants of promise, having no hope and without God in the world. [13] But now in Christ Jesus you who formerly were far off have been brought near by the blood of Christ. Eph 2:12-13 NASB

The names of tribes are given in Rev 7:5-8. It seems to be symbolic numbers and symbolic names, perhaps just noting the first fruits. Then it notes a numberless group of the saved, Rev 7:9-12.

But there is one strange thing in the first list. The tribe of Dan is not mentioned in the first list! There are twelve tribes listed. The tribe of Joseph, that is the tribe of Ephraim, is mentioned in verse 8, and also the tribe of Manasseh from Joseph is mentioned in verse 6 (which is called a "half-tribe" in passages like Jos 1:12), but the tribe of Dan is not mentioned! I cannot give you a sure answer here, but the tribe of Dan is mentioned as a serpent in the road in Jacob's (Israel's) prophecy about his sons on his death bed.

> [16] "Dan shall judge his people
>   As one of the tribes of Israel.
> [17]   Dan shall be a serpent by the way,
>   A viper by the path,

> That bites the horse's heels
> So that its rider shall fall backward." Gen 49:16-17 NKJV

"Dan shall judge his people." That could easily be a reference to Samson, of the tribe of Dan, who judged Israel in his day. Dan here also seems to be spoken of one who acts, shall we say, as a "snake in the grass." As an unseen and deadly foe who lurks nearby, and is able to unhorse the rider.

Jeremiah mentions the tribe of Dan because he says that God is going to send serpents among His people, among those of Dan, during an invasion to devour the land.

> [16] From Dan is heard the snorting of his horses;
> At the sound of the neighing of his stallions
> The whole land quakes;
> For they come and devour the land and its fullness,
> The city and its inhabitants.
> [17] "For behold, I am sending serpents against you,
> Adders, for which there is no charm,
> And they will bite you," declares the LORD. Jer 8:16-17 NASB

Does the seed of the serpent have something to do with the tribe of Dan? Is the beast of Revelation from the tribe of "Dan"? I don't know. That would only be speculation on my part.

After these things there is great rejoicing in heaven, Rev 7:10-12. Then one of the elders asked John, do you know where this crowd has come from, Rev 7:13? John tells the elder, you know, and he says they have all come out of the great tribulation, Rev 7:14a. Of course there are multiple periods of extreme tribulation spoken of in the Christian age. Paul says in 2Tim 3:1,

> But realize this, that in the last days difficult **times** will come. NASB

It says "perilous times" in the KJV. Clearly Paul is indicating that there would be multiple "difficult times," seeming to indicate these difficulties involve more than just the church (which of course they do). Also, multiple Scriptures point to one particular time which is more difficult than all the others. Wars and rumors of wars are just birth pangs compared to this particular time of stress, Mtt 24:7-8. Then Jesus says of some particular time, called "then,"

> For then shall be great tribulation, such as was not since the beginning of the world to this time, no, nor ever shall be. Mtt 24:21 KJV

So there will be one particular time of stress worse than all the others *ever!* Matthew 24 clearly speaks of *both* the destruction of Jerusalem and of the end of time, and the "problem" in Matthew 24 is separating the two. Some think that Mtt 24:21 (above) refers to the destruction of Jerusalem by the Roman armies in 70 AD. That was a great disaster, which has been well documented by the Jewish historian Flavius Josephus. It *was* a terrible scene. But was it really the greatest tribulation in all of history? With just a cursory knowledge of world history, that would seem at best to be hyperbole, exaggeration. The black plague in the Middle Ages killed many millions more, as did also the influenza epidemic in late World War I and extending into the 1920's. It has been the same for many tragedies in history, not to mention the Holocaust of World War II killing many more Jews than 70 AD. But the "great tribulation" of Jerusalem in 70 AD as hyperbole? Hyperbole, exaggerated language, is one of the indications of a symbol in prophecy. It was argued in *Prophecy Principles* that the destruction of Jerusalem in 70 AD is a type, symbolic, of the end of the world. You can read an extensive study of these things there.

Daniel also speaks of the greatest time of stress in all of history, and there it is emphatically associated with the end of the world and the resurrection from the dead.

> And at that time shall Michael stand up, the great prince which standeth for the children of thy people: and **there shall be a time of trouble, such as never was** since there was a nation *even* to that same time: **and at that time** thy people **shall be delivered, <u>every one</u> that shall be found written in the book.**
> Dan 12:1 KJV (*bold and underline emphasis added*)

Daniel then goes on to discuss the end of time and the general resurrection from the dead, "these to everlasting life, but the others to disgrace and everlasting contempt," Dan 12:1. So it seems Daniel is clearly talking about the end of the world. Is it possible that there are *two **greatest*** times of stress in all history? I think not. It seems both Jesus and Daniel are speaking of the same time of stress near the end of our present universe.

In Rev 7:13 it is very specific. These people have come out of literally and emphatically "<u>the</u> tribulation <u>the</u> great" (*tās thlipseōs tās megalās*, τῆς θλίψεως τῆς μεγάλης). That *great* multitude seen in John's vision in Revelation 7 are those who have triumphantly come out of that greatest time of stress at the end of time, out of that conflict yet to be described in detail in the book of Revelation.

They have made their clothes white in the blood of the lamb, Rev 7:14b. Now God will protect them, Rev 7:15. God will spread His tent, His tabernacle, over them. They will never hunger or thirst again, Rev 7:16. The lamb of God will be their shepherd forever more, Rev 7:17a. And He will wipe away every tear, Rev 7:17b.

These are, without a doubt, awesome pictures of our age.

VI. Trumpets of Warning, Revelation 8-11

⁴ Coming to Him as to a living stone, rejected indeed by men, but chosen by God and precious, ⁵ you also, as living stones, are being built up a spiritual house, a holy priesthood, to offer up spiritual sacrifices acceptable to God through Jesus Christ. ⁶ Therefore it is also contained in the Scripture,

> *"Behold, I lay in Zion*
> *A chief cornerstone, elect, precious,*
> *And he who believes on Him will by no means be put to shame."*

1Pe 2:4-6 NKJV

Now in this vision the last seal is about to be broken by the Lamb. Broken so we will know what is going to happen, Rev 8:1. There is "silence in heaven about the space of half an hour,." KJV. Everyone is waiting for the next part of the story. Now the seal is opened and seven angels were given seven trumpets in Rev 8:2. Trumpets will be talked about shortly, but first let us notice that these trumpets seem to come because of the prayers of God's people. Prayers of the saints are added to the incense.

> And another angel came and stood at the altar, having a golden censer; and there was given unto him much incense, that he should offer *it* with the prayers of all saints upon the golden altar which was before the throne. Rev 8:3 KJV

Now incense and prayers are associated with each other in Scripture. First let us notice that much of the Old Testament was symbolic. This is not meant to say that the Old Testament is false, or that its histories are not true. What I mean is that God had things happen, or built, or done, which were intended to be symbolic of other, later, things in history. It could even be said that God continually instructed His saints about the things that would happen much later, by nearer things which He had already caused to happen. The nearer things are "types," symbols, "shadows," or "patterns," of things to come.

> For the law having a shadow of good things to come, and not the very image of the things, ... Heb 10:1 KJV

So what does incense indicate in Rev 8:3? Incense is of course a sweet smell, a fragrant smell, made by burning certain spices or woods or oils, as in

> Oil for the light, spices for anointing oil, and for sweet incense,
> Ex 25:6 KJV

It was supposed to be something sweet, fragrant, to the Lord, as in,

> ... and shall burn it upon the altar *for* a sweet savour, *even* the memorial of it, unto the LORD, Lev 6:15

But what really smells sweet to the Lord? Moses burned incense and made atonement for the sins of the people, Num 16:47. So it seems to have the idea of putting a request before God.

Now God is a spirit, Jn 4:24. A spirit does not have flesh and bones, Lk 24:39. So God is not really focused on sweet smelling spices.

> "Bring your worthless offerings no longer,
>> Incense is an abomination to Me.
>> New moon and sabbath, the calling of assemblies —
>> I cannot endure iniquity and the solemn assembly."
>
> Isa 1:13 NASB

In fact, He cannot stand incense with sin. So what is really sweet to the Lord? David asks that his prayers be counted as a sweet incense.

> Let my prayer be set forth before thee *as* incense; *and* the lifting up of my hands *as* the evening sacrifice. Psa 141:2 KJV

The sacrifice Christians need to make is a sacrifice of praise.

> By him therefore let us offer the sacrifice of praise to God continually, that is, the fruit of *our* lips giving thanks to his name. Heb 13:15 KJV

In the description in Rev 5:8 it says the bowls of incense are added to the prayers of the saints. In Revelation 8 we see the prayers of the saints going up to the Lord as the smoke of the sweet smell of incense, out of the hand of the angel, Rev 8:4. The saints in Revelation 6 are like those in Revelation 5. They seem to be calling on God to act and do something. So the prayers and the incense are filled with fire from the altar in heaven, and it is thrown down to the earth, Rev 8:5. The result? Lightning and an earthquake. It seems the saints are calling for judgment on the earth. Judgment for wrongs done to them.

What are Trumpets for Anyway?

We use trumpets to announce things. For instance a special meeting of the people of God in Lev 23:24. Or perhaps they are sounded when the king is coming, or when some big announcement is about to the be made. In old time America they used to sound huge bells to announce things. Sound the bell when class starts, sound the church bell when it was time for church, because most people people did not have a clock. We see a similar use of trumpets in Num 10:10 to announce feasts. We also see trumpets used figuratively of great announcements which are to be made.

> Cry aloud, spare not, lift up thy voice like a trumpet, and shew my people their transgression, and the house of Jacob their sins.
> Isa 58:1 KJV

In modern times we also have warning sirens to warn of danger, but trumpets were often used to warn in ancient times! We see this in Num 10:9, and we see this usage as a warning in battle in Ezekiel.

> 2 "Son of man, speak to the sons of your people and say to them, 'If I bring a sword upon a land, and the people of the land take one man from among them and make him their watchman, 3 and he sees the sword coming upon the land and blows on the trumpet and warns the people, 4 then he who hears the sound of the trumpet and does not take warning, and a sword comes and takes him away, his blood will be on his *own* head." Ezek 33:2-4 NASB

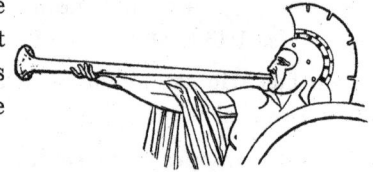

So seven angels have seven trumpets, to announce and warn.

The first trumpet of warning brings fire and hail mixed with blood. A third of the earth was burned up, and a third of the trees, and all of the grass of the earth, Rev 8:6. It seems to be speaking of a scorching of the earth which has not happened yet. Perhaps this is depicting a soaring of the intensity with which the sun is burning at some future time. Perhaps this is referring to the same thing talked about in Rev 16:8.

> And the fourth angel poured out his vial upon the sun; and power was given unto him to scorch men with fire. KJV

It is plainly talking about some scorching heat at some time in history as a trumpet of warning. Remember: these visions are overlapping, parallel, and cumulative.

Then the second angel sounded his warning trumpet. This does not seem to be the end, but it seems to point to very bad things coming to warn people. At this point something like a great mountain burning with fire was thrown into the sea, Rev 8:8a. Now what would a great burning mountain falling into the sea be called? I think we might call this a meteorite! Now some big meteorites have fallen on the earth before, to make blasts bigger than any nuclear bomb ever made. Scientists speculate what it would be like if we were hit by some tremendous meteorite. Of course we will get hit by one that will be very big, as we see here.

> 8 And the second angel sounded, and as it were a great mountain burning with fire was cast into the sea: and the third part of the sea became blood; 9 And the third part of the creatures which were in the sea, and had life, died; and the third part of the ships were destroyed. Rev 8:8-9 KJV

We are speaking here of an environmental catastrophe of, shall we say, apocalyptic proportions? I think so.

A small meteorite hit Russia in 2013, and pictures of its crashing and damage

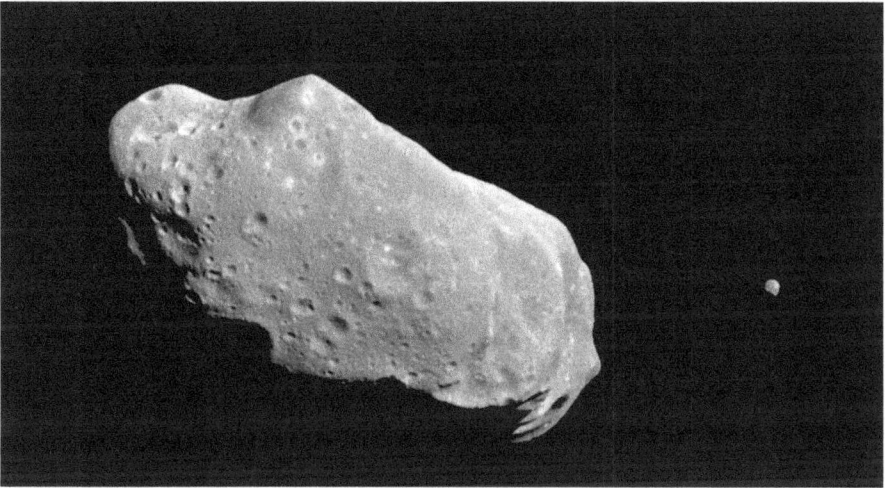

To give an idea of the scale of some of these things, asteroid Ida
even has its own moon circling it.

were news world wide. It was thought to be about 15 meters in diameter. A bigger one fell in Siberia about a hundred years ago. It was thought to have burst about 3 to 6 miles up in the air, being a small comet/asteroid/meteorite, but it left a tremendous impact in Tunguska, Russia. It knocked down all the trees in an area of approximately 770 square miles, on June 20, 1908. It equalled about

a 15 megaton atomic bomb, so it was far bigger in impact than any normal nuclear weapon. In the case of "the great mountain burning with fire" in Rev 8:8, a third of the sea turned to blood, and a third of the fish died, and a third of the ships at sea are sunk.

There seems to be general awareness in our times of the possibility of such things happening.

Scientists speculate what it would be like if we were hit by a large meteorite, and of course we will get hit by one that will be very big, as we see in, Rev 8:8-9. Men like to pretend that this earth is very near eternal, but God will dispel these illusions *before* the end. It seems that the "great

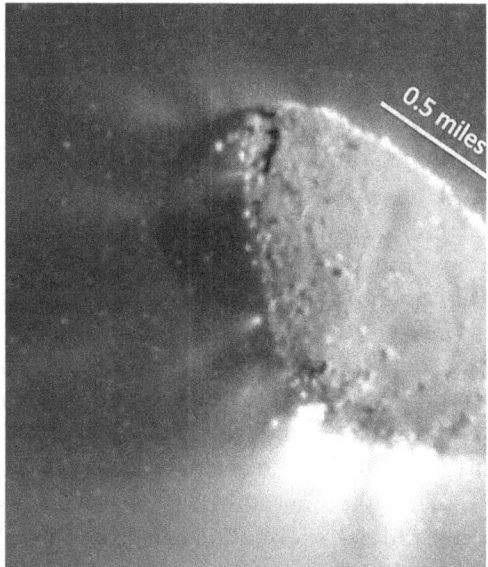

The Hartley asteroid, a very finite, small body, **still** spewing gas and snow, so it is still a relatively recent visitor to our solar system.

An Eyewitness Account of the Tunguska, Russia, Meteroite Impact, June 20, 1908

"At breakfast time I was sitting by the house at Vanavara Trading Post [65 kilometres/40 miles south of the explosion], facing north. ... I suddenly saw that directly to the north, over Onkoul's Tunguska Road, the sky split in two and fire appeared high and wide over the forest [as Semenov showed, about 50 degrees up—expedition note]. The split in the sky grew larger, and the entire northern side was covered with fire. At that moment I became so hot that I couldn't bear it, as if my shirt was on fire; from the northern side, where the fire was, came strong heat. I wanted to tear off my shirt and throw it down, but then the sky shut closed, and a strong thump sounded, and I was thrown a few metres. I lost my senses for a moment, but then my wife ran out and led me to the house. After that such noise came, as if rocks were falling or cannons were firing, the earth shook, and when I was on the ground, I pressed my head down, fearing rocks would smash it. When the sky opened up, hot wind raced between the houses, like from cannons, which left traces in the ground like pathways, and it damaged some crops. Later we saw that many windows were shattered, and in the barn a part of the iron lock snapped."

---

mountain burning with fire" in Revelation 8, as colossal as that will be, is just *sounding a warning of greater desolations coming!* This is not the end, but **warnings** of the end. This warning is by what we would call an astounding "natural disaster."

Then another trumpet of warning is sounded and a small star hits the earth in Rev 8:10. Now Scripture calls it a "great star" *astār megas* (ἀστὴρ μέγας), because it is a big disaster on the earth, but it would be small compared to most of the stars we see at night. What then would make it a star? It might be assumed it is giving off heat, not just being warmed by the sun or by going through the atmosphere. Perhaps it is also shining, not just from the sun, but it is also giving off light. At the point that it comes near the earth it evidently breaks up. Such is often called a "bolide." This seems to be common with large objects approaching an even larger object like the earth. This "star" falls on the waters of the earth and pollutes them, and makes a third of the waters of the earth bitter and undrinkable Rev 8:10-11. The text notes that lot of people die. Even so, this is really *just a warning* to sinful men!

Then the sun and moon are struck, Rev 8:12. Of course, most of the ancients did not realize it, but the moon gets its light from the sun. So if the sun does not have a strong light, it will affect the shining of the moon, naturally. The darkening of the sun and the moon, is included in every description in Scripture of the end of time. For instance, we see this in Isa 13:10. Again we see this in Isa 24:23, and also in Ezek 32:7-8. These passages are hyperbole (exaggerated language, symbolic) when you are talking about Israel and Judah of ancient times. However those ancient events are evidently symbolic of the end of the world, and the same language is literal when applied to the end of the world ("type" and "antitype," symbol and fulfillment). Jesus says this happens just before He comes again, Mtt 24:29-30. You can also find this in many other passages describing the end of time.

A third of the stars are also struck so that they do not shine, and it seems to say that a third of the day will not have the light of the sun, Rev 8:12.

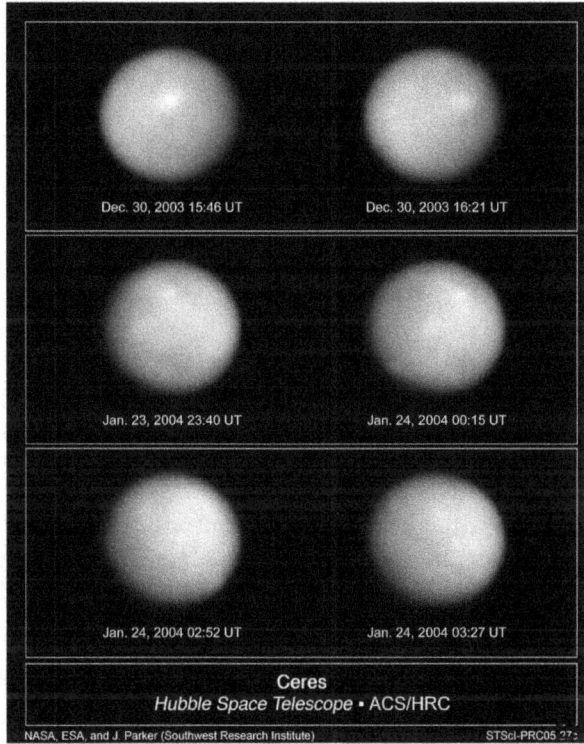

Ceres
Hubble Space Telescope • ACS/HRC

NASA, ESA, and J. Parker (Southwest Research Institute)   STScI-PRC05 27:

The largest of the asteroids is Ceres, which is approximately 590 miles in diameter, and some think it may be a true "mini-planet" with water/ice.

These are huge disasters that are being described. These are what we might otherwise call "natural" disasters. We now know that a large interplanetary impact with the earth is a very real possibility, and that is a constant subject of both scientific investigation, and speculation, and science fiction, and movies. Despite all of this, there are still three more trumpets of warning to come. Woe, woe, to those who dwell on earth, Rev 8:13. The worst of even the warnings are yet to come.

By the combinations of language which are used in chapter 8, it seems to be describing awesome physical disasters. At this point though, it seems to move on to describing terrible spiritual plagues as also coming. Lastly of course, judgement is coming. The Lord will gather us all before Him according to Mtt 25:31-33. We must all give an account of ourselves to God, Rom 14:12. **The "natural" disasters will get worse as men get worse.** "Time has been shortened, ... the form of this world is passing away," 1Cor 7:29-31 NASB. These tremendous disasters are just trumpets of warning!

So now you know some of the means God will use to try to wake up people when things are getting very bad morally. Revelation 8 seems to speak of ecological disasters, what we might even call "natural" disasters. Indeed, why not take the immediate literal sense of a passage if it fits the context, and this does.

The Abyss is Opened, Revelation 9

Revelation 9 at this point seems to make a transition to speaking of spiritual disasters.

Now some angels have already been sent for punishment into the abyss. The abyss is evidently a deep hole, a bottomless hole, a pit of punishment for the spirits of sinful angels and men, and this is talked about many places in Scripture. The demons in Luke 8 know that Jesus can send them into the abyss, and they are afraid to go. Jesus here is talking directly to the demons who are possessing the man in Lk 8:27, and the demons are answering through the man whom they seem to "possess."

> [30] Jesus asked him, saying, "What is your name?"
> And he said, "Legion," because many demons had entered him. [31] And they begged Him that He would not command them to go out into the abyss. Lk 8:30-31 NKJV

Peter says God did not even spare the angels who sinned and He threw them into pits of darkness, 2Pe 2:4.

Now in the first verse of Revelation 9 we see talk of a star falling from heaven into the abyss, Rev 9:1. Then we should ask why we should take the "star" in Rev 8:11 as literally being something we would call a "star," but then take the "star" of Rev 9:1 as symbolic of a great spiritual being. In fact this might be compared to the discussion of Psalm 22, where the "worm" and the "dogs" and the the "sword" were taken symbolically, and the "clothing," and the casting of lots, and the piercing of hands and feet as literal. (See pages 4-8.) The difference is context and common sense. The "star" in Revelation 8 is talked about in the context of bringing ecological catastrophes on the earth, and ruining water supplies. In contrast the "star" in Revelation 9:1 is talked about in context of a prison for spiritual beings, and their being released so they can mentally/spiritually, hurt men. The Greek phrase is "*tou phreatos tās abussou*" (τοῦ φρέατος τῆς ἀβύσσου) or literally of a pit which has no bounds. It is translated here the "bottomless pit" in many translations, including the NASB. Also, Jesus went to the abyss for you and me, for three days following His death, Rom 10:6-7.

> [6] But the righteousness of faith speaks in this way, "*Do not say in your heart, 'Who will ascend into heaven?'* " (that is, to bring Christ down *from*

above) ^{7} or, " 'Who will descend into the abyss?' " (that is, to bring Christ up from the dead). NKJV

In Romans 10 the word abyss (*abussos* ἄβυσσος boundless), is used without the word pit (*phreatos*). This place where Jesus went is clearly spoken of as being in the earth, both in Romans 10, and also in places like Mtt 12:40.

> For as Jonah was three days and three nights in the belly of the great fish, so will the Son of Man be three days and three nights in the heart of the earth. NKJV

Of course, angels are sometimes described as "stars" in Scripture. For example in Job 38:7.

> When the morning stars sang together, and all the sons of God shouted for joy? KJV

Here the angels of heaven are witnesses of some of the last acts of creation (it would seem they were themselves some of the first acts of creation), and these angels are called "sons of God" (compare Job chapters 1 and 2), and they are also called "stars," *kokav* כּוֹכָב. We see this again in Dan 8:10.

> And it grew up to the host of heaven; and it cast down *some* of the host and *some* of the stars to the ground, and trampled them. NKJV

I will not attempt to explain this relationship in Scripture between angels and "stars," but, however you view this relationship, it is clearly there.

Similarly we see Satan described as dragging these "stars" into revolt against God in Rev 12:3-4. Then we see Satan and all of his angles/demons being cast out of heaven, Rev 12:9. These passages will be dealt with in more detail later.

Clearly, at one time Satan had been in heaven, and he was still allowed there in Job's day, Job 2:1-2. In contrast, as Jesus is going to the cross, He sees Satan falling like lightning from heaven, Lk 10:18. Now Satan falls to the earth in Rev 12:9. Satan is confined in the abyss for a very long time, Rev 20:1-3. All of which will be discussed in more detail later.

But Satan is given the key to the abyss in Rev 9:1. It is translated "the bottomless pit" in the KJV and the NKJV and the NASB, but it is just the "Abyss" in the NIV.

Lastly we see that when the fifth angel sounds his trumpet, Satan (who seemingly is the "star from heaven which had fallen to the earth," Rev 9:1, and compare Rev 12:9) is allowed to open the abyss, and many more, obviously not literal locusts, but evidently demons are released, Rev 9:2.

> And he opened the bottomless pit; and there arose a smoke out of the pit, as the smoke of a great furnace; and the sun and the air were darkened by reason of the smoke of the pit. KJV

So we have a great demonic release starting in Rev 9:2-3.

Now men have been worshipping and serving demons all along through history, often times quite unconsciously. We all were once in bondage to these demons (Eph 2:2-3), who have never really, by their very nature, been "gods" (Gal 4:8). When we men have worshiped pagan "gods," we were really worshipping demons, according to 1Cor 10:20.

So do you really love demons, and not the LORD? Well perhaps then the proper thing is for you to have them! So the fifth angel sounds his trumpet, and Satan is allowed to give a sinful world the demons they really love.

Now the great demonic release is described figuratively in Revelation 9, and is described from other points of view in Revelation 19 and Revelation 20. It is a popular subject with the occult, and it is quite often pictured in occult movies and television shows, and you may have seen it in such shows. We saw in verse one that Satan is at some point allowed to open the abyss and to release its inmates. They are compared to millions of locusts here, but these locusts do not to hurt grass or trees or crops. They are sent only to harrass and afflict and torment sinful men who do not have the "seal of God," Rev 9:4. These are spiritual disasters.

That seal of the Christian is the Holy Spirit of God, living in the Christian, as has been discussed.

> [13] In Him you also *trusted*, after you heard the word of truth, the gospel of your salvation; in whom also, having believed, you were sealed with the Holy Spirit of promise, [14] who is the guarantee of our inheritance until the redemption of the purchased possession, to the praise of His glory. Eph 1:13-14 NKJV

So of course we are warned to not grieve the Holy Spirit, so that we do not lose this protection, Eph 4:30.

The demons are not *permitted* to kill, but only are allowed to torture sinful men, those not having the Spirit of God. They are permitted to torture sinful men for five months, Rev 9:5. This is apparently a terrible torment, like the sting of a scorpion it says. Notice again, *demons can only do what they are **permitted** to do*, what they have been given to do. It is much as it is with Satan himself as seen in Job chapters 1 and 2. It will be so bad that men will want to die, but death will elude them, Rev 9:6.

What are these locusts like? Like war horses, Rev 9:7. They have crowns indicating great power, and the faces of men, and they have hair like women, and teeth like those of a lion, Rev 9:8. Literal locusts out of the abyss makes no sense, nor having these descriptions. This is clearly figurative of millions of awesome evil spiritual creatures, who are only allowed to hurt sinful men.

> And they had breastplates, as it were breastplates of iron; and the sound of their wings *was* as the sound of chariots of many horses

running to battle. Rev 9:9 KJV

It is describing terrible agony being suffered by sinful men here on earth for a period of months. A plague more terrible than monster meteorites is here hitting the earth. The king of these demons is Satan, the angel of the abyss, whose name is "Destruction."

> And they had as king over them the angel of the bottomless pit, whose name in Hebrew is Abaddon, but in Greek he has the name Apollyon. Rev 9:11 NKJV

Despite all of these horrors, two more woes are coming, and four angels are released to kill one-third of all the people of the earth. So here the text seems to move to discussing demonic inspired man-made disasters.

> [14] Saying to the sixth angel which had the trumpet, Loose the four angels which are bound in the great river Euphrates. [15] And the four angels were loosed, which were prepared for an hour, and a day, and a month, and a year, for to slay the third part of men. Rev 9:14-15 KJV

There are several things which are prominent in this passage. First is that this slaughter of a third of mankind is supervised by four angels. Next that these angels are "bound," imprisoned, tied up, restrained at a known location here on earth: "the great river Euphrates." Third it seems that this great destruction is to be by war, a war of men against men. So it mentions the number of the troops for this incredible world war will be "two hundred million" men, Rev 9:16. The Euphrates is mentioned again in another vision, and again in connection with a terrible war, in Rev 16:12. It would appear that the vision in Revelation 16 is describing these same events from a different point of view. The next few verses seem to describe these things from a highly symbolic point of view.

> [17] And thus I saw the horses in the vision, and them that sat on them, having breastplates of fire, and of jacinth, and brimstone: and the heads of the horses *were* as the heads of lions; and out of their mouths issued fire and smoke and brimstone. [18] By these three was the third part of men killed, by the fire, and by the smoke, and by the brimstone, which issued out of their mouths. [19] For their power is in their mouth, and in their tails: for their tails *were* like unto serpents, and had heads, and with them they do hurt. Rev 9:17-19 KJV

Is this a terrifyingly symbolic representation of a modern war? Well obviously not if you have presupposed that prophecy cannot truly be "prophetic"! Right? Terrible times will come, 2Tim 3:1. Remember?

It appears to me that this is the preparation of sinful men for the great day of God which we see in Rev 16:14. I think we are seeing the actual battle in Revelation chapters 19 and 20. It appears they are being prepared for a battle in which they actually try to physically fight God.

Parts of the occult have all along planned for some truly horrifying wars to kill hundreds of millions of people. Alas, so far, as terrible as some of the wars of the twentieth century were, they only killed tens of millions of people, and nothing near one-third of all people. Still, a third of mankind is killed in these disasters, more than in any war in history to this point, Rev 9:18-19.

But men will still not repent in these incredible events of the last days, Rev 9:20. Repentance will not come to this sinful brood, afflicted by demonic powers in the last days, Rev 9:21.

There is a point of no return. A point from which we will never repent. We just will not consider it, no matter how sensible it seems. We need to seek the Lord while we can, and cling to Him and serve Him, before the night comes when no man can work, Jn 9:4.

The Angel and The Little Book, Revelation 10

We have seen God's servants being identified and marked with the seal of the Holy Spirit in an earlier part of Revelation. We have seen great trumpets of warning being sounded throughout the earth, and we have seen one picture of a great demonic release near the end of time.

Now we see a strong angel coming out of heaven,

> And I saw another mighty angel come down from heaven, clothed with a cloud: and a rainbow was upon his head, and his face was as it were the sun, and his feet as pillars of fire: Rev 10:1 KJV

Now angels are strong and very mighty creatures. They are stronger and mightier than men, 2Pe 2:11. Further, we see from Scripture that some angels are mightier than others. One angel in Revelation 20 is able to bind the evil angel, the Devil or Satan, by himself, Rev 20:1-2. Just one of the good angels is able to bind Satan *by himself!*

So some angels are stronger than others, and this one in Revelation 10 is a strong angel, a mighty angel in the KJV, and this angel is a dazzlingly glorious creature. This angel has a little book in his hand, Rev 10:2. He cries out with a loud voice, a voice like a lion when it roars, and when he cries out, seven thunders raised their voices, Rev 10:3.

Seven is the perfect number in Scripture, and this is evidently the perfect number of thunders, all of whom have something important to say. What do thunders have to say? It seems to be a message of anger and wrath and judgement. Thunders in Scripture are often associated with a couple of things. Thunders are associated with God speaking to men, as in Exodus 19.

16 Then it came to pass on the third day, in the morning, that there

were thunderings and lightnings, and a thick cloud on the mountain; and the sound of the trumpet was very loud, so that all the people who *were* in the camp trembled. ... [19] And when the blast of the trumpet sounded long and became louder and louder, Moses spoke, and God answered him by voice. [20] Then the LORD came down upon Mount Sinai, on the top of the mountain. And the LORD called Moses to the top of the mountain, and Moses went up. Ex 19:16, 19-20 NKJV

Here God is literally speaking with a voice like thunder. We see the people of God trembling at God's speaking and His presence in Ex 20:18. We see thunder as symbolically representing God's voice in many other passages, as it is in 2 Samuel 22 of God delivering David from his enemies.

[14] "The LORD thundered from heaven,
    And the Most High uttered His voice.
[15]   He sent out arrows and scattered them;
    Lightning bolts, and He vanquished them.
[16]   Then the channels of the sea were seen,
    The foundations of the world were uncovered,
    At the rebuke of the LORD,
    At the blast of the breath of His nostrils." 2 Sam 22:14-16 NKJV

Can you, my friend, speak this way? "Hast thou an arm like God? or canst thou thunder with a voice like him?" Job 40:9 KJV. Again, God's voice is *like* thunder in Psa 18:13. God is speaking in such a way. This is also in the New Testament, as when God speaks out of heaven and says to Jesus "I have both glorified *it*, and will glorify it again," KJV. But what did the people hear?

The people therefore, that stood by, and heard it, said that it thundered: others said, An angel spake to him. Jn 12:29 KJV

Thunder and hail and fire are also associated with God's judgment coming on men in Ex 9:23.

And Moses stretched forth his rod toward heaven: and the LORD sent thunder and hail, and the fire ran along upon the ground; and the LORD rained hail upon the land of Egypt. KJV

In Hannah's song she talks about those who oppose the Lord God, and here again we find thunder associated with final judgement.

"Those who contend with the LORD will be shattered;
    Against them He will thunder in the heavens,
    The LORD will judge the ends of the earth;
    And He will give strength to His king,
    And will exalt the horn of His anointed." 1 Sam 2:10 NASB

Again God made war on the Philistines with lightning and thunder.

And as Samuel was offering up the burnt offering, the Philistines drew near to battle against Israel: but the LORD thundered with a great thunder on that day upon the Philistines, and discomfited them; and they were smitten before Israel. 1 Sam 7:10 KJV

What will happen finally to the enemies of the Lord? Listen to Isaiah.

> [6] You will be punished by the LORD of hosts
>> With thunder and earthquake and great noise,
>> *With* storm and tempest
>> And the flame of devouring fire.
>
> [7]   The multitude of all the nations who fight against Ariel,
>> Even all who fight against her and her fortress,
>> And distress her,
>> Shall be as a dream of a night vision. Isa 29:6-7 NKJV

These are all consistent pictures of God drawing near to deliver His people

Hail and rocks falling on God's enemies from heaven is a uniform picture in God's word of God's judgment falling on those who oppose Him. Joshua's victory in Joshua chapter 10.

and to destroy those who oppose Him. All of this is very much in line with the pictures we see in the book of Revelation. The Bible does not tell us everything! There are secrets not discussed with us. It *does* tell us what we need to know, to do what we need to do, Deut 29:29. This is not a secret book, this book of Revelation. It is not a sealed book. What is written here is for all to know, if they will know, Rev 22:10. So what is written here is learning for all who will hear. John in our passage in Revelation 10 starts to write what is said by the seven thunders. He has heard what was said, it was information given to him, but some things are still not told to us.

> And when the seven thunders had uttered their voices, I was about to write: and I heard a voice from heaven saying unto me, Seal up those things which the seven thunders uttered, and write them not.
> Rev 10:4 KJV

Now ALL Scripture is inspired of God, 2Tim 3:16. We have everything we need for life and godliness if we use the whole Bible, if we *use* all Scripture including the Old Testament, and the New Testament and Revelation, 2Tim 3:16-17. John in his unique situation in Revelation evidently needed to know things we do not need to know, so he is told to not write these things.

Then the mighty angel has something to say, Rev 10:5. This holy angel from God tells when all of these things will happen, and he swears to the truth of these things with an oath by the Lord our God, Rev 10:6-7. What does he say? There is to be no more delay. No more delay about what? I think it is saying there will be no more delay in God finishing up His plan, and saving the saved and punishing the wicked.

Six angels have sounded their trumpets up through Revelation chapter 9. When the seventh angel is about to sound his trumpet, that means it is all over, Rev 10:7. We are looking, in what follows, at the end of a vision of the entire Christian age.

John is handed the little book, the book of prophecy. John is telling us these things. John is told to take the little book from the hands of the mighty angel which we saw at the beginning of this chapter. He takes the book, and he is told to eat it, to digest it, Rev 10:9a. He is told the result of digesting all of this material. The words will be sweet in your mouth, Rev 10:9b. They will be eloquent words, fit for the finest of speeches. But the message will be hard to take. In the end God's anger must fall on those who refuse to repent. It will taste pleasant, but will be hard on your stomach, Rev 10:9c.

Now John must tell us the hard message about what will come! John has to prophesy about a lot of peoples and nations and tongues and languages, Rev 10:11.

The time to get ready is now. There can be a point, even now, when God turns us over to our sins, as in Romans 1. There will definitely be a point when the gates of heaven are shut, and we begin to bang for entry from out of the darkness, Lk 13:24-28. Now is the time!

> again He designates a certain day, saying in David, *"Today," after such a long time, as it has been said:*
> *"Today, if you will hear His voice,*
> *Do not harden your hearts."* Heb 4:7 NKJV

Sparing the Temple of God, Rev 11:1-2

Now as we enter Revelation 11, John is having a vision of himself in heaven, and angels are revealing various things to him. He has heard six angels sound six trumpets, and has seen revealed various extraordinary things which will happen. Included are a meteorite and a star hitting the earth and working great devastation.

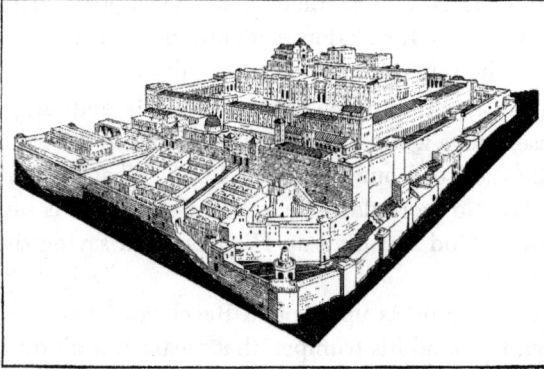

As the picture of this model illustrates, Solomon's temple was a huge public complex.

Then a strange thing happens. John is given a long measuring rod, one that is like a very long staff, a construction measuring rod. John is told to measure the temple of the Lord and its worshippers, Rev 11:1.

Now there are two words for temple in Greek. One word is *hieros* ἱερός, and this is a word which designates the entire grounds of the temple, where both priest and ordinary citizen can go. Now Jesus found men buying and selling on the temple grounds in Jn 2:14. When Jesus was teaching in the temple, He was teaching and preaching in the *hieros* ἱερός, the outer part of temple, as in Lk 19:47.

The other word for temple is the word *naos* ναός, a word for the sanctuary itself. This is the place where the priests themselves serve, where, for example, John the Baptist's father Zacharias went to serve in Lk 1:9, 21-22. Zacharias went into, not just the outer part of the temple, but into the inner sanctuary itself, the *naos*, where the angel Michael spoke to him.

There was the instance when Jesus was speaking of raising the temple of His body in Jn 2:19-21. The word He used in this instance was the word *naos* ναός. He was going to raise the inner part of the temple, He was going the raise the *naos* of His body.

Of course the true temple of the Lord is the church. It is people. Jesus' body is the true temple of the Lord, and the church is His body, Eph 1:22-23. Christ is of course the Savior of His body the church of our Lord, Eph 5:23. It goes without saying that death could not hold His body, Rom 6:9-10. We who are members of His body are the true temple of God, and that temple is holy.

[16] Know ye not that ye are the temple of God, and *that* the Spirit of God dwelleth in you? [17] If any man defile the temple of God, him shall

God destroy; for the temple of God is holy, which *temple* ye are.
1Cor 3:16-17 KJV

The Greek word for temple that is used here is the word *naos* ναός. So Christians, those who are truly owned by Christ, are the true inner temple of God, the *naos!*

> [19] What? know ye not that your body is the temple of the Holy Ghost *which is* in you, which ye have of God, and ye are not your own? [20] For ye are bought with a price: therefore glorify God in your body, and in your spirit, which are God's. 1Cor 6:19-20 KJV

Again the word temple here is *naos*. Christians are the true inner temple of God. God has made His people His dwelling place, His temple. As our human blood cleanses our human bodies, God has made for Himself a people cleansed and made holy by the blood of Jesus His Son. This is a temple built of people, a temple built of living stones, the true priests of the Lord.

> [4] Coming to Him *as to* a living stone, rejected indeed by men, but chosen by God and precious, [5] you also, as living stones, are being built up a spiritual house, a holy priesthood, to offer up spiritual sacrifices acceptable to God through Jesus Christ. [6] Therefore it is also contained in the Scripture,
>
> > *"Behold, I lay in Zion*
> > *A chief cornerstone, elect, precious,*
> > *And he who believes on Him will by no means be put to shame."*
>
> 1Pe 2:4-6 NKJV

True Christians are blood washed, blood bought, slaves of the Most High God, and priests dedicated to His service, Rom 6:17-18. Now there are a lot of people in the outer courts of God's temple, but they are not priests of the Most High.

John is directed to measure the inner parts of the temple. John is to measure the *naos* and the altar, Rev 11:1. He is specifically told to leave out the outer parts of the temple, to not measure those people, Rev 11:2a. Why is John told this? Because the outer courts of God's temple, those who are close, but not really priests of

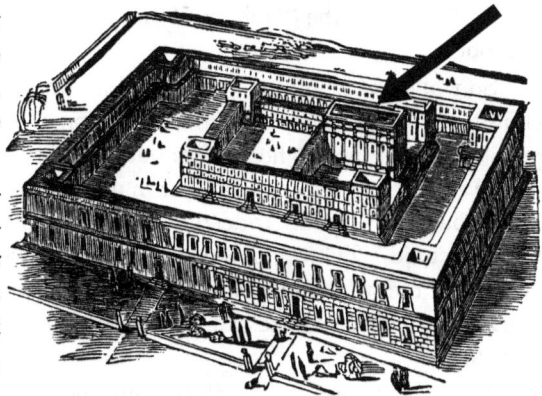

The "naos" of the temple, in contrast, is the much smaller "holy place" and the "holy of holies," (indicated by the arrow) where only the true priests of God can go.

the Most High, are to be given over to destruction!

> ... for it is given unto the Gentiles: **and the holy city** shall they tread under foot forty and two months. Rev 11:2b KJV

What would be the "holy city" of the Lord in Rev 11:2? It is the church. It is the heavenly Mount Zion, the mountain which cannot be touched, Heb 12:18.

> [22] But you have come to **Mount Zion** and to **the city of the living God, the heavenly Jerusalem**, to an innumerable company of angels, [23] to the general assembly **and church of the firstborn** *who are* registered in heaven, to God the Judge of all, to the spirits of just men made perfect, [24] to Jesus the Mediator of the new covenant, and to the blood of sprinkling that speaks better things than *that of* Abel. Heb 12:22-24 KJV (*bold and underline emphasis added*)

These are the ultimate spiritual answers. Remember,

> For the Law, since it has *only* a shadow of the good things to come and not the very form of things ... Heb 10:1 NASB

Some want us in these passages to forget the true, forget the spiritual, go back to the shadows. We should not do that. It is not that the Jews are not there in our present passage. Before these terrifying days of conflict they will have entered *en masse* the covenant of Jesus of Nazareth. They will also be part of those either protected or those given over to be "tread under foot." However, their conversion, which is in our time yet to happen, is a side story, which far precedes this present story.

Only the spiritual interpretation makes any sense in our present passage. In 70 AD the physical city of Jerusalem was captured and destroyed, *and the temple.* Yet there was no hope of the outer courts being taken, and not the *naos*, not the "Holy Place" and the "Holy of Holies." These *also* were taken and trodden under foot.

So what is the point of these terrible times to come? The outer parts of the church are to be given over to destruction. Those who visit, but are not true priests of God, those who profess but have not given their lives to Jesus, are given over to destruction, and "the nations" (plural not singular) will trample them down, Rev 11:2b. "Indeed, all who **desire** to live godly in Christ Jesus will be persecuted." 2Tim 3:12 NASB. Many will perish in those days who *desired* to do better, but who did not commit themselves *fully.* Though the number of Christians shall be as the sands of the seashore, only a remnant will be saved, Rom 9:27.

Now you know! It has always just been a remnant which will be saved. Many walk the path to destruction, Mtt 7:13; but only a few find the way to life. Only a remnant, Mtt 7:14. It isn't that they can't be saved. It is that they *won't* enter at the narrow gate, Mtt 7:13.

There has always been a remnant, as with Joseph and his brothers, from the descendants of Jacob, Gen 45:7. God promised He would protect a remnant of the Jews, 2 Kgs 19:30-31. That was promised. God will cleanse His people, and remove the blood from their teeth, and protect them, Zech 9:7. So also in Paul's day, "at this present time," there is only a remnant, Rom 11:5. The subject of a remnant is a major theme of Scripture from the beginning to the end, and of this grand theme we are merely touching the outlines, but it is also a factor in our text concerning the final days of conflict. The Lord knows those who are really His, 2Tim 2:19. God makes preparations to protect those who are really His.

Perhaps also forecasting this final scene, and/or perhaps an earlier difficult time, Isaiah says a destruction is determined which will result in righteousness.

> 20   And it shall come to pass in that day
>   *That* the remnant of Israel,
>   And such as have escaped of the house of Jacob,
>   Will never again depend on him who defeated them,
>   But will depend on the LORD, the Holy One of Israel.
> 21 The remnant will return, the remnant of Jacob,
>   To the Mighty God.
> 22   For though your people, O Israel, be as the sand of the sea,
>   A remnant of them will return;
>   **The destruction decreed shall overflow with righteousness.**
> Isa 10:20-22 NKJV (*bold emphasis added*)

There will be a highway for the remnant, Isa 11:16. To make yourself part of that true remnant, the *naos*, the inner temple of God, the specially protected ... ah, what an ambition!

> Now the just shall live by faith: but if *any man* draw back, my soul shall have no pleasure in him. Heb 10:38 KJV

Give yourself to God, completely, and do not hold back. Enter at the narrow gate. Walk in the narrow way. Give yourself to God and do not hold yourself back from His work, 2Tim 2:19.

Two Prophets to Come, Rev 11:3-19

John is having a vision of himself in heaven, and he is given a long measuring rod, one that is like a very long staff, Rev 11:1a. John is told to measure the temple of the Lord, Rev 11:1b. We have discussed those groups of the saints who will be protected in the desolations of the last times, the inner temple of the Lord, the true believers in Jesus Christ. But the outer courts of Christianity, those half-way believers and followers of the Christ, will be trampled down by the nations, Rev 11:2.

Then the Lord starts to talk of His two witnesses, Rev 11:3. It never specifically calls them "men." It does speak of them as if they were men. The Greek text uses the masculine form of nouns and pronouns to describe them, their clothing is mentioned, and they are testifying against a sinful world. It speaks of their being killed, and their corpses lying the street. The Lord says He will grant authority to his two witnesses. So these are authorized spokesmen of the Most High God Himself. These two witnesses are clearly prophets. We know they are authorized, for as the KJV says, they are given "power" by God. We know they are prophets because these two witnesses "prophesy" for twelve hundred and sixty days, Rev 11:3b. By the older Julian calendar (established by Julius Caesar in 46 BC), this would be exactly forty-two months, or three and a half years. (Each month in the calendar of that day was 30 days, with 5 extra days added to the year.) So here we are clearly confronted with the *fact* that late in the New Testament age, well after the first century, when things are going very badly, God will send two prophets to prophesy against the evil empire.

None of this really means that we do not have full revelation of the truth. We still have a message that will make us thoroughly furnished for every good work, 2 Tim 3:16-17. We still have the faith which was once for all delivered to the saints, Jude 3. God has still granted to us "everything pertaining to life and godliness," 2Pe 1:3. Those verses are sufficient to prove these points. The relation of these men to the New Covenant may be compared to the relationship of say Isaiah or Jeremiah to the Old Covenant. Could they add to or change Moses Law? No! Such was forbidden, Deut 4:2. Could they preach on the higher meaning of those texts, and tell men where disobedience was leading? Definitely so! So it will be with these New Testament witnesses who will prophecy for "twelve hundred and sixty days, clothed in sackcloth."

But Judgment Day is at hand, and Jesus is coming soon. These wicked men who destroy the church of the Lord, and seduce and persecute believers, *deserve* to be warned, and God sends men to warn the wicked. Now the two witnesses, the two prophets, have special powers from God. If anyone wants to try to kill these men, then fire comes down from heaven and destroys them, Rev 11:5, and they have the power to shut the skies so that it does not rain, Rev 11:6.

Now if you remember the story from the Old Testament, Elijah was able to call down fire from heaven. Remember he did it at the confrontation on Mount Carmel in 1 Kings. He prayed to the Lord for fire from God to light the altar he had built, and it happened, 1 Kgs 18:37-39. Elijah was also able to call down fire from heaven on his adversaries who were going to destroy him, more than once, as in 2Kgs 1:9-10.

Elijah was also able to "shut up the sky, so that rain will not fall." We are quoting the stated powers of the two prophets here, but it was first true of Elijah in history. The Apostle James commented on this.

> [17] Elijah was a man with a nature like ours, and he prayed earnestly that it would not rain; and it did not rain on the land for three years and six months. [18] And he prayed again, and the heaven gave rain, and the earth produced its fruit. Jas 5:17-18 NKJV

A number of things stand out in James comments. Elijah was just an ordinary man, but also one who was focused on God and His will, and his prayers had a powerful effect. Also, the period of time during which it did not rain in the time of Elijah *is exactly the same period of time for which these prophets are able to make it not rain!* It would appear that Ahab is a type of the man of lawlessness, the beast, and seemingly attempts will be made to get the beast to repent.

Besides, we should also remember that God said he would send "Elijah." If you remember, Elijah had not died like an ordinary man. In 2 Kings 2 it describes both Elijah and his successor Elisha walking along, both knowing that Elijah was soon to leave this world.

> [11] Then it happened, as they continued on and talked, that suddenly a chariot of fire *appeared* with horses of fire, and separated the two of them; and Elijah went up by a whirlwind into heaven.
> [12] And Elisha saw *it*, and he cried out, "My father, my father, the chariot of Israel and its horsemen!" So he saw him no more. And he took hold of his own clothes and tore them into two pieces.
> 2Kgs 2:11-12 NKJV

Later, some hundreds of years later, Malachi clearly warned that a final day of judgment was coming which would leave nothing for the evildoer.

> "For behold, the day is coming, burning like a furnace; and **all** the arrogant and **every** evildoer will be chaff; and the day that is coming will set them ablaze," says the LORD of hosts, "so that it will leave them neither root nor branch." Mal 4:1 NASB (*bold emphasis added*)

It is astonishing that so many scholars can read passages like this and not understand that such applies to the Second Coming. That is an amazing display of hardness of heart and of mind. This is *not* any ordinary day of judgement within history. Malachi says,

> "You will tread down the wicked, for they will be ashes under the soles of your feet on the day which I am preparing," says the LORD of hosts. Mal 4:3 NASB

That is plainly about the Second Coming of Christ for judgment. Additionally God said He was going to send someone before His second coming for judgment.

> "Behold, I am going to send you Elijah the prophet before the coming of the great and terrible day of the LORD. Mal 4:5 NASB

"Elijah" will be sent *before* that great and terrible day! It does say "Elijah," not just "like" Elijah. There is something about this text, and Elijah, which somehow makes Mal 4:5 entirely logical. But is this verse merely speaking super-literally so as to make a point? A man who did not die as ordinary men, is later to come back? Also of this Elijah it says,

> "He will restore the hearts of the fathers to their children and the hearts of the children to their fathers, so that I will not come and smite the land with a curse." Mal 4:6 NASB

Which seems to point to something *before* the end. Then John the Baptist was to be born in the first century BC, and the angel told his father Zacharias,

> "He will also go before Him in the spirit and power of Elijah, *'to turn the hearts of the fathers to the children,'* and the disobedient to the wisdom of the just, to make ready a people prepared for the Lord." Lk 1:17 NKJV

It is easy to see that Lk 1:17 matches Mal 4:6 in its intent. The angel does not say John the Baptist *will be* the prophet Elijah, but that he goes "in the spirit and the power of Elijah." It was natural then, that when the Pharisees asked John, "Are you Elijah?" that John would answer "I am not." Jn 1:21. He was not literally Elijah. Still later, after John's death, Jesus' disciples asked him,

> [11] And they asked Him, saying, "Why do the scribes say that Elijah must come first?"
> [12] Then He answered and told them, "Indeed, Elijah is coming first and restores all things. And how is it written concerning the Son of Man, that He must suffer many things and be treated with contempt?
> [13] But I say to you that Elijah has also come, and they did to him whatever they wished, as it is written of him." Mk 9:11-13 NKJV

So Jesus says the scribes were right, and Elijah did come first, and John the Baptist was this Elijah to come. His coming was in accord with what the angel said to Zacharias, that he was to turn the hearts of the fathers to the sons, and the disobedient to righteousness.

It is easily seen that in the intent John the Baptist matches the prophecy. Still, there are parts of the prophecy which do not quite seem to fit John the Baptist. God says by Malachi that this "Elijah" will come before "the great and dreadful day of the LORD," Mal 4:5 NKJV. Judgment day is plainly pictured in Mal 4:1-3, and indeed in *all* of Scripture that would definitely be a great and dreadful day. John the Baptist did come "before" that "day," yet he came *long before* that day, not at all close as is seemingly suggested in Malachi. Of course all of these are indications of a "type," a symbol in prophecy that has more than one fulfillment, much as it is with the "son" of David in 2 Samuel 7, that is fulfilled by both Solomon, and Jesus.

It is also easy to see that these prophets in Revelation 11 sound a little like Elijah, Rev 11:4-5. It does not say "Elijah," but they are like Elijah. Is it possible that Elijah and John the Baptist are *both* symbolic of these prophets? Elijah was able to call fire down from heaven on his enemies, as we have seen. In the same way it says of these two prophets,

> And if any man will hurt them, fire proceedeth out of their mouth, and devoureth their enemies: and if any man will hurt them, he must in this manner be killed. Rev 11:5 KJV

It must be said, though, that it is not clear whether this passage is speaking literally or metaphorically, but it seems to be metaphorical. It does seem to indicate that they *are* able to call down punishment and death on their enemies, with the result that no one dares to interfere with them.

Also these prophets are also a lot like Moses in Rev 11:6b. They have the power to turn waters to blood. If you will remember, Moses also had this power through the Lord his God. Pharaoh had hardened his heart, Ex 7:13. Evidently Pharaoh is symbolic of the god of this world, the beast which we will talk about later. The immediate result is that Moses turns the Nile to blood and all the fish die, and men cannot drink the water, Ex 7:20-21. These two prophets can also give these warnings of judgment as often as they like.

> ... and have power over waters to turn them to blood, and to smite the earth with all plagues, as often as they will. Rev 11:6 KJV

Remember also in Revelation 8 that one third of the sea was turned to blood, Rev 8:8-9. Also keep in mind that Moses cursed the land of Egypt with frogs, and flies, killed all of their livestock, and boils appeared on everyone, and a plague of huge hail, and of course hail is mentioned several times in the book of Revelation, for instance in Rev 8:7. These two prophets are a lot like Elijah, with a little bit of Moses mixed in. They are like Moses when he is trying to get the Pharaoh of this world to release God's people from their bondage. They have prophesied clothed in sackcloth, Rev 11:3, and they are the olives trees, and are the lamps of the Lord their God, Rev 11:4.

Then the ultimate adversary of God appears. The beast comes out of Sheol/Hades/the Abyss, the world of the dead. He "comes up out of the abyss," and makes war on the two witnesses, Rev 11:7 NASB. Remember that the abyss is where Jesus went for three days, as Paul tells us in Rom 10:6-7.

Finally these two witnesses finish their testimony to the sinful men on earth who will not listen to God or repent, and the beast kills the two prophets, the two witness, Rev 11:7. Their dead bodies will lie in the streets for three days. All the wicked men on earth will be happy for the deaths of the prophets at the hands of the beast, Rev 11:9-10. They are happy that no longer is anyone reminding them of the need to repent. The people will not allow them to be buried! So they lie in the streets of the great city that is symbolically called Sodom and Egypt. Now what city is "the great city" of Revelation? It is where Jesus was crucified, Rev 11:8b. You know what city that is. You know where Jesus was crucified. The great city of the book of Revelation is NOT the city of Rome.

Almost everyone tries to avoid the obvious impact of this verse, but it is still there. **It is plain**. It is told to us by symbolism, but it is not really obscure. *I cannot change it, nor can you!* Other Scriptures refer to earthly Jerusalem as Sodom. For instance in Isaiah 1 the prophet is talking to the rulers of Jerusalem.

> Hear the word of the LORD, ye rulers of Sodom; give ear unto the law of our God, ye people of Gomorrah. Isa 1:10 KJV

But it really goes all the way back to Moses, speaking of physical Israel.

> [32] For their vine *is* of the vine of Sodom, and of the fields of Gomorrah: their grapes *are* grapes of gall, their clusters *are* bitter: [33] Their wine *is* the poison of dragons, and the cruel venom of asps. Deut 32:32 KJV

This theme continues in the other prophets.

> I have seen also in the prophets of Jerusalem an horrible thing: they commit adultery, and walk in lies: they strengthen also the hands of evildoers, that none doth return from his wickedness: they are all of them unto me as Sodom, and the inhabitants thereof as Gomorrah. Jer 23.14 KJV

It is a theme in Scripture which cannot be avoided. Paul says of such language that they are an allegory of two covenants.

> [24] This is allegorically speaking, for these *women* are two covenants: one *proceeding* from Mount Sinai bearing children who are to be slaves; she is Hagar. [25] Now this Hagar is Mount Sinai in Arabia and corresponds to the present Jerusalem, for she is in slavery with her children. [26] But the Jerusalem above is free; she is our mother. Gal 4:24-26 NASB

The reader should be reminded that it is *not* the job of an expositor to explain *how* all of this will be, or necessarily *why* it is. Rather the job is merely tell you what it says, even if it seems odd or out of place. Often later events or study will make the incongruous seem apropos. Suffice it to say that there is a relationship of some sort between those clinging to a law of slavery and the great city which makes war on the saints, and that those who would belong to God must come out of her (Jer 52:6, Rev 18:4), in order to save themselves!

Then after 3-1/2 days they rise from the dead, Rev 11:11, and God calls them to heaven, Rev 11:12. Is this part of the resurrection at the second coming of Christ? I do not know. And a great earthquake came, Rev 11:13, and a great part of the great city is thrown down.

Then it plainly describes the end of the world.

> [18] And the nations were angry, and **thy wrath is come, and the time of the dead, that they should be judged,** and that thou shouldest give reward unto thy servants the prophets, and to the saints, and them that fear thy name, small and great; and shouldest destroy them which

destroy the earth. [19] And the temple of God was opened in heaven, and there was seen in his temple the ark of his testament: and there were lightnings, and voices, and thunderings, and an earthquake, and great hail. Rev 11:18-19 KJV

We will come back to these two witnesses one more time in a later passage in the book of Revelation. Terrible times will come in the last days, and here are some of the details. Are you ready? Whose side are you on? Can "your side" win in these circumstances?

VII. The Woman Above, the Dragon, and the Harlot, Revelation 12-14

Now we begin looking at the behind the scenes struggles which lead to the end of this universe. These are literally cosmic battles which affect all men.

The War in Heaven, Revelation 12

As we enter Revelation 12 we are entering a new section in the book of Revelation. The early chapters of the book of Revelation have been describing what the Christian Age looks like from the outside. It is what people see on the surface. First we saw how Jesus views His churches in this world. Then we saw a scene in heaven of the Lord Our God who rules over all. Then we had seven seals which were opened, and then seven trumpets of warning which were sounded, showing us how things look from the outside. We might even say, how things might look on the evening news, without relating events to our sins and significant national and religious happenings. The last part of Revelation 11, had the seventh trumpet sound, and the time of God's wrath came upon men, and the time to judge all men, Rev 11:18. Now comes a new section, and we get a look at the behind the scenes struggles of the Christian Age.

Then a great sign appears in heaven. The symbolism is of a woman clothed with the sun, and the moon under her feet, and a crown of twelve stars, Rev 12:1. Notice that this is a sign in heaven, and also the struggle continues on this earth. This woman was about to give birth to a child, Rev 12:2. Once more, you and I cannot get around this symbolism. It is clear and it is here. It is possible to take this woman as Mary the mother of Jesus. It is possible, and we might say that in one way it seems natural, at least to us as now conditioned by over a thousand years of history.

On the other hand, parts of the story told in Revelation 12 do not seem to fit Mary and Joseph, as least as far as we know. It does however seem to fit the people of God in our age. This woman's children also include all those "which keep the commandments of God," Rev 12:17 KJV. Now those who are led by the Holy Spirit of God are called "sons of God" in Rom 8:14. We are all sons of God through faith, Gal 3:26. Those who are peacemakers are called sons of God in Mtt 5:9. But *if* all men in the Lord are in some sense the sons of Mary the mother of Jesus, this is the only Scripture which speaks of it.

Instead I would suggest that the woman represents God's Holy people bringing forth the Christ at the proper time. "Jerusalem ... which is the mother of us all," Gal 4:26 KJV. Remember? We will read further, and you see what you think. After that, if you choose to interpret the woman in the vision in Revelation 12 another way, it is still true that all Christians are those "who keep the commandments of God," Rev 12:17.

After this another sign appears "in heaven." A red dragon in heaven, Rev

12:3. The "great red dragon" in verse 3 is the "great dragon" in Rev 12:9, "that old serpent, called the Devil, and Satan, ..." KJV. The devil was originally in heaven, and we see him appearing before God in heaven in Job 1:6-7. We have seen from Ezekiel 28 that the devil was at one time a mighty and good angel in heaven, Ezek 28:14; but then this mighty and beautiful angel sinned, Ezek 28:15. This caused this once beautiful creature to morph into what is a giant fiery lizard, and who has seven heads and ten horns, Rev 12:3.

We saw earlier that a beast or a monster in the book of Daniel is often an evil empire, as for instance in Dan 7:2-8. We are given examples of beasts or monsters as representing formidable human empires, such as the empires of Babylon, Medo-Persia, Greece, and Rome, and maybe something more! The horns often indicate individual rulers, like Alexander the Great, who is the single horn in Dan 8:8a-b. When Alexander died, he was replaced by four of his generals, represented by "four conspicuous *horns,*" who then divided up his empire, Dan 8:8c. Heads, as we all know, often represent the "head," the master/ruler, of something, and so also it is with Scripture. Diadems or crowns often indicate a right to rule, as we know and see throughout Scripture and in most of world literature. If you need to review these concepts, and see them in context and in action, look again in the earlier sections of "Prelude," and "Precursor Conflicts."

So there is precedent within the Word of God for the imagery we see in Revelation 12, which is in this case applied to Satan, the great dragon, and his kingdom of this world. Of this dragon, it tells us, "his tail drew the third part of the stars of heaven, and did cast them to the earth:" KJV.

The woman in Revelation 12 is about to give birth to a male child who is going to rule all nations with a rod of iron. You might think here of God's saints bringing forth the Messiah, or indeed of Mary about to bring Him forth. Mary, we should be able to see, fits at least part of this symbolism. The dragon is ready to devour this male child if he is able. The devil fails, and the male child is caught up to God in heaven. In so short a span of words is summarized both the attempts of Herod the Great to kill the child, and later attempts of the Pharisees and Sadducees and the Sanhedrin to quash this Messiah, and failing; and the Ruler's ascent to His Father in Acts 1. *Think about this one verse summary of Jesus' life in Rev 12:5, when you are trying to understand how prophecy works!*

Then it pictures an ongoing fight against the woman; a battle that does not mirror the life of Mary. The summation of the struggle leads to its climax at the end of our present age. "The woman" flees into the wilderness in verse 6. The Greek word is *erāmos* ἔρημος, or more literally the desert, as in the NIV, and *Weymouth New Testament in Modern Speech*, 1913, and others. Mary and Joseph we should note, did *not* flee to the desert, the wilderness, but to Egypt, and it was out of Egypt, not out of the wilderness, that they were called, Mtt 2:15. *We should always keep in mind that prophetic symbolism does not follow the primary rules of symbolism in English, and such double meanings and sliding from one subject to another, are common in Biblical prophetic literature.* These are differences from common English useages.

The woman flees to this desert, this uninhabited place, this wilderness if you will, for the same length of time that the two witnesses prophesy in Rev 11:3, and for the same amount of time that the holy city is trampled underfoot by the nations in Rev 11:2, for 1,260 days, Rev 12:6. It was covered in Revelation 11 about the *naos*, the true inner temple of God made of people, being spared from being trampled underfoot by the nations. I am trying to make sure you see all of the associations. This 3-1/2 year period does not fit Mary and Joseph, as far as we know. It does fit the periods of trouble described in Revelation 11, and this **IS** describing a period of trouble, and the sparing of the temple sanctuary (the *naos*). The children of the woman also are protected during these overwhelming conflicts. **This is a clear message** for these times of trial, and is consistent with the rest of Revelation and God's prophetic Word as a whole, especially Revelation 11. Still we must ask, is a distinction being made here between the woman and the rest of her children? It does seem so.

There is a war in heaven pictured according to Rev 12:7. Satan at one time appeared regularly before the Lord our God in heaven, as pictured in Job chapters 1 and 2, and other places. Now there is war. This war began *before* Adam and Eve were tempted in the garden. In this war Satan took away a third of the stars of heaven in Rev 12:4a. Stars represent angels in Rev 1:20, and other passages in the Old Testament, as in Job 38:7. So this evil angel revolted against God, and got a third of the angels of heaven to follow him. Michael and his angels threw Satan, "the dragon and his angels," out of heaven, Rev 12-7-8. Evidently this was about to happen as Jesus was going to the cross.

> And he said unto them, I beheld Satan as lightning fall from heaven. Lk 10:18 KJV

In at least one sense, it seems to have happened at the cross, that Satan and his angels are thrown down to earth, Rev 12:9. Thrown down to the "earth"! There is a phrase for you. As far as the ancients were concerned the universe was divided into heaven and earth, and the material creation was often thought of as "earth." We have similar concepts involved in the Old Testament Hebrew "earth" *erets* אֶרֶץ, Gen 1:1, and the New Testament Greek *gā* γῆ. In the NASB the Hebrew earth *erets* אֶרֶץ, is translated the earth, land: —country (2), earth (164), Earth (1), earthly (1), ground (20), land (46), and soil (16) times in the NASB. "God called the dry land earth," Gen 1:10. The Greek *gā* γῆ, is translated country (2), earth (164), Earth (1), earthly (1), ground (20), land (46), and soil (16) times in the NASB.

Both the Hebrew and the Greek samplings taken here are from the *New American Standard Exhaustive Concordance of the Bible*, General Editor Robert L. Thomas, Th. D., the Lockman Foundation. This is not meant as viewing the NASB as authoritative, but only trying to give the English reader a reference for the typical span of the translation of these words.

It would appear that quite often terms for the earth are used to contrast the material creation to what we call heaven. Scripture does, however, reflect an understanding that the throne of God is beyond even the material bodies of our "heavens." So when it is speaking of Jesus going to the throne of God beyond everything material, is says,

> He that descended is the same also that ascended up **far above all heavens**, that he might fill all things. Eph 4:10 KJV (*emphasis added*)

Similarly we see in Mtt 24:35 KJV,

> Heaven and earth shall pass away, but my words shall not pass away.

I think that in our present passage it is by metonymy clearly contrasting this material universe (the "earth"), with the ultimate residence of God "far above all heavens." Satan and his angels are thrown out of the place of the throne of God to this material universe.

Now the salvation and strength and the kingdom have come, according to Rev 12:10. This is the first century. Satan no longer has access to heaven to accuse us as in Job chapters 1 and 2 (cf Rev 12:10). Now we are able to overcome by the blood of Christ, Rev 12:11. Be happy heaven! Woe to the earth, because the devil knows he has but a short time left, Rev 12:12.

Now Satan persecutes the church, Rev 12:13. Plainly it is not speaking about Satan persecuting Mary, after he can no longer get a hold of Jesus! But the church is able to flee into the wilderness/desert, as indeed will later happen, for 1,260 days, or 3-1/2 years, or as it calls it here, "for a time and times and half a time," Rev 12:14 KJV.

> Therefore, behold, I will allure her, and bring her into the wilderness, and speak comfortably unto her. Hos 2:14 KJV

This is the protection of the temple sanctuary, the *naos*, of Rev 11:1. The devil then tries to destroy this remnant, but the earth helps the woman escape.

> And the earth helped the woman, and the earth opened her mouth, and swallowed up the flood which the dragon cast out of his mouth. Rev 12:16 KJV

How ironic for those who depend on this material world. Even "nature," if you will, helps take care of God's people when they have to flee from the ultimate persecutions at the end of our present age. Then the devil turns to make war on the rest "which keep the commandments of God, and have the testimony of Jesus Christ," Rev 12:17 KJV.

The Monster Comes, Rev 13:1-6

We saw the great dragon in Revelation chapter 12. The great dragon is Satan, and the great dragon was thrown out of heaven, as we see in Rev 12:9. The great dragon tried to destroy the Christ, Rev 12:3-4, but he was unable to do it. Then we saw the dragon making war on what is called in Scripture the church, those who keep the commands of God, Rev 12:17.

In Revelation 13 we see the dragon standing on the seashore, "on the sand of the seashore," Rev 13:1a NASB. It would appear his abode is now the abyss under the seas, and he stands on the seashore.

Perhaps you remember from the book of Isaiah that Satan is associated with a sea creature called Leviathan. The prophet treats this sea creature as a moral creature, an evil moral creature who deserves to be punished, and he says that God has appointed a day to punish him.

> In that day the LORD will punish Leviathan the fleeing serpent,
> With His fierce and great and mighty sword,
> Even Leviathan the twisted serpent;
> And He will kill the dragon who *lives* in the sea. Isa 27:1 NASB

Here Leviathan is also called a serpent, just like in Revelation 12, and he says that this dragon lives in the sea, Isa 27:1d. There are other Old Testament references, but this will do for now. If you remember Revelation 12 it pictures Satan as being cast down to the earth, and here in Isaiah 27 it pictures him as living in the sea, and in Rev 13:1 we see him coming to the sea shore. Then a monster comes up out of the sea.

> And I ... saw a beast rise up out of the sea, having seven heads and ten horns, and upon his horns ten crowns, and upon his heads the name of blasphemy. Rev 13:1 KJV

I have heard all sorts of supposedly scholarly arguments against characterizing this "beast" as a "monster." The Greek word is *thārion* θηρίον, and is variously translated as "beast (38), beasts (2), creature (2), wild beasts (3)." Luow and Nida (*Greek-English Lexicon of the New Testament Based on Semantic Domains*, 1988, 1989, United Bible Societies, New York, NY) says it includes "any living creature, not including man—'animal.'" Liddell and Scott says it is about "savage beasts," something that is wild and mean. In context I am not impressed with our many modern commentators in their dogmatism here. In modern everyday English of our time, any creature coming up out of the ocean that has ten horns and seven heads, we would call a monster. Period. This bizarre beast is, in context, regardless of any normal classical usage, is what we would call a monster in modern English. We also use the English word "monster" to apply to people. Dictionary definitions call a monster "an imaginary creature that is typically large, ugly, and frightening." and also,

• an inhumanly cruel or wicked person: *he was an unfeeling, treacherous monster.*

• often humorous a person, typically a child, who is rude or badly behaved: *Christopher is only a year old, but already he is a **little monster.***

• a thing or animal that is excessively or dauntingly large: *this is a **monster of** a book, almost 2,000 pages* | [as modifier] : *a monster 120-mm gun.*

• a congenitally malformed or mutant animal or plant.

New Oxford American Dictionary

All of which fits our subject as it is pictured here. Then let us revisit another subject. Almost all of our advisors want us to take the book of Revelation in isolation from the rest of Bible.

As I look back on those whom I have looked to for instruction on the Word of God, and on the Book of Revelation in specific, almost all of them wanted us to take the Book of Revelation by itself. Sometimes this was only by implication. Don't put it together with 2 Thessalonians 2. Don't put it with the Gospels. Don't put it with the Old Testament, and especially don't put it with Daniel or really any Old Testament prophet. Moreover, don't use your head and say, that seems to be the same thing talked about in this passage or another passage. It does not seem to matter what your interpretation is, just treat it in isolation, and you are not allowed to really link this to *anything else you read in Scripture.* Treat this all as mystifying, isolated topics, having nothing to do with *anything* either Scriptural or secular or in life!

I cannot think of anything more fatal to understanding than following this approach. Neither the Book of Revelation nor any other book of the Bible should be taken in isolation. Either intentionally or unintentionally, most of our advisors on prophecy seem determined to keep us from any real understanding of the book!

Now this monster has ten crowns and seven heads, and has many blasphemous names. We earlier looked at a beast or a monster in the book of Daniel as often being an evil empire, as for instance in Dan 7:2-6. Horns often indicated individual rulers, like in Alexander the Great, who is the single horn in Dan 8:8a-b, 21. We have given other examples which will not be discuss again here.

Now this monster comes up out of the sea. That may indicate merely that it comes from Satan in the sea (which would fit), or it might indicate that this is a great sea borne power, a great naval power. Now empires are described as beasts in the book of Daniel, and this empire/coalition/group has seven heads, seven centers of direction or instruction, Rev 13:1. The heads would do the thinking. This group has ten kings, ten diadems involved in its rule, Rev 13:1. This small base, the ten horns/kings would do the actual ruling, wield the actual power. The heads would do the thinking. The blasphemous names would mean that this group is making claims that only the True and Living God should make!

This beast is like a leopard, and its feet are like a bear, and its mouth is like a lion, Rev 13:2a-c. If you remember the book of Daniel, Babylon is described as being like a lion in Dan 7:4, and Persia is described as being like a bear in Dan 7:5, and Greece is described as being like a leopard in Dan 7:6. So this monster group is sort of like Greece and Persia and Babylon, all rolled into one. It is a Satanic coalition or empire or alliance! It is hard to know what to call it in context.

> ... and the dragon gave him his power, and his seat, and great authority
> Rev 13:2d KJV

The dragon stood on the seashore, and the dragon, Satan, gives this dragon-like group his own throne, and great authority. It may imply that it is a great naval power, but does not clearly say that here. Satan is allowed a lot of authority here on earth. He is described as the god of this age.

> In whom the god of this world hath blinded the minds of them which believe not, lest the light of the glorious gospel of Christ, who is the image of God, should shine unto them. 2Cor 4:4 KJV

We can see here that Satan is able to blind many men, and "mind control" will come up later! Now the "heads" would be the seven men who direct this monstrous group. Then one of these "heads" of this entity is killed.

> And I saw one of his heads as it were wounded to death; ...
> Rev 13:3a KJV

The system, this monstrosity coming out of the "sea" is called a "beast," a monster. Further, this individual "head" of Satan and his people, Rev 13:3, is also called **"the** beast" in the same verse and the following verses. This singular "him" is the personification of this system, and is the personification of this "red dragon having seven heads and ten horns." These are evidently synchronous traits of their evil spiritual master, his organization, and this man. He is a king or a high level leader for Satan.

Literally the Greek says that he is slaughtered to death (*esphagamenān eis thanaton*, ἐσφαγμένην εἰς θάνατον), Rev 13:3. The KJV basically says he receives a wound unto death. The NKJV says "mortally wounded," that is to say, wounded to death. The NIV says he had "a fatal wound," that is to say a wound that kills. We could go on.

But the fatal wound is healed, Rev 13:3b.

This is basically a contradiction. If you or I receive a fatal wound, then we are dead, and if we recover from a wound, then it was not fatal. **Period!** So what does this mean? It is the same with Jesus. One of heads of this monstrous evil empire is killed, and is raised from the dead! *Remember?* He comes with lying signs and wonders, 2Thes 2:9.

This man is the opposite of the Christ. The whole world is in awe of this one who is killed and then raised from the dead, and they follow him, Rev 13:3c. Because of these things they worship the dragon, Satan. **We are talking about the "the whole earth" worshipping Satan, vs 3.** Also they worship this individual beast as god, Rev 13:4. Who can fight against someone that you cannot kill? Everyone is in awe. This man is indeed a monster!

And the parallel: the sword strikes the worthless shepherd in Zechariah.

> "Woe to the worthless shepherd
> 　　Who leaves the flock!
> 　　A sword will be on his arm
> 　　And on his right eye!" Zech 11:17a-b NASB

But the "sword" is symbolic of violent death in Zechariah when it speaks of Jesus dying.

> Awake, O sword, against my shepherd, and against the man that is my fellow, saith the LORD of hosts: smite the shepherd, and the sheep shall be scattered: and I will turn mine hand upon the little ones.
> Zech 13:7 KJV

This passage is of course quoted of Jesus in Mtt 26:31, and again in Mark. Again the sword is symbolic of violent death in Psalm 22, when again it speaks of Jesus dying.

> Deliver Me from the **sword,**
> 　　My precious *life* from the power of the dog.
> Psa 22:20 NKJV (*bold emphasis added*)

The sword is symbolic of violent death when it says of the civil power, it "does not bear the **sword** for nothing,"Rom 13:4 NASB.

So the worthless shepherd is killed, and raised from the dead, "his fatal wound was healed," but they will not be able to restore all of his functions.

> "...   A sword will be on his arm
> 　　And on his right eye!
> 　　His arm will be totally withered
> 　　And his right eye will be blind." Zech 11:17b-c NASB

It will be, so to speak, a Satanic miracle of great proportions, but defective in its full effect. It will be effective enough to deceive most, and effective enough to *almost* deceive the elect.

> For there shall arise false Christs, and false prophets, and shall shew great signs and wonders; insomuch that, if *it were* possible, they shall deceive the very elect. Mtt 24:24 KJV

In Daniel, seemingly using Antiochus Epiphanes as a type, it says it is by no human hand that he will be killed.

... But he will be broken without *human* means.
Dan 8:25 NKJV (*bold emphasis added*)

Literally "without hand" KJV. Does he really die? Daniel 11 tells where he will die, near Jerusalem. And Habakkuk tells when this will happen. When he goes to oppress the church of God!

> [13] **You** went forth for the salvation of Your people,
>   For the salvation of Your anointed.
>   **You** struck the head of the house of the evil
>   To lay him open from thigh to neck.   Selah.
> [14] **You pierced with his own spears**
>   The head of his throngs.
>   **They stormed in to scatter us;**
>   Their exultation *was* like those
>   Who devour the oppressed in secret.

Hab 3:13-14 NASB (*bold emphasis added*)

"Without human agency," but "with his own spears," NASB. Is he in truth dead? When Jesus describes false christs, He seems to call him a corpse in Mtt 24:28.

> "Wherever the corpse is, there the vultures will gather." NASB

But it also says he is be thrown "alive" into hell in Rev 19:20. Clearly he seems to have been truly killed, yet to have survived. He makes tremendous claims.

> [5] And there was given unto him a mouth speaking great things and blasphemies; and power was given unto him to continue forty *and* two months. [6] And he opened his mouth in blasphemy against God, to blaspheme his name, and his tabernacle, and them that dwell in heaven. Rev 13:5-6 KJV

Notice again the period of time during which this empty braggart rages against God. It is forty-two months that he rules by God's allowance. That is the same as the forty-two months that the outer courts are trampled underfoot by the nations, and the same as the 1260 days that the two prophets prophesy against men's wickedness in Revelation 11, and the same as the "time, times, and half a time" that the "woman" flees into the wilderness. Only those who are lost will worship the beast, Rev 13:8.

Three and a Half Years of Severe Trouble, Rev 13:7-18

This monster is described as being killed and yet brought back from the dead, Rev 13:3a. The fatal wound was healed, Rev 13:3b. This man dies and is raised from the dead! Remember it was discussed in Revelation 11 that the beast comes out of Sheol, the world of the dead. He comes out of the abyss and makes war on the two witnesses, Rev 11:7. Remember that the abyss ("the deep," Rom 10:6-7 KJV) is where Jesus went for us for three days.

This very stressful three and a half years is described in a lot of ways. It is described as "time, times, and half a time," in passages like Rev 12:14. That is the time of trouble, and that is the time that the church is protected in the wilderness. It is described as forty-two months in passages like Rev 13:5. Forty-two months would be three and a half years. It is called 1260 days in passages like Rev 11:2-3. In the first century the general calendar used was not as accurate as ours. All twelve months had exactly 30 days, and 12 X 30 = 360 days in a year. So three and half years is 3-1/2 X 360 = 1260. So 1260 days is 42 months of 30 days each. Every effort is made in the text to make sure we understand that this is a literal 3-1/2 years, years of serious trouble for the church, world wide, *and also for "the world."* Not only the true church, but also all of the people who sort of half-way follow Jesus, or at least profess His name, will be oppressed. If anyone even only just "desires" to live godly in Jesus Christ, they will be persecuted, 2Tim 3:12.

The beast has some sort of rising from the dead, but they will not be able to completely heal him, Zech 11:17. Still the world will say, Who can fight against the beast? Rev 13:4. And the whole world will worship him.

The beast will make war on the church, world wide. It is called "the saints," in Rev 13:7. The word "saint" is the Greek word *hagios* ἅγιος, which means those who have been purified, those who have been washed in the blood of Jesus Christ for salvation. It means those who have been set aside for God's work! Have you been set aside for God's work? The book of Romans was written to those "called *to be* saints," Rom 1:7 KJV, as was the Corinthians, 1Cor 1:2 NKJV. It does not mean you are perfect, but it does means that you are owned by the Lord, and you have been cleansed by His blood. When Paul writes about giving to the Lord, he says, "Now concerning the collection for the saints," 1Cor 16:1.

The beast will fight and "overcome" the saints, Rev 13:7. He will "conquer" them as it puts it in the ESV and the NIV. That is what this word means. The Greek word used is *nikaō* νικάω, to have the victory. He will be victorious over the church, and he receives authority over all men, Rev 13:7. All men on earth will worship him.

> And all that dwell upon the earth shall worship him, whose names are not written in the book of life of the Lamb slain from the foundation of the world. Rev 13:8 KJV

Everyone who is not saved. The Lord knows those who are His, 2Tim 2:19.

Similarly, when speaking of the end of the world in Daniel 12, the angel says in the last part of Daniel 12:7,

> ... that *it shall be* for a time, times, and half *a time*; and when the power of the holy people has been completely shattered, all these *things* shall be finished. Dan 12:7 NKJV

I think it is talking about the same 3-1/2 years, and the power of the holy people being shattered. It is proper here to make some observations.

Necessary Conditions: A World-wide Revolt Against God.

This is about the man talked about in 2 Thessalonians 2, otherwise called "the beast."

> [3] Let no one in any way deceive you, for *it will not come* unless the **apostasy** comes first, and the man of lawlessness is revealed, the son of destruction, [4] who opposes and exalts himself above every so-called god or object of worship, so that he takes his seat in the temple of God, displaying himself as being God. 2Thes 2:3-4 NASB (*bold emphasis added*)

The word that is translated "apostasy" or "falling away" is the Greek word *apostasia* ἀποστασία, but it has a stronger meaning than the English word apostasy. It has the idea of conscious defection, and a revolt against God. Louw and Nida's, *Greek-English Lexicon of the New Testament Based on Semantic Domains*, says that it means.

> **to rise up in open defiance of authority,** with the **presumed intention to overthrow it** or to act in complete opposition to its demands — 'to rebel against, to revolt, to engage in insurrection, rebellion. (*bold emphasis added*)

It has a far stronger idea than of merely drifting away. This man will be preceded by a world-wide moral revolt against *all* authority. There will be an **open revolt** against God and ***ALL*** authority which will precede the coming of this man of lawlessness. Sexual lawlessness is also implied in Revelation 17. This man will be against ***ALL*** other gods, and anything else men might try to put before him. Everyone needs to listen to what God says about these things.

> If anyone is to go into captivity,
>> into captivity he will go.
> If anyone is to be killed with the sword,
>> with the sword he will be killed. ... Rev 13:10 NIV

Let me say though that I do not think most translations really give the sense of verse 10. It is a variation on the theme of Jer 15:2.

> "And it shall be that when they say to you, 'Where should we go?' then you are to tell them, 'Thus says the LORD:

> "Those *destined* for death, to death;
> And those *destined* for the sword, to the sword;
> And those *destined* for famine, to famine;
> And those *destined* for captivity, to captivity." NASB

So what does this mean? If God means for you to go into captivity, then you will go into captivity. If God means for you to be killed, then you will be killed! It is saying that God is in control even in these terrible times, and you cannot end up in prison or in a prison camp, unless God wants you to go to a prison camp! You cannot end up being killed, unless God wants you to be die at that time. God is still in control even when terrible things are happening. God looks after His own,

> Behold, the eye of the LORD *is* upon them that fear him, upon them that hope in his mercy; Psa 33:18 KJV

Once again,

> The angel of the LORD encampeth round about them that fear him, and delivereth them. Psa 34:7 KJV

There are many other such passages. God looks after His own, even in these terrible times which are to come. We need to be faithful, and patient, and accept those things we cannot change.

> ... This calls for patient endurance and faithfulness on the part of the saints. Rev 13:10c NIV

That is a superb paraphrase of the clear intent of the end of this verse.

Then another beast comes.

> And I beheld another beast coming up out of the earth; and he had two horns like a lamb, and he spake as a dragon. Rev 13:11 KJV

He is from below, from the earth, not from heaven. Notice the comparison of coming from above or coming from below in James.

> [14] But if you have bitter jealousy and selfish ambition in your heart, do not be arrogant and *so* lie against the truth. [15] This wisdom is not that which comes down from above, but is earthly, natural, demonic. [16] For where jealousy and selfish ambition exist, there is disorder and every evil thing. [17] But the wisdom from above is first pure, then peaceable, gentle, reasonable, full of mercy and good fruits, unwavering, without hypocrisy. [18] And the seed whose fruit is righteousness is sown in peace by those who make peace. Jas 3:14-18 NASB

This second beast in some ways looks as if it is just an innocent lamb, but it talks like Satan himself. He acts as a priest of the first beast, and makes everyone worship the first beast, who was killed and had some sort of resurrection, Rev 13:12. He even makes fire come down from heaven, Rev 13:13. Such is talked about in 2Thes 2:9.

> *Even him*, whose coming is after the working of Satan with all power
> and signs and lying wonders,

Satan is allowed in these final days to support his special man with powerful illusions and fantasies of authority. Abraham Lincoln is supposed to have
said, "You can fool some of the people most of the time, and all of the people,
some of the time; but you cannot fool all of the people all of the time." However,
this second monster fools, or suborns, everyone on earth, and they make an
image of the first monster, Rev 13:14.

More than that, they are able to make the image come to life, Rev 13:15a.
This special image is able to breath and speak as if it is alive. If anyone will not
worship the image, they are to be killed, Rev 13:15b.

Everyone must receive a mark of identification as belonging to this beast.
This mark will be on their right hand or on their forehead, Rev 13:16. *This is
NOT something invented by premillennialists.* This is Scripture. Absolutely *everyone*
has to have such a mark world-wide, or they cannot buy *anything* or sell *anything*,
Rev 13:17.

> And that no man might buy or sell, save he that had the mark, or the
> name of the beast, or the number of his name.

Necessary Conditions: Control of Commerce World-Wide.

If there is not comprehensive control of *all* commerce *prior* to this man coming to power, then it would not be possible to *require* and *enforce* this condition,
that all men have the mark of the beast on their right-hand or their forehead.

It would seem that *before* all of these things can happen, there must be absolute or very near absolute control of *every* transaction. The purchase of every
stick of chewing gum, every transaction for parking a car, every real estate purchase, every purchase of a hamburger or a hotdog, or of a shirt or shoes, *even
from individual to individual!* This is a daunting requirement, but necessary in order for the text to be reasonably possible. It would seem this level of control will
only come into play very near the end.

Necessary Conditions: Mystery Babylon must agree to a ruling false god.

There has not been any discussion yet about Mystery Babylon, but if world
trade is involved, she who is the master of these things must agree in order to
coordinate the compliance. This has not been proven yet from the book of Revelation. This is an involved subject, and we will return to it. You should keep
this comment in mind, and what I have said will become more apparent as we
go along.

*Necessary Conditions: God must **allow** this to happen.*

God has to think that the world is worthy to be turned over to such a monster, and that His saints are worthy of such a test. These are complicated subjects,
but I think such ideas are implicit in the story we see here. We should always
remember that the best way to avoid many tests is to be of such character that
such things are not necessary to prove us. A good example is the church at Philadelphia, which we have already studied, Rev 3:10.

On the other side of the coin, if we do not really *want to* serve or glorify
God, He may well turn us over to our sins, as is graphically depicted in Romans 1. God holds these things back until the proper time.

> [6] And now you know what is restraining, that he may be revealed in his
> own time. [7] For the mystery of lawlessness is already at work; only He
> who now restrains will do so until He is taken out of the way.
> 2Thes 2:6-7 NKJV

At the proper time God will allow such things to happen. When it is entirely proper. Of course, that has implications for both the world and the church.

This NEVER happened in the early centuries after Christ.

In the conflicts of the early history of Christianity, you had to offer incense
to Caesar, and you had to say, "Caesar is Lord." The magistrates would even
give you the incense to offer. After that, they would give you a certificate like the
one on the next page, and it was *not* necessary for buying food or buying anything or selling anything. The Caesars are only a type, a symbol, a prototype,
of the ultimate beast who will rule the entire world.

There was NEVER a "mark" which EVERYONE **had** to have.

In the early centuries there was plenty of pressure on the church to con-
form to the pagan world in which they lived. Many Christians were put to death
over a period of centuries. Even so, there was never any special mark of any
deity which everyone had to have before they could sell any goods or go to the
grocery store. This clearly has NOT happened, *yet!* With so much of prophecy
already happening, probably many thought that a universal mark might come
at any time, but it never happened! Such things are signs of either false prophecy,
or of a type/symbol/pattern in history.

This "Man" Will be Seated in "the Temple" as "God"!

Paul tells us this man will suppress the worship of anyone or anything beside himself.

> Who opposeth and exalteth himself above all that is called God, or that is worshipped; ... 2Thes 2:4a KJV

So this "man" (2Thes 2:3) clearly portrays himself as "God," and will not tolerate the worship of any other. This in effect will solve one of the world's greatest political problems. What is the true ground of being? What is the final truth? What is the unifying principle which will really allow all men to be truly united? Throughout history multiple "gods" and multiple centers of worship, including plants and trees, and even movie and entertainment "idols," have competed for what should be the true center of our lives. What is it that allows us to put all other things in order, in their place, and not being dominant, when they actually should be subordinate? For lack of such a focus we have political chaos, with many competing things trying to dominate our lives. Jesus, the very Son of God, the Master of Heaven and Earth and all that is under the earth, the Creator of all things, Who loved us, and died for us that we might be reconciled to Him ... He is the only true answer! But this child of Hell itself, this seed of the serpent, this mere man, who by nature is no god ... he says no. This beast says no, to Jesus, to everything right and good and holy. This man says no, I am the answer. I am the one who is truly master of heaven and earth, and all must worship me.

> ... so that he as God sitteth in the temple of God, shewing himself that he is God.
> 2Thes 2:4b KJV

He takes his seat "in the temple of God." Does this mean the literal temple in Jerusalem? When 2 Thessalonians was written (about the year 51 or 52 AD) the temple in Jerusalem was still standing. This would be the natural way to understand this verse, taking it as it stood. On the other hand, now in Christ a new temple is being built. A temple being made up of people. More than one apostle speaks of these things. Paul says,

> [16] Know ye not that ye are the temple of God, and *that* the Spirit of God dwelleth in you?
> [17] If any man defile the temple of God, him shall God destroy; for the temple of God is

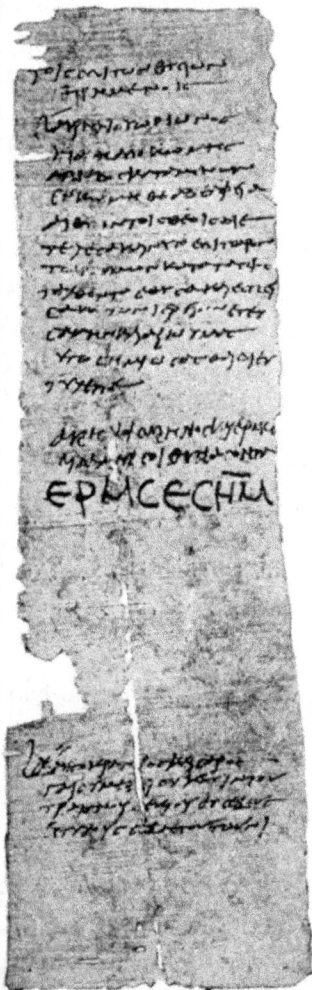

There **never** was a mark **everyone** had to have in the early centuries. Only a certificate, as seen here, which was issued for offering a pinch of incense (provided by the magistrates), and saying, "Caesar is Lord." And it was not needed for buying or selling.

holy, which *temple* ye are. 1Cor 3:16-17 KJV

Also the word for temple which Paul uses here is the Greek word *naos* ναός, which we discussed in the sections on Revelation 11, the word for the inner part of the temple where God dwells and only true priests can come. Peter also speaks of a temple made without hands, a temple made of people in whom the Lord God dwells.

> you also, as living stones, are being built up a spiritual house, a holy priesthood, to offer up spiritual sacrifices acceptable to God through Jesus Christ. 1Pe 2:5 NKJV

So the ultimate temple of God is made of people.

> ³ And there shall be no more curse: but the throne of God and of the Lamb shall be in it; and his servants shall serve him: ⁴ And they shall see his face; and his name *shall be* in their foreheads. Rev 22:3-4 KJV

Clearly many Christians will in these last days cave into pressure and receive the terrible mark of this impostor, so at least in some secondary sense we might well say that this monster "as God sitteth in the temple of God."

Or does he? How would a man take his seat in the church as God? Perhaps this is not impossible, but then again ... ? Look again at Revelation 11 as we discussed it in section VI. The true priests of God are pictured as protected from this man of sin, this man literally of lawlessness. So the beast is emphatically NOT enthroned among the holy priests of God of the *naos*, Rev 11:1. Then on the other hand, the outer courts of the temple are given over to the nations to "tread under foot." Thus, taken at face value, Revelation 11 does not sound like a church-temple made of people as a place where this monster is enthroned!

This is also the same picture we see in Revelation 12. It is not a picture of the dragon being enthroned in the church, rather it is a picture of God Himself giving the woman a place to flee to in uninhabited places, a place prepared for her so she will be safe for time, times, and half a time. Then the dragon pursues her there but is unable to get her, Rev 12:13-17.

This is similar to the picture we see in Revelation 13. This is not a picture of the beast being enthroned in the church as God, but of Satan, who cannot get the faithful to comply with his demands, then making war on the church.

> ⁷ And it was given unto him to make war with the saints, and to overcome them: and power was given him over all kindreds, and tongues, and nations. ⁸ And **all that dwell upon the earth shall worship him, whose names are not written in the book of life** of the Lamb slain from the foundation of the world.
> Rev 13:7-8 KJV (*bold emphasis added*)

None of these scenes from multiple visions presents a picture of Satan being enthroned in the church as "God." These arguments are not necessarily

202 Revealing the Christian Age

conclusive, but they do seem unanimous in pointing in other directions.

Then we come to the fact that Herod's temple, where both our Lord, and his apostles, and many early Christians, both preached and taught, was completely demolished in 70 AD, and to date has never been rebuilt. Many Jews *do* want to rebuild the temple in Jerusalem, and there have been for some time, plans being laid to rebuild the ancient temple to the Lord. Also it is plain from many Scriptures that at some future point God *will* for sure circumcise the hearts of the Jews.

> And the LORD thy God will circumcise thine heart, and the heart of thy seed, to love the LORD thy God with all thine heart, and with all thy soul, that thou mayest live. Deut 30:6 KJV

This is a statement of fact. Something God *will do*, which has NOT happened to date. Jeremiah says much later to the Jews,

> Circumcise yourselves to the LORD, and take away the foreskins of your heart, ye men of Judah and inhabitants of Jerusalem: lest my fury come forth like fire, and burn that none can quench *it*, because of the evil of your doings. Jer 4:4 KJV

Much later again, as it was shown in the early parts of this book, the prophet Malachi still views both priest and people as unfaithful to the Lord their God, and ripe for judgment. Then the prophet Stephen, whom the Jews murdered, testified to the Sanhedrin,

> Ye stiffnecked and uncircumcised in heart and ears, ye do always resist the Holy Ghost: as your fathers did, so do ye. Acts 7:51 KJV

That says many things, but it plainly shows us that the prophecy of God circumcising the hearts of the Jews as is seen in Deut 30:5-6 has **not *yet*** been fulfilled. There is a lot to say here, which should be said, but that is another subject. We only summarize that Scripture clearly forecasts the conversion of the Jews, as a group, before the Second Coming of Christ. Then it will be said,

> Now if the fall of them be the riches of the world, and the diminishing of them the riches of the Gentiles; how much more their fulness?
> Rom 11:12 KJV

Then another question comes for examination. ***If another temple is built,*** what will it have to do with the New Covenant? Moses' law plainly intended for the system of animal sacrifices to end when He is "pierced through for our transgressions, ... crushed for our iniquities." What a blasphemous heresy it would be to substitute the blood of bulls and goats for the blood of God's One and Only Son!

On the other hand, Herod's temple was used for New Testament worship in the book of Acts. Could not such a rebuilt temple similarly be used as a worldwide center for Christian worship, as Herod's temple should have been?

Then comes the prime question: does 2Thes 2:4 indicate that another physical temple will be rebuilt in Jerusalem and that the beast will take his seat as "God" in this yet to be rebuilt place of worship? Perhaps. This author is inclined to think so, but would not be dogmatic. It could be that other prophecies will throw a light on this. Or possibly we should merely remember what Jesus said,

> And what I say unto you I say unto all, Watch. Mk 13:37 KJV

What are the danger signs for Christians?

How will Christians be able to tell that we are coming near to this severe time of trouble? This may be a proper place to think about some of those precursor conflicts we studied in Section III.

We discussed earlier the original "abomination of desolation" which was placed in the temple in Jerusalem. This was in the early second century BC, and Antiochus IV Epiphanes removed the altar of the Lord, set up an image of Zeus in the temple, and had a pig sacrificed to Zeus. This idol of Zeus was the original "abomination." A long guerrilla war ensued between the Jews and Antiochus, and the Jews finally won, cleansed the temple, and reinstituted proper worship of the Lord our God.

Still, there were some other things which we noted there. There were parts of these prophecies that did not seem to fit, or were plainly unfulfilled. Antiochus IV, rascal which he was, and powerful though he was, did not and does not actually fulfill all of these prophecies. We noted in those discussions that these were the indications of what we chose to discuss under the Bible term of a "type." Those loose items of prophecy, which do not fit, are often the tip-off that one thing, perhaps near in history, is symbolic of something coming much later in history. The Bible calls these things variously as types, shadows, or patterns. I suggest that the modern term "prototype" might be a proper translation of some of these various terms.

Then in the gospels, Jesus verifies these suspicions about the original abomination merely being symbolic. In response to questions about when the temple in Jerusalem will be destroyed, and when the end of the age will come, Jesus tells us,

> When ye therefore shall see the abomination of desolation, spoken of by Daniel the prophet, stand in the holy place, (whoso readeth, let him understand:) Mtt 24:15 KJV

So Jesus verifies the suspicions expressed earlier about some of the prophecies in Daniel. We should note that Daniel also talks about "the time of the end," Dan 8:17, 19, and Dan 12:9. Jesus in fact seems to talk about these things as something which everyone will be able to see. Observe that Jesus is speaking of this abomination which ruins everything as standing in the holy place. Well, that might be a part of the temple in Jerusalem, and it would fit speaking of this "man" who "takes his seat in the temple of God, displaying himself as being God," NASB.

We have looked carefully at the idea of this "abomination" of which Jesus speaks as coming, as being the idolatrous images on Roman military standards, which would have been present when the Roman's offered their victory sacrifices to their gods, in the destroyed temple in 70 AD. "Images" of false "gods" *are* an abomination to the Lord. Still ... a victory sacrifice, offered *after* the Romans have conquered Jerusalem and burned the temple to the ground ... would be far too late an event to give any adequate warning that Christians might need to run for safety from impending destruction. At that point in 70 AD, the city of Jerusalem was already destroyed along with almost all of the millions of people within the city! (See the pictures and discussion on pages 68-69 in this volume.)

However, when the true abomination is standing in the temple, Jesus says in full,

> [15] When ye therefore shall see the abomination of desolation, spoken of by Daniel the prophet, stand in the holy place, (whoso readeth, let him understand:) [16] Then let them which be in Judaea flee into the mountains: [17] Let him which is on the housetop not come down to take any thing out of his house: [18] Neither let him which is in the field return back to take his clothes.
> Mtt 24:15-18 KJV

Some typical Roman standards ("flags" in our terminology). They did include pagan symbols. For instance, the eagle was a symbol of the pagan "god" Zeus.

When this abomination stands in the holy place, *that is the time to run. That is the time, if you are in Judea, to flee to the mountains.* **DON'T GO BACK INTO THE HOUSE TO GET** *ANYTHING!* **At this point, literally run for your life.** It will be bad for anyone who is pregnant at that time. We are supposed to pray that this will not happen in winter.

These parts do not actually fit the destruction of Jerusalem. The fleeing from Jerusalem *before* it was destroyed was severe, but not this severe. Pagan images on military standards in the temple simply were not the signal to avoid the destruction of Jerusalem in 70 AD. Rather it was when war came to Jerusalem with the *approach* of the Roman armies.

> "But when you see Jerusalem surrounded by armies, then know that its desolation is near." Lk 21:20 NKJV

Compare Mtt 24:6 which is rather speaking of the time of the end. In fact, history records that the Christians in Jerusalem did recognize this sign, and fled Jerusalem before the Romans cut it off with entrenchments.

Then as if to emphasize the point, Jesus says that if anyone says the Christ is here or there, or out in the wilderness, or in the inner room, DO NOT BELIEVE THEM.

> "See, I have told you beforehand." Mtt 24:25 NKJV

Then Jesus cinches it.

> "Wherever the corpse is, there the vultures will gather." Mtt 24:28 NASB

In Greek, the word for eagle (like the Roman eagle or the American eagle), and the word for vulture, is the same (*aetos* ἀετός). Thus both the KJV/NKJV and the NASB, are all correct! You just cannot make the double meaning come out in English! Vultures gather around a corpse. Remember: before the beast's fatal wound is healed ... he is a corpse. Then,

> ... and his deadly wound was healed: and all the world wondered after the beast. Rev 13:3 KJV

"The whole earth was amazed ..." NASB. This is an event noted world-wide.

Open Questions.

At some point what is called "an image of the beast" is made, Rev 13:15. They are even able to make the image breathe and speak, and everyone has to worship this image. Now when it says they are able to give this image "breath," the Greek word is *pneuma* πνεῦμα, which is the regular word for wind, *or* breath, *or* spirit, depending on the context. *Pneuma* in this context would plainly indicate that they are able to give breath to the image, *and it might indicate nothing more than this!* However, considering the extraordinary context in which we are speaking, might this also indicate they are able to revive his spirit? That would be an awesome piece of technology. Is this the corpse of the beast to which they have given breath and speech? Is this the new life from the fatal wound? On one hand it does seems to differentiate between the beast and his image, as in Rev 13:14. On the other hand, it seems to be the image which all have to worship. I will just ask the question: is it the corpse of the beast that is made into this "image"?

Keep in mind they will not be able to restore all of this worthless shepherd, Zech 11:17. There is a fuller discussion of this earlier in this work, and in *Prophecy Principles*. Or is this the ultimate joke on mankind of all time? Is it really a cadaver that is set up in the temple? A dead body which can breath and speak?

The remains of a man which all the world must worship? Will this be the "god" which *all* of this world must worship? Will the world's "god" merely be the ultimate golem of all time? A corpse worshipped as "god" would surely be an abomination to God, and hopefully to many men.

We took note of the fact in Revelation 11 that the great city is also symbolically called "Egypt," Rev 11:8. Look at God's judgment on Egypt in Isaiah 19. This is a multifaceted passage which includes some things which happened in ancient times, part of which is also a type of the final judgment on the Egypt of this world. A curious statement is made at the beginning of this oracle.

> The oracle concerning Egypt.
>> Behold, the LORD is riding on a swift cloud and is about to come to Egypt;
>> The idols of Egypt will tremble at His presence,
>> And the heart of the Egyptians will melt within them.
>> Isa 19:1 NASB

Part of this verse is readily understandable of the Second Coming of the Lord: "the heart of the Egyptians will melt within them." Then it says of this "Egypt" of the last days that, "The idols of Egypt will tremble at His presence." *Will this corpse-idol which is able to breathe and to speak, shake in his boots when he (and you and I, and everyone else) sees Jesus coming in the clouds?*

Is he really alive or not, after being killed? Evidently it will be hard for even the experts to tell. We have noted the ambiguity of some of the language concerning this beast's death, and there is one more piece of evidence we should bring up now. This beast is captured and "thrown alive" into hell in Revelation 19. At this point we should merely point out that Scripture seems to speak of this beast as if he is both alive, and not alive, after his fatal accident.

As Jesus suddenly came to the temple, so the beast will also suddenly come to the temple. Many have claimed and do claim to be the Christ. Many of these have also come to Jerusalem and I am sure some have made their claims in the temple of Jerusalem before they were chased away.

Then comes the final question. Is it when this man first claims to be "God" and comes to the temple that all the faithful must run for their lives? Or is it when the corpse is set up? I am inclined to think that the signal to run for your life is when the corpse is set up in the temple, which seemingly will be a worldwide witnessed event.

Also the beast has a number, 666, Rev 13:17. All letters had numeric values in both Greek and Hebrew, just like in Roman numerals. If you add up the number in this man's name, it equals 666. Scripture says it is the number of "man," verse 18. We are to watch so that we can be ready.

> Take ye heed, watch and pray: for ye know not when the time is.
> Mk 13:33 KJV

The Church Wins, Revelation 14

Now the prophet John has seen a distress filled vision of great trouble for the church of our Lord, *and for the world*. We saw in Revelation 12 that Satan first tries to destroy the Christ, and when that does not work he goes off to make war on those who keep the commandments of God, Rev 12:17. We saw in Revelation 13 that the dragon stood on the sands of the seashore, and a monster came out of the sea, Rev 13:1. That great dragon is the devil or Satan (Rev 12:9), who gave his authority to this monster, this beast, both this organization and this man, coming out of the sea, Rev 13:2.

We saw that some awesome false miracles and false signs were performed to make everyone think that this beast is a god. The entire world worships this beast. He overcomes the saints, Rev 13:7, and shatters the power of the holy people, Dan 12:7. Terrible times are described for both the church *and* the world.

Now the prophet is watching Christ rule in heaven, and the saints wear, not the name of the beast, but the name of the Christ, Rev 14:1.

Jesus does rule, even now, Rev 1:5. He rules over both all men and all kings and rulers and judges. He entered heaven after His resurrection, and was given a great nation which He will rule forever, Dan 7:13-14. He *now* rules among the kingdoms of men. God has given Him rule over all of the nations, Psa 2:7-8. Part of this is quoted in Heb 1:5. Jesus rules now, and whoever is willing to do something against Him, can only do those things Jesus *allows* them to do! Jesus *can* and *may* overrule at any point, and **often does**. If at any time, some ruler in this world displeases Him, Jesus may destroy them right then and there. So the rulers of this world, the kings, the dictators, the premiers, the prime ministers, the judges, are advised to worship and serve Him, Psa 2:10-12.

Jesus may take your life in a minute! Anytime, anywhere!

That is true for rulers and for you and me, and such things happen *every day*, although men often do not make the connections. The smart thing is to fear God and keep His commandments. The saints who do are pictured as on Mount Zion in heaven, Rev 14:1a. We have come to this heavenly Zion.

> [22] But **you have come to Mount Zion** and to the city of the living God, **the heavenly Jerusalem**, to an innumerable company of angels, [23] to **the general assembly and church of the firstborn** who are registered in heaven, to God the Judge of all, to the spirits of just men made perfect, Heb 12:22-23 NKJV (*emphasis added*)

Here in Revelation 14 some saints are pictured as being with their Lord in heaven, and singing to Him. John hears the sound of thunder in heaven, and he hears music, Rev 14:2. They sang a new song before their Lord. It mentions once again a special one hundred and forty-four thousand. The doomed on earth wear the name of the beast on their hand or their forehead, Rev 13:16-17. These saved ones, in contrast, wear the name of Jesus Christ on their forehead. They have been purchased out of this world, Rev 14:3b. They have not been fornicating. They are not defiled by sexual immorality. They follow Jesus wherever He goes. Jesus is their example, as Peter said,

> 21 To this you were called, because Christ suffered for you, leaving you an example, that you should follow in his steps.
> 22 "He committed no sin,
> and no deceit was found in his mouth."
> 23 When they hurled their insults at him, he did not retaliate; when he suffered, he made no threats. Instead, he entrusted himself to him who judges justly. 1Pe 2:21-23 NIV

This is what these saints on mount Zion in heaven have done. They are the first fruits of the saved. Not the full number of the saved, but they are the "first fruits to God and to the Lamb," Rev 14:4c. They are not liars, and they have been cleansed from all of their sins, Rev 14:5.

Another angel has the eternal gospel to be preached to all in Rev 14:6. **What is the command of God for the Christian age? "Fear God, and give glory to him; " Rev 14:7a** KJV. Fearing God is the beginning of wisdom, the start of being smart, Prov 1:7. This statement was *not* taken away at the cross of Jesus. It is *not* part of the Law of Moses, which is the books of Genesis through Deuteronomy, and was not taken away at the cross. This is part of the wisdom of God for all eternity. What is the center of all things?

> 13 Let us hear the conclusion of the whole matter: Fear God, and keep his commandments: for this *is* the whole *duty* of man. 14 For God shall bring every work into judgment, with every secret thing, whether *it be* good, or whether *it be* evil. Ecc 12:13-14 KJV

The angels in heaven during the Christian age confirm this is a central part of the gospel: walking in the fear of the Lord! Why continue in this walk? Because "the hour of his judgment is come" in Rev 14:7b. That time of judgment is of course when Jesus makes His Second Coming from heaven, 2Thes 1:7b-9. At this point the angel announces the fall of Babylon the Great.

> And there followed another angel, saying, Babylon is fallen, is fallen, that great city, because she made all nations drink of the wine of the wrath of her fornication. Rev 14:8 KJV

Before John is shown the story of Babylon the Great, her fall is announced. Of course literal Babylon of Old Testament times has fallen many centuries before. The area is still there but it is of no significance. Babylon the Great is keen on immorality. Fornication it is plainly. The Greek word here is *porneia* πορνεία, the word from which we get the word pornography, a writing about immoral sex, whether heterosexual or homosexual. The NASB translates this influence of Babylon the Great as **"the wine of the passion of her immorality,"** and the

ESV as **"the wine of the passion of her sexual immorality."** That word "pas-sion" is in Greek *thumos* θυμός, which is one of the normal words in Greek for just ordinary anger, or a bad temper. A good example is "rage"/"wrath/"furi-ous" in Lk 4:28. The KJV translates Rev 14:8 as "wine of the wrath of her forni-cation." That is a good literal translation, but it makes you wonder about the intent of the phrase. The old Revised Standard Version (1971) translated this as "the wine of her impure passion" which completely misses the impact of *thumos*. In the New Revised Standard Version (1989) that was changed back to the KJV "the wine of the wrath of her fornication." Perhaps the NIV 1984 gives the seem-ing intent of the passage,

> Babylon the Great, ... made all the nations drink the maddening wine of her adulteries." Rev 14:8

Ah, "the maddening wine" of her fornication. (Fornication, which is the text, takes in all adultery, but adultery does not take in all fornication.) It is a curious but plain fact of life that great sexual promiscuity also frequently gener-ates great anger. The jumps from "normal" sexual abuse to sadomasochism are indeed small. Sexual promiscuity generates a well documented anger at ourselves for being so simple as to so ruin ourselves. Then it generates anger toward those who would aid in this sort stupidity, as is also well documented, and frequently generates the beating of prostitutes, as continually shows up in the news. In fact, it is not going to far to note that quite often homosexuality and sadomas-ochism go hand in hand. A terrible retribution it is! "The maddening wine of her adulteries," is in all not a bad rendering. Perhaps "the maddening wine of her fornications," would be even better. Shakespeare well described the craziness of being driven by animal passions.

> The expense of spirit in a waste of shame
> Is lust in action;
>
> ...
>
> Enjoy'd no sooner but despised straight;
> Past reason hunted; and no sooner had,
> Past reason hated, as swallowed bait;
> On purpose laid to make the taker mad;
> Mad in pursuit, and in possession so ... Sonnet 129

Mad! Insane! Crazy! The "made ... drink" is all one word, *portizo* ποτίζω, which means to give someone a drink or to cause them to drink. There is some-one, a "she" who has made **"all** the nations" to drink of the intoxicating frenzy of her fornication. "She" has wide spread power and influence, and "she" has actually **made "all** nations" drink of her immorality, and by implication has made them drunk with this, shall we even call it, a "frenzy" of immorality. This would definitely fit a mystery of "lawlessness." In this case *sexual lawlessness is de-finitely implied, world-wide,* that drives everyone just a little bit crazy, a little bit angry, or maybe even more than just a little bit! All of this is in context with the coming of the beast in Revelation 14, and part of the great revolt against morality which precedes the coming of the beast, 2The 2:3.

The saints wear the mark of Jesus Christ, the Holy Spirit of God, Eph 4:30. In contrast, those receiving the mark of the seed of serpent, that terrible man of lawlessness, the beast from the abyss, and worships him, Rev 14:9; they will drink the full measure of the wrath of God, Rev 14:10. The smoke of their agony will go up forever and ever, Rev 14:11.

You must understand these things to be patient, Rev 14:12.

How blessed are all those who hold fast in those terrible times. **Blessed are all of those who die! ... from that point forward, Rev 14:13.** It is not terrible to die in those times. Rather it is blessed. *Provided you die in the Lord!*

Then John saw a vision of final judgement, Rev 14:14. The right time has come, the angel announces. It is time for the final harvest, Rev 14:15. It is implied that it is at the height of the power of the beast and Babylon the Great. Jesus compared the end of the age to a harvest of grain.

> [40] As therefore the tares are gathered and burned in the fire; so shall it be in the end of this world. [41] The Son of man shall send forth his angels, and they shall gather out of his kingdom all things that offend, and them which do iniquity; [42] And shall cast them into a furnace of fire: there shall be wailing and gnashing of teeth. [43] Then shall the righteous shine forth as the sun in the kingdom of their Father. Who hath ears to hear, let him hear. Mtt 13:40-43 KJV

The harvest is begun, Rev 14:16-18. The wicked are thrown into the winepress of God's wrath, Rev 14:19. What will the slaughter be like? The only close comparison would be this world in the flood of Noah's days.

> And the wine press was trodden outside the city, and blood came out from the wine press, up to the horses' bridles, for a distance of two hundred miles. Rev 14:20 NASB

Symbolic but true. This is clearly the end of one of these parallel visions. The next vision will offer more details. *Nothing* is more important than being ready for those times! Live for Christ and not for yourself!

This is actually a very simple story, of an awesome, guided, descent into wickedness, and its eternal consequences.

VIII. Bowls of Wrath,

Revelation 15-16

The previous page has an engraving by Albrecht Dürer (1471–1528) and is part of his vision of the bowls of wrath being poured out upon the earth. The Great Harlot sits on the seven headed dragon in the lower right. A monster indeed!

The Last Plagues Begin, Rev 15:1—16:11

Now we have seen in Revelation 13 that a tremendous period of stress three and one half years long is going to come on the entire world, and most especially on the church of our Lord. All the world will be required to worship one special seed of Satan, one man, one beast, one monster if you will, who receives the devil's throne and great authority. He will rule over the entire world, and will require all men to worship him.

Despite all of this, we saw in Revelation 14 that the church will win in the end. That all of those who perish because of righteousness in this great period of persecution are blessed, and their good works follow them, Rev 14:13.

Now plagues, or bad things, terrible disasters, have happened in this sinful world all along. The Greek word for plague is *plāgā* πληγή, means a blow or a punch or a beating. In the NASB it is translated "beat (1), beaten (m) (1), beatings (1), blows (1), flogging (m) (1), plague (3), plagues (10), wound (3), wounds (1)." It does not mean *just* a virus or an epidemic or a terrible sickness, as in the modern English sense of a plague, but it means any sort of severe blow which might fall on a person or a nation, or a planet.

Then the seven last plagues are announced.

> Then I saw another sign in heaven, great and marvelous, seven angels who had seven plagues, *which are* the last, because in them the wrath of God is finished. Rev 15:1 NASB

*These are the seven **last** plagues which will fall on this earth.*

No other plagues will fall after this, because with these blows on sinful men, God's wrath is going to be finished. Now obviously, if these are the seven last plagues which are to be, then it is speaking of things which will happen *just before* the end of time!

Then John saw what must be a vision in heaven. He saw an ocean made of glass mixed with fire, and he saw all of those who had been victorious over the beast, the monster, and his image, Rev 15:2. They were singing a song of joy and victory, Rev 15:3a. Great and marvelous is your name Lord, Rev 15:3b. Who will not fear and glorify the Lord our God, Rev 15:4a. Fear of the Lord is still a part of righteousness in the Christian Age. The church in the first century prospered walking in the fear of the Lord, Act 9:31. We are not to fear men, but we are to "rather fear him which is able to destroy both soul and body in hell," Mtt 10:28 KJV. The end is that we "might serve him without fear," Lk 1:74, but that would only be in consciousness of the awesome God whom we worship.

Now a lot of people fear the wrong things. We see repeatedly that the leaders of the Jews feared the reactions of the people, but the one who is acceptable to God is the one who fears Him, Act 10:35. We are straight out commanded to fear God.

> And if you call on the Father, who without partiality judges according to each one's work, conduct yourselves throughout the time of your stay *here* in fear; 1Pe 1:17 NKJV

> Having therefore these promises, dearly beloved, let us cleanse ourselves from all filthiness of the flesh and spirit, perfecting holiness in the fear of God. 2Cor 7:1 KJV

We are to work out our "salvation with fear and trembling," Phil 2:12 KJV. In contrast, of the wicked it says, "There is no fear of God before their eyes," Rom 3:18 KJV.

Now these brave ones, who have endured the test, did fear the Lord, and finally *all* will fear the Lord, and the reason is given.

> Who shall not fear thee, O Lord, and glorify thy name? for thou only art holy: for all nations shall come and worship before thee; for thy judgments are made manifest. Rev 15:4 KJV

Then John saw heaven opened, and saw the true temple in heaven, and seven wonderful angels were seen coming out of the temple in heaven, Rev 15:5-6. At this point the four living creature which we saw in Revelation 4 (presumably these creatures are cherubim?) gave the angels seven bowls full of the wrath of God, Rev 15:7. The temple in heaven was filled with smoke from the power and glory of God, and no one is able to enter the temple in heaven until these plagues are over, Rev 15:8. *The seven last disasters* are about to start on earth. The angels are commanded to start pouring out the wrath of the Lord our God, Rev 16:1. Men have known about God but have not worshipped Him. But they have worshipped a monster who is in no way god, and they have feared him more than they have feared the Lord God, and they have helped him persecute the saints of the Most High, and they are about to *begin* paying the price. Full warning is being given.

The first angel poured out the first bowl of wrath, and everyone who is worshipping the beast and has the mark of the beast comes to have terrible and detestable sores, Rev 16:2. It was mentioned earlier that near the end of time plagues would come on the earth, that were like Moses' plagues on Egypt of old. So it is in the present case.

[8] So the LORD said to Moses and Aaron, "Take for yourselves handfuls of ashes from a furnace, and let Moses scatter it toward the heavens in the sight of Pharaoh. [9] And it will become fine dust in all the land of Egypt, and it will cause boils that break out in sores on man and beast throughout all the land of Egypt." [10] Then they took ashes from the furnace and stood before Pharaoh, and Moses scattered *them* toward heaven. And *they* caused boils that break out in sores on man and beast. Ex 9:8-10 NKJV

It would seem that God has caused multiple great conflicts to happen in history as "types," symbolic, of the end of our present universe. The Greek word is *tupos* τύπος (compare Rom 5:14 in the NKJV, NASB and the ESV). The Greek word is variously translated as type, example, image, pattern, form, imprint, etc., and it occurs in our Greek New Testament in Jn 20:25, Acts 7:43-44, 23:25, Rom 5:14, 1Cor 10:6, Phil 3:17, 1Thes 1:7, 2Thes 3:9, 1Tim 4:12, Titus 2:7, Heb 8:5, and 1Pe 5:3.

In my first volume, *Prophecy Principles*, it was discussed in considerable detail the way our LORD used the destruction of Jerusalem in 70 AD as a type, symbolic, of the end of our universe. Also it can be seen from our present passage that one of the master types of the end of the world is the story of God working through Moses to bring about the deliverance of God's people from the Egypt of this world (cf. 1Cor 10:1-6ff). Egypt is a symbol of this world (compare Rev 11:8). Pharaoh is a type of the god of this world (compare 2Cor 4:4), especially as personified in that great man of Satan: the beast. The plagues on Egypt are typical of these plagues which will fall on sinful men at the end of time. If you want to understand the end of time better, and what men must do, you should study, among other things, the destruction of Jerusalem in 70 AD, and deliverance of Israel from Egypt in the fifteenth century BC. In Moses time the people of God fled Egypt to the wilderness before their intended entry into the promised land. In our present case, at the end of time, you will remember from the parallel vision in Revelation 12, that the church fled away from the dragon,

> ... into the wilderness, into her place, where she is nourished for a time, and times, and half a time, from the face of the serpent. Rev 12:14 kjv

Remember! It has been said from the first that the book of Revelation should not be studied in isolation. This is only an overview. Revelation should be studied in coordination with the book of Exodus, and Matthew 24, and many other texts, of which Paul says, "Now these things were our examples," 1Cor 10:6 KJV

This parallelism is between the end of time and the Exodus from Egypt. The final Exodus will be from this present world into the final promise land of what we call "heaven."

Then the second and third angels poured out their bowls. The pronoun is "his," the angel is described in the masculine sense. Even so, in much of traditional Western art angels are pictured as if they were women. Now the waters are turned to blood, Rev 16:3-4. This brings to mind what Moses did in Egypt.

> [20] And Moses and Aaron did so, as the LORD commanded; and he lifted up the rod, and smote the waters that *were* in the river, in the sight of Pharaoh, and in the sight of his servants; and all the waters that *were* in the river were turned to blood. [21] And the fish that *was* in the river died; and the river stank, and the Egyptians could not drink of the water of the river; and there was blood throughout all the land of Egypt. Ex 7:20-21 KJV

The logical question then would be: is this in Revelation 16 a parallel passage with Revelation 8 and Revelation 11? Many passages in Revelation are parallel. The beast is first mentioned in Rev 11:7 and is last mentioned in Rev 20:10, so there are many parallel passages in the book of Revelation. I am inclined to think these passages about waters turning to blood as overlapping/parallel passages. For sure it is a parallel to Ex 7:17-21, when Moses turned the waters of Egypt into blood.

Now you may remember that in a separate vision of the Christian Age we saw something like a mountain fall into the sea, what we would call an asteroid, and the sea became blood, Rev 8:8. That seemingly is a parallel vision, and it can be seen in Revelation 8 in literal terms, how it comes to be that the oceans themselves turn to blood, and the living creatures in the sea die. In Revelation 8 it would seem to describe it as it would appear from a global perspective, how the major waters are hit, and how overall a third of the creatures in the sea die. In contrast, in Revelation 16 it seems to describe this phenomenon as it would appear if you were on the shore of that sea into which the asteroid/meteorite falls: "and every living creature in the sea died." Rev 16:3 NKJV.

You may also remember another parallel passage in Revelation 11, when the two witnesses prophesy, and there it is clearly told that "they" (Rev 11:3) are the ones who "have power over the waters to turn them to blood," Rev 11:6 KJV. So it appears there is another parallel to Moses and Elijah. In Moses' day the people of Israel did not dare openly oppose the "god of this world" the Pharaoh /beast who rules all. If we looked at another parallel to these times, it would be oppressions of God's people by Antiochus IV Epiphanes in the second century BC. Antiochus IV was discussed earlier in "Precursor Conflicts." As the Pharaoh of Egypt is a type of the beast, so also is Antiochus IV. When it is speaking of those days in the book of Daniel, it pictures how it will be for many of God's people in those end days.

[33] "And those of the people who understand shall instruct many; yet *for many* days they shall fall by sword and flame, by captivity and plundering. [34] Now when they fall, they shall be aided with a little help; but many shall join with them by intrigue. [35] And *some* of those of understanding shall fall, to refine them, purify *them*, and make *them* white, *until* the time of the end; because *it is* still for the appointed time" Dan 11:33-35 NKJV

These valiant ministers give their lives to inform others while there is still time, in order to save them from eternal death in the lake of fire. All of this is very similar to the time of Antiochus IV. I think this is an accurate picture of how it will be for many knowledgable church leaders. They will be trying to warn all men. Keep in mind that we are told that we are to be,

> Not forsaking the assembling of ourselves together, as the manner of some *is*; but exhorting *one another*: and so much the more, **as ye see the day** approaching. Heb 10:25 KJV (*bold emphasis added*)

Most of the people of God will be in hiding. In the final last day they are crouching in their dungeons and prison camps (in literal bondage), or in their "deserts, and in mountains, and in dens and caves of the earth," Heb 11:38 KJV. **To be forewarned is to be forearmed.** But as Moses and Elijah openly opposed the powers of wickedness in their own day, so the two witnesses openly oppose the beast and the forces of wickedness in that final "forty *and* two months" (Rev 11:2-3), and no one dares to interfere with them until "the beast that ascendeth out of the bottomless pit shall make war against them, and shall overcome them, and kill them." Rev 11:7 KJV. *All through these events, God will have His witnesses before all men!*

Clearly there are many parallels here to the last days, including Elijah and Elijah opposing Ahab, the three and a half years of Jas 5:17, and the early chapters of Exodus when Moses is opposing the evil Pharaoh of Egypt. Clearly, both the Pharaoh and King Ahab are types of the beast of the last days, and should be studied in this light.

God is pictured in Revelation 16 as righteous in doing these things. Why? Because these men on earth have shed the blood of Christians, so they deserve to have to drink blood, Rev 16:5-7.

Then the fourth angel poured out his bowl, Rev 16:8. This angel's bowl is poured out on the sun, so men are scorched with heat, Rev 16:9a. So before the sun starts to fade, and it is dark even in the daytime, first the sun will become extra hot, and men are scorched with heat. Does it speak of a sun/star which is beginning to pulsate before it is totally extinguished? I think the parallel here is,

> These have power to shut heaven, that it rain not in the days of their prophecy:; ... Rev 11:6 KJV

And men slandered God, blasphemed God, called Him names, cursed Him, because they know that God is The One Who has control over these plagues. Then we see part of the purpose: that men would yet repent. However, even when these mighty demonstrations of power come, they are still not willing to repent, so now "the seat of the beast; and his kingdom was full of darkness; and they gnawed their tongues for pain," Rev 16:9-10 KJV. Are we looking at a dying/pulsating sun? The obvious parallel is in Exodus 10.

> [21] Then the LORD said unto Moses, Stretch out thine hand toward heaven, that there may be darkness over the land of Egypt, even darkness *which* may be felt. [22] And Moses stretched forth his hand toward heaven; and there was a thick darkness in all the land of Egypt three days: [23] They saw not one another, neither rose any from his place for three days: but all the children of Israel had light in their dwellings. Ex 10:21-23 KJV

They are in such agony that they chew on their tongues, but they still will not repent, Rev 16:10-11.

It appears these things happen *while* the church is oppressed and conquered. Now the story enters the final phase of God winning even in history. This is not the end of history, but these events are *in history*, just before the end. God is giving men some final time to see He is God, see His power and repent. But men will not be willing to repent. How very important it is to repent before we go too far!

The World Gathers for War, Rev 16:12-21

We have been looking at the last plagues, the last discipline from God, the last chastisements which fall on wicked men on this earth. These are the last burdens and trials which fall on men to try to get them to change from their evil ways. Only men are not repenting, but rather they are cursing God for bringing trouble on them, Rev 16:11.

So the sixth angel pours out his bowl and it dries up the Euphrates river, Rev 16:12a. This would be very severe drought to dry up the Euphrates. It is a mighty river system which flows all the way from the mountains of eastern Turkey near where Noah's ark finally landed, all the way to the Persian Gulf, some 1700 miles away. It would take quite a drought for this huge region to really dry it up. Then it tells us why it is to be dried up. To make way for kings and armies from the far east, Rev 16:12b. Now Satan is sending spirits out to deceive men.

> [13] And I saw three unclean spirits like frogs *coming* out of the mouth of

the dragon, out of the mouth of the beast, and out of the mouth of the false prophet. [14] For they are **spirits of demons**, performing signs, ... Rev 16:13-14 NKJV (*bold emphasis added*)

That dragon mentioned in verse 13 is Satan as can be seen from, Rev 12:9. The beast is that special head of Satan which is given authority by Satan, and who had a fatal wound, and that fatal wound was healed, as was seen in Rev 13:2-3. The false prophet is that special prophet, another beast, who speaks like a dragon, whom we saw in Rev 13:11. What are they really? Not "gods," for by nature they are not gods, Gal 4:8. There are many spirits which are not of God, 1Jn 4:1. Also it is easy to see from Scripture that in the last days men will listen to deceiving spirits and the things taught by demons, 1Tim 4:1. Our present text in the book of Revelation is clearly about the very last days, because here it is about very the last of the last seven plagues on the earth. So what are these demonic spirits doing? They are getting sinful men ready to fight ... ready to fight God! They are performing miraculous signs, Satanic miracles, Rev 16:14. The same thing is foretold in 2 Thessalonians 2 when it is speaking of what it calls "the man of lawlessness."

Even him, whose coming is after the working of Satan with all power and signs and lying wonders, 2Thes 2:9 KJV

A rising from the dead is just part of this deception. Notice that an angel of God helps set up this situation. "And the sixth angel poured out his vial upon the great river Euphrates," as we saw in Rev 16:12 KJV. In 2 Thessalonians 2 God helps these fraudulent messiahs and prophets to deceive all the wicked. They deserved this because they did not *want* to believe the truth.

[11] And for this cause God shall send them strong delusion, that they should believe a lie: [12] That they all might be damned who believed not the truth, but had pleasure in unrighteousness. 2Thes 2:11-12 KJV

God is going to come like a thief, Rev 16:15, ... **to the wicked!** The faithful are not in the dark to be surprised as by a thief.

[4] **But ye, brethren, are not in darkness, that that day should overtake you as a thief.** [5] Ye are all the children of light, and the children of the day: we are not of the night, nor of darkness.
[6] Therefore let us not sleep, as *do* others; but let us watch and be sober. 1Thes 5:4-6 KJV

It will be the same as in the days of Noah.

[26] "And just as it happened in the days of Noah, so it will be also in the days of the Son of Man: [27] they were eating, they were drinking, they were marrying, they were being given in marriage, until the day that Noah entered the ark, and the flood came and destroyed them all." Lk 17:26-27 NASB

Noah knew. He was not surprised. It will be same as in the days of Lot.

> [28] "It was the same as happened in the days of Lot: they were eating, they were drinking, they were buying, they were selling, they were planting, they were building; [29] but on the day that Lot went out from Sodom it rained fire and brimstone from heaven and destroyed them all. [30] It will be just the same on the day that the Son of Man is revealed." Lk 17:28-30 NASB

Lot knew. Lot was not surprised. *We will know if we are spiritually awake.* We will not know the day or the hour, but we will know when it is "**near.**"

> "Now when these things **begin to happen**, look up and lift up your heads, because your redemption draws near." Lk 21:28 NKJV

On the other hand, if we are getting drunk and partying, then that day will close on us like a trap, Lk 21:34.

The armies gathered at the Mountain of Megiddo, "Har-magedon." "Har" in Hebrew means mountain, and Megiddo is a place which is to the North-East of Caesarea, and South-West of Nazareth. So in the NASB it is called "Har-mage-don," and in the KJV and many other translations as "Armageddon." There has always been a lot of fighting around Megiddo, such as is seen in Judg 5:19. Invaders into Israel or Judah often had to travel through the pass at Megiddo. For instance, when good king Josiah came out to meet Pharaoh in battle in 2Kgs 23:29-30. So in Revelation 16 the forces of evil are gathering at Har-magedon to fight. The saints have already been suppressed. It seems they gather to fight against the coming of God Himself, Rev 16:14.

Is it meant to be literally at the place of ancient Megiddo? Perhaps. It does seem to indicate armies from the far east coming across the dry Euphrates River. Then again, it may just be symbolic of enemies of God's people gathering at a normal invasion point.

Then the last angel poured out the last bowl of God's anger. He pours it out into the air, Rev 16:17. It would appear that God's wrath is finished here with the Second Coming of Christ, and that in these last few verses of Revelation 16 it is about the end of our age, and the end of another of the parallel visions of Revelation. Then the greatest earthquake of all time comes on the earth, Rev 16:18. Babylon the Great, the great city which was spoken of earlier, is split in three parts, and it seems to say that all the cities of the nations fall at this time, Rev 16:19. The great city has been mentioned before in Rev 11:8. At this point the great city is given a symbolic name: "Babylon the great." Also ALL islands move, and ALL mountains fall, Rev 16:20. But ALL islands moving and ALL mountains falling would only be at the Second Coming.

Huge hailstones are mentioned here, and are often involved in God's victories. Huge hailstones fell on ancient Egypt to bring evil men to change their minds, Ex 9:22-26. God brought victory in Joshua's time in part by releasing huge stones (meteorites?) and huge hailstones on the enemy armies, Josh 10:11. What is it that precedes God when He comes out of heaven? Brightness, thick clouds, and hailstones, according to Psa 18:12. Again it can be seen in Psa 105:32. God comes with fire and hailstones in Isa 30:30. Lastly it should be remembered that God's vengeance on Gog and Magog (who have not been discussed at this point) includes fire and hailstones in Ezek 38:21-22. Remember we also ran into hailstones in Rev 8:7, and again we saw hailstones in Rev 11:19. It is one hundred pound hailstones, Rev 16:21.

When men go to fight against God, they are fighting Someone who they cannot overcome. How much more sensible to submit to God while we can!

IX. Babylon and the Beast Fall, Revelation 17-19

To Belshazzar, the king of ancient Babylon, portrayed in the picture on the preceding page:

> [24] Then was the part of the hand sent from him; and this writing was written. [25] And this is the writing that was written, MENE, MENE, TEKEL, UPHARSIN. [26] This is the interpretation of the thing: MENE; God hath numbered thy kingdom, and finished it. [27] TEKEL; Thou art weighed in the balances, and art found wanting. [28] PERES; Thy kingdom is divided, and given to the Medes and Persians. Dan 5:24-28 KJV

God will Destroy Babylon the Great, Rev 17:1-7

The discussion has been about the seven last plagues. Now the Oxford American Dictionary defines the American usage of "plague" this way.

> a contagious bacterial disease characterized by fever and delirium, typically with the formation of buboes (see **bubonic plague**) and sometimes infection of the lungs (**pneumonic plague**): : *an outbreak of plague* | *they died of the plague.*
> • a contagious disease that *spreads* rapidly and kills many people.
> • an unusually large number of insects or animals infesting a place and causing damage : *a plague of fleas.*

Now these entries are close to part of the Bible sense, and only lastly does the dictionary talk of the Bible sense of a divine punishment.

> • a widespread affliction *regarded* as divine punishment : *the plagues of Egypt.*

"Plague" is used in the Septuagint (LXX) Greek translation of the Old Testament in the modern American sense of the plagues of Egypt which Moses announced from the Lord, in passages such as Ex 11:1, and Ex 12:13. In Classical Greek, Liddell & Scott quote Hesiod and Aeschylus as calling a stroke of lightning a *plāgā theou* πληγη θεοῦ, literally a blow from God, or a blow from heaven in Sophocles.

Perhaps the nature of plagues in the Greek sense, and in the Bible sense, should have been emphasized more specifically. The Greek word is *plāgā* πληγή, which means a blow, a stoke with a club or a whip. It can mean a wound or a setback, a catastrophe. It comes from the word *plāssō* πλήσσω, which has the idea of flattening something out, pounding it out, beating something until it is laid out flat. In the Greek translation of the Old Testament it is used of the sons of Ammon being "subdued," Judges 11:33. When Jesus told the story of the Good Samaritan, the robbers beat the man, Lk 10:30, (*plāgā* πληγή), or the

Greek is more literal, it says they beat upon him, or some might say, "beat up on him." When Paul received an unjust condemnation before a court, it says that they beat him, Act 16:23, and the word again is the word plague (*plāgā* πληγή). Then it describes Paul's wounds in Acts 16:33, and the Greek word is that these are Paul's plagues (*plāgā* πληγή), his wounds.

And the beast's fatal wound in Rev 13:3, it is his fatal "plague." It is a plague, a blow, unto death (*ā plāgā tou thanatou*, ἡ πληγὴ τοῦ θανάτου).

When it speaks of the LORD crushing the Messiah in Isa 53:10, or bruising Him as in the KJV, "putting *Him* to grief," the Greek translation (LXX) uses the word for plague for crushing Him or bruising Him. Surely we considered Him smitten by the LORD our God, Isa 53:4. For sure, these things were no accident, for Jesus was "delivered by the determined purpose and foreknowledge of God," Acts 2:23 NKJV. It is used of a literal beating also in the LXX in Deut 25:2, of a man lying down and taking his beating.

God is going to flatten Babylon, beat her down.

One of the angels bearing the seven last plagues, then appeared to John in Rev 17:1, and told him judgment is going to fall on Babylon.

Now Babylon is described as a harlot, a prostitute she is called in the NIV. In the KJV she is described as "the great whore." This business harlot, offers immoral services to the kings of the earth, Rev 17:2a. I do not think this is just talking about sexual immorality here, although I think it would clearly include sexual immorality. Babylon is evidently "the fixer," the deal maker, the arranger. What is your problem as a king, as a ruler, as a judge? Is it a public problem, or is it a private problem? No matter, they will fix it! They will bribe, blackmail, extort money or influence or decisions ... as needed. They have the contacts in the dark world of crime and depravity. Whatever is your problem, they will fix it.

This Babylon also makes the world "drunk with the wine of her fornication," Rev 17:2 KJV. It seems to be saying drunk with wild sex, pleasure, pornography, lust, greed, the feeling of power, the absence of pain, the highs of drugs. Babylon is the center of selling immoral pleasure on our televisions, in movies, in our songs, in Hollywood, New York, Nashville, Chicago, London, Paris, Berlin, you name it.

The harlot rides on Satanism

> So he carried me away in the spirit into the wilderness: and I saw a woman sit upon a scarlet coloured beast, full of names of blasphemy, having seven heads and ten horns. Rev 17:3 KJV

John in this verse seems to be carried away to another place, a remote place, in what he calls a wilderness or a desert. It is as if he is seeing something which is in hiding, which is positioned in an obscure out of the way place. John seems to be seeing something which he has never seen before: this woman, this harlot. Then he sees that this woman *sits* on a scarlet beast/monster full of wicked and slanderous names, and the beast has seven heads and ten horns. This is clearly of the red dragon of Rev 12:3 and the verses which follow: "that old serpent, called the Devil, and Satan," Rev 12:9. Or no doubt we should say, she sits on this age long Satanic organization.

The harlot is NOT Satan or Satanism. She rides on Satanism, the beast's worldly organization. She *rides* on the beast which has seven heads and ten horns. Remember that the beast is first of all *the organization* (Rev 13:1) which has seven heads/directors, and ten centers of power (horns). Then we saw that one of those seven heads of the organization, had a fatal wound, but that wound was healed, Rev 13:3. The head that received this fatal wound is also called **the** "beast," and he is of the beast organization (Rev 13:1-3)! Also notice that the heads are seemingly public figures, but are not recognized for what they are.

Remember the beast (organization and man) both receive their powers from the dragon, Satan, **Rev 13:2**. And the dragon **IS** the devil or Satan, Rev 12:9a. **And the harlot rides this organization.**

The harlot is very, very rich, Rev 17:4a.

She is dressed in the most expensive of clothing, scarlet and purple, and she is wearing a lot of expensive diamonds and sapphires and pearls, and all sorts of costly stones and silver and gold. Further, the woman is very, very nasty. She drinking from a golden cup which is filled with the filthy fluids of fornication, Rev 17:4b. It describes it as "a gold cup full of abominations and of the unclean things of her immorality," in the NASB, as "full of abominations and filthiness of her fornication," in the KJV, as "filled with abominable things and the filth of her adulteries," in the NIV.

This harlot is a business entity of sorts, but she is also a religion. She is an occult religion, a special type of religion, a "mystery religion" is the Greek technical term. This is a religion that keeps their teachings secret between the members. These concepts are more fully discussed in *Prophecy Principles*.

> And upon her forehead *was* a name written, MYSTERY, BABYLON THE GREAT, THE MOTHER OF HARLOTS AND ABOMINATIONS OF THE EARTH. Rev 17:5 KJV

I think the punctuation may be misleading in many of our translations, including the KJV. When a first century reader saw this phrase they would not just think of something mysterious, but also of the very popular mystery religions which at times ran counter to civil law.

This religio-commercial entity is the mother of the abominations of the earth, Rev 17:5! She is their origin, their source.

This harlot drinks the blood of Christians, Rev 17:6.

She is in fact drunk on their blood, unable to think clearly, because of killing so many Christians and drinking their blood. John is awe struck.

It is not clear from the context whether this drinking of the filth of fornication, or of drinking the blood of saints is metaphorical, or literal, or both. First let us consider this subject from the viewpoint of a prostitute. Many people understand that even so-called "straight" *promiscuous* behavior is unclean, and is a breeder of disease and genetic problems (compare 1Cor 6:15-18). For a prostitute to engage in activities which are filthy, unclean, often becomes, so it seems, almost second nature, and such is constantly portrayed in American "entertainment" in the early twenty-first century. For those engaged in immoral behavior, over time, to treat filth as inconsequential is something commonly portrayed. It was certainly also very common in the first century AD. Paul comments on these things,

> [19] and they, having become callous, have given themselves over to sensuality for the practice of every kind of **impurity** with greediness. [20] But you did not learn Christ in this way,
> Eph 4:19-20 NASB (*bold emphasis added*)

"Impurity" in Eph 4:19 NASB could be more plainly translated as "uncleanness" as in the KJV or the NKJV, or even as "filthiness," as in the KJV Rev 17:2. This is one of the reasons for fornicators high disease rates. Most of this comes under the heading of sodomy, whether heterosexual or homosexual, and such *is* unclean, filthy. As religious entities, both the "mystery of lawlessness" (2 Thessalonians 2 and Revelation 13) and "Mystery Babylon" are portrayed as those whose true religious nature is deeply hidden from the public. John has to be taken away to an uninhabited place in order to see this harlot as she actually is. Her true nature is so foreign to John in these visions that he acts as if he has never seen such a thing, and he (and we) may never have, directly and openly. In the history of the occult in our world, a drifting into such immoral secret cults, and into criminal blood-cult activities, is also common. These things are discussed in much public occult literature. Such sometimes turned into open, public, activities, as with the ancient Canaanites, the Celts, the Aztecs, and some groups among our American Indians. In fact, it is often the horrendous criminal nature of many of these activities that provide the Satanic glue that so powerfully holds these groups together. The "Thugs" of India, and their worship of the black-mother-"goddess" Kali would be another public example (the Thugs of India are portrayed in Rudyard Kipling's *Gunga Din*). Some of this, at least with the beast and his worship, seems to be pictured in the book of Revelation as becoming once again public religion. I am inclined to take this drinking of the filth of fornication, and the drinking of the blood of Christians as metaphorical *and* literal. Not as an either or thing.

The angel then offers to tell John the secret of this powerful and immoral force in history, which rides on Satanism, Rev 17:7. This horrible, immoral entity is due for punishment. She is due to be flattened out by the Lord our God. It is coming. **Not at the end of history, but it is *within history* that it will come.**

Now we can be due a beating, and may get it.

The story is told of two officers who were at Pearl Harbor. They were witnesses to the start of the attack in December of 1941. What happened is accurately depicted in the 1970 movie "Tora, Tora, Tora!" They were walking along and saw a plane flying too low. One said to the other, look at how low that plane is flying, get his tag number. Then the plane, a Japanese plane, dropped a bomb, and they realized an attack was underway. They ran to the communications center and sent out a telegram to all stations. It read very simply: "Pearl Harbor is under attack. This is no drill."

God may come at an unexpected time for us, just as for Babylon the Great, Lk 12:45-46. The more we know, the better we can prepare and defend ourselves from Satan. But to know and not do?

> [47] And that servant, which knew his lord's will, and prepared not *himself*, neither did according to his will, shall be beaten with many *stripes*. [48] But he that knew not, and did commit things worthy of stripes, shall be beaten with few *stripes*. For unto whomsoever much is given, of him shall be much required: and to whom men have committed much, of him they will ask the more. Lk 12:47-48 KJV

My friends, we are in the middle of a giant battle for the souls of men.

THIS IS NO DRILL.

Seven Mountains, and Seven Kings, Rev 17:7-10

What are you wondering? the angel says. I will tell you about Mystery Babylon and the beast that carries her, Rev 17:7. Mystery in the sense of "mysterious" does seem to be the usage in this verse. There is also another incredulous thing here: it is the beast who carries the harlot. It is the same beast which has seven heads and ten horns! Again, heads means the heads of an organization, that is those who do the thinking and directing of the organization. Now in Revelation 13 one of the heads had a fatal wound, but the fatal wound was healed. Remember?

Horns, if you remember, represent power, for instance in passages like Psa 18:2, or again in passages like Psa 75:5. So it can mean either good power or bad power. It has also been shown that horns can also represent individual kings, or lines or families of kings. For instance, in the book of Daniel it talks about the Persian Empire as a ram, a powerful male sheep, with two large horns, and one horn is larger than the other, Dan 8:3. There the horns represent the kings of Media (the small horn), and the kings of Persia (the big horn). First the Medians ruled in the Persian Empire, and then the Persians ruled. The Persians were dominant longer and were more powerful. It tells us specifically this is what it means in Dan 8:20, so we can know this is true. Then the Persians were challenged by the Greeks, represented by a male goat with a conspicuous horn, Dan 8:5-9. The conspicuous horn is Alexander the Great, and the four horns are the four lines of kings who divided up his kingdom at his death. We know that this is true, because that is what it says in Dan 8:21-22.

So there are plenty of examples as to how we should take the symbolism in Revelation 17.

The monster which comes up out of the sea in Revelation 13, has seven heads which direct it, and it has ten kings or lines of kings under its power, Rev 13:1, and the horns have ten crowns/diadems, representing the right to rule. So these centers of power actually rule as crowned, or duly appointed, rulers.

Now the beast itself is of one of those heads, or one king of a line of those kings, Rev 13:3-4. The unsaved of this world will worship this monster, this beast, Rev 17:8.

Now this beast "was," Rev 17:8, "and is not." He was here on earth, but now, when John is seeing his vision, this beast is dead. This beast has gone to the place of the dead, called in Scripture *sheol* (Hebrew) or *hades* (Greek), or it is also called the pit or the abyss. There are good places to be, and bad places, in the world of the dead, but that is another discussion.

There is one further thing about this beast, who has formerly lived on earth. He is "about to come up out of the abyss," Rev 17:8 NASB, the place where Jesus went for three days, Rom 10:6-7 NASB, the place of the dead. Then from a short life here on earth the beast is again to "go to destruction," Rev 17:8 NASB. So he was on earth, but "now" (when John is writing) is dead, and will in the last times come to life, and then go to eternal destruction. It seems to be speaking of this former life of the beast, not of his being raised from the dead. This is speaking of a major time of Satanic pseudo-miracles, 2Thes 2:9-10. "Pseudo" in the sense that these actions do not prove what they purport to prove: the deity of this monster, and his right to rule.

The angel begins by describing the beast, the organization, overall.

> 9 "Here is the mind which has wisdom: The seven heads are seven mountains on which the woman sits. 10 There are also seven kings. Five have fallen, one is, and the other has not yet come. And when he comes, he must continue a short time." Rev 17:9-10 NKJV

Among the things to be noticed here is that **this is clearly multilayered symbolism**. Of course such is common in Bible prophecy with symbolism and fulfillment. Here we see such things raised to a new level. The seven heads are *both* seven kings and seven mountains. Seven kings we understand. Seven kings direct this enterprise, and they have ten horns, that is to say, ten centers of power, perhaps kings/rulers or powerful organizations, or lines of powerful men under Satanic control.

Now what are "mountains" symbolically? Mountains in Scripture quite often represent various religions, centered around some mountain or another. God's religion is centered on Mount Zion in Jerusalem. Many Old Testament verses could be cited, but Psa 2:6 will do. There is the mountain of Samaria for the Samaritan religion, and the mountains of Lebanon, and of course there is Mount Olympus for the so called "gods" of Greece. You can refer to Jn 4:20-22, and Psa 68:15-16 and many other passages.

The woman seemingly sits on seven kings and seven mountains, Rev 17:9. Now the mountains on which the harlot of Babylon sits, would in this context seem to mean that she sits on seven different religions! Babylon the Great, uses/advocates seven different religions to support her power. She rests on these religions. What are these seven religions? I think your guess is as good as mine. However these would clearly be key religions for the last two thousand years. You tell me! I would say that some of these probably would be religions that have been know by different names in different phases of our age.

Additionally, she also sits on seven kings, Rev 17:10. Here is clearly an out and out double meaning in verses 9-10, and it shows in our major translations, but the KJV translation, although saying it, does not make these things clear. Some want to say men can use a double meaning but God cannot!

Lastly, the beast is of one of these lines of kings/rulers, and is also a king, a ruler of some nation or group, an eighth king according to Rev 17:11.

It should be noted that liberal commentators are dogmatic that the seven kings are seven Caesars, and Mystery Babylon is the city of Rome! They cannot conceive of anyone speaking from beyond their own view and experience. The NIV translates the "mountains," as seven hills, in Rev 17:9, and Rome did sit on seven "hills," that is to say, "hills," not mountains.

In contrast to these ideas, the regular word for hills is *bounos* βουνός. In Rev 17:9 the word used is the regular word for "mountains," *oros* ὄρος. WHICH IS NOT THE SAME. You can see the word for mountain and the word for hill contrasted in Lk 3:5, where it says,

> Every valley shall be filled, and every **mountain** and **hill** shall be brought low; ..." KJV (*emphasis added*)

God will use these evil kings to destroy Mystery Babylon. God will put in their hearts to destroy this harlot who has drunk the blood of the saints, Rev

17:17. What then does the angel tell us?

> And the woman which thou sawest is that great city, which reigneth over the kings of the earth. Rev 17:18 KJV

Rome was a "great city," even though it sat on seven hills and not seven mountains. Rome did rule over many kings of the earth, and appointed them or deposed them, as may have suited Rome's senate or her emperors. Also Rome would clearly come to mind when this was read in the early centuries after Christ, *and* the book of Revelation *does cover*, not only the end of time, but also those early centuries after Christ. So far these things seem to fit.

But there is also some uneasiness here. First it would be with the "hills." Also the seven heads are part of the dragon, and these seven heads are not really of a Roman/Babylon, but of the dragon and the beast organization. And Mystery Babylon is not part of the seven heads, rather these are kings on whom the woman **sits**, Rev 17:9. Then what we see is that the great harlot, Mystery Babylon, **rules** *over* the kings/heads (the Caesars?), the governments of the earth, Rev 17:18.

You can call this a picture of Rome (Babylon?) resting on, sitting on the seven caesars, but then you have the harlot ruling over the Caesars, the heads. Thus, **the harlot is a distinct entity from the heads/mountains upon which she rests.** This will become even clearer when we take a closer look at this passage.

So a big part of the problem here is not Big Brother (civil government), but Big Mother, Mystery Babylon, the mother of harlots.

God is in control all the way. He can take care of us "*even* unto the end of the world," Mtt 28:20, *if* we will give our lives to Him!

Who are the Seven Kings? Rev 17:10-18

Or, who are the seven kings or *lines of kings?* It has been shown that a horn can be a line of kings, as for instance with the Medo-Persian kings in Dan 8:3, 20. Or a horn can be an individual king, like Alexander the Great in Dan 8:5-9, 21-22.

Zechariah 1 gives a good example of horns as kings or powers. Four horns have scattered Judah and Israel.

> [18] Then lifted I up mine eyes, and saw, and behold four horns. [19] And I said unto the angel that talked with me, What *be* these? And he answered me, These *are* the horns which have scattered Judah, Israel, and Jerusalem. Zech 1:18-19 KJV

But God will scatter these powers.

Then said I, What come these to do? And he spake, saying, These *are* the horns which have scattered Judah, so that no man did lift up his head: but these are come to fray them, to cast out the horns of the Gentiles, which lifted up their *horn* over the land of Judah to scatter it. Zech 1:21 KJV

Revelation 17 symbolism also covers seven kings, special kings, upon whom Babylon sits, Rev 17:9-10. The beast is of one of these lines of kings, and is also a king, a ruler of some nation or group, according to Rev 17:11. Also we have these seven heads in *both* Revelation 13 and Revelation 17.

If you read or listen to various liberal scholars, they emphasize how simple all of this is. You can see various lists from them. I have chosen to use the very popular (and very available in English) William Barclay, as an illustration of how these things frequently work out. In Revelation 13 the very readable Barclay list these heads as seven Caesars.

"Tiberius, A.D. 14-37; Caligula, A.D. 37-41, Claudius, A.D. 41-54; Nero, A.D. 55-68; Vespasian, A.D. 69-79; Titus, A.D. 79-81; Domitian, A.D. 81-96." *Daily Study Bible, Revelation, Vol. 2*, pg 110, Westminster Press, Philadelphia, 1960.

The obvious thing here is that he leaves out Caesar Augustus, the very first Caesar (if you leave out Julius Caesar!). Then in Revelation 17, Barclay gives **another** list of the seven heads, **a different list**. He lists the first five of the seven heads as,

"Augustus, Tiberius, Caligula, Claudius, and Nero." *Vol. 2*, pg 181.

He thinks these are the five fallen kings. These sorts of discrepancies are typical of the outright contradictions in liberal interpretations of the book of Revelation. But they think John was confused, not them, and they are very dogmatic as to how John was confused! Barclay thinks Vespasian is the one who is "one is" in Rev 17:10. That the one who has not yet come is Titus. Then comes the beast of Rev 17:11, who is Domitian. So Barclay seems to think "John" is writing this, making this up, during the time of Domitian, and pretending he is writing in the time of Vespasian, and that he is picturing Domitian as "the beast." Domitian began ruling in AD 81, and John's exile was toward the end of Domitian's reign (Domitian was assassinated in AD 96).

(Barclay overall is a good representative of the liberal/"scholarly" point of view on Revelation, and apocalyptic literature, from beginning to end. He presents these views in a readable non-technical fashion for the average adult reader. He does not believe that John the apostle wrote the book. He admits that tradition is consistent as to the apostle John writing the book, but he is ambiguous as to the date of its writing. *I really think that part of **the problem with the liberal point of view** is that they do not **like** the **message** of Revelation.* For them it is far too much like the Old Testament pictures of God, which they detest!

They have absorbed far too much of a Kabbalistic view of the Most High God as remote and detached from His creation, and as never intervening for anyone's benefit, or even worse from their point of view, for the doom of the wicked! That fits their naturalistic biases from the so called "Enlightenment," and their misinterpretations of both the Old and the New Covenants. Of course, for Bible believers, God is someone who does not change, Mal 3:6. So for the True God to hear the prayers of the saints, and to intervene in the affairs of men, is both consistent, and proper. **Here are the real issues!**)

Domitian, though he was a monster in many ways, really does not fit the picture of the beast, in hundreds of different ways! Even on the surface this does not fit the time lines of which John writes in Revelation chapters 11, 12, and 13. Let us take something simple here: Domitian ruled about fifteen years, essentially claiming to be a "god" from the first, not the mere three and half years that the beast is to rule as some sort of "god"! So here, and in other places as well, Domitian is at best a "type." Yet some like to pretend it written to fit the Emperor Domitian.

Then comes the next part: the book of Revelation has the beast, one of the heads of the dragon organization, ***destroying Mystery Babylon*** *within history!* The "beast" will destroy "Babylon" "in one hour," Rev 18:10.

So the standard out of the box liberal interpretation has the caesars destroying the Roman Empire! That should be an incredible interpretation in anyone's book. Further Rome did not fall in a single day, much less a single hour. Rome was 1500 years in falling, according to Gibbon's *Decline and Fall of the Roman Empire*, **and was not destroyed by a Caesar, but by multiple foreign invasions, over many centuries!**

Further, in the book of Daniel it was shown, the Roman Empire is clearly described as **"a"** "beast," Dan 7:7, 19, 23. If you view Scripture as a unity, that would seem to put the Roman Empire on the "beast" side of the imagery in Revelation 17, **NOT** on the Babylon the Great side of this imagery. Also that fits the context in Revelation chapters 17 and 18, as has been shown.

So Barclay, like most liberals, views Revelation as a fake prophecy, which failed in the first century! He does not say it plainly, but, like many liberals, he does in effect say it. Generations of ministers who knew that premillennialism would not stand up to examination in the light of Scripture, were ready to believe there was an alternative to Scofield and his like, have bought into these interpretations, sometimes not fully realizing that these men meant that the book was a *false prophecy!*

The sorts of contradictions which have been demonstrated with William Barclay, you can also do with most of the mainline liberal commentators. *They fit only to a point.* Now bits and pieces of this *do* fit the Caesars and Rome, and the first century ... **but not all of it.** Similarly, bits and pieces fit Mohammed, and Napoleon, and Hitler, and Mussolini, and so on. But not all! For better or for worse, I am emphasizing here what does *not* fit. So what is to be seen here?

The Caesars and the Roman Empire are *at best* types and patterns, symbolic of the final world order, and the persecutions of the end. Not the ultimate fulfillment. There will be more discussion of this later.

So who are the seven kings? I do not know! I do not have enough information to know! The last part of Daniel 11 does not fit Antiochus IV Epiphanes or any king we know. Perhaps some of the verses in Daniel 11 apply to both Antiochus IV and the times of the beast, and possibly more especially to understanding the final beast.

> [33] "And those of the people who understand shall instruct many; yet *for many* days they shall fall by sword and flame, by captivity and plundering. [34] Now when they fall, they shall be aided with a little help; but many shall join with them by intrigue. [35] And *some* of those of understanding shall fall, to refine *them*, purify them, and make *them* white, *until* the time of the end; because *it is* still for the appointed time." Dan 11:33-35 NKJV

I think this is like Dan 12:4, where the angel told Daniel,

> But thou, O Daniel, shut up the words, and seal the book, *even* to the time of the end: many shall run to and fro, and knowledge shall be increased. KJV

It appears these things will become clearer as the time gets closer. The beast is one of the seven heads of the Satanic organization, Rev 13:1, 3, and similar verses in Revelation 17. Further, it seems the beast is one of the seven kings upon whom Mystery Babylon sits, Rev 17:11. Mystery Babylon, it seems, is supported by seven religions, and by **seven** kings or lines of kings!

Additionally, it can be seen that the beast uses the ten horns of Satanism, Rev 13:1. Satanism is supported by **ten** powers who have not yet received a kingdom, and the beast persuades them (who did not yet have power, perhaps they are royal princes or members of a Satanic nobility!) to work with him to destroy Mystery Babylon, Rev 17:12-13, 16.

Now ten kings, ten horns, line up with the beast, Rev 17:12. *It does look as if they are related to the ten horns of Dan 7:24.* They have just one purpose, and that is to give their power and authority to the beast, Rev 17:13. They will make war on Jesus, but they will not win, Rev 17:14.

Now the harlot sits on seven kings, and seven religions and many "waters" or nations, Rev 17:15. However, the heads, the kings, resent this dominance over them by the harlot. Once more it should be pointed out, she "reigns over the kings of the earth," Rev 17:18 NKJV. The beast and the ten kings hate the harlot, Rev 17:16. They will ruin Mystery Babylon, and burn her with fire, and eat her flesh.

For God hath put in their hearts to fulfil his will, and to agree, and give their kingdom unto the beast, until the words of God shall be fulfilled. Rev 17:17 KJV

So God Himself puts it in the mind of the beast and the ten kings to destroy Babylon. They hate Mystery Babylon.

Clearly in the overall context of Revelation, ancient Rome is distinctly here. But if you put it in the context of the heads of the beast being the caesars, and Mystery Babylon being Rome itself, then what you have is the Caesars deliberately destroying Rome, *their own power base*. So was Rome really the Great city?

The Fall of Babylon the Great, Revelation 18

In Revelation 17 there was an organization of ten kings, and another king called the beast, Rev 17:12. They are organized against Mystery Babylon, the harlot who rules over the kings of the earth, Rev 17:18. Their job is to destroy the great harlot, Mystery Babylon, *because the Lord our God has said it*, Rev 17:17. Is the harlot, Mystery Babylon, the great city Rome? Let us look further into our subject.

As one enters Revelation 18, they see another angel announcing Babylon's fall.

And he cried mightily with a loud voice, saying, "Babylon the great is fallen, is fallen, and has become a dwelling place of demons, a prison for every foul spirit, and a cage for every unclean and hated bird!"
Rev 18:2 NKJV

Notice that the description in verse 2 is seemingly taken from the prophets Jeremiah and Isaiah, in passages like Isa 21:9.

And, behold, here cometh a chariot of men, *with* a couple of horsemen. And he answered and said, Babylon is fallen, is fallen; and all the graven images of her gods he hath broken unto the ground. KJV

Babylon of old, after her fall to the Medes and the Persians, is pictured in the Old Testament as a place where only wild creatures can live, and where only thorns and briars can grow.

[11] But pelican and hedgehog will possess it,
  And owl and raven will dwell in it;
  And He will stretch over it the line of desolation
  And the plumb line of emptiness.
[12] Its nobles — there is no one there
  Whom they may proclaim king —
  And all its princes will be nothing.

[13] Thorns will come up in its fortified towers,
    Nettles and thistles in its fortified cities;
    It will also be a haunt of jackals
    And an abode of ostriches.
[14] The desert creatures will meet with the wolves,
    The hairy goat also will cry to its kind;
    Yes, the night monster will settle there
    And will find herself a resting place. Isa 34:11-14 NASB

The Septuagint Greek translation of the Old Testament (which is often abbreviated as LXX) says in Isa 34:14,

"Demons shall meet with donkey–centaurs and call one to another;"
A New English Translation Of The Septuagint, Ed. Pietersma and Wright, 2007, Oxford University Press.

The KJV translates the hairy goats as "Satyrs" here. In other words, it is what many would call "goat demons," as in Lev 17:7 in the NASB, and just as John takes them in Rev 18:2. Jer 50:39 is a similar passage, and the LXX translates it this way:

"Therefore phantoms shall live in the islands, and daughters of Sirens shall inhabit her; she shall never again be inhabited forever."
A New English Translation Of The Septuagint.

Mystery Babylon seems to be compared to Sodom and Gomorrah.

Therefore shall her plagues come in one day, death, and mourning, and famine; and she shall be utterly burned with fire: for strong *is* the Lord God who judgeth her. Rev 18:8 KJV

You may remember that the "great city" is called Sodom in Rev 11:8. Mystery Babylon of the New Testament will be very much like Sodom of old in her destruction. Jeremiah wrote of ancient Babylon along such lines.

As God overthrew Sodom and Gomorrah and the neighbour cities thereof, saith the LORD; so shall no man abide there, neither shall any son of man dwell therein. Jer 50:40 KJV

Why is Mystery Babylon to be so destroyed? Babylon has ruined the nations, has in fact ruined the world.

For **all** nations have drunk of **the wine of the wrath of her fornication**, and the kings of the earth have committed fornication with her, and the merchants of the earth are waxed rich through the abundance of her delicacies. Rev 18:3 KJV (*bold and underline emphasis added*)

All nations have drunk of her passionate immorality. All the kings of the earth have fornicated with her, and have "become rich by the wealth of her sensuality," NASB. It is not merely because she has drunk the blood of saints, but also because she has seduced "all nations."

Come out of her Christians, we are told in Rev 18:4. That clearly implies that many Christians will be involved in Mystery Babylon! (On the other hand, Revelation does *not* seem to imply that Christians will be involved in the beast organization, the mystery of lawlessness!)

Come out of Mystery Babylon, Rev 18:4. That way you will not participate in her punishment. The Lord our God has remembered her sins, Rev 18:5. Her sins are as high as heaven! Pay her back double, is what God says. To the degree that she has glorified herself, bring punishment on her.

> Therefore shall her plagues come in one day, death, and mourning, and famine; and she shall be utterly burned with fire: for strong *is* the Lord God who judgeth her. Rev 18:8 KJV

Most of the kings of the world will cry about her passing. They have had intimate relations with her, and drunk deep of her wine, and the merchants have become rich "from the power of her luxurious living," Rev 18:3 ESV They will look from a distance at her destruction, for fear of being involved in the terrible retribution that has come upon her. She will fall "in one hour," Rev 18:10. Not just in one day, but in one hour!

Ancient Babylon did fall in a single day, as recorded in ancient history, for instance by the Greek historian Herodotus. For a major empire to even fall in one day was a difficult thing in ancient times. But one hour? Literally?

Rome, of course, did not fall in one day, much less in one hour. In fact, with her far flung armies and administration, it would have been almost impossible for Rome to have fallen in a single day. Gibbon's *Decline and Fall of the Roman Empire* is six volumes long, and covers over 1400 years, from the first century onward to the fifteenth century. Falling in one day, or in one hour, does not fit ancient Rome.

Rome did not require a mark of the Emperor to buy or sell. They only issued a certificate that you had offered incense to the Emperor, and it was not needed for buying and selling. A special mark of a "god" before you could buy or sell anything? That will come later! Remember, this was covered in section VII about "The Woman Above, the Dragon, and the Harlot," pgs 199-200.

So how does the rest of the prophecy fit Rome? The answer is simple: Rome is viewed as iron legs and feet, that can stomp all others into oblivion, Dan 2:40. She has the strength to crush and shatter all opposition. How else is she viewed? As a monster with iron teeth, that can devour and crush and smash others and trample them under her feet, Dan 7:7. So the normal picture of Rome in prophecy is of power and might and strength, and incredible endurance which no one can resist. That fits with history. Ancient Rome had incredible power and discipline and stamina to deal with threats or rebellions or defeats. Defeats? Rome had plenty of them, but absorbed them, and rebuilt her forces and kept on coming! Seduce people? Fix them up with harlots or riotous pleasures? Help them make money so as to gain control of them? Rome has no need to do such. She can merely order them around, demand money as she needs it, and stomp them into the dirt if they resist!

Babylon the Great, on the other hand, seems to rule by seduction, by cunning, by immoral influence, by the grand deal that is sealed with overwhelming luxury and passion, and demonic spirits. Everything unclean and nasty is her specialty, and "the maddening wine of her adulteries," Rev 18:3 NIV, makes everyone just a little drunk and reeling with intoxication in dealing with her. Rome in contrast ruled by the iron-spiked boot. Babylon rules by immorality like a harlot, Rev 18:3. She sells herself like a prostitute. But Rome has no need to sell herself. Rome can beat and smash, grind to pieces, and stomp into the ground any who dare to oppose her. There is some parallel with the ten horns. In opposition to this picture of ancient Rome, Babylon rules by making *others* rich. "and the merchants of the earth grew rich from her excessive luxuries." Rev 18:3 NIV. She can transfer her factories and reroute her trade if they disobey. Rome, however, *did **not*** rule by making others rich, but by *using **others*** to make ***herself*** rich.

The Conclusion:

The picture in Revelation only partially fits Rome! No passage we have examined consistently fits Rome all the way. No doubt, many ancient Romans, both Christian and pagan, also thought the same if they read the book of Revelation, with much wondering! If Revelation was meant to be a fake prophecy about ancient Rome, it would be the height of stupidity to write it this way. In contrast, the book of Revelation is written as if it is consistent, following some design that may not always be apparent to us.

Remember from our previous studies: when what is told does not completely fit the immediate object in history, that is often a sign of the immediate object being symbolic of something else in the future. The immediate object is what the Bible would call a "type" or a "shadow" or a "pattern." It is a prototype of something. Even more discrepancies will be visible as we go along.

The merchants cry because of losing sales, Rev 18:11. Now the great harlot is very religious (after a fashion), and very open minded (except about Christianity)! Remember she evidently sits on seven religions, and plays patty-cake with them all. But she is very anti-Christian in outlook.

> I saw the woman, drunk with the blood of the saints and with the blood of the martyrs of Jesus. And when I saw her, I marveled with great amazement. Rev 17:6 NKJV

She sells herself, bodily. She sells seduction and immorality. She sells a little of everything. Notice that Mystery Babylon is to some degree *contrasted with **many*** *of the merchants!* The merchants are crying because of the loss of the extraordinary sales they were having through Mystery Babylon, Rev 18:11. In fact it seems to speak as if this means the end of abundant luxurious sales, "for no man buyeth their merchandise any more," KJV. What was Mystery Babylon responsible for selling?

> [12] The merchandise of gold, and silver, and precious stones, and of pearls, and fine linen, and purple, and silk, and scarlet, and all thyine wood, and all manner vessels of ivory, and all manner vessels of most precious wood, and of brass, and iron, and marble, [13] And cinnamon, and odours, and ointments, and frankincense, and wine, and oil, and fine flour, and wheat, and beasts, and sheep, and horses, and chariots, and slaves, and souls of men. Rev 18:12-13 KJV

A better question might be, what does she not sell. She also sells people: women, children, young men, you name it. What does Scripture say of the masters of Mystery Babylon?

> ... for **thy merchants** were the great men of the earth, ... Rev 18:23c KJV

Notice that these descriptions are like the descriptions of Tyre and Sidon, on the coast of Palestine, in the Old Testament prophets. Tyre and Sidon *also* are plainly intended as types or symbols of this one-world New Testament age religio-commercial empire, which dominates world trade!

Isaiah 23 describes in some detail the fall of the harlot Tyre, and her eventual return after being decimated by the Babylonians.

In Ezekiel 27 it describes the luxurious trade of Tyre. She used many other peoples in her army, and they made many a splendid display.

> [10] "Persia and Lud and Put were in your army, your men of war. They hung shield and helmet in you; they set forth your splendor. [11] The sons of Arvad and your army were on your walls, *all* around, and the Gammadim were in your towers. They hung their shields on your walls *all* around; they perfected your beauty." Ezek 27:10-11 NASB

So in the type, in the symbolism, there was some degree of military power also. Tyre traded to the ends of the then know world, all the way to Tarshish /Spain, Ezek 27:10. This is followed by an extensive list of the breadth of her trade. She picked up materials in one place and sold them in other places. Her merchants' ships were evidently able to dominate the entire Mediterranean trade world, but evidently without her having Mediterranean wide military power. Then when Tyre falls, the picture is much like that of Mystery Babylon of the New Testament.

> [27] "Your wealth, your wares, your merchandise,
>   Your sailors and your pilots,
>   Your repairers of seams, your dealers in merchandise
>   And all your men of war who are in you,

> With all your company that is in your midst,
> Will fall into the heart of the seas
> On the day of your overthrow.
> [28] "At the sound of the cry of your pilots
>> The pasture lands will shake.
> [29] "All who handle the oar,
>> The sailors *and* all the pilots of the sea
>> Will come down from their ships;
>> They will stand on the land,
> [30] And they will make their voice heard over you
>> And will cry bitterly.
>> They will cast dust on their heads,
>> They will wallow in ashes.
> [31] "Also they will make themselves bald for you
>> And gird themselves with sackcloth;
>> And they will weep for you in bitterness of soul
>> With bitter mourning.
> [32] "Moreover, in their wailing they will take up a lamentation for
>>> you
>> And lament over you:
>> 'Who is like Tyre,
>> Like her who is silent in the midst of the sea?'"
>
> Ezk 27:27-32 NASB

Tyre brought so much luxury to so many places, and so much good employment in so wide a range of goods, from raising horses, to stealing men and women as slaves, that many throughout the world regretted her passing. All of this is pertinent to understanding modern Mystery Babylon. Further, as was pointed out with Roman power and any present entity, Tyre was **not *all*** *of trade* in the Mediterranean world, and many merchants and manufacturers survived her fall, to lament the loss of business, but Tyre did dominate Mediterranean trade for an extended period of time.

Also it was showed in section II under "And a Demonic Man from Satan," it appears that the "beast" is in some sense a "king" of Tyre/Mystery Babylon. In that light, the description of the death of the King of Tyre is pertinent, and it is here that the data on the death of the beast of Revelation 13 might can be tied together. This one who claims,

> ... 'I am a god,
>> I sit in the seat of gods
>> In the heart of the seas';
>> Yet you are a man and not God,
>> Although you make your heart like the heart of God
>
> Ezek 28:2 NASB

Further, if this beast is also one of the merchant princes/kings of Tyre/ Babylon, then it is no wonder that Mystery Babylon trusts the beast, and is undone by his treachery toward her!

As was showed earlier, two different deaths are described for the King of Tyre. One it seems for the "type," and one for the "anti-type," the fulfillment. The death of the ancient King of Tyre I think is described in Ezek 28:10.

> "'You will die the death of the uncircumcised
> By the hand of strangers,
> For I have spoken!' declares the Lord GOD!" NASB

And I think the death of the anti-type, the fulfillment, the beast, is described in Ezek 28:18.

> ... Therefore I have brought fire from the midst of you;
> It has consumed you,
> And I have turned you to ashes on the earth
> In the eyes of all who see you. NASB

He dies without any human agency (Dan 8:25), and by his own spears (Hab 3:14), by "fire from the midst of you"!

Babylon seems to be a religio-commercial empire, that also rules over kings and presidents and dictators, and *rules over/facilitates commerce*. But her power is to be broken, and it speaks as if luxury is to be lost forever.

> "The fruit you long for has gone from you, **and all things that were luxurious and splendid have passed away** from you **and** *men* <u>**will no longer**</u> **find them**. Rev 18:14 NASB (*bold and underline emphasis added*)

There is no recovery from this final time of loss! What a dramatic prophecy, and one that clearly does not apply to the demise of ancient Tyre or ancient Babylon, or ancient Rome! The corporate heads, financial officers, company presidents, and merchant princes are scared, Rev 18:15. Once again it is emphasized that the destruction all happens in one hour.

> [16] And saying, Alas, alas, that great city, that was clothed in fine linen, and purple, and scarlet, and decked with gold, and precious stones, and pearls! [17] **For in one hour** so great riches is come to nought. And every shipmaster, and all the company in ships, and sailors, and as many as trade by sea, stood afar off, [18] And cried when they saw the smoke of her burning, saying, What *city is* like unto this great city! Rev 18:16-18 KJV (*bold emphasis added*)

The sailors are crying in their beer! But be happy Christians! Babylon had drunk and become drunk with the blood of the saints and the witnesses to Christ. God is the One who has judged her, *within history!* Rev 18.20 NASB,

> "Rejoice over her, O heaven, and you saints and apostles and prophets, because God has **pronounced judgment** <u>**for you**</u> against her."

Babylon the Great will completely disappear. It will be like throwing a boulder into the ocean, according to Rev 18:21.

> And a mighty angel took up a stone like a great millstone, and cast *it* into the sea, saying, Thus with violence shall **that great city Babylon** be thrown down, **and shall be found no more at all**. KJV

It is proper to discuss both ancient and modern Babylon together. One is symbolic of the other. She is just like Babylon of the Old Testament times. The city of chaos is broken down, Isa 24:10-11. Compare Jeremiah's prophecy of Babylon in Jer 25:10-11. She was to sink never to rise again as a city.

> [63] And it shall be, when thou hast made an end of reading this book, *that* thou shalt bind a stone to it, and cast it into the midst of Euphrates: [64] And thou shalt say, **Thus shall Babylon sink, and shall not rise from the evil that I will bring upon her**: and they shall be weary. Thus far *are* the words of Jeremiah. Jer 51:63-64 KJV (*bold emphasis added*)

That was a bold prophecy in the sixth century BC about ancient Babylon. Most cities are established for sound geographical reasons, and do not easily disappear. Even if they are totally destroyed, often nothing more than geography is needed to dictate their rebuilding. Even so, Jeremiah boldly says of the ancient mega-city of Babylon, that she will be destroyed and sink out of sight like a stone thrown into the water. It will also be the same for New Testament Mystery Babylon the Great.

> [22] And the voice of harpers, and musicians, and of pipers, and trumpeters, **shall be heard no more at all in thee**; and no craftsman, of whatsoever craft he be, **shall be found any more in thee**; and the sound of a millstone **shall be heard no more at all in thee**; [23] And **the light of a candle shall shine no more at all in thee**; and the voice of the bridegroom and of the bride **shall be heard no more at all in thee**: for thy merchants were the great men of the earth; for by thy sorceries were all nations deceived.
> Rev 18:22-23 KJV (*bold emphasis added*)

But there are weddings in Rome today. And music, and dancing, and workmen and craftsmen of all crafts, and light of lamps. *The Ancient Roman Empire fits **part** of the prophecy, **but only part**.* She is clearly symbolic of the ultimate rule of money and pleasure in New Testament times by Mystery Babylon the Great, the mother of harlots, and the source of all the wars on earth.

Remember 2 Samuel 7, the prophecy of building a temple for the Lord? This is fulfilled by Solomon according to 1Kgs 8:20, and it is fulfilled by Jesus according to Heb 1:5. Solomon is only symbolic of Jesus, and parts of the prophecy only fit Solomon, and parts of the prophecy only fit Jesus, and parts fit both but in different ways. Notice also that when one king or kingdom or event, symbolizes another king or kingdom or event, **BOTH are considered fulfill-**

The remaining ruins of ancient Rome are surrounded by a vibrant modern city. She was not a city which sank never to be inhabited again, like a millstone thrown into the sea, to be desolate forever. Rome is only a type.

ments! So Rome *is indeed* **a** fulfillment, but not the ultimate one. She is at best a type we are to learn from.

Also notice that it says, "thy merchants were the great men of the earth," Rev 18:23. It apparently indicates that Mystery Babylon has merchants, and as was noted, evidently not *all* merchants are automatically part of Mystery Babylon. The Greek word for "great men" is *megistan* μεγιστάν. Thayer says it is a word used for "the grandees, magnates, nobles, chief men of a city or a people, the associates or courtiers of a king ..." Those of Babylon are the ruling men of the earth, like the princes of Tyre and Sidon.

Yes, this does *in part* look like ancient Rome, but not as a whole, not in full. Ancient Rome is symbolic of the ultimate religio-commercial empire of the Christian Age which will come to rule over and seduce all the nations of the world.

Then give attention to the summary.

... for by thy sorceries were all nations deceived. Rev 18:23b KJV

The Greek word used here is *pharmakeia* , and it is the word from which we get the word pharmacy. Louw and Nida in the *Greek-English Lexicon of the New Testament Based on Semantic Domains*, say this word indicates "the use of magic, often involving drugs and the casting of spells upon people − 'to practice magic, to cast spells upon, to engage in sorcery ...'" It is often translated as "witchcraft," and could easily be so translated that way here. The NET Bible translates it as "magic spells." The full description here could also easily take in the international drug trade of the last four centuries. Certainly it does seem to indicate that **some sort of *mind* control *of the world*,** is being *exercised by Mystery Babylon*. This mind control it indicates in Revelation is part of the reason for her sales and her power, and part of the reason why her merchants are the great men of the earth.

Several things should again be noted. This does not, and never would, indicate Rome, especially a Rome being destroyed by one of her Caesars. Once more, *Rome's forte was not seduction or mind control, but the power of iron, and the tenacity and endurance of her armies.* **Mystery Babylon** in comparison **owes her power to seduction, and sensuality,** a feminine sort of mastery in **enticement and pleasure and hypnotic control of her subjects. She is the master of illusion.**

Many cities have been proposed as "the great city," including Rome, Constantinople, Paris, Berlin, London, New York, and others. You run into phrases like, "Babylon on the Hudson" (meaning New York), or "Babylon on the Thames" (meaning London). It should be pointed out that such associations, while not being complete in the New Testament sense, may not be entirely out of line. Remember that Mystery Babylon is evidently an age long entity. Remember that Mystery Babylon is,

> ... THE MOTHER OF HARLOTS AND OF THE ABOMINATIONS OF THE EARTH. Rev 17:5 KJV

At times we may be witnessing the working of one of the daughter harlots Mystery Babylon has produced: a tentacle and not the octopus. On the other hand, we may be witnessing the harlot herself in one of her up and down stages, striving for world mastery that seems to continually elude her and the beast until just before the end. Mastery in trade, like mastery in politics and many other things, is often an elusive commodity, that time and again slips away from one's grasp. Even if achieved, mastery requires considerable diligence to maintain. It is for reasons such as these that a convincing case can sometimes be made for some of these other identifications.

Once it is understood that something beyond Rome is being portrayed, it is easy to see that Mystery Babylon does not yet have her full power in history, *although she has great world-wide power, all through the Christian age*, and even now. I think we have watched her movies and shows and seduction. We bought some of her goods in her stores. You and I may have worked for one of her corporations. Why is she brought down so terribly? Why will all of this happen? Because she is full of the blood of Christians, on which she has become drunk, and she is the cause of **all** the bloodshed on the earth, Rev 18:24.

Review in your mind what I have described to you. **Notice carefully that I have NOT told you *who* the beast is, *or who* Mystery Babylon the Great is. In** fact *the names they may use in history may change often*, so that might not even be a useful activity even if I wanted to try. This has been an analysis of what the Biblical symbolism tells us, and some things which can be ruled out as final answers. **Even so, I think the description is complete enough that if you or I run across them in our day to day activities, or in the media, their footprints will be unmistakable, and we can take warning.** He who has ears to hear, let him hear.

Mystery Babylon is a Christian-Age-long religio-commercial entity. And she is *completely* destroyed *within* history.

The Wedding Feast, and the Last Battle, Revelation 19

Then John heard something like a loud voice, saying that salvation and glory belong to the Lord our God, Rev 19:1. Why has salvation come now? Why does it belong to God? Because His verdicts, His judgments, are true, Rev 19:2. It is because the Lord has brought judgment on the evil harlot, for,

> And in her was found the blood of prophets, and of saints, **and of all that were slain upon the earth**. Rev 18:24 KJV (*emphasis added*)

That is an astounding statement, and very inclusive! What a dramatic statement of prophecy of the Christian age! This harlot is along with other things, a bloody and murderous entity. As has been said repeatedly, this has been going on for over 2,000 years. And yes, salvation and glory belong to God because God has avenged the blood of His servants, Rev 19:2c.

You see, Mystery Babylon has not just sold things, not just herself, not just things and materials, not just people ... but Mystery Babylon, the religio-commercial world-wide empire, has hated Christ and Christians, and has murdered them, and drunk their blood. Mystery Babylon lost her bearings, and her place because she became drunk with the blood of Christians, Rev 17:6.

Hallelujah! The smoke of Babylon rises forever! Rev 19:3. The twenty-four elders and the four living creatures agree, and are singing God's praise, Hallelujah! Rev 19:4. A voice from the throne sang, Hallelujah! Rev 19:5. Rejoice, for the marriage of the Lamb is near, Rev 19:7. The saints are engaged to be married to our Lord, we were betrothed to Him. Paul said to the Corinthians of the first century.

> 2 For I am jealous over you with godly jealousy: for I have espoused you to one husband, that I may present *you as* a chaste virgin to Christ.
> 3 But I fear, lest by any means, as the serpent beguiled Eve through his subtilty, so your minds should be corrupted from the simplicity that is in Christ. 2Cor 11:2-3 KJV

We were told to forget our old family, our old house. We will be one with our Lord. We will now wear His name. Foreigners will seek our favor,

> ¹⁰ Listen, O daughter,
>> Consider and incline your ear;
>> Forget your own people also, and your father's house;
> ¹¹   So the King will greatly desire your beauty;
>> Because He *is* your Lord, worship Him.
> ¹²   And the daughter of Tyre *will come* with a gift;
>> The rich among the people will seek your favor.
> Psa 45:10-12 NKJV

In place of our fathers will be our sons in the Lord, Psa 45:16-17. There is definitely promised to the faithful a productivity and a posterity in the world to come, but that is a side point, only implied in Revelation 19. The saved are given fine wedding clothes to wear. The righteous deeds of the saints, Rev 19:8. Who gave us these righteous deeds? The Lord is the One.

> LORD, You will establish peace for us,
>> Since You have also performed for us all our works.
> Isa 26:12 NASB

Incapacity on our part is not a valid objection to our coming and serving! Blessed are those invited to the marriage supper, Rev 19:9. Despite this, many have despised this invitation, just as the parable which Jesus told.

> ¹   And Jesus answered and spake unto them again by parables, and said, ² The kingdom of heaven is like unto a certain king, which made a marriage for his son, ³ And sent forth his servants to call them that were bidden to the wedding: and they would not come. Mtt 22:1-3 KJV

So the Master did all He could to fill His house for the great wedding party, Mtt 22:9-10. Nevertheless, there finally comes a decision point, and an answering time in all of our affairs.

> ¹¹ And when the king came in to see the guests, he saw there a man which had not on a wedding garment: ¹² And he saith unto him, Friend, how camest thou in hither not having a wedding garment? And he was speechless. ¹³ Then said the king to the servants, Bind him hand and foot, and take him away, and cast *him* into outer darkness; there shall be weeping and gnashing of teeth. Mtt 22:11-13 KJV

Many have been invited, but few have been chosen, Mtt 22:14. Blessed are those who are invited, and who arrived clothed in righteousness, to the most exclusive and joyous party of all time.

John was ready to worship this awesome angel, who was delivering such a message of joy to him, Rev 19:10. But John was told, no, do not do that. Some insist on the worship of angels, which can cheat us out of our prize, Col 2:18.

Faithful angels do not accept worship as gods. Sometimes though, angels have accepted such worship, 1Cor 10:20. Even so, despite their awesome nature, they are by nature not really gods, Gal 4:8.

Then the final battle comes, and Jesus appears, Rev 19:11. He is faithful and true and wages war in righteousness. He *is* powerful. He *will* call all of us to account. Pictures of Jesus as weak, never able to oppose or deliver *anyone*, are inaccurate. He came the first time to deliver us, and show us the way to trust in God who delivers in righteousness and truth. He rules the nations *now*, in restraint, mercy and righteousness, and is in the process *now* of smashing His enemies, Psa 2:10-12. He *now* gives men the opportunity to repent and come to the side of righteousness and justice and peace. As has been shown all through this book, He can and does operate in history, and often brings both men and nations to account even *within* history, to encourage and stimulate to change the irresolute. But then, finally, He will bring this short period of amnesty to a close, and He will appear in majesty and glory. His eyes are like fire, and He has a special name of honor which only He knows, Rev 19:12. He has a robe dipped in blood, Rev 19:13. His name is the Word of God! Remember?

> [1] In the beginning was the Word, and the Word was with God, and the Word was God. [2] The same was in the beginning with God. [3] All things were made by him; and without him was not any thing made that was made. [4] In him was life; and the life was the light of men. [5] And the light shineth in darkness; and the darkness comprehended it not. Jn 1:1-5 KJV

And the armies of heaven are coming with our Lord at the last day, Rev 19:14. The Lord is gathering His armies for battle on the last day. They are coming from a far away country, from the farthermost extremes of the universe. It will for sure be magnificent, scary.

> [4] A sound of tumult on the mountains,
>   Like that of many people!
>   A sound of the uproar of kingdoms,
>   Of nations gathered together!
>   The LORD of hosts is mustering the army for battle.
> [5] They are coming from a far country,
>   From the farthest horizons,
>   The LORD and His instruments of indignation,
>   To destroy the whole land.
> [6] Wail, for the day of the LORD is near!
>   It will come as destruction from the Almighty.
> [7] Therefore all hands will fall limp,
>   And every man's heart will melt.
> [8] They will be terrified,

> Pains and anguish will take hold of *them;*
> They will writhe like a woman in labor,
> They will look at one another in astonishment,
> Their faces aflame.
> ⁹ Behold, the day of the LORD is coming,
> Cruel, with fury and burning anger,
> To make the land a desolation;
> And He will exterminate its sinners from it. Isa 13:4-9 NASB

They are clothed in white linen, and ride white horses, Rev 19:14. Our Lord will slay the nations, and stamp them down in the winepress of His anger, Rev 19:15. Jesus is alone King of Kings and Lord of Lords, Rev 19:16.

Gather all the birds to eat the dead corpses! Rev 19:17. They will eat the dead until they are gorged with the flesh of men, Rev 19:18. This is a consistent picture of that Last Day which is given in Scripture. At that final time, evidently the beast and his armies, in their final act of defiance, will literally be gathered to fight against God.

> And I saw the beast, and the kings of the earth, and their armies, gathered together to make war **against him** that sat on the horse, and against his army. Rev 19:19 KJV (*emphasis added*)

This is the same battle described in Revelation 16.

> ¹³ And I saw three unclean spirits like frogs *come* out of the mouth of the dragon, and out of the mouth of the beast, and out of the mouth of the false prophet. ¹⁴ For they are the spirits of devils, working miracles, *which* go forth unto the kings of the earth and of the whole world, to gather them to the battle of that great day of God Almighty.
> Rev 16:13-14 KJV (*emphasis added*)

The same battle is described here and Revelation 19, and also in many other passages of Scripture. They gathered at a certain place.

> And he gathered them together into a place called in the Hebrew tongue Armageddon. Rev 16:16 KJV

What will it be like when the battle starts? The people will be terrified. Rather than march in order to their doom, the soldiers of the nations will begin to fight each other on that last day, as is told in many passages.

> And the beast was taken, and with him the false prophet that wrought miracles before him, with which he deceived them that had received the mark of the beast, and them that worshipped his image. **These both were cast alive into a lake of fire burning with brimstone.** Rev 19:20 KJV (*emphasis added*)

The stars will not give their light when Jesus comes to punish the world for its sin.

¹⁰ For the stars of heaven and their constellations
> Will not give their light;
> The sun will be darkened in its going forth,
> And the moon will not cause its light to shine.
¹¹   "I will punish the world for *its* evil,
> And the wicked for their iniquity;
> I will halt the arrogance of the proud,
> And will lay low the haughtiness of the terrible.

Isa 13:10-11 NKJV

It will be an all inclusive day at the last. Earth and heaven will shake and tremble, in that day, Isa 13:13. The rest, all those who do not know God and who will not obey the gospel, will be killed by the flaming fire of Jesus second coming, Rev 19:21.

> ⁷ ... when the Lord Jesus shall be revealed from heaven with his mighty angels, ⁸ In flaming fire taking vengeance on them that know not God, and that obey not the gospel of our Lord Jesus Christ: ⁹ Who shall be punished with everlasting destruction from the presence of the Lord, and from the glory of his power; ¹⁰ When he shall come to be glorified in his saints, and to be admired in all them that believe (because our testimony among you was believed) in that day. 2Thes 1:7b-10 KJV

This present period of amnesty will be over, as will the offer of amnesty. Everything which can be shaken to pieces will be.

> ²⁶ Whose voice then shook the earth: but now he hath promised, saying, Yet once more I shake not the earth only, but also heaven. ²⁷ And this word, Yet once more, signifieth the removing of those things that are shaken, as of things that are made, that those things which cannot be shaken may remain. ²⁸ Wherefore we receiving a kingdom which cannot be moved, let us have grace, whereby we may serve God acceptably with reverence and godly fear: ²⁹ For our God is a consuming fire. Heb 12:26-29 KJV

We have received an unshakeable nation, Heb 12:28-29.

So ends another of the visions of the book of Revelation.

X. Excursus: What Might This Look Like in History?

It is only as we come near to the end of our story, that we are in a position to put some of these parts together, to form some sort of coherent picture. These are big things on the ground, but despite that, they are only parenthetical subjects in the grand scheme of things, God working in history, the master subject of Scripture and the book of Revelation.

Any answer we have here, which does not fit the first century, and the Christians of the early centuries, cannot be the subject of the book of Revelation, for obviously our subject concerns those immediate readers of the early centuries. Also any answer we give here which does not fit the end of world history, universe history, cannot be our subject, because our subject is by these accounts in the book of Revelation also very much in operation very near the end of history. The final beast, the final man of lawlessness, comes very near the end of all history, and uses Mystery Babylon to come to power and to conquer the church, and then **destroys Mystery Babylon <u>within</u> history!** Then, the beast is personally destroyed by Jesus Second Coming, and is thrown *alive* into hell, Revelation 19. The climactic events that lead to the end of time, all have the Mystery of Lawlessness *and* Mystery Babylon as active players, *until very near the end of time!*

Additionally, any answer we give here which does not fit the bulk of history during Christian age, does not fit the subject of the book of Revelation. These two mystery entities **are clearly viewed as age long powers** which concern Christians here on the earth *all through our age*, and these are *powers of whom Christians must be **wary** all through our age.* Thus the relevance of this book.

So there is an imposing set of limitations on how our views of Mystery Babylon and the Mystery of Lawlessness must be formulated. I hope to produce here an overview which will be useful to the saints of our age for some time into the future, perhaps even hundreds of years into the future, if the Lord wills. However, to have a discussion relevant to current readers, what can be seen of these histories for most of the Christian age, will only summarized.

This discussion will concentrate on the relatively recent past: the 19th and 20th centuries. That is close enough to produce abundant materials for discussion, and distant enough to allow a degree of dispassionate consideration. It is a discussion of people and organizations and tactical *modus operandi* which does not step on the toes of the living. The overall principles apply, it would seem, to all of the history of our age. Hopefully by doing this, the *types* of operations which would seem to be typical for most of the Christian age can be seen. **<u>Nothing</u> here is secret, only things not widely known.**

Part of the issue here is to distinguish between lookalikes, and the real thing. We are even told that the great harlot is the mother of harlots! How do you discern between mother and daughter? Have you identified the octopus, or have you mistaken a tentacle ... for the octopus? A part for the whole? Or a wannabe for the real thing? Many a researcher has mistaken a subordinate organization for the master "mystery of lawlessness" or "Mystery Babylon the Great." When guarding a nation, such mistakes may be tragically significant. For the individual trying to avoid a cesspool of iniquity, it might not make much difference. Both of these "mysteries" are predatory occult groups.

A Lawless Entity: Satanism at Work

"**The mystery of lawlessness is already at work**," 2Thes 2:7 NKJV, in the first century AD. These words in context indicate the existence of a mystery religion, an occult or at least semi-secret religion, that is characterized by lawlessness, and that has been in existence *at least* since the first century AD. The wording used in 2 Thessalonians 2 *could* indicate organizational continuity. At a minimum it indicates *doctrinal* continuity, which will last until the end of time, when it produces "the **man** of lawlessness" (2Thes 2:3 NASB), who opposes the worship of any except himself (2Thes 2:4), and is accompanied by "all power and signs and lying wonders" (2Thes 2:9), and is personally destroyed by Jesus' Second Coming (2Thes 2:8). The specter of the beast as an organization in Rev 13:1-2 almost immediately presents the prospect of an organizational continuity. On the other hand, if you think the doctrinal unity option is correct, it would suggest occult groups which change and morph, and one group perhaps supersedes another, but the groups overall, down through history, believing generally the same things. (And if you think it through, these are not *necessarily* mutually exclusive views.) Unless of course you want to propose two such men at the end of time, this man of lawlessness in 2 Thessalonians 2 is the same as the beast of Revelation 13, and in fact, the grand outlines in both passages are similar. "The synagogue of Satan."

If a person wanted to get an overview of the religion of Satan, perhaps there is no better source than Richard Cavendish's, *The Black Arts*, Capricorn Books, NY, 1967. Cavendish is a British historian, educated at Oxford. *The Black Arts* is very concise, but does outline the teachings in enough detail that, if one is familiar with first and second century AD gnosticism, it is easy to see the links. Cavendish's scholarly, but distasteful, 24 volume encyclopedia *Man, Myth and Magic*, is widely praised, and is considered a must have by many public libraries. Your author has even seen it in some High School libraries. Often Cavendish tells you their claims, and what they say of the things they saw or did, and just leaves it at that, without passing any judgment. Neither of these works are for children, or for the unstable.

Cavendish in *The Black Arts* starts out by telling us that, "The driving force behind black magic is hunger for power," pg 1. Further he says, "The magician sets out to conquer the universe." pg 3. He gives as an example of what he called, "The most notorious and most brilliantly gifted of modern magicians, Aliester Crowley ..." Crowley worked at various times for both British and German intelligence, and claimed "that he was the Beast himself ... He often signed himself 'The Beast 666' or TO MEGA THERION ..." pg 119.

Cavendish ties all of their doctrine to the Jewish Kabbalah (he spells it Cabala), a writing in 12th and 13th century AD Spain, of early Christian age "Gnostic" doctrine. In the Kabbalah the worship of Satan is sometimes discussed as being the "left hand path," "the other side," or the "emanation of the left," or the "dark emanations." Cavendish shows the relationship between names and numbers and the names of powers, and astrology and ritual magic. Much of this is being vividly portrayed in many modern movies and television shows. Cavendish comments that "genuine Satanists have probably always been rare, as they are today." That is no doubt correct, and he reviews some of the history of groups which have been publicly accused of Satanism. Among other things, he does discuss human sacrifice as part of all of this (for instance pgs 239, 248-249). He mentions times when people have been accused of such, and at times gives various examples such as, "In 1841 treasure hunters in Italy murdered a boy as a sacrifice to a demon which they believed would find buried treasure for them." pg 249.

What would such groups look like when they work in public?

Their dominant characteristic is lawlessness. We should always remember that, "sin is lawlessness," 1Jn 3:4 KJV. Satanic groups are generally against the status quo, and are trying to break it down into chaos, anarchy and, widespread lawlessness, in preparation for their special man. Generally speaking *whoever* is in control, in charge, they will oppose. *Whatever* is accepted as an authority, they would be against, and will be constantly trying to undermine it. They are perpetual revolutionaries, and intrigue is their specialty. They are against *any* authority among men, *any* controlling person *or* group *or* tradition. They oppose almost all law and discipline of any sort. They often will work hard to try to stop the punishment of anyone. (Although they sometimes punish their own with the utmost of severity.) They work for children to be raised without any restraint. They are, like their master, basically anti-man, anti-human being. They truly seek the ruin of all. They oppose everything which is good for men, and support everything which is unhealthy for men. They are always for "freedom" and absence of all control. "Do what you will!" is one of their key sayings.

From time to time people involved in such things come to light. Sometimes it is from the criminal side with some of the most reprehensible of crimes. Sometimes "great" men are involved, and that evidently included Samuel Clemens, or "Mark Twain" as he was known (although he was "outed" before he really wanted to be). Sometimes groups are accidentally exposed, like the devil worshipping "Hell Fire Club" of 18th and 19th century England. That club included some of the most prestigious men in England of that time. Members included the head of Britain's postal system, and the First Lord of the Admiralty, at a time when the British navy was one of the most powerful military entities on earth. The licentious Benjamin Franklin, during his time in England, was a member under the pseudonym of "Brother Benjamin of Cookham."

Then there are men like the aristocratic super-star, the Duc De Richelieu, Louis Franquois Armand Du Plessis. He was rich, good looking, and brilliant. He had a successful career as a French general and diplomat, and he rates a full statue in the Louvre museum in Paris. He was also a very lawless man, and was in and out of trouble almost all of his life. He was in and out of prison in the French Bastille three times. He had sex appeal to the ladies much like a modern rock-star. When in the Bastille he was even visited by princesses. Because of constant adulteries, he was time and again fighting duels, but once even had two high-born ladies fight a duel over him! He was also very much into the occult. Most of this was of course hidden, but on occasion such did peek out. Hugh Noel Williams tells part of this in his biography, *The Fascinating Duc De Richelieu, Louis Franquois Armand Du Plessis (1696-1788)*, Methuen and Co. Ltd., London, 1910. (I could not help but laugh when Williams described Richelieu's carousing as "gallantries.") On one occasion,

> "... they brought two Franciscans to a country-house, where they made them say a Mass, then after the consecrations, the wafers were given to two he-goats, one white and one black, with the intention of seeing the devil ..." pg 105

But it seems there was more to the story than abusing the Mass.

> "The rendezvous, for the evocation of the devil, was a quarry near Vienna, to which they proceeded at night. It was summer, and the incantations were so long that the day was beginning to break, when the quarrymen, who were on their way to their work, heard such piercing cries that they came running up, and found a man dressed as an Armenian, bathed in blood and at his last gasp. It was apparently the pretended magician, whom these gentlemen ... had just immolated in their vexation." pg 106

The *New Oxford American Dictionary* defines "immolate" as to "kill or offer as a sacrifice, esp. by burning."

The men involved were of high enough station to not be held accountable for their crimes, as also is common in modern America. One of the "gentlemen" involved, however, seemed to lack the funds to purchase his "innocence," and so had his life ruined by the incident. Most of such incidents await judgement day for the truth to be told, but such incidents can be seen now and again on the peripheries of history, though the miscalculations of evil men. Richelieu died in his nineties. When he was eighty-five, one witness described him as looking like he was sixty-five. And history? My desktop *Encyclopedia Britannica* does not even mention the Duc, nor does the English Wikipedia as of this writing (the French and German Wikipedia do have short articles about him). History is sprinkled with such evil men, Christian age long. For such fleeting "victories" men sometimes sell their eternity, and God accepts their bargain.

Another profile which is common for Satanic groups, is something like the Jewish Frankist groups. The Frankists were named after a false messiah, Jacob Frank (1726-1791). They also were accidentally exposed, in this case by orthodox Jews. They had the general traits of lawlessness, but, so far as is generally acknowledged, were not explicitly Satanic. They did use a lot of the vocabulary of Satanic groups, claiming to follow "the left hand path," "the other side," following the "dark emanations," etc. Except for qualifiers such as we have given, they sure fit the mold.

Then an additional profile which is common for such groups can be seen in the traits of the Arab secret society known as the Assassins. We will let the *New Oxford American Dictionary* give a summary:

> assassin ... noun ...
>
> • (Assassin) historical a member of the Nizari branch of Ismaili Muslims at the time of the Crusades, when the newly established sect ruled part of northern Persia (1094–1256). They were renowned as militant fanatics, and were popularly reputed to use hashish before going on murder missions.
>
> ORIGIN mid 16th cent.: from French, or from medieval Latin assassinus, from Arabic ... 'hashish eater.'

This Arab group used mind control and drugs (especially hashish, as you can see above) to produce a level of professional assassins in their group. Hypnotism ("spells," Deut 18:11 NASB and the NKJV. "Charms," KJV) and drugs have always been part of the occult. The Greek word for "witchcraft" (or "sorcery") in Gal 5:20 is *pharmakeia*. From the word *pharmakeia* we get the word "pharmacy." Their power was wider than is indicated by the above quote. The Assassins completely dominated the Arab world for an extensive period of time, and were only destroyed by powers external to the Arabs.

One more profile group should probably be noted: the "Bavarian Illuminati." This was a Masonic sect involved in revolutionary activity, and the leaders at the highest levels worshipped Satan. This group was also revealed by accident. A courier for the group was carrying messages by horseback, and was struck by lightning in a small Bavarian town. The police started going through the papers, became suspicious, and began monitoring the Illuminati lodges in Bavaria, and finally conducted a series of raids, resulting in a large trove of documents, which were then widely publicized and published.

The Illuminati organized the very anti-Christian French Revolution, using Grand

Orient Masonry as a front. The term Illuminati meant to be Enlightened (with the light of Satan). Many famous men were members of this group, including some Americans. After they were exposed they went under cover, but continued to operate. It was a well known entity in political circles in France and the United States in the late 1700's and the early 1800's. This author does not know of any *verifiable* information as to whether this particular group still exists, but names, fronts, and pretences can change quickly in the occult world. *There is a great deal of misinformation about the Illuminati. Much you may read about the Illuminati is only hearsay, and rumor, or even outright invention. It has even become a modern subject for novels and movies.*

Are there any original sources of information available about this group in English? Yes, and two of them with which this author is familiar with have stayed in print almost continuously. They may even be available as free downloads on the internet. They are:

> Robinson, John, *Proofs of a Conspiracy Against All The Religions And Governments of Europe.* Robinson was a prestigious Scottish "Professor of Natural History." Western Islands, Boston, Los Angeles, reprint © 1967.

> Barruel, A. (1741-1818), *Memoirs Illustrating the History of Jacobinism*, Real-View-Books, Fraser, MI, 1995, ISBN0-9641150-5-0. This is from a 1798 translation.

Barruel is the more readable and informative. He was in France and was running in Masonic circles as much of this was unfolding. Also he later had access to the documentary materials which had been seized and published. He outlines a very records intensive order, but there is no discussion of the source of the considerable amounts of money needed to fund such an order. I think we are discussing the "mystery of lawlessness," or at least one of its close fronts.

So I am offering you more than one *historical example* of the *types* of organizations that would fit *the general descriptions given in Scripture.*

There is obviously much more to say. One of the key concepts of Satanism is to "Do what you will." Like everything else here, you find hairsplitting about this, but it basically means: do whatever you want to do. No law!

Another of the key concepts in the Kabbalah and a lot of occult literature is that before Satan can be revealed as the "true" god of heaven and earth, first the entire earth must go through a period of total chaos, total lawlessness. Then and only then will people be ready for the world-wide worship of Satan. (Compare this with the earlier discussion of 2Thes 2:3 as being about a deliberate revolt against God!) This chaos is called many things in occult literature, including being the ultimate "Sturm und Drang," the great storm and stress. In Scripture this period is often prophetically called "the uproar of the nations."

What does Thessalonians and Revelation tell us of such groups?

Basically it tells us that such groups have been around for a long time. They are powerful and influential, but they work deep in the background. A council of seven men rule their organization, and they will work until their man, one of the seven, is enthroned as "god." Their power is backed by ten rulers or lines of rulers (horns). So what we have implied from Revelation is coalitions of powerful subterranean groups.

It should be clear that such groups work together to infiltrate centers of power, wherever and whatever they be. They are subtle and relentless. They are driven by his lowness below, in the abyss. Obviously, they are *completely* ruthless in seduction, and entrapment, and extortion, and blackmail, and murders where suitable. They seem to favor a conservative religious cover for general operations, with a pacifist sort of tinge, if possible. Like the Hell Fire Club, they are often found in the centers of power.

Further, although members of the mystery of lawlessness are often used to help Mystery Babylon, they hate her. Babylon takes advantage of these services, uses them, needs them, but often does not adequately reward the services of these groups. Might we also add, Babylon often despises these groups whose services she requires.

And one thing should be pointed out. Implicit in these groups is a recognition of the true God and His Son Jesus of Nazareth. Only, by decision, or entrapment, they have *knowingly* decided to oppose the true God, and *consciously* side with Satan.

Dominating World Trade and Commerce

One of the key traits of Mystery Babylon is that she to some degree "owns" world trade. It depends on her, she makes it work.

> [11] And the merchants of the earth shall weep and mourn over her; for no man buyeth their merchandise any more: [12] The merchandise of gold, and silver, and precious stones, and of pearls, and fine linen, and purple, and silk, and scarlet, and all thyine wood, and all manner vessels of ivory, and all manner vessels of most precious wood, and of brass, and iron, and marble, [13] And cinnamon, and odours, and ointments, and frankincense, and wine, and oil, and fine flour, and wheat, and beasts, and sheep, and horses, and chariots, and slaves, and souls of men. Rev 18:11-13 KJV

She is not all of world trade. Other parts of manufacturing and trade, profit from Mystery Babylon, but are not really part of Babylon the Great.

The merchants of these things, **which were made rich by her,** shall stand afar off for the fear of her torment, weeping and wailing,
Rev 18:15 KJV (*emphasis added*)

But Mystery Babylon is the organizing entity, the dominating entity. It seems to describe, once again, morphing coalitions of men with similar outlooks, serving it appears, some sort of pantheon of religions in the background. It seems plain in the book of Revelation that she was in existence in the first century AD, and that she has been in existence all through the Christian age. She *sits* on *the **organization*** called "a beast," (Rev 13:1), *and* on the seven heads and the seven mountains. (Out of that organization *one of its heads* then becomes "**the beast,**" Rev 13:3.) Mystery Babylon rests on seven religions, and many nations, peoples, and tongues. The seven religions? A couple of them would obviously be Satanism and what we would call "mother earth" cults. No doubt the names by which these cults have been called during the last two thousand years have changed from time to time. She is obviously in existence in the first century, and will be in existence until near the end of time. She hates Christianity as much as the mystery of lawlessness does. She will be destroyed *within* history. I have made the argument in other places that she was established sometime after the 6th century BC, Zech 5:5-11. That would imply that Mystery Babylon predates Christianity by perhaps several hundred years!

What would we see *if*—perhaps I should say *when*—we ran into Babylon in our everyday life?

No, This is NOT about "Free" Enterprise

The really big money is not made by free enterprise. The big money is made by monopolistic controls, and shutting down the competition, or hampering them, or denying them financing or access to markets.

A Wall Street Journal article on September 13-14, 2014 was, "Competition is for Losers," by Peter Theil. The author says "Americans mythologize economic competition, **but it's actually the opposite of capitalism**. If you want to create and capture lasting value ... look to build a monopoly." (*emphasis added.*) Calling it "The Monopoly Way," the article goes on to say that,

> "Creative monopolies aren't just good for society. They're powerful engines for making it better." pg C2

First it might be well to acknowledge that sometimes there *are* economies of scale to be had with private enterprise or government monopolies, and sometimes things can be accomplished which can be done no other way. A Bible example would be Joseph's mandatory food storage program in Genesis chapter 41 and following, which ended up saving Egypt and other nations from starvation. At other times there is only greater waste and pillage.

Some instances of how monopolistic America is showed up on the internet in the early 21st century. Two visuals and an article by a Mike Shedlock (Nov 2, 2013) showed that "10 Corporations Control Nearly Everything You Buy, 6 Media Corporations Control Nearly Everything You Read or Watch." One of the charts states that "In 1983, 90% of American media was owned by 50 companies ... In 2011 that same 90% is controlled by 6 companies." (If not still on the internet, the reader can possibly find these visuals at one of the archive sites, for example archive.org.) There is an extensive literature about such phenomena, and many social and academic studies. An internet search on "monopolies," "cartels," "syndicates," etc., will at this time turn up many books.

Many people talk about "market economies," but in truth the big money has always been made by special "arrangements" which eliminate, or cripple the competition. So what would be the public face of this Mystery? In ancient Rome it would be the combines of rich and powerful senators who by government license / monopolies (the first corporations) plotted to dominate trade in this or that, thus looting her provinces for the benefit of Rome. In later history it would be seen in the likes of Venice, the Hanseatic League, The East India Company, the monopolies of ancient, medieval and modern nations, and the virtual monopolies of the modern world. Business produces taxes, so the business face of society, ends up focusing the government face. "Free Enterprise"? These words are *often* no more than a cloak, a facade. They would like to be free to run you out of business, if they can.

What sort of words might be used to describe this when we see it?

"The Fraternity," "The Money Power," "free enterprise," "Free Market," "Big Business", "the Association," conglomerates, monopolies, cartels, Capitalism, multinationals, syndicates, Trusts, "Big Finance," "the Network," "the Cooperators," "The Hidden Hand." You may see other pseudonyms tomorrow.

Global Inc., An Atlas of the Multinational Corporation, by Medard Gabel and Henry Bruner, The New Press, NY, 2003, says that,

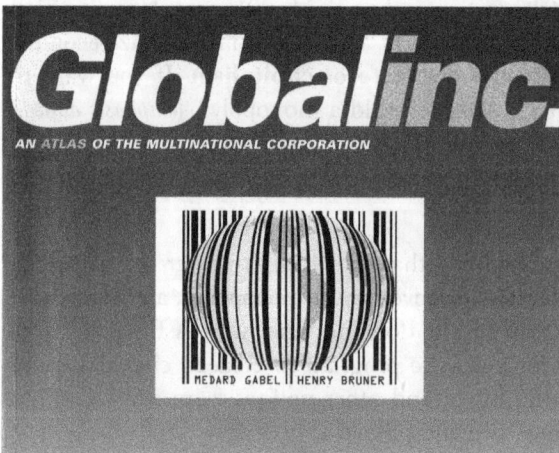

"With more than 63,000 multinational enterprises and 821,000 foreign subsidiaries ... the 1,000 largest account for 80% of world industrial output." pg 7

The size of some major multinationals is astonishing. Steve Coll in *Private Empire, ExxonMobil and American Power,* Penguin

Books, NY, 2012, points out that if ExxonMobil were a nation-state, it would be the 21st largest nation in the world. For instance, in 1999 ExxonMobil earned $228 billion, more the total Gross Domestic Product of Norway, pg 66. To say that in power and influence they dwarf many smaller countries in the world is a huge understatement. Other measures of these things come up from time to time. The Wall Street Journal (WSJ) of May 1, 2017, pg A1, says that Apple Computer's $250 billion mountain of cash, was more than the foreign currency reserves of both Great Britain and Canada combined. Then in a September 23-24, 2017 WSJ article titled "Amazon Takes Over the World," an article by Scott Galloway says that the *increase* on value of "Amazon, Apple, Facebook, and Google ... since the recession of 2007-09 ... approaches the GDP of India." Kings and presidents are often overwhelmed by these powers. Another article by Scott Galloway, WSJ, September 30–October 1, 2017, calls these same corporations "The Four Horsemen of Big Tech," making similar comparisons! In other eras it might be other entities/industries/factions: insurance, railroads, shipping, spices, drugs, or even literal robber barons.

There are even multiple fictional representations of what the Bible calls Mystery Babylon. It might be mistaken for the fictional "Trade Federation" in the Stars Wars series of movies, Episode I (and a very negative view it is). Or the "N.I.C.E" corporation in C. S. Lewis' *That Hideous Strength*. In the end of Lewis' book the "N.I.C.E" corporation is destroyed by a resurrected Druid magician (Merlin), and pagan "gods" descending from "the spheres"! You may see other representations of Mystery Babylon in fiction.

You may see and read of others objecting to Mystery Babylon's dominance. It is a known entity, under many different names, and many do not like it. Such was the obvious object of Karl Marx's *Das Kapital* (and it was Marx who in the mid 1800's invented the term "capitalism.") Or you can see books like Noam Chomsky's *Profit Over People, Neoliberalism and Global Order*, Seven Stories Press, NY, 1999. The brilliant Dr. Chomsky is a professor at the Massachusetts Institute of Technology (MIT), a self-confessed anarchist, a long standing left wing political activist, and author. His book is about what Scripture would call "Mystery Babylon the Great," and he very much dislikes it, and argues that it is unjust. Chomsky says the United States is a "state capitalist democracy," pg 47, a "business run society par excellence ..." pg 60, and speaks of a fake "free market," pgs 34-37. It is also true that this book carries on some of what many would call

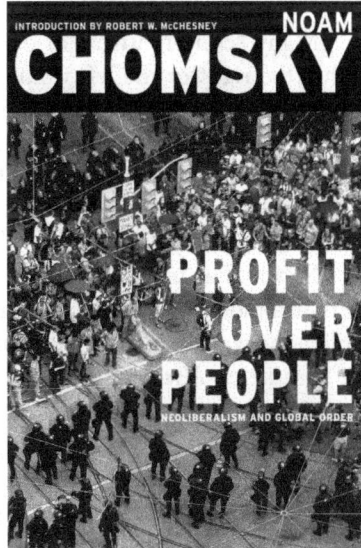

"pro-communist" rants, for instance, about what Chomsky considers the unjust treatment of Communist Cuba by the United States. But the subject overall is the often over-the-top dominance of multinational corporations in American affairs. For instance, under a heading of what he calls, "The "corporatization [sic] of America"" he notes,

> "A current variant is called "minimizing the state," that is, transferring decision-making power from the public arena to somewhere else: "*to the people,*" *in the rhetoric of power*; to *private tyrannies,* **in the real world**. ..." (*emphasis added*)

> "The so-called "free trade agreements" are one such device of undermining democracy. They are designed to transfer decision making about people's lives and aspirations into the hands of private tyrannies that operate in secret and without public supervision or control." Chomsky *Profits Over People,* pgs 132-133

Many "conservatives" also make the same points. I do not think anyone of either the right or the left would agree with everything Chomsky says (I don't). Still, his clear target is what the communists call "capitalism," and the public face (front) of what the book of Revelation calls "Mystery Babylon the Great." And he makes many telling points.

No, This is Nothing New. A Christian Age Long Phenomenon.

So who has to deal with this Babylon the Great during history? The answer is that almost everyone has to: rulers, businessmen, workers, shoppers. If you notice the warnings in Revelation 18, *they almost speak as if you could be a worker or an executive for Mystery Babylon for years, and think it is alright or even good, not really realizing what you have become a part of!*

> [4] And I heard another voice from heaven, saying, Come out of her, my people, **that ye be not partakers of her sins, and that ye receive not of her plagues**. [5] For her sins have reached unto heaven, and God hath remembered her iniquities. Rev 18:4-5 KJV (*bold emphasis added*)

This is of course a **command** to Christians, **and is part of the reason that the warnings and teachings of prophecy are pertinent to the entire Christian Age**. Also the command implies that it is plain enough for Christians to understand what is said, recognize these entities when they run across them in history, and can obey the command. We are dealing with the same essential entities throughout the entire Christian Age.

Babylon Merely Uses the Mystery of Lawlessness!

One of the key things to see: Mystery Babylon is a *religio-commercial entity*. Yes, there is evil religion in the background, but it is deeply hidden, except for its animosity against Christ. Evidently both of these key "mysteries" have a *need* to hide! On the hatred of Christ, and everything Christian both Babylon and the Mystery of Lawlessness agree. Babylon has great power through money and trade, and through seduction. She is an impressive power on her own. Her strength and endurance are great ... especially because she sits on "many waters," Rev 17:1, that is to say, on many "peoples and multitudes and nations and tongues," Rev 17:15. If someone is foolish enough to oppose her, she can remove presidents and setup presidents, through the strings she can pull. Almost no one can be elected without her support. She can bring nations to great prosperity and luxury through her trade, or she can bankrupt presidents and nations. She can transfer her manufacturing sources to other shores. But such things as that takes time.

Now obviously it is true that sometimes she can marshall force on her own. The East India Company and her armies is an example. Venice also had her armies and naval fleets. But that is not the forte of Mystery Babylon. Her forte is seduction and illusion and money and economic power, with religion in the deep background, even further it is remote in "the desert."

But what does she do for covert warfare and what does she do for enforcement? She is not organized for force, she is organized for trade and money. It takes more than money, and more than seduction, and it often takes more than her great endurance. Sometimes it takes "executive action," and great precision in duress against those who are reluctant to "cooperate." To worm her way into the privileged positions to extort great wealth, often she also needs the cunning and the brutal powers of enforcement in intrigue which only an entity organized for exerting force can provide. Assets and money can only go so far, useful though they be.

Babylon, so it seems from our text, relies for enforcement, for muscle, on two entities: 1. civil government (she rules over the kings of the earth, Rev 17:18) ... and 2. the mystery of lawlessness which is the *organization* called "a beast" in Rev 13:1. These *two sets of powers* it seems are her first line of immediate enforcers, when such is needed, and they are needed all along.

Both the East India Company and Venice were, it seems, sort of marriages between the harlots and kings.

Nonetheless, the harshest discipline on earth is in the bowels of the Satanic occult. Here are men and women who have been born or lured into this and that wrong until suddenly they find themselves forced to participate in the most gruesome and disgusting of crimes. Some have said that to enter Satanism is to be involved in progressively more, and more, gruesome murders. From this point they are no longer really drivers, but are driven. If they succeed, great rewards await them, and they are *promised* recurring lives of iniquity (reincarnation)! What a surprise death will be, Heb 9:27!

If at any point the adepts hesitate, they know that they will be the victims of these same hideous crimes: torture, rape, pedophilia, murder, drinking of blood, cannibalism, and every reprehensible act which can be imagined. The number of Satanists in our world are thankfully minuscule. Their influence, however, in part because of partnering with Mystery Babylon, is very great. The internal control exercised over those who know "the deep things of Satan" (Rev 2:24), is almost absolute. They can be ordered to do absolutely anything and they will do it. They are the ultimate "agency" from which no one can ever really retire. It is bondage that leads to hell itself. So they often make the most dependable of agents. The best a victim, an adept, can even hope for is that by very good fortune, they might be able to sneak away without triggering their own execution. There is absolutely nothing alluring about this. This is a hideous enterprise.

The woman "rides" the beast!

The beast is the one that bears these economic powers to victory. The beast, the organization, is even one of the main keys to controlling "the kings of the earth."

> ... and I saw a woman **sitting on** a scarlet beast, full of blasphemous names, having seven heads and ten horns.
> Rev 17:3 NASB (*bold emphasis added*)

The woman needs the beast. The woman rides the beast. The woman relies on the beast, very much as she relies on the civil powers to provide muscle, violence, when it is needed. Babylon has her victories every day ... in dollars and cents, in Marks and Pounds and Yens. And the Mystery of Lawlessness, though very necessary, sits in the background, and never has its ultimate fulfillment.

> And the ten horns which thou sawest upon the beast, these shall hate the whore, ..." Rev 17:16 KJV

The beast and the harlot are NOT a unity.

They are different powers, with different objectives and motives. The conflicts between the beast and the woman is part of the core reason that these forces have never had total success world-wide. God, among other things, uses them to foil each other, to prevent any ultimate victory they might have, *until the right time.*

Two, perhaps three, other points should be made. First, I have not emphasized it, but especially in the Mystery of Lawlessness, they make a point of "converting" or capturing or raising men and women of the very highest intelligence. The top levels do indeed include many brilliantly intelligent men and women in earthly terms.

Second, these powers do include "seven heads and ten horns, and upon his horns ten crowns" Rev 13:1 KJV, which indicates both worldly wealth and power. So the picture in the horror movies, of some Satanists as being well-to-do decadents whose homes at times include some old castles, has a certain flavor of truth to it. And, very understandably, there are frequent outbreaks of outright insanity in individuals and families involved in Satanism.

Third, these groups will have their "day" of victory of sorts. No one seems to notice it, but Scripture *clearly* tells us **that one day, for a short time, the entire world will worship Satan!** Satan is clearly the dragon with seven heads, and ten horns and seven crowns/diadems, Rev 12:3, 9. The dragon, Satan (Rev 12:9), then spawns "a beast" organization which also has "seven heads and ten horns, and upon his horns ten crowns," Rev 13:1. Then one of the heads of this "beast" organization becomes *the* "beast," Rev 13:3. Then it says,

> [3] ... And **the whole earth** was amazed and followed after the beast;
> [4] **they worshiped the dragon** because he gave his authority to the beast; **and they worshiped the beast** ...
> Rev 13:3-4 NASB (*bold emphasis added*)

That is all very plain, for one with eyes to see. What a remarkable prophecy to be made in the first century of our era. A prophecy which transcends even the most outrageous attempts to deny the authenticity of the book of Revelation!

A Capsule Look at Some Recent History

This is perhaps a good time to look at some recent history, and how some of these things can work out in our present day. In this brief review we are looking at *things which are past!* Organizations used and methods of operations change over time, and some of the organizations and methodology which are described here, 1) may *not* have been current in, say, 700 AD, and 2.) may not be current today! Sometimes it is easier to point out things in the past with more impartiality, than it is to discuss current affairs, that are to a greater extent embroiled in the propaganda mind-muddles of our times.

The purpose of this section is to document
the ***types*** of *modus operandi* which
would be involved in an entity
like Mystery Babylon.

First we will take a look at *Tragedy and Hope, A History of the World in Our Time*, by Carroll Quigley, 1966, First Printing MacMillan Co, NY. The book (about a thousand pages, with no index) is evidently in public domain, but at least some of the "pdf" versions on line are poorly edited and shortened. I have used the New Millennium Edition, Unabridged, Dauphin Publications, ISBN 978-1-939438-22-9 (year and location not given).

Carroll Quigley was a professor of history at Georgetown University in Washington, DC, and was a dedicated tool of what *he calls* "the Eastern Establishment." His book is mainly an economic history from approximately 1870 to 1960. In the main, Quigley's book follows the propaganda mainstream of the Establishment. He is writing for a liberal elite left, and he does sometimes discuss things that are intended for this group, about which the population overall knows very little. Not everything he says is true, however, Quigley does provide a readily available source for a variety of subjects which are not widely known, but which can also be documented in many other places.

Quigley mentions the existence of a large "Anglophile network" (English loving, network), which operates in ways which are secret, or semi-secret. This is really an economic history of this powerful Anglo-American group, really an extensive, loosely organized, front group (not a mystery cult), which had a great impact on the 20th century. Quigley is proud of this organization, says much of its secrecy is unnecessary, and perhaps even counter productive.

> "In fact, this network, which we may identify as **the Round Table Groups,** has no aversion to cooperating with the Communists, or any other groups, and frequently does so. I know of the operations of this network because I have studied it for twenty years and was permitted for two years, in the early 1960's, to examine its papers and secret records. I have no aversion to it or to most of its aims and have, for much of my life, been close to it and to many of its instruments." Quigley,
> *Tragedy and Hope,* pgs 690-691
> (*bold emphasis added*)

Quigley goes on to name some of the people instrumental in starting this group. We should stop right here to make some points about the Round Table Groups and about Mystery Babylon. *Mystery Babylon is by definition seated on many nations, many peoples,* and is in particular seated on seven heads and ten horns. In contrast, what Quigley calls *"the Round Table Group" or the "Establishment"* is an English-speaking entity, founded mainly on the British Commonwealth and the United States. We could even call this a regional or ethnic (English-speaking) group. Whatever Quigley is talking about is *much smaller* than the international scope of Mystery Babylon.

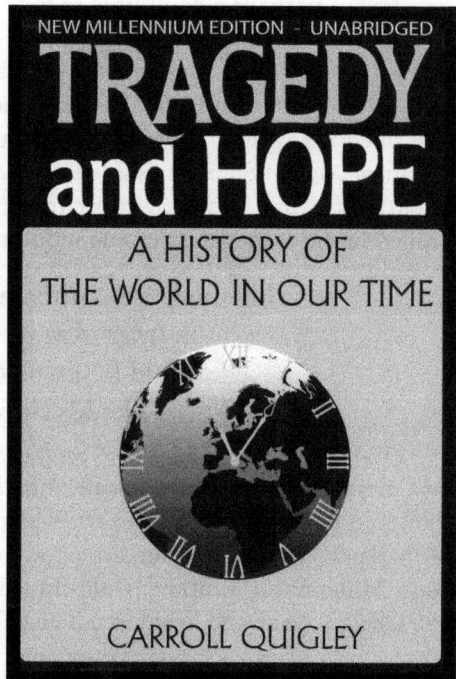

NEW MILLENNIUM EDITION - UNABRIDGED

TRAGEDY and HOPE

A HISTORY OF THE WORLD IN OUR TIME

CARROLL QUIGLEY

Even so, Quigley's discussion of this "network" is interesting for seeing how things often work down through history, *and that is the purpose in this part of the discussion.* He says of this group,

> "There does exist, and **has existed for a generation**, an international Anglophile network **which operates, to some extent, in the way the ... Right believes the Communists act."**
> Quigley, *Tragedy and Hope,* pg 690 (*emphasis added*)

What does that mean? In practical terms it means that this group practices infiltration, subversion, entrapment, bribery, blackmail, extortion, and on occasion violent overthrow of their adversaries. This is the way many people would describe a mafia, or drug cartel. Some have indeed called this "a legal mafia." So, if we are paying attention, we can see he is describing a formidable and ruthless organization! He identifies many names and organizations, some of which still exist. He says of the American branch of operations,

> "... the American branch of this organization (sometimes called the **"Eastern Establishment"**) has played a very significant role in the history of the United States in the last generation."
> *Tragedy and Hope,* pg 691 (*emphasis added*)

Bankers seem dominant in this group, although many "industrialists" are also included. He tells us of the American branch.

> "The American branch of this **"English Establishment"** exerted much of its influence through five American newspapers (The New York Times, New York Herald Tribune, Christian Science Monitor, the Washington Post, and the lamented Boston Evening Transcript)."
> *Tragedy and Hope,* pg 693 (*emphasis added*)

Quigley does add much praise for this group.

> "The chief aims of this elaborate, semi-secret organization were largely commendable: to coordinate the international activities and outlooks of all the English-speaking world into one (which would largely, it is true, be that of the London group); to work to maintain peace; to help backward, colonial, and underdeveloped areas to advance toward stability, law and order, and prosperity along lines somewhat similar to those taught at Oxford and the University of London (especially the School of Economics and the Schools of African and Oriental Studies)." *Tragedy and Hope,* pg 694

Quigley even points out,

> **"The element of secrecy is one of the outstanding features of English business and financial life."** pg 359 (*emphasis added*)

> "... they were almost equally devoted to secrecy and secret use of financial influences in political life." pg 38

A Rule of Money.

In his book, Quigley gives many examples of how this group operates. At the center of these efforts is one of the most misunderstood facets of our modern world: money and banking.

One of the things coming out of any informed discussion of banks and banking is about what some call the "fractional reserves system." Banks are in fact licensed to create money out of nothing. As Quigley demonstrates in his discussion of the founding of the bank of England, this is even true when a country is on a "gold standard," and is absolutely true when a country uses "fiat money" (as opposed to a gold or silver standard). Most of the world is now on fiat money. To document this "creation of money," Quigley quotes some experts, a "chancellor of the Exchequer."[1]

> "In January, 1924, Reginald McKenna, who had been chancellor of the Exchequer in 1915-1916, as chairman of the board of the Midland Bank told its stockholders: "I am afraid the ordinary citizen will not like to be told **that the banks can, and do, create money** ... And **they who control the credit of the nation direct the policy of Governments and hold in the hollow of their hand the destiny of the people**."" *Tragedy and Hope,* pg 236 (*emphasis added*)

Quigley even gives more quotes. Throughout the book he names men and corporations, and points out that the banks use the money they create for their own benefit. It even goes further than what Quigley spells out. On a national level, the central banks are often the ones creating money out of nothing, and then loaning that money to their own governments at interest! Local banks still operate on the fractional reserves principles.

Quigley does make the case that much of this has faded in importance, but many would say, "Not so that anyone can tell." A book of recent years is John Perkins', *Confessions of an Economic Hit Man,* A Plume Book, Penguin Group, NY, 2006. Perkins was a representative for large financial interests, and was working to ensnare third world countries into "infrastructure" loans which would not really help these countries, and from which those countries would never be able to extricate

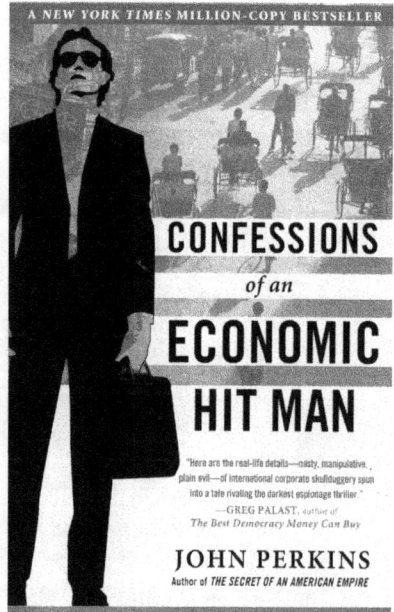

---

[1] A position roughly equal to the U.S. Secretary of the Treasury.

themselves, and whose debt over time would grow and grow.

Quigley describes in some detail how banks have grabbed control of the finances of almost all nations, and how they have operated. They were persuading governments to accept the private control of money. Quigley goes on to say that *it was necessary to* "**conceal, or even to mislead, both governments and people about the nature of money and its methods of operation.**" pg 39. He notes that really **"even central banks were private institutions"** pg 40 (*emphasis added*), "technically" pg 44. As William Gladstone, British chancellor of the Exchequer (roughly equal to the U. S. Secretary of the Treasury), 1852, said,

> ""the hinge of the whole situation was this: the government itself was not to be a substantive power in matters of Finance, but was to leave **the Money Power** supreme and unquestioned."" Quigley, *Tragedy and Hope*, pg 45 (*emphasis added*)

There were "close private associations between these private, international bankers and the central bank itself." pg 41. "... **they funneled capital to enterprises which yielded control and away from those who resisted**." pg 44. "... **they ... generally reduced competition**," pg 45, Quigley, *Tragedy and Hope*, (*emphasis added*). Quigley goes on to quote Sir Drummond Fraser, vice-president of the Institute of Bankers, who said,

> ""The Governor of the Bank of England must be the autocrat who dictates the terms upon which alone the Government can obtain borrowed money,"" *Tragedy and Hope*, pg 45

These are ALL things which can also be documented from multiple points of view and a wide range of sources.

Quigley goes on to give many examples of their influence and control in Britain, the United States, and Europe. In the United States **in 1930**, *200 corporations* **held 49.2% of the assets** of *40,000 corporations*, pg 53. They held only 32% in 1909. AT&T was controlled by J. P. Morgan and Co., and had more assets than twenty-one states. He flatly states that it was Morgan and Company that was "precipitating" the panic of 1907, pg 53. He speaks also of the "systematic exploitation" of farmers, and says President McKinley was opposing these forces, pg 54 (and was killed we might note).

Of such operations in Europe, Quigley references a well known quote from German financier and industrialist Walter Rathneau.

> "As early as 1909, Walter Rathenau, who was in a position to know (since he had inherited from his father control of German General Electric Company and held scores of directorships himself), said, **"Three hundred men, all of whom know one another, direct the economic destiny of Europe and choose their successors from among themselves.""** *Tragedy and Hope*, pg 44-45 (*emphasis added*)

Quigley additionally notes that, "Business hates competition." pg 327

Quigley points out that there was a semi-religious side to all of this (even as was also true of Nazism, as is commonly noted). One of the principals of the Round Table Group, Lionel Curtis, wanted this to lead to "... the Kingdom of God on earth." He said "men should strive to build the Kingdom of Heaven here on earth." After World War I, he said, "The world is in the throes which precede creation or death," pgs 105-106. I think that Curtis, like others of that time, was expressing his desires and plans, rather than what actually happened.

None of This Rule is Absolute. Only God's Rule is Absolute!

These are by no means permanent things. Babylon rules by illusion, seduction, and conniving. Quigley paints a picture of evolving groups and coalitions.

> **"In no country was the power of these great complexes paramount and exclusive,** and in no country were these powers able to control the situation to such a degree that they were able to prevent their own decline under the impact of world political and economic conditions ..." Quigley, *Tragedy and Hope,* pg 389 (*emphasis added*)

> "individuals or groups are unable to maintain their positions in the complex flux of modern life," *Tragedy and Hope,* pg 390

Notice Quigley calls them "complexes." He is giving examples here from the twentieth century, and goes on to say that groups succeed groups. Such things as cartels and trusts and syndicates are ever changing, and are perpetually insecure. I think what Quigley points out here is consistent with the representations we see in the book of Revelation and the rest of the prophets.

Legally and structurally these "cartels," shall we call them, want to present themselves as ambiguous targets to their workers, the people overall, and to the governments that they work under. This is easily seen by tracing the relevant financial structures in any section of the economy: shoes, housing, finance, food stuffs, clothing, you name it, for almost any twenty year period during the last century. For the employees involved these are often dismaying machinations, with endless (and seemingly useless) corporate changes, sales and buy-backs, and switching or laying off of personnel. There are many books and business articles on these subjects. Such changes can keep even high level personnel useful, while not fully realizing the purposes which they are serving. The men who are really calling the shots are often deep in the background, and many times can only be identified in retrospect. It would be a full time job just to keep track of these changes. Our national governments do have such specialists, and there are constant struggles for leverage on all sides. Some of the books quoted in the following sections on war sprang from such government investigations of these things (especially the volumes *Trading With the Enemy,* and *The Crime and Punishment of I. G. Farben).* Governments and these entities are quite often in opposition to each other, and in the end it is a combination of the beast and ten "kings" which completely overthrow Mystery Babylon in history. Mystery Babylon and government are NOT the same thing! Also full of good quotes is G. Edward Griffin's excellent monetary history, *The Creature from Jekyll Island, A Second Look at the Federal Reserve*, American Media, Westlake Villiage, CA, 1998.

Another point should be made here. These men are quite often not smarter or more intelligent than their competition. Quite often the biggest profits are not made by being smart or clever, but rather by rigging the system, by putting in a "fix" so that things come out a certain way, by making sure it is NOT a level playing field. Their arrogance and disdain for others often breeds fatal overconfidence. Then if at some point the "fix" no longer produces the desired results, these men often never see their decline coming, and are washed away before they understand what is happening. I think the popular "Dilbert" cartoons of the late 20th and early 21st centuries are a picture of what it looks like at the office level ... when these groups rule at the top.

> For it is written, I will destroy the wisdom of the wise, and will bring to nothing the understanding of the prudent. 1Cor 1:19 KJV

These men make *many* mistakes. They are good at plots and manipulations and falsifications, but *often times* even their plots and fixes are poor and do not work. Despite these misses, often more money is made with such manipulations, than by hard work and diligent business practices. Then if their plans have completely failed, *yet* they still control the creation and distribution of money, *or* they still have the ear of the king and contribute to his purse, they can always create new monopolies later.

These groups are in our time especially voracious consumers of intelligence at all levels. This is often under the euphemism of "big data." With the interlocking of ownerships and working relationships, the significance of "privacy policies" is often negligible. These huge collection efforts are tremendously valuable to them, so much so that they will often pay us for help in collecting our data (memberships, discount clubs, etc.). Often it is our national governments going to these organizations for information, not the other way around. This information seems to be used (in order I think) for economic, political, and religious purposes. The truth is, the lead corporations collecting personal information are themselves predatory businesses, as can be easily seen by even a superficial review of their histories as seen in Establishment news sources.

Lastly, remember that these are not just individuals. These are dark, powerful, and rapacious *organizations*, that have teeth. On the inside, and also at the last day, there is nothing here that is pretty. Even so, many in the outer circles of such groups are not really aware of the purposes which they serve. They are merely trying to "get ahead." So we have many warnings in Scripture.

> But they that will be rich **fall into** temptation and a snare, and into

many foolish and hurtful lusts, which drown men in destruction and perdition. 1Tim 6:9 KJV (*emphasis added*)

... Come out of her, my people ... Rev 18:4 KJV

The Economics of War.

The second Apostle James, the half brother of Jesus, pointed it out:

[1] Where do wars and fights *come* from among you? Do *they* not *come* from your *desires* for pleasure that war in your members? [2] You lust and do not have. You murder and covet and cannot obtain. You fight and war. Yet you do not have because you do not ask. [3] You ask and do not receive, because you ask amiss, that you may spend *it* on your pleasures. Jas 4:1-3 NKJV

Wars are about money and the power to do whatever pleases you. Someone wants the prosperity that you have, or you want the prosperity that someone else has. We should not sugar coat our frequent focus on the world and personal prosperity. James also points out

[14] But if you have bitter envy and self-seeking in your hearts, do not boast and lie against the truth. [15] This wisdom does not descend from above, but *is* earthly, sensual, **demonic**. [16] For where envy and self-seeking *exist*, confusion and every evil thing *are* there. Jas 3:14-16 NKJV

The translation is literally correct in "demonic" here. It is the Greek word *daimoniōdās* δαιμονιώδης. We can cross that line from the spiritual to the demonic in an instant, not merely in pagan worship, or human sacrifice, but also in mere selfish ambition.

In the discussion of these things it is well to note the money to be made from war. One way to see this is from quotes like the following from Marine Corps Major General Smedley Butler. Butler pointed out,

"... that the average profit of Du Pont from 1910 to 1914 was only $6 million, but it soared to $58 million between 1914 and 1918. ... Bethlehem Steel had been $6 million to $49 million; for International Nickel, $4 million to $73 million."

Jules Archer, *The Plot to Seize the White House, The TRUE Shocking Story of the Conspiracy to Overthrow FDR*, Skyhorse Publications, 1973, 2007, 2015.

Just using the above figures, it would seem that four years of war is worth ten times the equivalent years of peace time profits! The method here is very rudimentary. Even so, the above figures are based on publicly available data and should give some idea of what is involved.

These things do not count the fact that in a war you might be able to completely knock out your competitors and dominate the markets all to yourself, and use war to enforce the economic rape of a country or region. Such calculations go into war. At the end of World War II for instance, all of America's competitors had been ruined, and she had unfettered domination of world trade.

General Smedley Butler plainly said war is "largely a matter of money," Archer, pg 130. As a Marine Corps officer he had personally been involved in some of America's gunboat diplomacy in Central America, mainly to enforce Wall Street contracts by force, to take some leader out who wished to oppose Wall Street, or even to literally "fix" some "American supervised" elections. Butler elaborated on these things at times.

> "There are things I've seen, things I've learned that should not be left unsaid. War is a racket to protect economic interests, not our country, and our soldiers are sent to die on foreign soil to protect investments by big business." General Butler as quoted in Archer, *The Plot to Seize the White House,* pg 207. [This book documents an Establishment attempt to overthrow President Franklin D. Roosevelt in a coup, using two-time Medal of Honor winner General Butler as front man. Butler refused to be involved, and testified against the conspirators before Congress. The men and organizations involved were too big and important for them to ever be prosecuted.]

> "[War] is conducted for the benefit of the very few at the expense of the masses. Out of war a few people make huge fortunes ..."
> General Butler in Archer, *The Plot to Seize the White House,* pg 219

> "I spent 33 years ... being a high-class muscle man for Big Business, for Wall Street and the bankers. In short, I was a racketeer for capitalism. ..." General Butler in Archer, pg 118

Quigley comments on our entry into World War I.

> "the United States was inveigled into the war by a conspiracy of international bankers and munitions manufacturers eager to protect their loans to the Entente Powers or their wartime profits from sales to these Powers;" *Tragedy and Hope,* pg 180

The more you know of these schemes, the more you realize how unconscionable they are.

Moreover, we should not think that this preeminence of money in war is a new thing. Thucydides (455 BC to 400 BC) in his history of the war between Athens and Sparta quotes the Spartan King Archidamus as saying,

> "... war is a matter not so much of arms as money, for it is money alone that makes arms serviceable ... Let us therefore provide ourselves with money first, instead of being carried away prematurely by the eloquence of our allies ..." *Thucydides,* with an English translation by

Charles Forester Smith, Vol I, Cambridge, Massachusetts, Harvard University Press, 1980, pg 141 (Book I, LXXXIX).

Also Thucydides quotes Pericles,

"Again, it is accumulated wealth, and not taxes levied under stress, that sustains war." pg 243 (Book I, CXLI)

You can find such sentiments from many phases of history. Frederick the Great of Prussia (1712-1786) was an extremely able strategist, tactician, and combat general. He maintained the independence of his kingdom against what would be considered overwhelming odds. That was in the old flintlock rifle days, when many think that grit and not finances were predominant. Frederick said there were three things necessary to wage war: "Money, money, and money!" And it was Thomas Jefferson who said in 1813, "the perpetuation of debt, has drenched the world in blood, and crushed its inhabitants under burdens ever accumulating." Merrill D. Peterson, ed., *Thomas Jefferson: Writings*, NY, Library of America, 1984, pg. 1282. Indeed, the money to be made in financing and supplying war is not a new thing.

The Setup and Profiting from War.

Most people are not aware of the machinations that go into creating wars. Pat Buchanan in *Churchill, Hitler and the Unnecessary War*, Three Rivers Press, 2008, gives us an interesting quote on war.

"[W]ar is the creation of individuals not of nations.—Sir Patrick Hastings, 1948, *British barrister and writer.*" pg *xii*

Naturally, if someone is attacking us with intent to rob or kill us, it does make sense for us to resist. On the other hand, sometimes *both sides* in a war have much less noble motives than self defense. An exceptional read from this point of view is Eugene G. Windchy, *Twelve American Wars, Nine of Them Avoidable,* iUniverse, Bloomington, IN, 2014, which covers from the 1790's to World War I. For instance, he makes the case that it was the Russians who really started World War I. Further he says that the British actually wanted a war with Germany so that she could stop

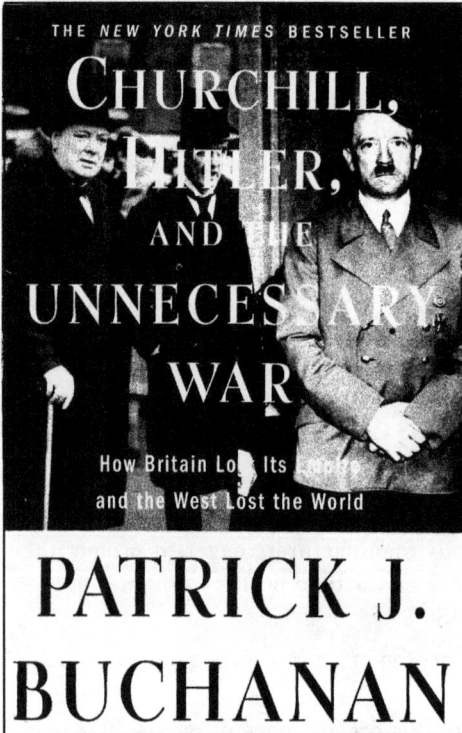

Germany's *commercial dominance* of Europe. That point of view is definitely contrary to the propaganda templates you and I were taught in school. However several British historians have pointed out that Germany was not guilty of initiating World War I, including A. P. J. Taylor, and Russell Grenfell. Woodrow Wilson, in speeches in St. Louis, and St. Paul, said in 1919,

> "This war, in its inception, was a commercial and industrial war ... The German bankers and German merchants and the German manufacturers did not want this war. They were making conquest of the world without it, and they knew it would spoil their plans." Buchanan, pg 48

Quigley by the way mentions that it was "the Russian mobilization which precipitated the war." *Tragedy and Hope,* pg 190.

Another book which argues that World War I *and* II were unnecessary, is Patrick J. Buchanan in his New York Times Bestseller, *Churchill, Hitler and the Unnecessary War, How Britain Lost Its Empire and the West Lost the World*, Three Rivers Press, 2008. He does not really deal with the financiers setting up the Communists and the Nazis in power, but still makes a powerful case. Buchanan's work is readable, balanced, and well documented.

Where they have the influence, the financial powers seem to try to use the end of one war to create the next war. If, for example, you use the end of World War I as a starting point, the badly conceived Versailles Treaty was used to lay the ground work for a future war. An American delegate to Versailles, Henry White, said in protest, "now we are doing hell's dirtiest work." Buchanan, pg 75. In fact, while World War I was still going on, the financing of Communism was begun by the Western financial systems, and starting in the 1920's of fascism and Nazism ... just to get things going good. There is a great deal of documentation on this. One source on Nazism is *Wall Street and the Rise of Hitler*, by Anthony Sutton, GSG Associates, San Pedro, CA, 2002. Sutton, a Stanford University scholar, documents that Hitler was financed into power by a combination of German, British, and American financiers and industrialists.

No one likes to admit it, but the notorious paramilitary "brown shirts" of Germany were a direct result of the Versailles Treaty, and was part of Germany trying to be ready to defend herself. The legal army they were allowed by treaty

Here is the incredible story of the American financiers who provided the money and matériel Hitler used to launch World War II.

WALL STREET AND THE RISE OF HITLER

Antony C. Sutton

was insufficient for the chaos following World War I. It actually looks like Versailles was *intended* to destabilize Germany for take over by the Communists (part of some deal?), and it is a wonder that she escaped such between 1919 and 1930. The "brown shirts," the "SA," then proved a double edged weapon, that in the long run *did help* destabilize Germany. At their height the "brown shirts" had three million men in uniform. (Imagine the money it takes to put three million unemployed men into uniform, and get them to dance to your tune!) Hitler started as an army political spy in 1919. Captain Ernst Rohm was part of the "Black Reichswehr" which financed Hitler in the period of 1920-23, and then the army stopped this flow of money because of the fiasco of the Munich Putsch, Quigley, pg 310. Following this, industrialists supported the Nazi 1924-1932, Quigley, pg 310, 315.

Quigley is interesting because, while many liberals try to treat Hitler as if he was "Right wing," Quigley points out that the Nazis were very anti-Christian and anti-Western, not really "conservative" at all. He points out the Nazis were "not clearly a party of the Right, but were ambiguous," pg 311. He also speaks of "the forces of irrationality represented by fascism," pg 606.

> "In spite of Hitler's verbal attacks on Communism, his real hatred was directed at the values and traditions of Western Civilization and Christian and middle-class ways of life."
> Quigley, *Tragedy and Hope,* pg 585

That, if you think about it, is obviously true of these genocidal maniacs. Hitler responded to his donors. Quigley comments,

> "Fascism is the adoption by the vested interests in a society of an authoritarian form of government in order to maintain their vested interests and prevent reform of the society." *Tragedy and Hope,* pg 397

Quigley says, the "Nazi system was dictatorial capitalism" pg 325, and presents some of the evidence of Nazism as "corporate capitalism," pg 325-331, a section well worth reading.

And "capitalism"? Shall we attempt a serious definition? Something beyond the sterile falsehoods of our dictionaries which make it sound as if capitalism is merely "private property" versus "government ownership." *The New Oxford American Dictionary* comes close in a sub-point under "capital" as,

> • people who possess wealth and use it to control a society's economic activity ...

Good to a point, for "capitalism" is far more than an individual using money for private investment. It is a social and ethical value. **Let us try this:**

capitalism, *n.,* A system which views it proper for private wealth (capital) to dominate *all things* in behalf of wealth. For government or religion or other ethical and political considerations to dominate is to be considered invalid. *nf.*

This narrow interest point of view captures the moral essence of the conflicts we have seen, and is closer to reality than the pseudo-definitions we often see.[1] Thus, all things are "moral" ... *if* they make money. Still, "You cannot serve God and wealth." Mtt 6:24. There are many, many, things worth more than money.

There is a wealth of fascinating stories to tell here, parts of which are also told by Quigley. As World War II came near, powerful financial and commercial interests did everything they could to make sure that both sides had whatever they needed to get a really good war started. When the war started, many of the leading parts of the American Eastern Establishment did business with both sides, throughout the war. This story is told in considerable detail, with full documentation, by Charles Higham in *Trading With the Enemy*, Barnes and Noble, 1983, 1995. Higham calls the plotters "the Fraternity." Some of the details are simply outrageous. At one point early in World War II, one American oil company's tankers in the Caribbean had German crews and were actually refueling German U-boats at sea! In fact, Western corporations knowingly furnished fuel to Hitler through Spain, up to 1944, with grudging consent from the Treasury Department. (Clearly affecting things like the U. S. operations in Italy in 1943.)

Another interesting book in this light is *The Crime and Punishment of I. G. Farben. The Unholy Alliance Between Hitler and the Great Chemical Combine,* by Joseph Borkin, Barnes and Noble, NY, 1978, 1997. I. G. Farben was the most powerful cartel/company in Germany, and included many companies with whom Americans are familiar. Most do not realize this, but there were actually three prison camps at Auschwitz. Two of them were directly run by I. G. Farben in making, or attempting to make, synthetic chemical products using slave labor.

Just to give an idea of how intense all of this was, a German lawyer for I.G. Farben, August von Knieriem **flew to New York** for a trial **while World War II was still going on** (July 13, 1944) concerning the U.S. government's seizing of

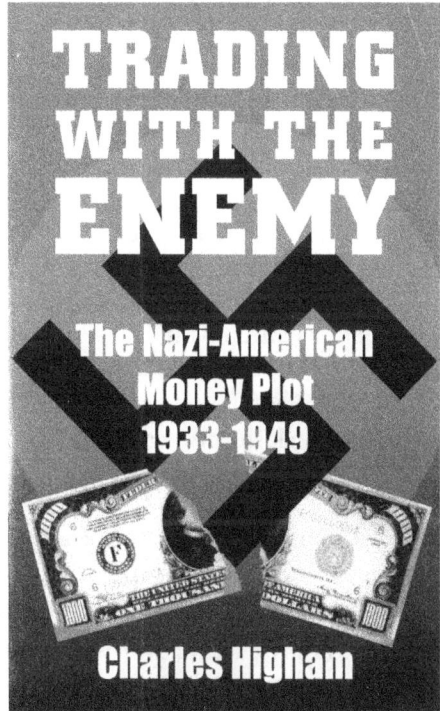

[1] Alternately, some see capitalism as being a term for that now rare entity, true "free enterprise," and call the monopolists "mercantilists." Clearly, useages vary.

I.G. Farben's synthetic rubber patents, Higham, pg 61. Final judgment was not given until September 22, 1947 by Judge Charles Clark, who stated that,

> "Standard Oil can be considered an enemy national in view of its relationship with I.G. Farben after the United States and Germany had be become active enemies." Higham, *Trading With the Enemy, The Nazi-American Money Plot, 1933-1949*, Barnes and Noble, 1983, 1995, pg 62

Standard lost their claims. Then as World War II came to an end, there also came the setup for future wars. A favorite tactic then came to be splitting countries as a way to insure future conflict. Quigley tells us the Round Table Group pushed the partition of India-Pakistan, Ireland and Palestine, pg 765. Additionally we had East and West Germany, North and South Vietnam, and North and South Korea. (That last one still could be used to trigger another war). The Russians wanted to split Japan also, but General Douglas MacArthur personally prevented that one, and for this, and other reasons, the Eastern Establishment has an undying hatred for MacArthur. He could have been president and he knew it. He would not be their man.

As this book is being written the mega powers are setting up ISIS from scratch for a clash between civilizations. These are not a small stakes games.

What Might All of This Cost?

Not counting the money, according to Pat Buchanan, in *Churchill, Hitler and the Unnecessary War*, World War II cost approximately fifty million lives, pg 112. Only about 35% of those casualties were military.

> "If any question why we died, / Tell them, because our fathers lied."
> Rudyard Kipling, Buchanan, pg 372

Or a monetary way to evaluate wars would be to take a casual look at the national debt of the United States of America as is related to war. The following figures were taken from http://en.wikipedia.org/wiki/national_debt_of_the_ united _states, June, 2018. Prior to the American Civil War, our national debt was a only $65 million. By 1866 it was $2.7 billion. (Again, Windchy in *Twelve American Wars, Nine of Them Avoidable,* demonstrates that the American Civil War was very preventable.) By 1913 our national debt had been reduced 55%, but by the end of World War I it was $25.5 billion! Perhaps it should also be pointed out that had the United States *not* intervened in World War I, the Kaiser would have still been the emperor of Germany, *and Hitler never would have happened!* Then by the end of World War II our national debt was $251.43 billion, nearly ten times as much as at the end of World War I! So, just take the over $200 billion that World War II cost. That was money **created** based on American credit (there was no combination of men that had it anywhere in a safe)! It was spent for airplanes, ships, rifles, bullets, bombs, shells, trucks, tanks, gasoline, you name it, to win a war that was very real by that time. So that $200 billion plus was *also* **"earned"** by various corporations supplying war. Truly staggering sums of money are involved in war, *all through history*. Mull over these figures a little and you will come to understand the financial interests that seek to create wars. The apostle James had it right about war!

Should we also mention that as of 2013, because of the way we choose to fight it, America's ten year plus Iraq-Afghanistan war, will cost the taxpayers $4 trillion to $6 trillion, per Enesto Londono, *The Washington Post*, March 28, 2013. And there is no end in sight. Has it occurred to you that this looks a lot like the endless Eur-Asian wars in George Orwell's futuristic novel, *1984*?

> [3] When He opened the second seal, I heard the second living creature saying, "Come and see." [4] Another horse, fiery red, went out. And it was granted to the one who sat on it to take peace from the earth, and that *people* should kill one another; and there was given to him a great sword. Rev 6:3-4 NKJV

Really unrealistic, that book of Revelation. Right?

The real point to be made is that these are *not* new things, but in fact, age long things, beginning sometime *before* our present era. An ancient example might be Julius Caesar's invasion and looting of Gaul in the first century BC, when Gaul was technically an ally of Rome! No! Such shenanigans are not new.

And **Many** *Spectacular Misses.*

Again, the humanity and fallibility of these groups should be emphasized. At times though it may seem that they are somehow superhuman, both to themselves and often also to us, their misses are often huge, both personally and organizationally.

Take for instance the setup for having a giant "World War III" in the twentieth century. In terms of the death of "useless eaters," it would have been a masterpiece. In terms of money to be made, it would have been marvelous. In terms of political manipulations with a view toward their New World Order, it would have been without parallel. In an "under the table" sort of manner, the Western "Establishment" endlessly supported creaking and bumbling Communists tyrannies, which otherwise would have almost immediately collapsed under their own weight. These communist revolutionaries have proved from the first to be inept nation builders. From the 1920's forward conservative writers and researchers wondered why the Western governments and the financial and industrial giants of the West, would again and again rescue the Marxist tyrannies from oblivion. These tyrannies would never have lasted without nearly continual Western help, and ongoing modern technological injections. There were always excuses and misleading "reasons," which never seemed to really standup to examination.

But alas! The grand war never happened! When it came right down to it, both the Russian Central Committee and the Soviet General Staff were *not* suicidally inclined, and were very levelheaded plotters and planners, and *did have* some care about what happened to their own nation. They were *not* going to be lured into a general "world war" as Hitler was, unless winning was a sure thing, an absolute certainty, which, of course, it never was.

Then when it was made clear in the 1980's that the Russian bear was not going to dance to the beat, these systems were not long in collapsing. Western financiers refused to continue funding them. (In a sideways sort of way they even admit that!) Still, despite failing in their ultimate objective, hundreds of billions of dollars were made in financing the buildup, both East and West!

Also clearly, **the blood of literally tens of millions** of resisters to Communist tyranny, over a period of about seventy years, was not only on the hands of Stalin and Beria and the like, but **was also on the hands of thousands of genteel Western bankers and industrialists.** It was also on the hands of Mystery Babylon the Great.

These men are a long way from any sure thing, powerful though they be in their own way. It is actually very difficult to arrange a good old fashioned world war! You need what the Disney cartoon called, "a villain that is willin'."

How should you view the examples in this "Excursus"?

Once again, I am not claiming to have positively identified either the Mystery of Lawlessness or Mystery Babylon the Great in any definitive sense, especially not in any intelligence sense. Nor do I claim to have either the resources or the ability to do so.

Even so, we can see from the book of Revelation that these *are* identifiable entities, and they have probably been so identified many times in history. The beast, with the help of "ten kings," will be able to so identify Mystery Babylon as to be able *to completely destroy her,* top to bottom, root and branch, all the way to the ground, *within history!* Additionally, the book of Revelation gives identifying marks which we would not be able to readily retrieve from historical data, and probably not even from easily obtainable intelligence data.

The examples I have given in this "Excursus" are only of *the **kinds** of operations* which can be seen in history *which would fit the general imagery given in the book of Revelation,* of entities creating wars to achieve money and power. The reader should also keep in mind that the externals of these groups change with time. So many of the externals may appear different a century from now.

On one level we cannot avoid bearing the brunt of these world-wide operations. Government itself, like the family, is also ordained of God (Romans 13, etc.) and is not *per se* the enemy. Both Mystery Babylon and the Mystery of Lawless subvert government in so far as they are able, even though in the final analysis, "... he is a minister of God to thee for good. But if thou do what is evil, be afraid ..." Rom 13:4 KJV. We should carry out our rightful and proper parts in protecting and defending our own peoples. Good Bible examples of these things would be Joseph in Egypt, Jonathan the son of Saul, and Daniel in ancient Babylon.

This has been an analysis of the *kinds of operations* that would be involved in such entities as Revelation describes. Further, this book has barely touched the clear evidence for these sorts of operations in history. Operations of such size cannot be completely hidden, but the media cartels by and large will not point out the evidence. They should not be your only source of information.

Review in your mind what I have described to you. I have NOT told you who is the beast is, or who is Mystery Babylon the Great. In fact the names and fronts they may use in history may change so often, it probably would not be a useful activity, even if I wanted to try. These entities are trying to hide, and are very good at hiding.

What is the objective in this section? That the reader be well enough informed, that if he runs across such operations in his daily life, he may have the good sense to flee active involvement in such evil things. **Sometimes you just need to walk away, and you should so order your life so that you can do that if the need arises.** And there are men who do just that, both Christian and non-Christian, all along in history. Such also seems to be a major purpose of the book of Revelation. For the Christian dealing with such entities in history, whether you have come up against the real thing, or only a lookalike, or a daughter harlot, or perhaps even a "wannabe," may be a moot point, and not worth trying to decide. It should also be pointed out that much of this is in no way obscure or uncertain. It should not take a rocket scientist to see that the slave trade of old, or the international drug trade of the past four centuries, is an organized part of Mystery Babylon, as was also Auschwitz, and Treblinka.

> And I heard another voice from heaven, saying, Come out of her, my people, that ye be not partakers of her sins, and that ye receive not of her plagues. Rev 18:4 KJV

To be forewarned is to be forearmed. Jesus rules in the kingdom of men *now!* As God used ancient Assyria and Babylonia to serve His purposes in Old Testament times, so He uses these entities (and you and me) as He sees fit, to accomplish *His* purposes. It is to protect the righteous, and punish wicked nations, peoples or churches, and advance *His* kingdom and the gospel of peace, *all along* (Acts 17:26-28)! **There is a plan.** Jesus will continue to rule until the last enemy is destroyed, 1Cor 15:25-26. Things may be out of *our* control, **but they are *NOT* out of control!** The LORD our God will completely destroy these worldly powers when He is ready.

Blessed is the man who serves His purposes, who aligns himself with God's eternal order of righteousness and peace. He will have the victory in the end.

> [25] But that which ye have *already* hold fast till I come. [26] And he that overcometh ... to him I will give power over the nations; [27] And he shall rule them with a rod of iron ... [29] He that hath an ear, let him hear ... Rev 2:25-27, 29 KJV

What does Revelation Tell Us About Mystery Babylon?

These entities are not anything new. I do not say this. Scripture says this. Revelation basically tells that this is the way things have "worked," with adaptations for the cultures and the times and technology, all through the Christian age. What are we told?

> And **in her was found the blood** of prophets, and of saints, and of **all that were slain** upon the earth. Rev 18:24 KJV

What an inclusive statement of affairs! What a bold and staggering prophetic announcement of fact!

And the beast and the kings allied with him? They hate the harlot.

> [16] And the ten horns which thou sawest upon the beast, these shall hate the whore, and shall make her desolate and naked, and shall eat her flesh, and burn her with fire. [17] **For God hath put in their hearts to fulfil his will,** and to agree, and give their kingdom unto the beast, until the words of God shall be fulfilled.
> Rev 17:16-17 KJV (*bold emphasis added*)

At the last, following the seeming defeat of Christianity, and then of Mystery Babylon, the Mystery of Lawlessness can go about creating a new world order on a basis of what Winston Churchill called "arrested development." There would be no "soaring to the skies" here. Cut the tap roots of a dynamic and prosperous mankind, to produce a permanently moldable, pliable, and manageable world. A forever restrained bonsai world. Man then becomes an eternal mental and moral and spiritual midget, grinding away in the service of Satan, eternally. So at least the organization of the beast intends.

> He who digs a pit will fall into it,
>   And he who rolls a stone, it will come back on him.
> Prov 26:27 NASB

XI. Conflict, Judgment, and Redemption, Revelation 20-22

And he carried me away in the spirit to a great and high mountain, and shewed me that great city, the holy Jerusalem, descending out of heaven from God,

Rev 21:10 KJV

Satan Bound and Released, Rev 20:1-6

At the end of Revelation 19 we saw the beast and the false prophet being thrown into the Lake of Fire. In other words, they were thrown into hell, Rev 19:20. We have also seen that the beast is evidently described as the "man of lawlessness" in 2Thes 2:3. Both entities are described as being worshipped by the entire world, 2Thes 2:4/Rev 13:8. Both of them are described as being destroyed by the second coming of Christ, as in 2Thes 2:8/Rev 19:20. We saw the beast gathered all the armies of the earth to fight against Jesus Second Coming in Rev 19:19. Clearly this is a "Star Wars," "Independence Day," sort of encounter. Compare Psalm 2 one more time. Lastly we saw "the rest" of the armies destroyed by the sword out of Jesus mouth, Rev 19:21. At the end of time Jesus will come to destroy all of the disobedient with His flaming sword, as we see in many places in Scripture, including, 2Thes 1:7-9.

So it appears that Revelation 19 is the end of a vision, and it ends with the second coming of Jesus Christ.

We are beginning a new vision in Revelation 20. Now we see another vision of the entire age. Like many of our earlier visions, it encompasses the entire Christian age, but it goes even further. It summarizes the entire Christian age in a few verses and then goes beyond this age and this universe to describe the world, the universe, to come. Previous visions have included the Second Coming, but this gives more details of what happens at the end of the age, that is to say at the Second Coming, and also what happens after that!

First we see a great angel coming down out of heaven, with a chain of some sort. A chain with which to tie up spiritual beings. This single angel grabs Satan and binds him, Rev 20:1-2. Here in Revelation 20 we see a single angel tying up Satan for what it calls a thousand years, Rev 20:2. Just like a donkey is tied up in Mtt 21:2 (and it is the same Greek word, *deō* δέω).

So one certain angel in heaven is in fact more powerful than man, and even more powerful than this mighty evil angel, the devil or Satan! And this one unnamed angel both ties up Satan for "a thousand years," and casts him into the abyss, Rev 20:3. Now we know that the evil angels, the demons, do not want to go to the abyss. We see this clearly in Lk 8:31 NASB, where the demons pleaded not to be thrown into the abyss before their time. The beast, we are told, comes up from the abyss. Remember passages like Rev 11:7, and others? Other angels are also in prison, and it seems to also talking about the abyss in 2 Pe 2:4.

> For if God spared not the angels that sinned, but cast *them* down to hell, and delivered *them* into chains of darkness, to be reserved unto judgment; KJV

So many of the rebellious angels are confined to the abyss (the bottomless pit, KJV) for most of the Christian age.

> [2] And he laid hold on the dragon, that old serpent, which is the Devil, and Satan, and bound him a thousand years, [3] And cast him into the bottomless pit, and shut him up, and set a seal upon him, that he should deceive the nations no more, till the thousand years should be fulfilled: and after that he must be loosed a little season. Rev 20:2-3 KJV

Lastly let us remember that Jesus also went to the abyss for three days, for you and me, Rom 10:6-7 NASB. The NASB is accurate to the Greek in Romans 10, and in Rev 20:3 where it translates the KJV "bottomless pit" as "the abyss."

Then notice the evil angels are only restrained for a time. They are only restrained for what it calls a thousand years, *perhaps* which is only symbolic of a very long time in human terms! At the last they are to be released! They are restrained so that they cannot deceive the nations it says in Rev 20:3. Then, they and Satan, are to be released, Rev 20:3, 8.

Among other things, 1.) we should not make more out of something than what is said. 2.) We should indeed remember that the term "a thousand years" is sometimes used in Scripture metaphorically of a long time. For instance in the psalms.

> For a thousand years in thy sight *are but* as yesterday when it is past, and *as* a watch in the night. Psa 90:4 KJV

Again, as in,

> even if he lives a thousand years twice—but has not seen goodness. Do not all go to one place? Ecc 6:6 NKJV

And Satan unrestrained? Unhindered? What would that be like?

A cursory look at Scripture will tell us what sort of abilities Satan has, and instruct us concerning what he could do to us *if* he were unrestrained. We see for instance in the book of Job. Satan would wreak much havoc, however ... he needs permission for that. Look at Job 1:12-20. Satan asks for permission to test Job, and God answers him.

> And the LORD said unto Satan, Behold, all that he hath is in thy power; only upon himself put not forth thine hand. So Satan went forth from the presence of the LORD. Job 1:12 KJV

With this *permission*, Satan then is able to stir up a raiding party to take all of Job's oxen and donkeys (500 yoke of oxen, and 500 female donkeys, Job 1:3), and kill the servants tending them. Then he is able to cause lightning from heaven to burn up the sheep (7,000 of them, Job 1:3) and their shepherds with them. Then he is able to stir up another raiding party to steal all of Job's camels (3,000 of them, Job 1:3), and to murder all of their keepers. Job was a very wealthy rancher by any standards. Lastly Satan is able to cause a straight-line wind to hit the house where Job's seven sons and three daughters were feasting, and caused the house to collapse and kill them all! All in the same day. All by the instigation of Satan. All by the allowance of God. Then again, on another day, Satan appeared before the Lord.

> Then the LORD said to Satan, "Have you considered My servant Job, that there is none like him on the earth, a blameless and upright man, one who fears God and shuns evil? And still he holds fast to his integrity, **although you incited Me against him, to destroy him without cause.**" Job 2:3 NKJV (*emphasis added*)

In the Gospels we see Satan can take things out of men's hearts.

> "When anyone hears the word of the kingdom, and does not understand *it*, then the wicked *one* comes and snatches away what was sown in his heart. This is he who received seed by the wayside." Mtt 13:19 NKJV

We see also in Scripture, and in life, that sometimes Satan can enter a man. For instance a man like Judas, who seemingly cannot control his desire for money. He was already stealing from the communal purse of Jesus and the apostles, Jn 12:6. So it tells us,

> And Satan entered into Judas who was called Iscariot, belonging to the number of the twelve. Lk 22:3 NASB

And Satan can put ideas into our heart.

> And supper being ended, the devil having now put into the heart of Judas Iscariot, Simon's *son*, to betray him; Jn 13:2 KJV

In Old Testament times it says that Satan was against Israel, and he got to them by seducing their leader, a godly man, David son of Jesse.

> And Satan stood up against Israel, and provoked David to number Israel. 1Chron 21:1 KJV

So here is action against a nation, by luring a good leader into wrong doing, with the evil motive on Satan's part of hurting a nation! Again back to the gospels, we see Peter trying to talk Jesus out of going to His death.

> [22] Then Peter took Him aside and began to rebuke Him, saying, "Far be it from You, Lord; this shall not happen to You." [23] But He turned and said to Peter, **"Get behind Me, Satan! You** are an offense to Me, for you are not mindful of the things of God, but the things of men." Mtt 16:22-23 NKJV (*bold emphasis added*)

So here is a godly man, Peter the apostle chosen by our Lord Himself, and Jesus answers him as if Satan himself was in Peter, in trying to get Jesus to try to avoid the cross.

Satan is allowed to tempt men, to try to lure them to sin, 1Cor 7:5. Satan can and does blind men, **in fact *ALL* who do *not* turn to Jesus the Christ are blinded by Satan, 2Cor 4:4. *And the whole world is under his power, 1Jn 5:19.*

Further Satan can also cause disease and physical harm. Paul the apostle was richly blessed with spiritual gifts, and there was evidently a danger that pride would take hold of him, and perhaps even destroy him. So in our text we are told Satan was *allowed* to physically afflict Paul, give him some illness that hurt physically.

> [7] Because of the surpassing greatness of the revelations, **for this reason,** to keep me from exalting myself, there was given me **a thorn in the flesh, a messenger of Satan to torment me — to keep me from exalting myself!** [8] Concerning this I implored the Lord three times that it might leave me. [9] And He has said to me, "My grace is sufficient for you, for power is perfected in weakness." ...
>
> 2Cor 12:7-9 NASB (*bold emphasis added*)

This "thorn" was for Paul's own good, so he would always keep in mind the mortal and the transient nature of this life. But it was Satan who was, once again, *allowed* to afflict him! Here we have the Lord our God, even using Satan's malice, to work eternal good for those who are His. Compare Rom 8:28.

Satan can sometimes also hinder us from doing things. Even Christians, 1Thes 2:18.

And Satan restrained? Bound? What would that be?

Satan's wrath and power is great. Angels are more powerful than men, 2Pe 2:11. However, the truth is that Satan cannot do just *anything* he wants, anymore than you or I can. He cannot tempt you beyond what you are able to bear. He can try to lure you to sin, but he is not *allowed* to tempt you beyond what you can bear.

> There hath no temptation taken you but such as is common to man: but God *is* faithful, who will not suffer you to be tempted above that ye are able; but will with the temptation also make a way to escape, that ye may be able to bear *it*. 1Cor 10:13 KJV

Obviously, this is speaking of limits that vary with different individuals. It is a picture of God tracking and caring for each individual. Of course you can throw that protection away, and sometimes that is what we do. Romans 1 describes situations where men willingly reject God, and God turns men over to their sins. Satan does deceive most for most of this age, 2Cor 4:4.

First it should be acknowledged that there are yet some very good times to come to *this world* because of Christianity. Not heaven on earth, but some good and significant side effects of Christianity yet to come. Often these are confused with prophecies of heaven, and they are at times mentioned side by side. "... and **the voice of weeping** shall be **no more** be heard in her, **nor the voice of crying**," Isa 65:19 KJV. "No more" could only be applied to a permanent heaven. But then also there is a day when,

"No longer will there be in it an infant who lives but a few days, ...

> For the youth will die at the age of one hundred
> And the one who does not reach the age of one hundred
> Will be thought accursed." Isa 65:20 NASB

That? *That* would never fit heaven where there is <u>no death</u>, *nor* does it fit world history so far! And Scripture cannot be broken! Jn 10:35.

Now as a donkey is "bound," tied up, tethered, as in Mk 11:2 (the word is *deō* δέω), so also Satan is "bound," tied up, tethered, in Rev 20:2 (the very same word in Greek). Notice that Jesus speaks of the binding of Satan as beginning during His ministry on earth, Mtt 12:28-30! Now a donkey may be tied to a post, fence or a rail to restrict the animal so he can barely move, *or* so he can graze only in one area, *or* so he cannot reach Aunt Emma's peaches, or Martha's green beans.

So Satan is tethered to the Abyss under the sea for a purpose: "that he should deceive the nations no more," Rev 20:3 KJV. *Then* I think it will truly be that "mine house shall be called a house of prayer **for all the people**," Isa 56:7 KJV. Compare also passages like Psalm 98, some of which speak of "the world to come," and some of this world. The nations will be, for one extensive period awakened, receptive to the gospel. It will be glorious times. Mystery Babylon will still exist, and also the "mystery of lawlessness." Evil men and seducers will still grow worse and worse, but the blinders, so to speak, will be taken off the nations, and there will be a rich harvest. "And this gospel of the kingdom shall be preached in all the world ... then shall the end come," Mtt 24:14 KJV. Who says? Jesus, Revelation 20, and many other Scriptures. Also the Spirit expressly says that toward the end, Satan and his demons "must be loosed a little season," Rev 20:3, 7, etc.

And Satan Released?

We saw earlier the demons being released from the "abyss." That is the Greek word is in Rev 9:1, but it is translated "the bottomless pit" here in many of our translations. The beast himself comes up out of the abyss, where he has been restrained, Rev 11:7. He existed at one time upon the earth, but does not now, but will come later for a short time upon the earth, and then go to destruction! He "was, and is not; and shall ascend out of the bottomless pit" Rev 17:8 KJV, and go the destruction. It appears that he is one of the few exceptions to Heb 9:27.

The demons in Revelation 9 rose from the abyss to afflict the evil men who are upon the earth, Rev 9:2-6. The bottomless pit, the abyss, will be opened at God's command in the last days. The demons will go forth for a particular purpose: to deceive the entire world to gather them for battle, Rev 9:14-16, and Rev 16:13-14. Remember? It verifies this Satanic release and its purpose in Rev 20:7-8a.

> [7] And when the thousand years are expired, **Satan will be loosed out of his prison,** [8] and shall go out **to deceive the nations** ... KJV

It does seem one or more of the Caesars are symbolic of the beast. They are a "type," a "shadow," a "pattern," of the final beast. Now which one or ones? I would not be dogmatic. Many have been proposed Nero, Domitian, Diocletian, and others. Remember, the beast has been on the earth before, that is before John writes the book of Revelation. He "was, and is not; and shall ascend out of the bottomless pit," Rev 17:8 KJV, and go to his destruction. Your guess may be as good as mine, or maybe even better. Take your pick! Read a little history.

Even so, Satan is restrained for a long time. Imprisoned! He has boundaries he cannot cross. Shall we speak of him like a dog on a chain? Rev 20:2-3. He may be mean but he cannot do all that he really wants to do, either to hurt men, or to deceive men. Remember also, when we have a type and an anti-type, a symbol and a fulfillment, *both are spoken of as fulfillments!*

So when the prophecy in 2 Sam 7:12-16 speaks of both Solomon and Jesus, Solomon is spoken of as a fulfillment in 1Kgs 8:19-20, and Jesus is spoken of as a fulfillment in Heb 1:5!

I think it is proper to say that one or more Caesars partially fulfilled the picture of the beast in for instance Revelation 13. Many Christians went to their death, who did not worship the Caesars or serve him as a god. So it says,

> [4] And I saw thrones, and they sat upon them, and judgment was given unto them: and I saw the souls of them that were beheaded for the witness of Jesus, and for the word of God, and which had not worshipped the beast, neither his image, neither had received his mark upon their foreheads, or in their hands; and they lived and reigned with Christ a thousand years. [5] But the rest of the dead lived not again until the thousand years were finished. ... Rev 20:4-5a KJV

But in addition remember, that a lot of things, for instance in Revelation 13, did NOT happen in the early centuries after Christ. For instance, there was no mark you had to receive to allow you to buy or sell anything. Remember? Surely many early Christians thought that a "mark" must be coming at any time. But it never came. So the Caesars are a type, yes! *And thus they **are** a fulfillment!* But they fall far short, are clearly not the ultimate fulfillment. In this light we might compare the many types of the Christ who was to come. There was Joseph, Moses, David, Solomon, the passover lamb, and many others. But Jesus was the final, the ultimate fulfillment of the prophecies of the Christ.

So according to Revelation 20, those saints that suffered at the hands of the Caesars, they came to life and ruled with Christ for a thousand years, Rev 20:4. I think the early Christian martyrs are clearly pictured in Rev 20:4.

> But the rest of the dead lived not again until the thousand years were finished, Rev 20:5 KJV

Is the first resurrection that we have in baptism, rising to walk with Jesus in newness of life?

> [3] Know ye not, that so many of us as were baptized into Jesus Christ were baptized into his death? [4] Therefore we are buried with him by baptism into death: that like as Christ was raised up from the dead by the glory of the Father, even so we also should walk in newness of life. Rom 6:3-4 KJV

Is this meant to be a type and anti-type? A symbol and a fulfillment? For whoever rises to walk in newness of life with Jesus, the second death, will have no power, Rev 20:6. That would indeed fit baptism. It won't be very long. We must work and be ready.

The "thousand years" Fulfills Old Testament Prophecy?

Now we have talked about Satan being both bound for much of the Christian Age, and then being released for a short while just before the end of time. That period during which Satan is like a vicious dog on a chain, is described as a thousand years, Rev 20:2. Now this is a very symbolic passage. I do not think anyone thinks we can bind a spiritual creature, like Satan, with a literal chain, say made of steel. So the "chain" is not made of, say, 4140 steel, or 316L stainless steel. The chain is of something which can be used to restrain a spiritual being, bind him it says in almost all of our translations.

And Satan is not a literal snake, or a literal dragon. He is a powerful renegade angel. Even so, he has at times appeared as a snake, and it looks like he has also appeared as a dragon, a dinosaur we might say, at times. So he is symbolically called both a snake and a dragon.

So is the thousand years a literal 999 years plus 1, of 365-1/4 days? Or is it just symbolic of a very long period of time, and if so, of what period of time does it speak?

The thousand years is clearly a period of prosperity for Christianity. Many speak of the thousand years as the period of the fulfillment of all Old Testament prophecy. It does picture many of the martyred saints, those who died for Christ during the early Christian centuries, as ruling with Christ during this period of time, Rev 20:4. We have also seen that baptism is a resurrection from the dead, as described in for instance, Rom 6:3-4, as has just been shown. Further we have seen that if we have this resurrection from death and sin, then the second death, hell itself, has no effect on us. So baptism itself may also be in view in, Rev 20:6. *If taken in this way, also it would picture Christians both dead and alive as ruling with Christ during the Christian age.* You may remember Paul talking about Christians as *having been seated* with Jesus in the heavenly places.

⁵ even when we were dead in trespasses, made us alive together with Christ (by grace you have been saved), ⁶ **and raised _us_ up together, and made _us_ sit together in the heavenly _places_** in Christ Jesus, ⁷ that in the ages to come He might show the exceeding riches of His grace in _His_ kindness toward us in Christ Jesus.

Eph 2:5-7 NKJV (_emphasis added_)

Eph 2:5-7 likewise often strikes people as being strange, as does Rev 20:4. Our being seated with Christ is past tense (aorist indicative in the Greek). In opposition to Revelation 20, Paul statements are not in the middle of a highly symbolic passage, _but does seem in many ways to say roughly the same thing as Rev 20:4._ He _has_ seated us with Him. (The same as Rev 20:4? If not, why not?) Might this then be speaking of _all_ Christians ruling with Christ now? Of the prayers of the saints having the ear of their Lord, and their requests going up before the Lord with the smoke of incense, Rev 8:5; and leading to trumpets of judgment, Rev 8:6ff?

Plainly, much of Old Testament prophecy is now being fulfilled. It is being fulfilled in New Testament Christianity, and the preaching of the gospel. Acts chapter two by itself gives examples. Peter says that the men speaking in other languages on the day of Pentecost are not drunk, Acts 2:15. Peter says in Acts 2:16-17 this is a fulfillment of Joel 2:28. Peter goes on to quote Psa 132:11, that God would put one of David's sons on his throne, and Peter says this has been fulfilled in Jesus' resurrection, Act 2:30-33. (Part of Rev 20:4? If not, why not?) So Peter is making the point Jesus is in the process of fulfilling Old Testament prophecy, and that Jesus will rule until He puts down all of His enemies, Act 2:34-35.

We saw earlier in the book of Revelation that many Christians were being martyred for the sake of Christ. They were pictured as underneath the altar, having been sacrificed for Jesus' sake.

And they cried out with a loud voice, saying, "How long, O Lord, holy and true, until You judge and avenge our blood on those who dwell on the earth?" Rev 6:10 NKJV

These are told to be patient until their full number are completed. Then we saw in chapter 8 that trumpets of warning were coming. How did they come? The prayers of the saints were going up to God, asking for God to intervene.

And the smoke of the incense, _which came_ with the prayers of the saints, ascended up before God out of the angel's hand. Rev 8:4 KJV

What then was the result of the prayers of the saints?

And the angel took the censer, and filled _it_ with fire of the altar, and cast it into the earth: and there were voices, and thunderings, and lightnings, and an earthquake. Rev 8:5 KJV

Then followed the trumpets of warning to a world that has rejected God and abused His people: hail and fire, something like a great mountain is thrown into the sea, a third of the sea was turned to blood, and signs in the sun and moon ... *all in response to the requests, the prayers, of the saints!*

> [5] even when we were dead in trespasses, made us alive together with Christ (by grace you have been saved), [6] **and <u>raised</u> <u>us</u> up together, and made <u>us</u> sit together in the heavenly *places* in Christ Jesus,**
> Eph 2:5-6 KJV

> [12] For He will deliver the needy when he cries,
>> The poor also, and *him* who has no helper.
> [13] He will spare the poor and needy,
>> And will save the souls of the needy.
> [14] He will redeem their life from oppression and violence;
>> And precious shall be their blood in His sight.
> Psa 72:12-14 NKJV

> [7] And shall not God avenge his own elect, which cry day and night unto him, though he bear long with them? [8] I tell you that he will avenge them speedily. Nevertheless when the Son of man cometh, shall he find faith on the earth? Lk 18:7-8 KJV

Is it possible that all of these are parallel passages with Rev 20:4? Is it possible that they are all viewing the same thing from different points of view, both literally and metaphorically?

You who are righteous, hear the words of the prophets. Are you abused and oppressed? Follow your LORD, 1Pe 3:20-23. Trust Him ... to the end! Raise your voices in petition to your LORD and your King. He will deliver you, not only *from* death, but *in spite of death*, even as it was with His very own Son! All you peoples! Watch! You will see it happen with your own eyes!

> ... Here is the patience and the faith of the saints. Rev 13:10 KJV

Could all of this be part of the fulfillment of those who "lived and reigned with Christ a thousand years," Rev 20:4? Those who are saved do "come to life" even during this life!

As Paul describes in 1 Cor 15:25-26, the last enemy Jesus will put down will be death. Paul says then will be fulfilled:

> [54] When the perishable puts on the imperishable, and the mortal puts on immortality, then shall come to pass the saying that is written, "Death is swallowed up in victory." [55] "O death, where is your victory? O death, where is your sting?" 1Cor 15:54-55 ESV

Here Paul is quoting from Isa 25:8, and Hos 13:14, and indicating that these prophecies will only be fulfilled at the last, when Jesus puts down the final enemy of death! So Christ is presently *in the process* of finishing the fulfillment of Old

Testament prophecy. The question I am posing is: Does the thousand years, the "millennium" complete the fulfillment of Old Testament prophecy?

Note what the Old Testament says will finally happen. The preaching of the gospel was to begin in Jerusalem, Isa 2:2-3. At the last Jesus will end war FOREVER! That is what it says in Isa 2:4. The peace of that day will be so complete that a baby will be able to play with a cobra, and weaned child with a viper, Isa 11:8-9. It will be just like it says in Isaiah 2 that there will be no more war. It says the same thing in Psa 46:9, and in many Old Testament passages. When Old Testament prophecy is finally complete, there will be no more war forever!

But look at what happens *after* the Millennium. When the thousand years is completed, **then** Satan will be released, Rev 20:7. **Then** Satan will deceive all the nations **so they will make war on the church and on God Himself**, Rev 20:8. They are described as led by Gog and Magog, Rev 20:8. Magog is one of the first descendants of Japheth, one of the main heads of the Gentile peoples, the nations of this earth, Gen 10:2. Evidently Rev 20:8 is parallel to Ezekiel chapters 38 and 39. These chapters are *also* about Gog and Magog attacking and overwhelming God's people. Listen to what it says in Ezek 38:1-4, and what it calls Gog, who is evidently a prince, a king, a leader against God's people. These vast armies will fight against God's people.

> [15] "Then you will come from your place out of the far north, you and many peoples with you, all of them riding on horses, a great company and a mighty army. [16] You will come up against My people Israel like a cloud, to cover the land. It will be in the latter days that I will bring you against My land, so that the nations may know Me, when I am hallowed in you, O Gog, before their eyes." Ezek 38:15-16 NKJV

Now nothing like Ezekiel 38 and 39 HAS EVER HAPPENED! Further, however you may interpret the thousand years, according to Revelation 20 this happens *after* the millennium! I would say it is obvious that John (or really God) wants us to compare what he writes here in Revelation 20, with Ezekiel chapter 38 and 39! They are gathering to make "war," *polemos* πόλεμος, Rev 20:8 NASB. They surround God's people in war, and are about to completely wipe them out, Rev 20:9a. This is *after* the thousand years of, Rev 20:7.

So war does not end *forever* as in prophecies like Isa 2:4, and in Psa 46:9, and many other passages, until <u>AFTER</u> the thousand years! The thousand years is **NOT** the fulfillment of the balance of Old Testament prophecy. The "millennium," the thousand years, does **NOT** bring permanent peace and prosperity.

The only lasting peace is *after* the second coming! *The premillennialists are confusing prophecies of the Christian-Age with prophecies of heaven*, and **imagining** a heaven of earth! It is true that some of the blessings of the wide spreading of the gospel will be "types," symbolic, of heaven. Still, the fulfillment of that ultimate reign of peace, is only *after* the thousand years, and *after* that greatest conflict of all time, at the end of time!

And if the "thousand years" does NOT complete Old Testament prophecy, why would we suppose Jesus would come to earth *a second time,* to rule, and ... prove what?

Christ *already* rules heaven *and* earth (1Cor 15:24-26, Mtt 28:18, etc.) and the Second Coming (after the "thousand years," however you figure that) is the **beginning** of the *completion* of the Old Testament prophecy! And only a Second Coming is spoken of: not a second, and then a third. How are God's people rescued from this final battle? By Jesus coming to repay their enemies with affliction, 2Thes 1:6. Jesus comes in flaming fire to give us relief, 2Thes 1:7. So it is with fire from heaven that Jesus rescues us, Rev 20:9b. It is the Second Coming which we are seeing in the end of Rev 20:9, at the end of the final battle.

Jesus will deal out retribution to those who do not know God, and do not obey the gospel, 2Thes 1:8. Everyone who does not know God will be eternally destroyed, and will be banished from God's presence forever, 2Thes 1:9. And God will be glorified in His faithful saints, 2Thes 1:10.

Gog, and Magog Make War, Rev 20:7-8

Then we come to another description of the final battle. This is an elegant summary of this battle in a mere three verses.

Demonic Releases

First we are told that Satan, and by implication also his helpers, his demons, are to be released so that they might work unrestrained.

> And when the thousand years are expired, Satan shall be loosed out of his prison, Rev 20:7 KJV

Here we might say is a time notice of sorts. This will occur *after* the thousand years are completed, however you might interpret the "thousand years." At that time Satan is released for a specific purpose: "to deceive the nations."

When in the book of Revelation we first saw a Satanic/demonic release, it was in chapter 9, it was a horrible thing. It was arranged by a special angel who had fallen to the earth, and who had been given the key to the abyss. Remember also that the beast comes up out of the abyss, Rev 11:7, 17:8. Could this be part of our overlap in visions? Could this be talking about the same thing, or parts of the same thing? I think so.

In Revelation 9 this release from the abyss appears to be demons who only afflict those *without* the seal of God, and which was discussed in detail earlier. The demons there seem to have the symbolic appearance of some awesome locusts dressed in armor. ***The affliction of these locusts seems to lead to a great conflict and war.*** Four angels are released *at the great river Euphrates*, and they are prepared to kill a third of mankind, Rev 9:14-15.

John said he heard the number of the armies and what he heard was two hundred million. A description of a great conflict follows, and in the end of chapter 9 people still refuse to repent of their sins, and then this leads to the vision of the temple of God being overrun, but the *naos*, the sanctuary of the temple, being protected. Two prophets are rebuking the world for its sins, and finally the beast comes up out of the abyss and kills the two prophets. That was the first context of demonic release in our parallel visions of the book of Revelation.

The second description of the demonic release in the book of Revelation, if you wanted to call it that, is in Revelation 16. The first thing we see is that it also has to do with war, and with the great River Euphrates being dried up. The *Euphrates* is dried up for the kings of the east, who are coming to make war, Rev 16:12. Such repetition of names and traits are common in prophecies which are intended to be parallel and overlapping and cumulative. *A good example of such things, to study similar usages, would be the various prophecies of Christ coming to this earth the first time.*

It is at this point that we see specific actions by Satan to deceive the nations. Three evil spirits show themselves. One comes out of the mouth of the dragon, that is to say, out of the mouth of Satan. The second evil spirit is out of the beast, the Satanic man who claims to be the one and only "god." The third spirit comes out of the mouth of the false prophet who did incredible signs and demanded that everyone worship the first beast.

What are these "spirits of demons," "three unclean spirits like frogs," (Rev 16:13-14 KJV) doing? They are performing signs, the implication is that these are Satanic "miracles" of a sort, for the kings of the earth, to prepare them for battle "on the great day of God, the Almighty"? The place of battle is Armageddon! This is followed by a description of the end of the world. So we have some overlap in the general subject of a Satanic release, and it seems to be for the general purpose of gathering huge armies to make war, *seemingly* ... against *God Himself*, as daunting as such a subject sounds.

The specific purpose is "to deceive the nations ... **to gather them together to battle**: the number of whom *is* as the sand of the seas," KJV. So numberless masses of troops are gathered for a war, a war that they must be deceived into fighting? That would certainly fit the war seemingly against God in Revelation

16. That would also seem to fit the war pictured in Revelation 19, which also it would seem is against God. It is against the King of kings and the Lord of lords, and the outcome is that the beast and the false prophet are captured alive and thrown alive into hell! Indeed, the final battle is seen in more than one place.

Relating to Gog and Magog

There are other associations with this battle/war as described in Revelation 20. Satan is released from his prison in the last days to deceive the nations of the earth, and the nations are given a name: Gog and Magog. Thus it is, for better or for worse, that to understand Revelation 20, we will need to sort out Ezekiel chapters 37 through 39, in which Gog and Magog figure are major figures.

Gog and Magog have an early history in Scripture. Noah's three sons were Shem, Ham, and Japheth. From these three men and their wives came all the peoples of the earth. From Ham came Mizraim (Egypt), Cush (Ethiopia), and Canaan. From Shem came the Semites of the earth, including the the Arameans (which includes Syrians), and the Assyrians (sons of Asshur), and the Hebrews (or to put it in a Greek sort of way, the 'Ebrews) descendants of Eber, Gen 10:21. Basically all the rest of mankind came from the very prolific descendants of Japheth. This evidently includes most of what we call Caucasians, and most of what we call Asians. So the sons of Japheth includes most of the world.

Among the prominent sons of Japheth are Magog, Tubal and Meshech (Gen 10:2). Then, it just happens, that all of these are mentioned in Ezekiel 38 as invading Israel !

> [1] And the word of the LORD came to me, saying, [2] Son of man, set thy face against Gog, the land of Magog, the chief prince of Meshech and Tubal, and prophesy against him, [3] and say, 'Thus says the Lord GOD, Behold, I *am* against you, O Gog, the chief prince of Meshech and Tubal. Ezek 38:1-3 KJV

So Gog and Magog are mentioned in both Revelation 20, and in Ezekiel chapters 38 and 39. Both are mentioned in the general context of making war on God's people. It seems pretty obvious that our Lord in Revelation 20 wants us to examine Ezekiel 38-39. When using terms about early patriarchs in both passages, it seems obvious that in both passages it is using the names of these early patriarchs as symbolic of the huge numbers of their descendants. So we will begin by looking at Ezekiel 37 to 39, and the context there, and *then* look at Revelation 20, to see what relationship might exist between the two.

The Spiritual Awakening of the Jews, Ezekiel 37

To examine Ezekiel chapters 38 and 39 we will first start with chapter 37. This is the chapter about God raising physical Israel from spiritual death. It starts off with Ezekiel seeing a valley full of very dry bones, and Ezekiel being instructed to prophesy to these bones, and to make them come to life. The bones begin to rattle and shake, and bone joins to bone, and sinews and ligaments begin to appear on the bones and muscles and skin comes on these corpses. Lastly God puts the breath of life into these renewed bodies. God told Ezekiel,

> Then he said unto me, Son of man, these bones are the whole house of Israel: behold, they say, Our bones are dried, and our hope is lost: we are cut off for our parts. Ezek 37:11 KJV

In a time of the Jews being dispersed all over the world, God says,

> And shall put my spirit in you, and ye shall live, and I shall place you in your own land: then shall ye know that I the LORD have spoken it, and performed *it*, saith the LORD. Ezek 37:14

This renewing of God's people never really seemed to happen after the first gathering from captivity took place. The prophets, including specifically Zechariah and Haggai and Malachi, seem to view Israel as still in their stiff-necked and rebellious mode. Then the second dispersion of Israel took place, as prophesied by Jesus the Christ, in 70 AD, and as also prophesied by Isa 11:11, and Zech 10:8-12 and other passages. And the promised spiritual resurrection of the Jews ... ? It has never happened ... even to this day! *Could the period of the Jews turning to Jesus of Nazareth in faith be a key part of "the thousand years"?* I think it very well could be. It is obviously spoken of in prophecy as a period of glory for the gospel, but that also is another story.

Then following this chapter about the spiritual renewal of Israel, first comes Ezekiel chapter 38, about an invasion of Israel by Gog and Magog and all of their hosts. For a different treatment of what these names mean, see the discussion of "Victory over Christianity, Gog and Magog," in *Prophecy Principles*.

Huge numbers of troops and peoples are pictured as being allied with Magog, peoples from all over the world. They are told to prepare themselves, because they will be summoned to attack Israel, "in the latter years," Ezek 38:8 KJV. Ezekiel 38 seems to be *after* some regathering of Israel. It is to,

> ... the land that is restored from the sword, **whose inhabitants have been gathered from many nations to the mountains of Israel which had been a continual waste;** but its people were brought out from the nations, and they are living securely, all of them. Ezek 38:8 NASB (*bold emphasis added*)

So you could take Ezekiel 38 as something that happens *after* Israel's spiritual renewal. That is a possible inference, but not a necessary one, given the way prophecy is written. Always keep in mind that prophecy is almost *never* strictly linear. Rather the syntax is conversational, with subjects being dropped and then brought up again, and other things being injected in between, just like in extended human conversations.

God clearly indicates at the beginning of Ezekiel 38 that He is against Gog, who is a leader of "Rosh, Meshech and Tubal," Ezek 38:2 NASB. Also God clearly indicates in Ezekiel 38 that **He** will smash this confederation which is attacking God's people.

A War With Gog and Magog, Ezekiel 39

Then let us look for a moment at Ezekiel 39. Similarly it starts off,

> ¹ "And you, son of man, prophesy against Gog, and say, 'Thus says the Lord GOD, "Behold, I am against you, O Gog, the prince of Rosh, Meshech, and Tubal; ² and **I will** turn you around and lead you on, bringing you up from the far north, and **bring you against the mountains of Israel**." Ezek 39:1-2 NKJV (*bold emphasis added*)

Then, very much like Revelation 19 and other descriptions of the last battle of all time, it pictures the corpses of the soldiers who have opposed God, as just lying out in the open, with the birds of the air and the beasts of the field being free to feed on their corpses, in a great supper which has been prepared for them by the Lord.

Then we have a special ending of Ezekiel 39. The first thing we see is that the corpses have to be buried, although it says it will take a long time. Then it says that the nations will know that God has favored the house of Israel.

> ²³ "The Gentiles shall know that the house of Israel went into captivity for their iniquity; because they were unfaithful to Me, therefore I hid My face from them. I gave them into the hand of their enemies, and they all fell by the sword. ²⁴ According to their uncleanness and according to their transgressions I have dealt with them, and hidden My face from them." Ezek 39:23-24 NKJV

Then God points to a regathering and a spiritual renewal.

> ²⁵ Therefore thus says the Lord GOD, "Now I will bring back the captives of Jacob, and have mercy on the whole house of Israel; and I will be jealous for My holy name— ... ²⁷ When I have brought them back from the peoples and gathered them ..." Ezek 39:25, 27 NKJV

First let us take Ezekiel 39 firmly in hand. **Let us say for sure, *that nothing like this has _ever_ happened* !** Some Jews are pictured as *already* living in Palestine in Ezekiel 39. Then the invasion by this vast coalition is smashed, and the burials take years and it results in Israel being renewed! I am reminded of stories of the American Battle of Gettysburg in 1863. For years after that battle, unburied bones were still being found, or turned up by a plow. No invasion of Palestine by so broad a coalition, that results in the invasion being completely smashed, and Israel being spiritually renewed in the process, **has _ever_ happened _in any way_!** A Babylonian coalition invaded in 586 BC (it was in fact a Semitic invasion, we might add). However it was not this broad of a coalition, and it did not end this way. There was a Roman invasion after the revolt in 67 AD, mainly of the sons of Japheth, but not by this broad a coalition, and it surely did not end like Ezekiel 39.

Let us also notice that the end of Ezekiel 39 seems to point to the spiritual raising from the dead of the Jews, **and that *also* has _never_ happened!** Then it seems to lead to a full blessing of Israel, and peace, and a *full* drawing of the Jews to Palestine.

> ²⁶ after they have borne their shame, and all their unfaithfulness in which they were unfaithful to Me, when they dwelt safely in their *own* land and no one made *them* afraid. ²⁷ **When I have brought them back from the peoples and gathered them out of their enemies' lands, and I am hallowed in them in the sight of many nations,**
> Ezek 39:26-27 NKJV (*bold emphasis added*)

It does appear that Ezekiel 39, as presented here, seems to relate to Ezekiel 37 and their rising from the dead spiritually, and it seems to precede it, to continue life here on earth as the followers of Jesus the Christ, that they always should have been, in an excellent manner, and in peace. **Notice carefully that Israel seems to have peace here on earth *after* this invasion is repelled!**

Another War With Gog and Magog, Ezekiel 38?

Now let us notice some contrasts between Ezekiel chapter 38 and chapter 39. In Ezekiel 38 it pictures God's people living in a Palestine that *had been* a waste.

> After many days thou shalt be visited: **in the latter years** thou shalt come **into the land** *that is* **brought back from the sword,** *and is* **gathered out of many people, against the mountains of Israel,** which have been always waste: but it is brought forth out of the nations, and **they shall dwell safely** all of them.
> Ezek 38:8 KJV (*bold emphasis added*)

It appears that in Ezekiel 38 it is *following* the spiritual resurrection of Israel from spiritual death, as pictured in Ezekiel **37,** *and* Ezekiel **39,** and they start out living in peace, already restored from the scorches of war, and are surprised by this invasion of Gog and Magog!

Although Ezekiel 38 *also* pictures an invasion by Gog and Magog, but here it seems to be a worldwide sort of thing! The armies of Gog and Magog seem to be *sweeping the entire earth instead of just Israel*. They show up at Sheba, south of Israel. They show up at Dedan, which similarly seems to be talking about peoples to the south on the Persian Gulf. Also it seems to picture the armies of Gog and Magog coming to Tarshish (Spain). The armies of Gog and Magog are **not** invading Sheba and Dedan and Tarshish, rather they are sweeping Sheba and Dedan and Tarshish looking for certain people. In Ezekiel 38, when the armies are sweeping the earth for the children of God, the peoples of the earth are surprised.

> 'Sheba, Dedan, the merchants of Tarshish, and all their young lions will say to you, "Have you come to take plunder? Have you gathered your army to take booty, to carry away silver and gold, to take away livestock and goods, to take great plunder?" ' Ezek 38:13 NKJV

The peoples of the earth are surprised at this sweeping of the earth looking for the children of God! So Ezekiel 38 seems to be picturing a worldwide sweep *against God's people.* They are not assaulting the fortifications of Israel, rather they are going up "against My people Israel," Ezek 38:16.

> [11] and you will say, 'I will go up against the land of unwalled villages. I will go against those who are at rest, that live securely, all of them **living without walls and having no bars or gates,** [12] to capture spoil and to seize plunder, to turn your hand against the waste places which are *now* inhabited, and against the people who **are gathered** from the nations, who have acquired cattle and goods, **who live at the center of the world.'** Ezek 38:11-12 NASB (*bold emphasis added*)

Notice that the war against God's people in Revelation *also* seems to be worldwide, and against a people who are not in fortified cities, but rather living in "camps" "at the center of the world"!

> **They went up on the breadth of the earth** and surrounded the camp of the saints ... Rev 20:9 NKJV

Could it be that Ezekiel 38 and 39 are speaking of two separate wars against "Israel," separated in history by perhaps even hundreds of years?

Two wars that are in many particulars the same, but also in many particulars different. However, *both* result in a failure of the coalitions against "Israel"?

Then notice another difference in the two invasions. The invasion in Ezekiel 38 seems to end in what we would call the end of time, the end of this present universe! God comes here in fire.

> "For in My jealousy and in the fire of My wrath I have spoken: "Surely in that day there shall be a great earthquake in the land of Israel," Ezek 38:19 NKJV

The mountains of Israel are a long way from the sea, but in Ezekiel 38 it is not only the mountains which quake at God's coming, but also the fish in the sea and the birds of the air, and **"all the men that *are* on the face of the earth"** (38:20 KJV), will shake at God's presence. As the search for God's people is worldwide (and includes all Christians, not just those of the Jews), so it would appear the intervention by God is worldwide, so that,

> ... and the mountains shall be thrown down, and the steep places shall fall, and **every** wall shall fall to the ground.
> Ezek 38:20 KJV (*bold emphasis added*)

The mountains will fall down? The steep places will collapse? "... **every** wall will fall to the ground"? There is only one time when **all** of this will happen to "**all** ... men," Ezek 38:20. At the end of time!

> Then the sky receded as a scroll when it is rolled up, and **every mountain and island was moved out of its place**.
> Rev 6:14 NKJV (*bold emphasis added*)

Remember? This was discussed earlier. Remember also that discussions of "what will be" in prophecy do not always follow a linear format, rather they follow a conversational format, weaving in and out of talking about, say, two happenings in history which are in some ways similar. This was first illustrated with a discussion of 2 Samuel 7 in *Prophecy Principles*, and it has been shown how these sorts of things work in many prophetic passages.

A conclusion on Ezekiel chapters 37 through 39 ?

Ezekiel 37 is about the spiritual transformation of the Jews in their great time of stress *in the latter days*. This results in the conversion of Israel as a nation to Jesus Christ, as described in Zechariah chapter 13, and many other passages. Ezekiel 38 *in contrast* is about *the end time* of stress, when the beast is revealed, and an attempt is made to round up and kill all Christians worldwide. Ezekiel 38 then is parallel to our text in Rev 20:7-9. Ezekiel 39 then seems to drop back and describe *that special time of stress* which *leads to* the conversion of the Jews, and their living in peace. Such going back and forth between topics is common in prophecy, and is easy to illustrate in, for instance, Isaiah chapters 40 to 66.

A Synthesis of the Accounts of the Final Conflicts

The conflict which is visualized in Rev 20:7-9 is the final assault on Christianity. The armies of the world are assembled to round up and destroy all Christians worldwide. This core of righteousness is not an entity which can be persuaded away from Jesus the Christ. They are not people who can be seduced, nor "made drunk with the wine of her immorality," nor intimidated into abandoning the Christ. For the beast and his armies to *not* have their ultimate work of evil unhinged by the truth of God, both the *naos* **and** those who only "desire to live godly in Christ Jesus," must be destroyed, annihilated, completely. The signal for this battle to start, seems to be when we see,

> "... 'abomination of desolation,' spoken of by Daniel the prophet, standing in the holy place ..." Mtt 24:15 NKJV

This last battle against Christianity, seems to begins with sweeping the earth with millions of soldiers looking, not for loot, but for people. This is called in Revelation 16 the battle of Armageddon, the key battle against God's people. A three and a half year worldwide reign of terror has begun. The church at this time will have both strong gentile *and* Jewish components, cannot buy nor sell *anything* worldwide. The church flees into the wilderness, to a place prepared for her there, where God again cares for His people in the wilderness, Rev 12:14.

> "Therefore, behold, I will allure her,
>> Bring her into the wilderness
>> And speak kindly to her." Hos 2:14 NASB

It will be terror on the whole world in these days. For their wickedness in oppressing those who had done them no wrong, the plagues of Egypt and more will come upon the earth, including darkness and burning heat, and asteroids, and water turned to blood. Gog and Magog will come very close to overcoming the church, and in human terms will seem to have accomplished that. Jesus said,

> ... Nevertheless when the Son of man cometh, shall he find faith on the earth? Lk 18:8 KJV

Just when it seems that the beast has won,

> For when they say, "Peace and safety!" then sudden destruction comes upon them, as labor pains upon a pregnant woman. And they shall not escape 1Thes 5:3 NKJV

> ... *it shall be* for a time, times, and half *a time*; and when the power of the holy people has been completely shattered, all these *things* shall be finished. Dan 12:7 NKJV

So just when it seems the beast has won,

> [7] ... the Lord Jesus will be revealed from heaven with His mighty angels, [8] In flaming fire taking vengeance on them that know not God, and that obey not the gospel of our Lord Jesus Christ:. 2Thes 1:7-8 KJV

So it is described in Revelation 20 as Gog and Magog surrounding the Christians, the church of our Lord, to destroy them, and then,

> ... fire came down from God out of heaven, and devoured them. Rev 20:9 KJV

My friends, we are still living in a Bible story!

Reward and Punishment, Rev 20:10 to 21:8

The last battle, the battle in which Satan once and for all tries to wipe out the church, the battle in which the kings of the earth try to take a stand against God, and try to defeat Him ... that battle is over.

That battle is described in Revelation 19 and Revelation chapter 20, and in many other passages of prophecy. The effect these assaults on the church have on the oppressors is described in "the seven last plagues."

You probably remember that in Rev 16:16 that battle is called Armageddon, or as it says in the NASB "Har-Magedon" (that is, the mountain, Hebrew "*Har*" הַר, of Meggido). That battle is over. Satan and the beast and his armies have been decisively defeated, in fire and hail, in turning to fight each other rather than suicidally fight the angels, and in just plain old running for cover. The church of Our Lord has been decisively saved. There is more to tell from relevant prophecies which have not been examined in this cursory overview.

Now comes the true end of things. Satan first of all is punished. The devil or Satan is thrown into the lake of fire, along with the beast and the false prophet, Rev 20:10.

If you remember Revelation 19, then you remember that the beast and the false prophet are thrown alive into the lake of fire, "and shall be tormented day and night for ever and ever," Rev 20:10 KJV.

Notice that Satan and the beast have already been condemned by the courts of heaven. They have already had their notices by prophets and the angels of God. This has happened *during history* and is described in the book of Daniel. In Dan 7:9-11, it may also be describing the condemnation of the early types of the beasts in New Testament Roman times. The final beast seems to be in mind in Dan 7:12.

> As concerning the rest of the beasts, they had their dominion taken away: yet their lives were prolonged for a season and time. KJV

God appears and heaven and earth flee away, and there is no longer any place to be found for the old universe, Rev 20:11. The heavens and the earth pass away with fire.

> [10] But the day of the Lord will come as a thief in the night; in the which the heavens shall pass away with a great noise, and the elements shall melt with fervent heat, the earth also and the works that are therein shall be burned up. ... [12] Looking for and hasting unto the coming of the day of God, wherein the heavens being on fire shall be dissolved, and the elements shall melt with fervent heat? 2Pe 3:10, 12 KJV

And the universe is rolled up like an old coat, and put away, Heb 1:11-12. But God endures as the same, Psa 102:26-28. The same yesterday, today and forever! All the dead appear before the Lord Our God, Rev 20:12.

And I saw the dead, small and great, stand before God; and the books were opened: and another book was opened, which is the book of life: and the dead were judged out of those things which were written in the books, according to their works. KJV

This is also described in Mtt 25:31-33. There is "big data" in heaven which no human organization can match. Earth and sea give up their dead, and they are judged by their works, Rev 20:13. Death and Hades are thrown into the lake of fire, Rev 20:14. Anyone not found in the Book of Life is given over to death. They are thrown into the eternal lake of fire, Rev 20:15.

Who shall be punished with everlasting destruction from the presence of the Lord, and from the glory of his power; 2Thes 1:9 KJV

God has known for a long time who would make it and who would not. If God is all knowing, then He had to know this too, or He isn't all knowing. So God chose those who would follow Him, from before the foundation of the world, Eph 1:4. He predestined us to adoption as sons, Eph 1:5. I did not say that! God said that! Our names have been written in the Book of Life since the foundation of the world, Rev 17:8. God has made His decisions by foreknowledge, 1Pe 1:1-2. He lets us *prove* who we really are, tries to change us if we are on a wrong path, but He foreknew us.

Then John saw the passing away of heaven and earth, and the sea was no more, Rev 21:1. Then the new Jerusalem came down out of heaven, Rev 21:2. There is a Jerusalem below, a Jerusalem just of this earth, just of this world.

Now this Hagar is Mount Sinai in Arabia and corresponds to the present Jerusalem, for she is in slavery with her children. Gal 4:25 NASB

But there is a Jerusalem above, and we are a part. "But the Jerusalem above is free; she is our mother." Gal 4:26. Jerusalem above is the church of which we have been a part, the heavenly Jerusalem.

22 But **you have come to Mount Zion** and to the city of the living God, **the heavenly Jerusalem**, to an innumerable company of angels, 23 **to the** general assembly and **church of the firstborn** *who are* registered in heaven, to God the Judge of all, to the spirits of just men made perfect, 24 to Jesus the Mediator of the new covenant, and to the blood of sprinkling that speaks better things than *that of* Abel. Heb 12:22-24 NKJV (*bold emphasis added*)

At this point in Revelation we will truly see the heavenly Jerusalem in her glory and majesty, and God will then live among His people Rev 21:3. Then people will see the difference.

16 Then they that feared the LORD spake often one to another: and the LORD hearkened, and heard it, and a book of remembrance was written before him for them that feared the LORD, and that thought

upon his name. [17] And they shall be mine, saith the LORD of hosts, in that day when I make up my jewels; and I will spare them, as a man spareth his own son that serveth him [18] Then shall ye return, and discern between the righteous and the wicked, between him that serveth God and him that serveth him not. Mal 3:16-18 KJV

There will be no more crying or tears, Rev 21:4. That has been repeated more than once in the prophecies of the age which is yet to come. For instance in Isa 65:19.

> "I will also rejoice in Jerusalem and be glad in My people;
> And there will no longer be heard in her
> The voice of weeping and the sound of crying. NASB

There will be no death and no decay, so your bones will flourish like the new grass, Isa 66:13-14. Do you like new things? Do you? God will make all things new, Rev 21:5. The government will rest on Jesus.

> [6] For unto us a child is born, unto us a son is given: and the government shall be upon his shoulder: and his name shall be called Wonderful, Counsellor, The mighty God, The everlasting Father, The Prince of Peace. [7] Of the increase of *his* government and peace *there shall be* no end, upon the throne of David, and upon his kingdom, to order it, and to establish it with judgment and with justice from henceforth even for ever. The zeal of the LORD of hosts will perform this. Isa 9:6-7 KJV

And of posterity there?

> A little one shall become a thousand, and a small one a strong nation: I the LORD will hasten it in his time. Isa 60:22 KJV

The wolf will live with the lambs, Isa 11:6-7, and a little boy will be able to lead them. The nursing child will play with a cobra, and a little boy will be able to stick his hand in a vipers nest, Isa 11:8. None will hurt another on that Holy Mountain in that final age of glory, Isa 11:9. "In the mount of the LORD it will be provided." Gen 22:14 NKJV. Jesus says it is done, Rev 21:6. He who overcomes will inherit these things, Rev 21:7. Eternal bliss *follows* the "thousand years." But the cowardly and unbelieving will be destroyed, Rev 21:8.

The Greater Jerusalem, Rev 21:9-27

Now earlier in the book of Revelation we saw seven angels who had seven bowls containing the seven last plagues which would come upon the earth. This was in Revelation chapters 15 and 16, although the story of the last plague stretched all the way to the end of chapter 19. Now one of those seven angels invites John to see the bride, the wife of the Lamb, Rev 21:9.

Now the Lamb, as we all know, is Jesus the Christ, the lamb which takes away the sins of the world, Jn 1:29. He is our Passover lamb from God, and by His blood God passes over our sins, and overlooks our wrong doing, 1Cor 5:7, *if* we have the wit to grab ahold of such a wonderful gift!

But who is the wife of the lamb? It is a political unit. It is a city.

> And he carried me away in the spirit to a great and high mountain, and shewed me that great city, the holy Jerusalem, descending out of heaven from God, Rev 21:10 KJV

That is what we have come to in Jesus: the heavenly Jerusalem, as we have shown from Heb 12:22-23. As you well know by now, there are two Jerusalems. First there is a present Jerusalem. It is in slavery with all of her children, Gal 4:25. It obviously includes most of the present day Jews of the early 21st century. It is called Sodom and Egypt in Rev 11:8. Now you may not like these verses, but there they are, and they are very plain, that the great city in the book of Revelation becomes what Gal 4:25 calls "present Jerusalem." It is called Sodom and Egypt in prophecy, for instance in the prophet Isaiah.

> [10] Hear the word of the LORD, ye rulers of Sodom; give ear unto the law of our God, ye people of Gomorrah. [11] To what purpose is the multitude of your sacrifices unto me? saith the LORD: ... [12] When ye come to appear before me, who hath required this at your hand, to tread my courts? ...
> [21] How is the faithful city become an harlot! it was full of judgment; righteousness lodged in it; but now murderers. Isa 1:10-12, 21 KJV

I do not think "the great city" is centered there now. She has not yet reached the fulness of her power, obviously. Babylon will ride on the coattails of a Christianized Jewish nation, and after what is seemingly an extended period of time, first seduce many of them into iniquity one last time. Then in a last surprise attack, will join with the beast in trying to completely destroy Christianity. It will *seem* she has succeeded. But God will intervene and rescue the *remanent* of His people. Jerusalem below will be completely destroyed, Revelation 18 because God ordained it. "... and fire came down from God out of heaven ..." KJV to destroy those surrounding the camp of the saints.

But Jerusalem above is our mother, Gal 3:26! The heavenly Jerusalem. And heavenly Jerusalem is once again a city. Once again she will come down out of heaven from God. Formerly we gentiles were banned from this city, Eph 2:12. Through Jesus we have become part of this city. We are fellow-citizens with the saints of old, the faithful of the Old Testament, Eph 2:19.

Now Satanists and anarchists and many modern liberals are anti-man, anti-maturity, anti-civilization, anti-city. However, the heavenly Jerusalem is by definition a city, and what a city! The ideal place to live according to Scripture is a city. A city, a civilization, without sin or any wrong doing or decay. How big is this square city? It is immense. This is truly a dazzling city, with impressive walls, and twelve gates for the twelve tribes of Israel. An angel has a measuring rod to measure the city, and it is fifteen hundred miles high and wide and long, with three gates on each of her four sides, Rev 21:16. The foundation stones are named for the twelve apostles, Rev 21:14.

By any measure this city will dwarf even Babylon the Great, even when she reaches her height later in the Christian age. This city of Revelation 21 is like a small planet. And the walls? They are over 200 hundred feet high, Rev 21:17. The original says the walls are 144 cubits high, with a cubit being about 18 inches.

How then are we to take these measurements? *I think we should take them like the thousand years of Revelation 20.* These measurements are symbolic of immense size, beyond what we can imagine, but very probably nothing like the immensity and grandeur which we will see someday. Like the dimensions of the temple in the prophet Ezekiel, it is meant to convey the idea of something beyond what men can conceive or carry out. The walls are made of the costliest of stones: japer, sapphire, emeralds, etc., Rev 21:18-20. The gates are made of pearl, Rev 21:21. So what is this saying? I think it is saying that this city is rich beyond human imagination, and these are the only images which may be somewhat appropriate. However, there was no temple there, Rev 21:22. Why? Because God will no longer live in a temple made with hands. It was Jesus purpose to build it, Mk 14:58. Rather Jesus is building a temple made of purified people, the saints of the Most High God, Eph 2:20-22. We are living stones in a spiritual temple.

> [5] you also, as living stones, are being built up a spiritual house, a holy priesthood, to offer up spiritual sacrifices acceptable to God through Jesus Christ. [6] Therefore it is also contained in the Scripture,
> *"Behold, I lay in Zion*
> *A chief cornerstone, elect, precious,*
> *And he who believes on Him will by no means be put to shame."*
> 1Pe 2:5-6 NKJV

This is the more perfect tabernacle, not of this creation, Heb 9:11, 24. No need for a power grid. God will be its light, Rev 21:23.

> [19] "The sun shall no longer be your light by day,
> Nor for brightness shall the moon give light to you;
> But the LORD will be to you an everlasting light,

And your God your glory.

20 Your sun shall no longer go down,
 Nor shall your moon withdraw itself;
 For the LORD will be your everlasting light,
 And the days of your mourning shall be ended."
Isa 60:19-20 NKJV

There will be no gang wars there. There will be no more violence there.

> Violence shall no more be heard in thy land, wasting nor destruction within thy borders; but thou shalt call thy walls Salvation, and thy gates Praise. Isa 60:18 KJV

Everyone will be righteous there, Isa 60:21. The final fulfillment of all prophecy will be in that heavenly Jerusalem. The nations (plural) will walk by the light of God, Rev 21:24. The gates will never be closed, Rev 21:25. This city will be completely and finally secure *forever!*

There will be no night. We will not need any rest, Rev 21:26. In a present universe blighted by sin and death, it is a blessing that sensations can pass. It is a blessing that hurt and loss can pass away, that feelings of inadequacy and embarrassment can fade, that the smell of death is no longer so strong in our nostrils. But where death and decay and entropy are no longer operating principles, then it is possible to enjoy beauty and life and song and the fragrance of good things *forever*, without ever tiring of them. Goodness forevermore in perfection. The glory and honor of all the nations will flow into heaven, Rev 21:26. Of course the same thing is said in many other passages.

> "Therefore your gates shall be open continually;
> They shall not be shut day or night,
> That men may bring to you the wealth of the Gentiles,
> And their kings in procession." Isa 60:11 NKJV

Only nothing unclean or filthy will be there. Only those whose names are written in the Lamb's book of life will be there, Rev 21:27.

You wouldn't want to miss it for the world!

The Road to Paradise, Revelation 22

In Genesis 1 we see God creating the heavens and the earth, Gen 1:1-5. Then we see God making man, Gen 1:27. At first there was no one to manage God's creation, Gen 2:4-7. Plainly though, man was made to rule. Man was made to be God like, Gen 1:26. Man's job was to be the boss, under God, Gen 1:28. Man was **made** to live in a perfect environment that was watered by a river in Western Turkey/Northern Iraq, Gen 2:8-10-14. It was meant to be a perfect existence. Without wrong, or evil, in full fellowship with God. Also man was given a helper. Someone to share his destiny, to be his companion, Gen 2:18. So God formed woman from part of man.

Man was given a job. Man was born to be useful, to manage, to tend, to cultivate ... in the perfect job, in the perfect place, in a fabulous garden, in a paradise, because paradise, *paradeisos* παράδεισος in Greek, means a garden or a park, Gen 2:15. However, man and his companion fell into sin, and lost their position, Gen 3:22-24. Man was ruined. We were ruined.

> [12] Wherefore, as by one man sin entered into the world, and death by sin; and so death passed upon all men, for that all have sinned: [13] (For until the law sin was in the world: but sin is not imputed when there is no law. [14] Nevertheless death reigned from Adam to Moses, even over them that had not sinned after the similitude of Adam's transgression, who is the figure of him that was to come. Rom 5:12-14 KJV

Then the Lord saw that the wickedness of man was great on the earth, and that every intent of the thoughts of his heart was only evil continually. Gen 6:5. We have been ruined! Can the leopard change his spots? Jer 13:23. Our righteousness is as filthy rags, Isa 64:6.

> [10] As it is written, There is none righteous, no, not one: [11] There is none that understandeth, there is none that seeketh after God. [12] They are all gone out of the way, they are together become unprofitable; there is none that doeth good, no, not one. Rom 3:10-12 KJV

Creation was ruined. The earth no longer naturally brought forth its fruit. Only with toil and frustration can man now produce fruit, Gen 3:17-19. Man's sin affects his environment. Man finally becomes so evil that God destroys the land, Gen 6:6-8. It has been that way down through history. So Isaiah writes,

> [4] The earth mourns *and* fades away,
> > The world languishes *and* fades away;
> > The haughty people of the earth languish.
> [5] The earth is also defiled under its inhabitants,
> > Because they have transgressed the laws,
> > Changed the ordinance,
> > Broken the everlasting covenantt.
> [6] Therefore the curse has devoured the earth,
> > And those who dwell in it are desolate.
> > Therefore the inhabitants of the earth are burned,
> > And few men *are* left. Isa 24:4-6 NKJV

Things are not what they are supposed to be! This is not the way life is supposed to be. We sense this. We recognize this. Then comes redemption through Jesus.

> [6] For when we were yet without strength, in due time Christ died for the ungodly. [7] For scarcely for a righteous man will one die: yet peradventure for a good man some would even dare to die. [8] But God commendeth his love toward us, in that, while we were yet sinners, Christ died for us. Rom 5:6-8 KJV

Jesus Christ is the new Adam of a new race of men, men born not of flesh but of the Spirit of God.

> [20] But now is Christ risen from the dead, *and* become the firstfruits of them that slept. [21] For since by man *came* death, by man *came* also the resurrection of the dead. [22] For as in Adam all die, even so in Christ shall all be made alive. [23] But every man in his own order: Christ the firstfruits; afterward they that are Christ's at his coming. 1Cor 15:20-23 KJV

Now you may say, 'Well I don't deserve the death that comes by Adam.' And that may be so, but that is the way sin works, it destroys all we hold dear, and all those around us. But here is the other side. Now you have *sins of your own*. Now you deserve to die for *your* iniquity, and now *you* don't *deserve* the righteousness that is in Jesus! God will redeem us, Isa 44:23. David says,

> I have been young, and now am old; yet have I not seen the righteous forsaken, nor his seed begging bread. Psa 37:25 KJV

He will take care of you, Mtt 6:30-33. He will fulfill all our needs, Phil 4:19. We will live in houses we did not build, have vineyards we did not plant, and rule over creation as we were intended to rule, Heb 2:5-8. And this is all through Jesus. We will judge the world, 1Cor 6:2-3. And we will live in the perfect place, Rev 22:1-7. It is a garden. The paradise of God.

Everything that is wrong with us ... or with the world ... is corrected in Jesus Christ, and in Christ alone. How do we get these rich and precious gifts? We must give our hearts and minds and lives to Jesus, Mk 16:15-16.

Don't love this world, 1 Jn 2:15. Do whatever Jesus says, Heb 5:9. Overcome by faith, 1 Jn 5:3-4. And what will you have? The paradise of God, Rev 2:7.

You won't be hurt by the second death, Rev 2:11. You will receive the hidden manna, Rev 2:17, the food of God. You will have authority over the nations, Rev 2:26-28. God will not erase your name, Rev 3:5. You will be a pillar in God's house, Rev 3:12.

> To him that overcometh will I grant to sit with me in my throne, even as I also overcame, and am set down with my Father in his throne. Rev 3:21 KJV

XII. Retrospect

More Unfinished Business

The precursor conflicts, and their obvious relationship to the book of Revelation, have been discussed. An overview and synopsis of the book of Revelation has been given. Admittedly, not all synthesis of the relevant parallel passages in Scripture and the book of Revelation has been done. A little bit of synthesis of Zechariah and Revelation has been done, but there is still much that has been unexamined. I have not even touched the idea in Zechariah 5 that the harlot herself is worshipped as a "god." Also, although obviously ancient Tyre and ancient Babylon are types of Mystery Babylon the Great, I have not really done systematic synthesis of these accounts. Further, obviously the Pharaoh of ancient Egypt, and Ahab king of Israel, and the king of ancient Babylon, are all types of the beast, the man of lawlessness. Once again I have not really done any systematic synthesis of these accounts. Nor the prospect from other prophets that some kings of Assyria are also types of the "beast," and that the beast somehow comes out of "Nineveh." Additionally, many works have done a more thorough job of discussing the relevance of the ancient caesars, while I have concentrated on what was lacking in ancient Rome as a fulfillment of prophecy. This is only an overview. I can only admit what this brief study has not been really covered.

Final Instructions

There is a river of life.

And he showed me a pure river of water of life, clear as crystal, proceeding from the throne of God and of the Lamb, Rev 22:1 NKJV

The panorama of what will happen is described in Psalm 46. It is there we see *a seven verse synopsis of the book of Revelation* given to men by the sons of Korah hundreds of years before Jesus came.

⁴ There is a river whose streams make glad the city of God,
     The holy dwelling places of the Most High.
⁵ God *is* in the midst of her, she will not be moved;
     God will help her when morning dawns.
⁶ The nations made an uproar, the kingdoms tottered;
     He raised His voice, the earth melted.
⁷ The LORD of hosts is with us;
     The God of Jacob is our stronghold.   Selah.
⁸ Come, behold the works of the LORD,
     Who has wrought desolations in the earth.
⁹ He makes wars to cease to the end of the earth;

He breaks the bow and cuts the spear in two;
He burns the chariots with fire.
[10] "Cease *striving* and know that I am God;
I will be exalted among the nations, I will be exalted in the
earth." Psa 46:4-10 NASB

A "river whose streams make glad the city of God"? This seems to be the
same river described in Ezekiel chapter 47 and Rev 22:1. Now the temple is on
Mount Zion in Jerusalem, at a height of approximately 3,000 feet, and there are
no rivers on this approximately 3,000 foot high mountain. But Ezekiel sees water flowing out from the house of God.

> Afterward he brought me again unto the door of the house; and,
> behold, waters issued out from under the threshold of the house
> eastward: for the forefront of the house stood toward the east, and the
> waters came down from under from the right side of the house, at the
> south side of the altar. Ezek 47:1 KJV

If you went about 1500 feet down the stream, it was ankle deep, Ezek 47:3.
In another 1500 feet it reached your knees, Ezek 47:4a. Then another 1500 feet
it was hip deep, Ezek 47:4b. In an additional 1500 feet it was too deep to cross,
Ezek 47:5. And half the river flows toward the Dead Sea, and half of it flows toward the Mediterranean, and it makes both oceans to be of fresh water instead
of salt water! Ezek 47:8. This is an impossibility in earthly terms. A river that
starts on a 3,000 foot mountain top and in a little over a mile it is too deep to
wade! It definitely does not describe the city of Jerusalem here on earth. In fact,
when King Hezekiah diverted a mere spring of water and brought it within the
walls of the city, it was a major accomplishment, 2Kgs 20:20. These seem to be
the marks of a symbolic description. Ezekiel's temple is seemingly symbolic of
the greater tabernacle in heaven. The place where God "will dwell in the midst
of the children of Israel <u>forever</u>," Ezek 43:7 NKJV. But only heaven is "forever."

> But Christ came as High Priest of the good things to come, with the
> greater and more perfect tabernacle not made with hands, that is, not
> of this creation. Heb 9:11 NKJV

Your author *thinks* another temple will probably be built in earthly Jerusalem. It may serve as another type, but it will not be Ezekiel's long anticipated
temple. It is physically impossible for men to build Ezekiel's temple here on
earth. Jesus has already entered the more perfect tabernacle not of this creation,
the true temple which will be eternal. All kinds of fish were swimming in this
river, Ezek 47:9. Beside the river were trees on either side, which bear fruit all
year long, and the leaves of the trees are for healing, Ezek 47:12. We will need
much healing. It seems Ezekiel is describing the river of the water of life in heaven. This book is a unity!

The tree of life will be there, Rev 22:2. There will be organic healing for the

nations. There will no longer be a curse in this new universe, Rev 22:3. We will
"serve" the Lord there. No man has ever seen God at any time, Jn 1:18. We see
dimly now, as if we were looking at Him through a very bad mirror, 2Cor
3:18a. However seeing the Lord in just this feeble way is changing us day by
day, 2Cor 3:18b. But in heaven we will see God face to face. God Himself will
be our light. Things will once again be like they should have been from the
first. Everything I am telling you is true, Rev 22:4-6.

Blessed is he who *heeds* the words of this prophecy, Rev 22:7. This is a prophecy to understand and obey! The book of Revelation is understandable. Do we
have to understand all of it? Well, is there any book of the Bible where we really
understand *all* of it? Can we misuse it? Yes! Just as we can misuse any of the
Scriptures.

> [15] and consider *that* the longsuffering of our Lord *is* salvation—as also
> our beloved brother Paul, according to the wisdom given to him, has
> written to you, [16] as also in all his epistles, speaking in them of these
> things, in which are some things hard to understand, which untaught
> and unstable *people* twist to their own destruction, as *they do* also the
> rest of the Scriptures. 2Pe 3:15-16 NKJV

Obviously we can and often do misuse the book of Revelation just like we
often misuse the rest of Scripture. Still, we *can* also understand the book of Revelation and heed it, and obey the truth that is taught here, just like we can the
rest of Scriptures, and there is a blessing there.

> Behold, I come quickly: blessed is he that keepeth the sayings of the
> prophecy of this book. Rev 22:7 KJV

So you and I need to heed what we have heard. Don't worship angels, we
are told, Rev 22:8-9. That will rob us of our prize, Col 2:18. Don't seal up this
book, Rev 22:10. Preach and teach it. A necessary part of this book is something
that can be understood and obeyed! "The time is near" He says, Rev 22:10.
Outside of the city is everything wicked and vile.

> For without are dogs, and sorcerers, and whoremongers, and
> murderers, and idolaters, and whosoever loveth and maketh a lie.
> Rev 22:15 KJV

Jesus is the promised seed of David, and this book is "for the churches,"
Rev 22:16.

Don't add or take away from this book, Rev 22:18-19.

> He that is unjust, let him be unjust still: and he which is filthy, let him
> be filthy still: ... Rev 22:11a-b KJV

I think the Lord here is mocking those who cannot make up their minds to
really give their lives to the Lord, instead of seeking money or pleasure or comfortable rest. America and the church have been blinded by the wealth of the

sensuality of Mystery Babylon, Rev 18:3b. **_We_** have drunk of the wine of the anger of her immorality, and have become spiritually drunk, Rev 18:3a. Not just the big cities. It is even in the rural places. Our worldliness, our neglect of the local church, our children and our grandchildren, are part of the witness of our failures. God and His ways are on our list ... but He is most often not first! In our own time, the 20th and 21st centuries, the world has converted the church to worldly things, rather than the church converting the world to heavenly things.

> ... and he that is righteous, let him be righteous still: and he that is holy, let him be holy still. Rev 22:11c KJV

> 12 And, behold, I come quickly; and my reward *is* with me, to give every man according as his work shall be. 13 I am Alpha and Omega, the beginning and the end, the first and the last. Rev 22:12-13 KJV

There, He says it again. That is repeated over and over, and you and I will fully realize it when our short life is over and we soon stand before the Lord of Glory.

Blessed are those who are washed and clean, Rev 22:14.

The washing starts in baptism, Acts 22:14, and continues with the Word and the service of our Lord. Now is the time to come, Rev 22:17. He is coming quickly, He again emphasizes, Rev 22:20.

> The grace of our Lord Jesus Christ be with you all. Amen. Rev 22:21 KJV

Do not ignore the call. Do not fail to give Him everything!

Why the World Thinks it is Important to Not Believe This Book

There are two important points to be made here.

First, the World System wants us to think that God, even if He exists, would never actually do *anything*, either for us or against us. Thus, in their Kabbalistic logic, there is a *need* for man to in effect act as God, and to act on his own, independent of God, and possibly even in opposition to this remote do-nothing God, that is the product of their imagination.

Now if that is the conclusion that they want to drive us to, in preparation for their god-man whom they will reveal at the proper time, then the last thing they want you to realize is that the Lord our God is active and powerful, and He constantly interfaces with men, and raises them up, or puts them down, as pictured in both the book of Revelation *and* all of Scripture. They want us to be insensible to, and blind to, His working to turn us from foolish and destructive ways. They do not want us to realize that God has now for us, as He always has,

> [26] "... determined their preappointed times and the boundaries of their dwellings, [27] so that they should seek the Lord, in the hope that they might grope for Him and find Him, though He is not far from each one of us; [28] for in Him we live and move and have our being, as also some of your own poets have said, 'For we are also His offspring.' "
> Act 17:26-28 NKJV

To realize these things, would undercut their Satanic plans to replace God, to reveal their own god-man as the center of an anti-Christ new world-order.

Then the Second Point: Understanding these things as described in the book of Revelation would cause a very appropriate wariness of the world, and the world systems as described in 1Jn 2:15-16.

> [15] Love not the world, neither the things *that are* in the world. If any man love the world, the love of the Father is not in him. [16] For all that is in the world, the lust of the flesh, and the lust of the eyes, and the pride of life, is not of the Father, but is of the world. KJV

So then we would do what Jesus said to do.

> And what I say unto you I say unto all, Watch. Mk 13:37 KJV

This wariness of their designs is counter productive to these systems, so it very well suits their purpose to disrupt any real understanding of Revelation. **If you grasp the basic message of Revelation, it is way too easy to identify the outline of these groups in history.**

If you really believe this book, you will give your power and your service to God, instead of to these men who want to play god, "for one hour," Rev 17:12.

"Behold, I have told you in advance."
Jesus of Nazareth, 30 AD
Mtt 24:25 NASB

320

Index

Biographical Information

Neal Fain was born in Georgia and converted to Christ in Dallas, Texas in 1962. He attended Harding University from 1965 to 1967, preaching as a student, graduating with a degree in Bible and Biblical Languages. He lived in Alaska for over 30 years, both preaching and teaching, and much of that time self-supporting. He retired from a major oil company in 1999, followed by preaching in North Carolina. He is now retired to Tennessee, preaching, teaching, researching and writing.

From listening to popular views, he early took a rationalistic view of prophecy, and only slowly realized its importance to the entire Christian age, not as an "accidental" extra, but as something needed for both conduct and preparedness, "a lamp shining in a dark place." This volume is an outgrowth of his earlier book *Prophecy Principles*.

www.ingramcontent.com/pod-product-compliance
Lightning Source LLC
Chambersburg PA
CBHW060243100426
42742CB00011B/1626